PORTRAYING THE AZTEC PAST

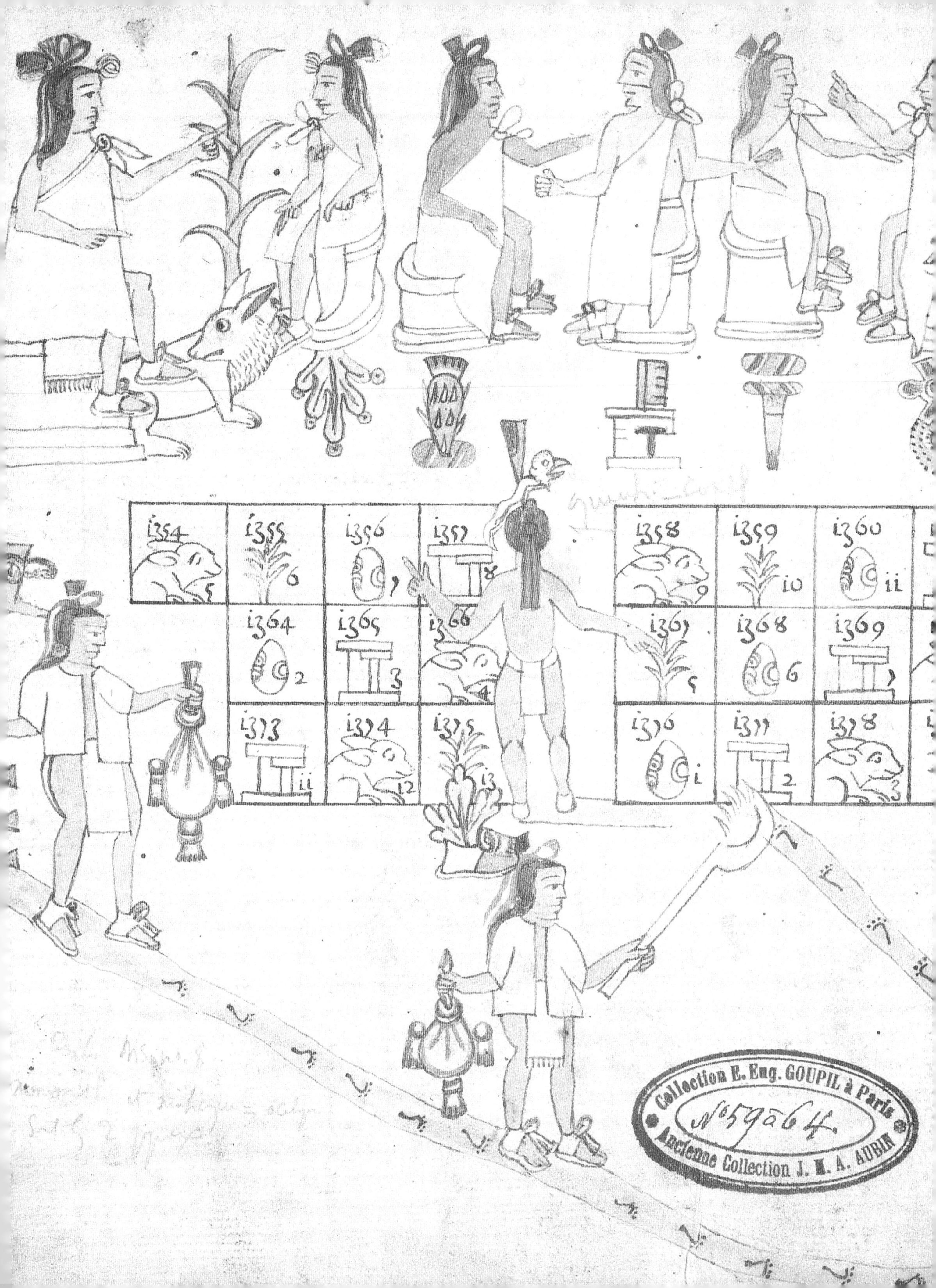
1354
1355
1356
1357
1358
1359
1360
1364
1365
1366
1367
1368
1369
1373
1374
1375
1376
1377
1378
Collection E. Eug. GOUPIL à Paris
Ancienne Collection J. M. A. AUBIN

PORTRAYING THE AZTEC PAST

The Codices Boturini, Azcatitlan, and Aubin

ANGELA HERREN RAJAGOPALAN

UNIVERSITY OF TEXAS PRESS · AUSTIN

RECOVERING LANGUAGES & LITERACIES OF THE AMERICAS

This book is a part of the Recovering Languages and Literacies of the Americas publication initiative, funded by a grant from the Andrew W. Mellon Foundation.

All images from the Codex Boturini are courtesy of CONACULTA-INAH-MEX; reproduced with permission of the Instituto Nacional de Antropología e Historia.

Material from Angela Herren Rajagopalan's essay "Early European Book Conversations and Legitimized Mexica History in *Codex Aubin*," in *Constructing Power and Place in Mesoamerica: Pre-Hispanic Paintings from Three Regions*, edited by Merideth Paxton and Leticia Staines Cicero (University of New Mexico Press, 2017), is used with permission.

Printed in the United States of America
First edition, 2019
First paperback reprint, 2022

The paper used in this book meets the minimum requirements of ANSI/NISO Z39.48-1992 (R1997) (Permanence of Paper). ♾

A NOTE ON SPELLING AND TRANSLATIONS

Unless otherwise indicated, translations from Spanish and French are mine. Unless otherwise noted, all references to the Codex Aubin text derive from the translation by Debra Nagao found in appendix 2. Following scholarly conventions, I have not used diacritical marks on Nahuatl words and have often chosen modern spellings for clarity. Except in quoted matter, I generally use the standard form of names rather than the reverential (e.g., Ecatl rather than Ecatzin).

Library of Congress Cataloging-in-Publication Data
Names: Rajagopalan, Angela Herren, author.
Title: Portraying the Aztec past : the codices Boturini, Azcatitlan, and Aubin / Angela Herren Rajagopalan.
Other titles: Recovering languages and literacies of the Americas.
Description: First edition. | Austin : University of Texas Press, 2018. | Series: Recovering languages and literacies of the Americas | Includes bibliographical references and index.
Identifiers: LCCN 2018003954
ISBN 978-1-4773-1607-8 (pbk. : alk. paper)
ISBN 978-1-4773-1608-5 (library e-book)
ISBN 978-1-4773-1609-2 (nonlibrary e-book)
Subjects: LCSH: Manuscripts, Nahuatl. | Nahuatl language—Writing. | Aztecs—History. | Codex Boturini. | Codex Azcatitlan. | Codex Aubin.
Classification: LCC F1219.54.A98 R34 2018 | DDC 972—dc23
LC record available at https://lccn.loc.gov/2018003954

doi:10.7560/316061

For my parents, Joseph and Michele Herren

CONTENTS

Tables

ACKNOWLEDGMENTS

THIS PROJECT HAS ROOTS in my doctoral dissertation in art history at the Graduate Center of the City University of New York (CUNY). I am deeply grateful to Eloise Quiñones Keber, my thesis advisor, for introducing me to the world of Mesoamerican manuscripts, sharing her expertise, and guiding me through my initial studies of Codex Boturini, Codex Azcatitlan, and Codex Aubin. I also thank Judy Sund, Katherine Manthorne, and Diana Fane for serving on my dissertation committee and providing support and helpful feedback. Courses with Guilhem Olivier and Esther Pasztory furthered my interest in and understanding of Mesoamerican art. A summer course in Oapan, Guerrero, with Jonathan Amith gave me an elementary foundation in Nahuatl. As a graduate student, I worked with Diana Fane as an intern and a research associate in the Department of the Arts of Africa, the Pacific, and the Americas at the Brooklyn Museum of Art. I am thankful to her for fostering my love of the object and all that its material qualities can tell us. My book has benefited from the opportunity to connect viscerally with and learn from original objects and archival materials.

For facilitating just that, I acknowledge the many institutions that have offered me access and assistance during my dissertation years and beyond. Madame Monique Cohen, former conservateur général in the Département des Manuscrits, Division Orientale of the Bibliothèque Nationale de France, generously allowed me access to the original Codex Azcatitlan and related materials. Carolusa González, former guardian of the Bodega de Códices at the Biblioteca Nacional de Antropología e Historia, enabled my study of the original Codex Boturini and kindly provided me with digital images. I thank her and the individuals at the Instituto Nacional de Antropología e Historia for providing me with the resources and permission to share my study of this special manuscript. The British Museum allowed me to work with the original Codex Aubin, which led to my interest in the manuscript's binding. My hunt for the source of Codex Aubin's endpapers began at the British Library and brought me to collections at Princeton University Library, Yale University Library, the University of Manchester Library, New York Public Library, the Morgan Library & Museum, and finally the Ahmanson Murphy Aldine Collection at the University of California, Los Angeles Library, where I found a match. The librarians at the J. Murrey Atkins Library at the University of North Carolina, Charlotte (UNCC) have offered continual support with interlibrary loans.

The research, travel, and conference presentations that went into the development of this book would not have been possible without financial support. In graduate school a Mellon Fellowship for Dissertation Research from the Council on Library and Information Resources allowed sustained work in Mexico, Paris, and London. A Sylvan C. Coleman and Pamela Coleman Art History Fellowship from the Metropolitan Museum of Art supported research, writing, and stimulating conversations with colleagues. Funding, including a Program Dissertation Fellowship, from the Graduate Center at CUNY facilitated my progress and my professional development. As a faculty member in the Department of Art and Art History at UNCC, I have enjoyed continued institutional support. In addition, fellowships and grants from the Consortium in Latin American and Caribbean Studies at the University of North Carolina Chapel Hill and Duke University, the Southern Regional Education Board, and the National Endowment for the Humanities have furthered my research. A Fulbright-García Robles Scholar Grant allowed me a year in Mexico to advance the book project and share ideas with colleagues. I am especially grateful to Karen Cordero and my colleagues at the Universidad Iberoamericana for hosting me and for helping to organize a joint conference with UNCC.

I am profoundly grateful to the many scholars and friends who have offered advice and support for this project over the years. Among them, I wish to acknowledge María Castañeda de la Paz and Federico Navarrete, who invited me to participate in "Más allá de Aztlan: Taller en torno al Códice Azcatitlan," an especially fruitful symposium at the Universidad Nacional Autónoma de México, co-sponsored by the Instituto de Investigaciones Antropológicas and the Instituto de Investigaciones Históricas. Their ideas have often stimulated my thinking. I thank Merideth Paxton and Byron Hamann for reading and commenting on my work on Codex Aubin. Elizabeth Morán and Ruth Anne Phillips provided helpful feedback on many parts of the manuscript. I especially thank Ruth Anne Phillips for providing editorial assistance on the book. I thank Debra Nagao, Doris Heyden, Alessandra Russo, Patrice Giasson, Karla Burgueño, Fico Lage, and Felipe Falcón for helping me to find a home in Mexico City. I am grateful for the support of scholars and friends like Jennifer Wagelie, Harvey Stark, Rachel Gonzalez Levy, and my colleagues at UNCC.

I am fortunate to work with an excellent team at the University of Texas Press. I thank Theresa May, former editor-in-chief, and Kerry Webb, senior acquisitions editor, for their interest in my project. My manuscript has been greatly improved by manuscript editor Lynne Chapman and the excellent work of copy editor Kathy Lewis.

This book would not be possible without the abundant and unconditional love and support of my family: Srikanth and Ava Rajagopalan; Joseph and Michele Herren; Raj and Vatsala Rajagopalan; Shelley, Derryl, Emily, Max, and Riley Halpern; Kavitha Rajagopalan and Matthew, Leela, and Krishna Young.

PORTRAYING THE AZTEC PAST

CHAPTER 1

INTRODUCTION

Portraying the Aztec Past

HERE IT IS TOLD AND PUT FORTH how the ancient ones, those called and named Teochichimeca, people of Aztlan, Mexitin, Chicomoztoca, as they sought and merited the land here, arrived and came into the great altepetl, the altepetl of Mexico Tenochtitlan, the place of renown, the sign, the site of the rock tuna cactus, in the midst of the waters; the place where the eagle rests, where the eagle screeches, where the eagle stretches, where the eagle eats; where the serpent hisses, where the fish fly, where the blue and yellow waters mingle—where the waters burn; where suffering came to be known among the sedges and reeds; the place of encountering and awaiting the various peoples of the four quarters; where the thirteen Teochichimeca arrived and settled, where in misery they settled when they arrived.

Behold, here begins, here is to be seen, here lies written, the most excellent, most edifying account—the account of [Mexico's] renown, pride, history, roots, basis, as what is known as the great altepetl began, as it commenced: the city of Mexico Tenochtitlan in the midst of the waters, among the sedges, among the reeds, also called and known as the place where sedges whisper, where reeds whisper. It was becoming the mother, the father, the head of all, of every altepetl everywhere in New Spain, as those who were the ancient ones, men and women, our grandmothers, grandfathers, great-grandfathers, great-great-grandparents, great-grandmothers, our forefathers, told and established in their accounts and exemplified for us on paper what was done in their accounts, what they left for us who now live, who have issued from them.[1]

The passage above, drawn from the writings of a Nahua noble named don Fernando Alvarado Tezozomoc, reflects an early seventeenth-century perspective on the purposes of recording Mexica migration history.[2] As he summarizes, the migration story existed as a record produced by the ancestors for their descendants. It provided them with an understanding of who they were and where they came from ("those called and named Teochichimeca, people of Aztlan, Mexitin, Chicomoztoca"). It recorded a physical journey wherein the Mexica earned their right to the land ("as they sought and merited the land here") and the process of transition from a period of suffering ("where suffering came to be known . . . where in misery they settled when they arrived") to greatness ("It was becoming the mother, the father, the head of all, of every altepetl everywhere in New Spain").

The Mexica migration history, sometimes described as a rags-to-riches tale, is recorded in several sixteenth-century central Mexican indigenous manuscripts that take alphabetic, pictorial, and hybrid forms. In this history the Aztecs, of Chichimec ancestry, depart from their homeland of Aztlan, in the twelfth century.[3] They leave this island city at the behest of their god Huitzilopochtli, who will lead them through a 200-year journey. Upon landing at Colhuacan or Teocolhuacan, a place that is sometimes conflated with Chicomoztoc and Quinehuayan, they meet up with other tribes. Huitzilopochtli causes the Aztecs to separate from the others and offers them a new identity, renaming them the Mexica and providing them with the things that they need to survive the peregrination. In exchange for this support, he requires sacrifice. After a long and dangerous journey punctuated by many lengthy stops, they arrive at Chapultepec in the Basin of Mexico region. Despite continuing hardships, they manage to intermarry with the Acolhua people of Colhuacan, a group that claimed prestigious Toltec ancestry. Eventually the Mexica see the eagle on the nopal cactus and sacred springs, which indicate that they have reached the promised land (an island in Lake Texcoco that was located at the center of present-day Mexico City). Soon after settling on this site, the Mexica quarreled. While the Tenochca Mexica occupied Tenochtitlan, later capital of the Mexica Empire, the dissidents (Tlatelolca Mexica) established Tlatelolco on the northern part of the island.

Taken as a whole, the Mexica migration narratives offered a vision of Mexica identity that set this group apart from all others. The Mexica were the only people that claimed Aztlan as a homeland. While the makers of Mixtec and Puebla-area manuscripts emphasized longevity in a certain region, the *tlacuiloque* (artist-scribes; singular *tlacuilo*) that produced manuscripts in the Basin of Mexico chose the concept of a migration to represent where their people came from and how they got to their new homeland. In Acolhua histories this journey was referenced only through a record of the arrival of Chichimecs in the Basin of Mexico.[4] In Mexica histories, however, it was the journey itself that forged their identity. As the last of several groups to enter the Basin of Mexico region, the Mexica used migration history to emphasize that they had earned their right to the land. This history helped to legitimate the Mexica political position in the Basin of Mexico by recording the early battles, alliances, and claims to land. At the end of the migration history, the foundation of Mexico Tenochtitlan (and Tlatelolco) marked the point at which the Mexica came into their own. These histories, often coupled with ruler genealogies and accounts of early conquest events, provided an ideal platform for different *altepeme* (city-states; singular *altepetl*, literally, "water-hill") to establish their claims to the land, the legitimacy of their ruling dynasties, and their identity as distinctive peoples with unique histories.

Before the arrival of the Spanish, Mexican histories like the one described here would have been recorded using a pictographic (iconographic) writing system. The glyphic images presented information through pictorial representation (images that bear a resemblance to what they depict), ideograms (images that convey ideas or abstract concepts), and phonetic referents (language-based or rebus writing). At times the glyphs carried multiple meanings and functioned in more than one capacity. The *tlacuiloque* were generally men and often passed down their skills from father to son. They produced painted manuscripts in temples and palaces and used them in a variety of circumstances and settings. The manuscripts were not bound books (codices in the true sense of the word) but were painted on hide, paper, and cloth. They frequently took the form of a screenfold or accordion-style document. The *tlacuiloque* were often the primary users of the books that they painted, interpreting them for audiences that desired access to the historical, calendric, economic, social, and religious information contained therein. Painted histories of the Mexica migration were not created as static, unchanging records but as visual anchors that partnered with a vibrant oral history tradition. Later alphabetic records of these oral accounts suggest that trained orators honored the crucial thrust of the narrative but adapted it to suit their audience. They could, for example, emphasize or expand certain aspects of the history or delight their audience by inventing dialogic exchanges between long-dead ancestors.

Though some pre-Hispanic manuscripts still seemed to be circulating in the sixteenth century, many were destroyed during the Spanish conquest (1519–1521). As Dominican friar Diego Durán described in his historical account, the Spanish conquest of Mexico ended in 1521 with a long and drawn-out battle fought against the fiercely resistant inhabitants of the city and their ruler Cuauhtemoc. Although Hernando Cortés ordered the Spanish conquistadors and their allies to release all captives after his victory, the city had been devastated. As Durán reports:

> The dead on that day were over forty thousand men and women, who, rather than fall into the hands of the Spaniards, knowing of the cruel death they could meet at the hands of those men and their Indian allies, threw themselves and their children into the canals. The stench of corpses was so great that, even though bodies were continually disposed of outside the city, many were left and the evil smell was unbearable for a long time.[5]

In the aftermath of the conquest, Cortés destroyed the religious structures of the former city as he rebuilt on its ruins, ordering that "the temples be demolished, the idols broken, the city razed, and the canals filled in."[6] Although the role of the *tlacuiloque* probably continued in areas outside the city center, the social structure that supported the artist-scribes in Tenochtitlan and Tlatelolco had been irrevocably altered.

Few manuscripts could have survived the wholesale destruction that the Spaniards visited upon the capital of the Mexica Empire, and those that did would have been subjected to a new force of opposition in the persons of the arriving mendicant friars. The first friars, including Pedro de Gante, arrived in Mexico in 1523. A group of twelve Franciscan friars arrived in 1524, followed by the Dominicans in 1525, and the Augustinians in 1533. Like Diego de Landa in Yucatan, Juan de Zumárraga, the first bishop of Mexico, sought to destroy indigenous manuscripts. Even some Nahua participated in the destruction of the emblems of their former cosmology as they embraced Christianity. As Durán writes, "The Christian religion began to grow and the Indians took to it with love and willingness. After the Christian fathers had preached to them, they began to abandon their idols. They broke them, mocked them, stepped on them, and demolished the *cúes* [temples] where these images had been." Religious opposition, coupled with the pestilence and poverty that ensued after the conquest, severely undermined the surviving *tlacuiloque*.[7]

Nonetheless, oral histories continued to be recounted, *tlacuiloque* continued to produce painted manuscripts, and cultural narratives like the Mexica migration story continued to circulate among Nahua intellectuals in central Mexico. Although Spanish Christian hostility toward native manuscripts persisted to greater and lesser degrees throughout the sixteenth century, indigenous and mestizo *tlacuiloque* still found value in the pre-Hispanic pictorial writing system and used it to reach their audiences and record information about indigenous culture. While some manuscripts were produced for Spanish political and religious officials, others (like Codex

Boturini, Codex Azcatitlan, and Codex Aubin, the three manuscripts at the heart of this study) were made by and for indigenous populations. As with the migration account described in the epigraph above, the *tlacuiloque* who created these three manuscripts sought to celebrate and preserve a shared history. For the Mexica descendants who resided in Tenochtitlan and Tlatelolco before and after the conquest, the tale of their ancestors was a source of "renown, pride, history, roots, basis" that forged a sense of communal identity.

As the ruins of Tenochtitlan were razed and rebuilt to create Mexico, the capital of what would become New Spain's viceroyalty, European centers of education were established. Younger Nahua began to learn new communicative strategies in the monastery schools established by the friars. As early as 1523 or 1524 Franciscan friar Pedro de Gante established a school in Tetxcoco. A few years later he moved to San Francisco, the main Franciscan monastery in Mexico City, where he established the Colegio de San José de Belén de los Naturales.[8] In this school, which catered primarily to the children of indigenous elites, students learned Spanish, Latin, and how to read and write alphabetic script.[9] By 1536 Juan de Zumárraga had established the first school of higher education. Students who excelled in their early education came to study at the Colegio de Santa Cruz in Tlatelolco, where they received a humanist education with a focus on theology and the liberal arts. Over the course of the sixteenth century European-style images circulated ever more widely in books, woodcut prints, and church decor. *Tlacuiloque* in the post-conquest period accessed new methods of recording and consuming knowledge and often combined these with older pre-Hispanic central Mexican graphic systems in inventive and strategic ways.

Codex Boturini, Codex Azcatitlan, and Codex Aubin differ from other pictorial accounts of Mexica migration produced in central Mexico after the conquest. In contrast to the others, these three manuscripts list the same migrating groups in the same order and the same four god-bearers, although Codex Azcatitlan includes additional leaders as well. These manuscripts also offer the longest and most complete accounts of the origin, migration, and foundation of the Mexica. Their itineraries are closely aligned in comparison to other manuscripts (table 1.1).

The itineraries of Codex Boturini and Codex Aubin are essentially identical up to the point where Codex Boturini breaks off due to damage. Codex Azcatitlan includes most of the stops listed in Codex Boturini and Codex Aubin and adds some additional locations. In some cases the discrepancies are due to varying levels of pictorial detail in the account. For example, the Place of the Broken Tree, found in Codex Boturini and Codex Aubin, may very well be located at Colhuacan, a site that Codex Azcatitlan does include. Codex Boturini visually conveys that Cuextecatlichocayan was a site they passed through but that they did not set up an establishment until they arrived at Coatlicamac. Codex Azcatitlan does not depict this intermediate location, but it does record Coatlicamac. Codex Azcatitlan includes Chicomoztoc, a site that does not appear in Codex Boturini and Codex Aubin, but Chicomoztoc is frequently conflated in scripted accounts with Colhuacan, Quinehuayan, and even Aztlan. Although major discrepancies in dating and minor discrepancies in itinerary indicate that the *tlacuiloque* drew on at least one other source, Codex Azcatitlan's migration account is in large part consistent with the accounts found in Codex Boturini and Codex Aubin.

These three manuscripts also differ from other pictorial accounts of Mexica migration in their formats and in the way that they organize time. In contrast to the Tira de Tepechpan and Codex Mexicanus, which utilize a continuous stream of year signs that run horizontally through the middle of the page, these three group the date signs into blocks, placing the compositional emphasis on events rather than the unbroken flow of time.[10] Codex Mendoza depicts only the foundation of the Mexica. The Mapa Sigüenza does not use date cartouches and takes a cartographic approach. Codex Telleriano-Remensis and Codex Vaticanus A mix elements of Mexica migration history with Chichimec sources from Puebla.[11]

Table 1.1.
Comparison of the Mexica Migration Itineraries in Codex Azcatitlan, Codex Boturini, and Codex Aubin

CODEX AZCATITLAN	CODEX BOTURINI	CODEX AUBIN
Aztlan [–1 Flint (1168)]	Aztlan [–1 Flint]	Aztlan [–1 Flint]
		Quinehuayan [–]
Colhuacan [–]	Colhuacan [–]	Colhuacan [–]
	Broken Tree [–]	Broken Tree [–]
	Cuextecatlichocayan [–]	Cuextecatlichocayan [2 House–2 House]
Tepemaxalco [2 House (1169)–3 Rabbit (1170)]		
Chicomoztoc [4 Reed (1171)–11 Rabbit (1178)]		
Coatlicamac [12 Reed (1179)–13 Flint (1180)]	Coatlicamac [2 House–3 Flint]	Coatlicamac [2 House–2 Reed]
Huacaltepec [1 House (1181)–2 Rabbit (1182)]		
Huixachtitlan [3 Reed (1183)–5 House (1185)	*Huixachtitlan [8 Flint–11 Reed]*	*Huixachtitlan [8 Flint–11 Reed]*
Coatepec [6 Rabbit (1186)–1 Rabbit (1194)]		
Tezcatepec [2 Reed (1195)–6 Reed (1199)]		
Xiuhcocan [7 Flint (1200)–3 House (1209)]		
Tula [4 Rabbit (1210)–10 House (1229)]	Tula [4 House–9 Reed]	Tula [3 Flint–9 Reed]
	Atlitlalacyan [10 Flint–6 House]	Atlitlalacyan [10 Flint–7 Rabbit]
Huehuetocan [–]		
Tlemaco [11 Rabbit (1230)–12 Flint (1244)]	Tlemaco [7 Rabbit–11 Rabbit]	Tlemaco [8 Reed–12 Reed]
	Atotonilco [12 Reed–3 Reed]	Atotonilco [13 Flint–3 Reed]
Apazco [13 House (1245)–3 Flint (1248)]	Apazco [4 Flint–2 Reed]	Apazco [4 Flint–2 Reed]
Tzompanco [4 House (1249)–6 Reed (1251)]	Tzompanco [3 Flint–6 Reed]	Tzompanco [3 Flint–6 Reed]
Xaltocan [7 Flint (1252)–1 Reed (1259)]	Xaltocan [7 Flint–10 Reed]	Xaltocan [7 Flint–10 Reed]

Table 1.1., cont.

CODEX AZCATITLAN	CODEX BOTURINI	CODEX AUBIN
Acalhuacan [2 Flint (1260)–6 Flint (1264)]	Acalhuacan [11 Flint–1 Reed]	Acalhuacan [11 Flint–1 Reed]
Ehecatepec [–]	Ehecatepec [2 Flint–5 Reed]	Ehecatepec [2 Flint–5 Reed]
Tolpetlac [7 House (1265)–12 Rabbit (1270)]	Tolpetlac [6 Flint– 13 Reed]	Tolpetlac [6 Flint– 13 Reed]
Cohuatitlan* [13 Reed (1271)–8 Flint (1292)]	Cohuatitlan [1 Flint–7 Reed]	Cohuatitlan [1 Flint–7 Flint]
Huixachtitlan* [–]	Huixachtitlan [8 Flint–11 Reed]	Huixachtitlan [8 Flint–11 Reed]
Tecpayocan [9 House (1293)–2 Reed (1299)]	Tecpayocan [12 Flint–2 Reed]	Tecpayocan [12 Flint–2 Reed]
Pantitlan [3 Flint (1300)–5 Rabbit (1302)]	Pantitlan [3 Flint–6 Reed]	Pantitlan [3 Flint–6 Reed]
	Amallinalpan, border of Azcapotzalco [7 Flint–1 Reed]	Amallinalpan, border of Azcapotzalco [7 Flint–1 Reed]
	Pantitlan [2 Flint–5 Reed]	Pantitlan [2 Flint–5 Reed]
	Acolnahuac [6 Flint–9 Reed]	Acolnahuac [6 Flint–9 Reed]
	Popotlan [10 Flint–13 Reed]	Popotlan [10 Flint–13 Reed]
	Techcatitlan [1 Flint–4 Reed]	Techcatitlan [1 Flint–4 Reed]
**	Atlacuihuayan (Tacubaya) [5 Flint–8 Reed]	Atlacuihuayan (Tacubaya) [5 Flint–8 Reed]
Chapultepec [6 Reed (1303)–8 Reed (1331)]	Chapultepec [9 Flint–2 Reed]	Chapultepec [9 Flint–2 Reed]
Acocolco [–]	Acocolco [–]	Acocolco [–]
Contitlan, Colhuacan, Acatzintitlan, border of Tizaapan–Colhuacan [9 Flint (1332)–12 Reed (1335)]	Contitlan [3 Flint–6 Reed], Colhuacan	Contitlan, border of Tizaapan–Colhuacan/Tizaapan, border of Colhuacan; Acatzintitlan [3 Flint–6 Reed]
Mexicatzinco [–]		Mexicatzinco [7 Flint–7 Flint]
Nexticpac [–]		Nexticpac [8 House–11 Flint]
Iztacalco [–]		Iztacalco [12 House–13 Rabbit]
Mixiuhcan/Temazcaltitlan [–]		Zoquipan/Temazcaltitlan [1 Reed–1 Reed]
Mexico Tenochtitlan [5 Rabbit (1354)–6 House (1381)]		Mexico Tenochtitlan [2 Flint–]

Note: Italics indicate locations that appear at another point in the itinerary. Shaded areas are nearby or closely related.

* There is a glyph that relates to this site, but it is not glossed.

** The sites of Tepetzinco and Tenayuca are depicted, but the glosses do not indicate that the Mexica stayed there and there are no associated date blocks.

Although Codex Boturini, Codex Azcatitlan, and Codex Aubin all use pictographic images and glyphic signs to record narratives based on shared source material, they differ substantially in execution. In each case, the *tlacuiloque* who created these manuscripts used different formats, styles, and communicative strategies. Codex Boturini is damaged and breaks off just before the arrival at Tenochtitlan. Codex Azcatitlan and Codex Aubin go on to include imperial history as well as conquest and postconquest events. While these manuscripts have been incorporated in studies that explore Mesoamerican history, politics, and visual traditions, this book focuses in particular on the role of the artist-scribe. Through an analysis of the materials, stylistic traits, facture, and narrative qualities of these manuscripts, I examine how individual *tlacuiloque* produced their histories and how their decisions to present or recontextualize a shared Mexica migration history reflect shifting cultural identities.

My point of entry in approaching these manuscripts has been to attend first to their materiality and facture. My premise is that the physical state of the manuscript (its paper, its binding, how the artist applied paint to its surface) can provide clues as to how these artists worked and, in some cases, shed light on who these artists were. The studies presented here contribute to our understanding of their makers and their circumstances of production. For example, chapter 6 connects the Codex Aubin *tlacuilo* to the Colegio de Santa Cruz in Tlatelolco and provides evidence that he bound his manuscript there in 1576. I am also interested in how the narrative qualities of the migration history are presented and manipulated. Codex Boturini presents a Mexica migration history that offers a shared vision of cultural identity that stood to unite different *altepeme* subject to the Mexica Empire. Codex Aubin offers a vision of how this narrative of Mexica identity might be contextualized in a Spanish Christian environment. Codex Azcatitlan draws out the implied Tlatelolca presence in this narrative and makes it explicit. It also uses the Mexica migration history as a conceptual framework for presenting elite Mexica history. My study has benefited from work with the original manuscripts. Throughout this study I make extensive use of sixteenth- and seventeenth-century sources and archival documents. The book is organized as three case studies. Each manuscript is taken in turn, drawing links and connections among the manuscripts throughout.

Codex Boturini

Codex Boturini is referred to at times as the Tira del Museo or Tira de la Peregrinación de los Mexica. Named after eighteenth-century collector Lorenzo Boturini Benaduci, it is the oldest of the three manuscripts and currently resides in the Museo Nacional de Antropología in Mexico City. This screenfold manuscript consists of a long strip of native paper, 19.8 cm high and 549 cm long, pleated to create an "accordion-style" document with folios of roughly equal size.[12] The twenty-one and a half leaves each measure approximately 25.4 cm in width. A *tlacuilo* versed in pre-Hispanic pictorial traditions created the manuscript. Consistency in the representation of figures and forms throughout the manuscript indicates that the *tlacuilo* worked alone. The only alphabetic writing consists of a few largely illegible Nahuatl glosses in sepia that label and explain some of the glyphs in the manuscript; they are not integrated with the composition and appear to have been added at a later date.

Chapter 2 examines the compositional techniques and erasures of the Codex Boturini *tlacuilo* to elucidate how his decisions enact subtle shifts in meaning. Examination of the lines and erasures reveals that the *tlacuilo* started from his source (perhaps an oral account or a pictographic model) and created an original composition, carefully considering how to communicate his history in precise visual terms. Based on this understanding of his working methods, I compare the Codex Boturini's opening pages to those of Codex Aubin, analyzing apparent discrepancies between the two and arguing that the Codex Aubin *tlacuilo* probably copied Codex Boturini directly. Analysis of the material qualities of Codex Boturini and its manufacture suggests that we cannot rule out a pre-Hispanic or conquest-era production. Additionally, this chapter examines evidence that the manuscript is unfinished. The second half of this chapter considers the narrative arc of Codex Boturini, articulated in spare and neatly rendered figures, and how it charts the vision of Mexica identity proffered by the *tlacuilo*. I point to ways in which the *tlacuiloque* working later in the century used this narrative as a paradigm, modifying and modulating this vision of Mexica identity to fit their social exigencies (a subject explored at greater length in the ensuing chapters).

Codex Azcatitlan

Chapters 3 through 5 address Codex Azcatitlan. This manuscript is archived in the Bibliothèque Nationale de France. Named for a gloss that appears on folio 1v, the manuscript currently consists of twenty-five leaves of European paper painted front and back and bound together like a book. It is unclear whether the sheets of European paper were painted first and then bound or vice versa. Inconsistencies in the narrative content indicate that a few leaves have been lost. The leaves measure 21 cm high and 28 cm wide. The images flow across the facing pages, adapting the continuous content of a pre-Hispanic accordion or screenfold document to the two-page spread of a bound book. The path that guides the protagonists in the migration segment drops off on one page and appears in the same spot when the page is turned. The manuscript conveys a cohesive narrative content, linking the Mexica migration to subsequent historical events. The first half of the manuscript replicates and expands the migration history of Codex Boturini. The second half records a ruler history, conquest history, and postconquest history. While it is hard to pin down a production date, historian María Castañeda de la Paz has proposed that it was made in the second half of the seventeenth century.[13] New analysis in chapter 5 indicates that the chronology recorded in the manuscript ends deliberately in 1527, shortly after recording the death of Cuauhtemoc, the last *huey tlatoani* (great ruler) of Tenochtitlan. Analysis of Codex Azcatitlan is complicated by its unfinished state. Draft lines, empty spaces in the composition, and the sporadic use of color indicate that Codex Azcatitlan's *tlacuiloque* did not finish their project. The partial compositions, however, often provide valuable insights into their working processes.

Chapter 3 examines how the two *tlacuiloque* who produced this manuscript worked and interacted. Close study of the stylistic qualities of these two hands indicates that the manuscript was made in a hierarchical workshop environment. The greatest interaction between these two artists occurs in the migration segment of the manuscript. The master artist takes on the more important narrative content at the beginning and end of the migration, gradually allowing the apprentice to take over painting the various stops that form the bulk of the peregrination. Both *tlacuiloque* adapt and expand the Codex Boturini narrative to experiment with introduced European stylistic techniques, to record details visually that might have once been shared orally, and to promote Tlatelolca identity. Close reading of the master *tlacuilo*'s opening and closing scenes shows that he emphasized that the Mexica legacy belonged to both the Tenochca and the Tlatelolca. Scholars like María Castañeda de la Paz and Federico Navarrete have previously commented on the Tlatelolca presence but characterized it as a secondary or "hidden" narrative subsumed within a Mexica Tenochca document.[14] This study recasts our understanding of the Tlatelolca presence, arguing that it is not hidden but forthright and explicitly there from the very beginning of the manuscript. A reading of the pages depicting Acamapichtli's reign indicates that Tlatelolco's Tepanec ancestry continues to figure prominently in the imperial history. While this chapter focuses on those parts of the narrative that are most informed by well-established paradigms, it also provides an overview of the master artist's structure and compositional shifts. Because the narrative content of Codex Azcatitlan's second half has received limited scholarly attention, the following two chapters present a new reading of conquest and postconquest content, enabling an examination of how the Mexica migration history functions in the larger context of the manuscript.

Chapter 4 addresses the conquest history and identifies the important role of Ecatl, an indigenous Tlatelolca warrior who is sometimes referred to by his Christian name, don Martín, or in honorific form as Ecatzin. This section of the manuscript consists of four two-page compositions executed by the master *tlacuilo*. Comparison of the events recorded in these images to their representation in other sixteenth-century historical accounts indicates that the *tlacuilo* celebrated indigenous victory and presented indigenous defeat as the inevitable result of cosmic destiny. In this brief account of the conquest the *tlacuilo* casts Ecatl as a cosmic hero, defending the Fifth World (or Sun) that the Mexica believed themselves to be living in from destruction. Though the images read as one unified European-style "scene," compositional and stylistic analysis indicates that the *tlacuilo* compresses or overlays discrete temporal moments.

Chapter 5 provides a reading of the final post-conquest pages of the manuscript, which have heretofore been opaque and poorly understood. This chapter argues that the master *tlacuilo* adapts his history to a cosmic template that reflects cyclical conceptions of time. This new reading indicates that the postconquest history addresses major events of the years 1521 to 1527. As in the previous parts of the manuscript, the *tlacuilo* presents an indigenous perspective and does not adjust or modify narrative and pictorial content to cater to a Spanish audience. Furthermore, this chapter argues that the *tlacuilo* uses the narrative and cosmic thrust of the migration story as a template to enhance the meaning and import of his annals in the second half of the manuscript. As recorded in Codex Azcatitlan, the Mexica migration records a great cycle from the departure from Aztlan to the foundation of the twin cities of Tenochtitlan and Tlatelolco. The separation of the Tlatelolca from the Tenochca and the enthronement of their first rulers serves as the end of the migration history and a hinge to the elite Mexica history adumbrated in the second half of the manuscript. This second great cycle then ends shortly after the death of Cuauhtemoc, a ruler of both Tenochca and Tlatelolca ancestry. Taken as a whole, Codex Azcatitlan is a Mexica narrative that posits the Tlatelolca as equals to the Tenochca and documents their intertwined narrative from its cosmic origins to the new era that begins after the Spanish conquest.

Codex Aubin

Codex Aubin, named after a nineteenth-century French collector, now resides in the British Museum. Codex Aubin is a small manuscript painted on European paper and bound as a book. This annals history includes accounts of the twelfth-century migration of the Mexica people from Aztlan to Tenochtitlan, a history of Mexica rulers, and a record of significant events that marked the first half-century following Spanish hegemony. While the narrative content of the Mexica migration history is identical to that of Codex Boturini, the *tlacuilo* used both indigenous pictographic images and alphabetic Nahuatl text to record his histories, effectively creating a "bilingual" or hybrid work that could communicate to individuals versed in traditional pre-Hispanic writing systems or to Nahuatl speakers who had learned to read and write alphabetic script in their native language. The colonial segment records events related to San Juan Moyotlan, indicating that the manuscript was likely made for local use.

Chapter 6 argues that the *tlacuilo* who produced Codex Aubin emulated compositional and structural elements of early printed books as a way to lend authority to the pre-Hispanic history that he presented. This chapter offers the first close study of Codex Aubin's binding, which includes recycled endpapers from an early sixteenth-century Latin edition of Julius Caesar's *De Bello Gallico*. Comparison between the printed book and the painted manuscript highlights the break from the format of traditional pre-Hispanic annals. While the *tlacuilo* reproduces Codex Boturini's narrative faithfully, he carefully alters the format of the document and makes strategic choices about how and when to lodge his content in script or glyph. In changing these aspects, he mediates the reception of this history. It is presented from the point of view of a Christian: the powerful deity Huitzilopochtli is cast as a "devil," and Mexica origins are perhaps framed as akin to Europe's classical pagan past. This study offers a more nuanced understanding of the Codex Aubin's dates of production, proposing that the document was begun in the late 1550s or early 1560s and bound in 1576. Chapter 6 also places the manuscript in historical context by examining how the *tlacuilo*'s choices reflect sixteenth-century educational practices, epidemic disease outbreaks, and the climate of censorship created by Spanish Catholicism and Inquisition practices. While the Codex Aubin *tlacuilo* records his history in Nahuatl, for a Nahua audience, he couches his history in a format and conceptual framework that would have been familiar to the Spanish, arguably to ensure the preservation of his cultural legacy.

In a brief concluding chapter I use the findings of this study to consider how these objects might have circulated among Nahua intellectuals in the post-conquest period. While these manuscripts are linked by their shared narratives and probably intersected in the sixteenth and seventeenth centuries, we know for certain that their lives as objects came together in the eighteenth century in the hands of Lorenzo Boturini Benaduci. The epilogue to this book charts the early movements of these three manuscripts, from their first appearance in Boturini's inventories to the museum and library collections where they are currently located. The two appendices facilitate the arguments in this study and may serve as a resource for scholars interested in these manuscripts and in Mesoamerican history more generally. Appendix 1 offers an English translation of the Nahuatl glosses in Codex Azcatitlan. Appendix 2 contains an English translation of the Nahuatl text in Codex Aubin. This translation shows continuous blocks of text (like much of the original Codex Aubin) and does not reflect Dibble's paragraph breakdowns, which were provided to facilitate reading and allow for line-by-line comparison with the original Nahuatl.

This book does not and cannot address all aspects of these manuscripts. It sheds light on the materiality and facture of these manuscripts and contributes to our understanding of the identity of their makers and on some of the strategies used to create and portray their histories. Such a study contributes to the body of literature that examines how these manuscripts function and how pre-Hispanic history is visualized, recorded, and thought about in the colonial period. As Dana Leibsohn suggests, the particularities of historical enterprise can lead to a broader purchase on the fashioning of pre-Hispanic history.[15]

This book builds on and contributes to a broad literature on early colonial Mesoamerican manuscripts, both painted and scripted. In the last thirty years scholars like Elizabeth Hill Boone and others have directed scholarly attention to Mesoamerican painted manuscripts of the pre-Hispanic and colonial periods as a crucial source for understanding indigenous history and agency. Their work has led to a better understanding of how these visual systems work, how we might categorize them, how they communicate, and how they intersect with spoken language and performance. While digitized editions of Mesoamerican manuscripts are increasingly available, that has not always been the case. Monographic studies with facsimile reproductions like those of Frances Berdan and Patricia Rieff Anawalt, Walter Lehmann and Gerdt Kutscher, Eloise Quiñones Keber, and Robert Barlow and Michel Graulich have been tremendously valuable during the course of this study.[16] Though Robert Barlow originally wrote his comments on Codex Azcatitlan in the mid-twentieth century, they are still an important starting point. My work has much in common with recent studies of early colonial painted manuscripts, such as those by Lori Boornazian Diel and Eduardo de J. Douglas.[17] Like the latter, I consider some of the narratives in my study to be literary, even poetic, works as well as historical documents. The works of Angélica Jimena Afanador-Pujol, Dana Leibsohn, and Alessandra Russo have informed my thinking about the processes of making these manuscripts and the individual choices that the *tlacuiloque* make when navigating between different communicative systems and audiences.[18] I rely on Federico Navarrete and especially María Castañeda de la Paz, two scholars who have addressed these three codices at length.[19] My material analyses are inspired by the work of Diana Magaloni Kerpel, and I have found the work of Barbara Mundy especially helpful in conceptualizing how the events recorded in Codex Azcatitlan's conquest and post-conquest history correspond to the actual physical space of Tenochtitlan and Tlatelolco during and after the conquest.[20] Since the narratives and histories of Codex Boturini, Codex Azcatitlan, and Codex Aubin are frequently recorded in other Nahuatl scripts, I refer regularly to the work of Nahuatl scholars like Arthur J. O. Anderson, Susanne Klaus, James Lockhart, Susan Schroeder, Kevin Terraciano, and Camilla Townsend.[21]

While these centuries-old manuscripts may seem obscure and arcane to those outside the world of Mesoamerican manuscripts, their narrative contents and iconographic elements continue to be an important locus for Mexican identity today. The eagle on the nopal cactus, a symbol of the foundation of Mexico-Tenochtitlan, is perhaps the most famous image from the Mexica migration narrative and appears on the Mexican flag. Codex Boturini's narrative is etched into the courtyard façade of the Museo Nacional de Antropología, Mexico's largest and most comprehensive museum. The following chapters chart some of the decisions and working methods of *tlacuiloque* whose manuscripts respond to the question of what it means to be Mexica, what it means to be Mexica-Tlatelolca, and what it means to be Mexica in a Spanish Christian context.

CHAPTER 2

CODEX BOTURINI

A Pictographic Paradigm

IN RECENT DECADES several studies have worked to interpret the pictographic writing of Codex Boturini and its narrative (plates 2.1–2.22). In 1991 Dinorah Lejarazu Rubin and Manuel Hermann Lejarazu updated existing information on the manuscript and published their interpretation along with a facsimile edition.[1] This study offered a thorough iconographic and paleographic analysis of the manuscript, identifying the basic pictographic components of the Mexica migration. In the same year, Elizabeth Hill Boone illuminated aspects of the narrative construction in Codex Boturini and related manuscripts.[2] She argued that the shared elements in these narratives could be understood as registering a transformative ritual performance. In 2002 María Castañeda de la Paz investigated the migration histories depicted in Codex Boturini, Codex Azcatitlan, and Codex Aubin, offering a close study of selected glyphs.[3] Taking a political perspective, her analysis suggested that differences in the manuscripts stemmed from both colonial innovations and the individual histories of different ethnic groups, while the underlying shared narrative offered a cohesive history to the heterogeneous groups inhabiting the Basin of Mexico. In a 2000 study focused on aspects of visual narration, historian Federico Navarrete employed Mikhail Bakhtin's concept of the "chronotope" to examine the graphic conventions used to record time and space in Codex Boturini; he argued that the single line used to connect the year-bearers in the manuscript was an important pre-Hispanic convention that persisted into the colonial period.[4] In 2010 Rafael Tena explored the chronology of the manuscript.[5] Patrick Johansson Keraudren's reading of the manuscript, published in 2015, is one of the most comprehensive to date.[6] These and other studies have expanded our understanding of Codex Boturini and its relationship to other migration narratives. This chapter builds on this scholarly foundation to explore issues of facture and examine how Codex Boturini's narrative defines Mexica identity.

What sets the first part of this study apart from most others is that it is based on an analysis of the original manuscript and further study of the Museo Nacional de Antropología's high-quality digital reproductions.[7] Due to the value and delicate nature of Codex Boturini, the original manuscript is not easily accessed by scholars and has rarely been exhibited since the early part of the twentieth century.[8] A recent exception was the Instituto Nacional de Antropología e Historia (INAH) exhibition "Códices de México, memorias y saberes" at the Museo Nacional de Antropología in 2014–2015, which featured forty-four codices. As part of an initiative to make the manuscripts more accessible, INAH launched the website *Códices de México* in September 2014 and published a digital edition of Codex Boturini in 2015, accompanied by a scholarly text by Patrick Johansson Keraudren.[9] Good color images of Codex Boturini have been inconsistently available until this excellent digitized edition.

The first part of this study focuses on the original manufacture of Codex Boturini, contributing visual and archival evidence to our understanding of the manuscript as unfinished and arguing that it likely served as a direct model for Codex Aubin. The discussion begins with an overview of the paper, pigments, and construction. Further analysis of the lines, erasures, and compositions reveals the subtle shifts that the *tlacuilo* made to enhance the accuracy and specificity of the information that he recorded. These observations help us to understand his process, which may provide insight into the production of other painted manuscripts. Understanding the *tlacuilo*'s process also facilitates a useful comparison with Codex Aubin. While the Codex Azcatitlan *tlacuiloque* freely and confidently modified the core narrative presented in Codex Boturini, the Codex Aubin *tlacuilo* hewed closely to the Boturini paradigm. Even as he adapted the visual and narrative content to the new format of a bound book, he attempted to record the narrative with accuracy and fidelity.

The second part of this chapter builds on existing glyphic and narrative studies to take a closer look at how Codex Boturini's record of events registers Mexica identity, pointing to areas where the narrative paradigm converges with and diverges from Codex Aubin and Codex Azcatitlan. While the underlying shared narrative unites the three manuscripts, their material, stylistic, and narrative differences indicate that the manuscripts function differently. The formal and material aspects of Codex Boturini imply a function intimately linked to oral and performative traditions. In such a context Mexica cultural identity would have served to unify political and social factions in the Basin of Mexico, to justify Mexica rule, and to contextualize ritual practices like human sacrifice. The unfinished nature of the manuscript and its lack of pigmentation, however, indicate that this potential was perhaps not fully realized. Because of its traditional function, and its likely early production date, I consider Codex Boturini a paradigm for Codex Aubin and Codex Azcatitlan. Comparisons with these two codices introduce some of the differences explored in greater depth in the following chapters.

Codex Boturini: A Work in Progress

Among the pictographic annals relating central Mexican history, Codex Boturini is one of the most pre-Hispanic in materials and style. While eighteenth- and nineteenth-century inventories and references describe Codex Boturini as an "original" or pre-Hispanic manuscript, twentieth-century scholars have questioned these assumptions. The criteria proposed for considering Codex Boturini a colonial manuscript are uniformly based on style, composition, and narrative qualities rather than on the paper, pigments, or screenfold format. These criteria include the grouping of date glyphs, the depiction of the broken tree on folio 3 (plate 2.3), the use of a simplified line, the lack of color, and the rendering of drapery folds, eyebrows, and ears.

Until the mid-twentieth century Codex Boturini was considered a pre-Hispanic manuscript. In the 1920s, when anthropologist Paul Radin included Codex Boturini in his study of "The Sources and Authenticity of the History of the Ancient Mexicans," he described it as a pre-Columbian manuscript and suggested that it may have been produced in the time of Moteuczoma the Elder.[10] His work was based on the writings of nineteenth-century scholars Manuel Orozco y Berra and José Fernando Ramírez, who also described the work as pre-Columbian.

Art historian Donald Robertson was one of the first to reassess the pre-Hispanic dating of several manuscripts. For him, the primary basis for interpreting Codex Boturini as colonial was the grouping of date glyphs. Robertson believed that the pre-Hispanic prototype for this manuscript would have had a continuous sequence of time units running in an undisturbed horizontal linear fashion, much like Codex Mexicanus. He writes: "We propose that the editing of the component parts of such Mexican historical chronicles is a Colonial activity wherever it is found, since there is no example of a Pre-Conquest manuscript using this 'edited' form."[11] While this proposal is worthy of consideration, Robertson, like all manuscript scholars, faced the challenge of trying to understand these works in a restricted context. We have only a limited number of pre-Hispanic manuscripts from the Mixtec and Maya cultures, so comparisons must be qualified. It is equally possible that the concentration of the date blocks is a late pre-Hispanic activity or that it is a compositional device particular to central Mexico.

Citing a personal conversation with ethnologist Wigberto Jiménez Moreno, Robertson also brought forward the image of the broken tree on folio 3 as grounds for colonial dating. Although the tree's roots are shown in a typically pre-Hispanic manner, he argued that many-branched trees with clumps of leaves had not been found in pre-Columbian imagery and thus indicated European influence in the Codex Boturini. Robertson pointed out the tree on folio 22 of Codex Mendoza as a more pre-Hispanic example, explaining: "The native tradition is to draw a tree with three branches, a single leaf at the end of each."[12] Robertson's argument is complicated by the fact that Codex Mendoza is a definitively colonial manuscript and that other types of tree imagery do exist. For example, on folio 19 of the pre-Hispanic Codex Borgia there is an image of a tree, broken in several places, that has visible roots as well as at least thirteen branches with clumps of stylized foliage on the ends. The more rounded tufts of leaves in Codex Boturini may be an early colonial innovation, but the broken tree is not an unambiguous marker of colonial provenance.

Pablo Escalante has proposed additional stylistic criteria, pointing to the lack of color and extreme simplification of the human figures in Codex Boturini as indicative of colonial status. The significance of color use is often discussed in relation to pre-Columbian painting, and the absence of flat washes of color within the forms outlined in black is notable. As this study shows, however, the lack of colors beyond black and red likely results from the unfinished nature of the manuscript. Escalante has also cited the extreme simplification of the figures, the representation of eyebrows, and the naturalism of the ears depicted at the end of the manuscript.[13] Sometimes the occasional folds in the drapery are cited as further evidence of colonial manufacture. These stylistic choices indicate, but do not establish with complete certainty, a postconquest dating. If these are postconquest innovations, they are limited and subtle, probably reflecting a production date in the first half of the sixteenth century. We cannot completely rule out the possibility that it was made before or during the conquest.

If we consider the original manufacture of Codex Boturini, its materials and format correspond to early European descriptions of Mesoamerican manuscripts sent back to Spain. Writing from his privileged place as an educator of young noblemen in the Spanish court of the early sixteenth century, the Italian humanist Peter Martyr was one of the first scholars to take an interest in the material aspects of the native manuscripts of Mexico. As a chronicler for and later member of the Spanish Council of the Indies formed in 1510, Martyr had direct access to reports from the New World and was acquainted with the treasures, officials, and explorers returning from abroad.[14] Peter Martyr's comments on the structure of the native manuscripts that he observed, described in a letter to Pope Hadrian, indicate that the earliest manuscripts sent back to Spain were similar in construction to the Codex Boturini:

> They do not bind them as we do, leaf by leaf, but they extend one single leaf to the length of several cubits, after having pasted a certain amount of square leaves one to the other with a bitumen so adhesive, that the whole seems to have passed through the hands of the most skilful [*sic*] bookbinder. Whichever way this book was opened, it would always present two sides written and two pages appear, and as many folds, unless you extend the whole of it.[15]

The research of paper scholar Hans Lenz indicates that, rather than being bituminous, the adhesives employed in pre-Hispanic Mesoamerica were made from the roots of plants in the Orchidaceae family as well as from the sap of trees called *Enterolobium cyclocarpum* of the family Leguminosae.[16]

As in Martyr's description above, and like almost all extant Mesoamerican manuscripts accepted as pre-Hispanic, Codex Boturini is a screenfold.[17] Though early catalogue entries describe the manuscript as being made from agave or maguey, its appearance and construction indicate that the *tlacuilo* used *amatl* (a type of paper produced from the inner bark of the wild fig tree). This type of paper was commonly employed in the pre-Hispanic period and in the early part of the sixteenth century, before the establishment of the first mills in New Spain made European-style paper more widely available. It was called *amatl* in the Nahuatl language and *amate* in the Hispanicized form.[18]

In his *History of the Indians of New Spain*, Franciscan friar Toribio de Benavente (called Motolinía) described two types of native paper in common circulation in the first half of the sixteenth century:

> From the *metl* good paper is made. The sheet of paper is as large as two sheets of our paper. Much of it is made in Tlaxcallan and it is used in a large part of New Spain. Other trees from which paper is made grow in the warm region, and from these trees a great quantity used to be obtained. The tree and the paper are called *amatl*, and from this name is derived the name *amate* which is applied to letters, to books, and to paper, though for books they have also a special name.[19]

Metl (or maguey) paper comes from the agave plant and produces paper slightly lighter in color and finer in texture than that of Codex Boturini. Furthermore, whereas maguey paper was produced from washed and boiled fibers and could be made in various sizes, the dimensions of the tree dictated the size of *amatl* paper. To create longer manuscripts, it was necessary to glue smaller pieces together. The visible seams on the obverse of Codex Boturini indicate where the pieces of plant fiber, varying slightly in size, have been adhered. These adhesions generally correspond to the pleats in the manuscript. Additional pieces of *amatl* have been glued as reinforcements at the seams on the reverse.

Once the manuscript pages were glued together, the *tlacuilo* began the process of painting Codex Boturini by applying a type of gesso that filled the pores of the paper and created a more even painting surface. While Codex Boturini has not undergone chemical analysis, analyses of similar bases used in other codices, such as the preconquest Codex Colombino and the postconquest Codex Selden, have shown them to be a mixture of calcium sulphate and calcium carbonate (commonly known as gypsum, chalk, or limestone).[20] Several entries for such substances are described in Franciscan friar Bernardino de Sahagún's *Historia general de las cosas de Nueva España* (Florentine Codex) in the section "which telleth of that of which colors [are made]; that which improves colors."[21] While some Mesoamerican manuscripts are painted on both sides, gesso appears only on the obverse of Codex Boturini. The *amatl* reinforcements that disrupt the painting surface on the reverse indicate that the *tlacuilo* only intended to paint one side of the long paper strip.[22]

Because adequate color reproductions have not been widely available until recently, Codex Boturini is at times described in scholarly literature as being without color.[23] Due to its unfinished state, the manuscript lacks solid color fill within the lines framing the forms, but the *tlacuilo* employed both red and black pigments. He used black to produce the bulk of the manuscript and a faint red line to connect the date cartouches that help direct the reader through the meander pattern of the date blocks. The use of color is so limited that many photographic reproductions render the manuscript in black and white.[24] Copies often reproduce this red line as a black line equal in density to the line used to create the glyphic forms. The red and black pigments used to produce the pictographic forms match descriptions in the Florentine Codex of natural pigments available to the pre-Hispanic and early colonial period *tlacuilo*.[25]

As has often been noted, of the many pigments used in the pre-Hispanic period, black and red held special significance. The Nahuatl term *in tlilli, in tlapalli* (literally, "the black [ink] and the red [ink]") referred to the characters and images in the manuscripts and by extension to writing, painted books, and knowledge in general.[26] Don Domingo Francisco de San Antón Muñón Chimalpahin Quauhtlehuanitzin (Chimalpahin), for example, writes: "Here begins, here starts, the account of the ancient life and organization of the year count of the ancient Mexica Tenochca as they told it, as they put it forth, as they organized it in the black and the red."[27] Arthur J. O. Anderson and Charles E. Dibble translate *in tlilli, in tlapalli* in the Florentine Codex as "the writings." Along with books and paintings, they are described as the domain of priests or wise men called *amoxoaque*: "Once again they embarked and carried off the writings, the books, the paintings. . . . They carried the writings, the books, the paintings. They carried the knowledge; they carried all—the song books, the flutes."[28] Similarly, the words of a Nahua elder, addressing the first twelve friars in Tenochtitlan shortly after their arrival in 1524, describe the *tlamatinime* (native scholars) as "those who have in their power the black and red ink, the pictures."[29]

WORKING OUT THE COMPOSITION

Few previous studies have focused on the *tlacuilo*'s application of pigment, quality of line, and practices of erasure.[30] These revealing aspects of the manuscript provide valuable information about how the *tlacuilo* worked and contribute evidence to support the idea that Codex Boturini is an unfinished manuscript. Essentially, the *tlacuilo* carefully worked out his compositions in draft before committing to them through the use of lines of thick dark pigment. Underneath the heavy black forms that compose the narrative pale black draft lines can occasionally be glimpsed. The pale red draft lines are never covered over with darker pigment. Now barely visible in some places, these lines reveal how the *tlacuilo* worked out how to connect date glyphs and place signs. These red draft lines and the lack of additional colors suggest that he had not finished the project. The various points of erasure are especially telling, showing how the *tlacuilo*'s draft process allowed him to alter unsuccessful compositions, correct mistakes, enhance the aesthetic qualities of the manuscript, or make slight adjustments in how the manuscript communicated. The nature of the changes suggests that the *tlacuilo* worked out his composition from left to right and from beginning to end.

The application of black and red pigments suggests that the *tlacuilo* worked out the composition of the black year-bearers and glyphic forms first, before

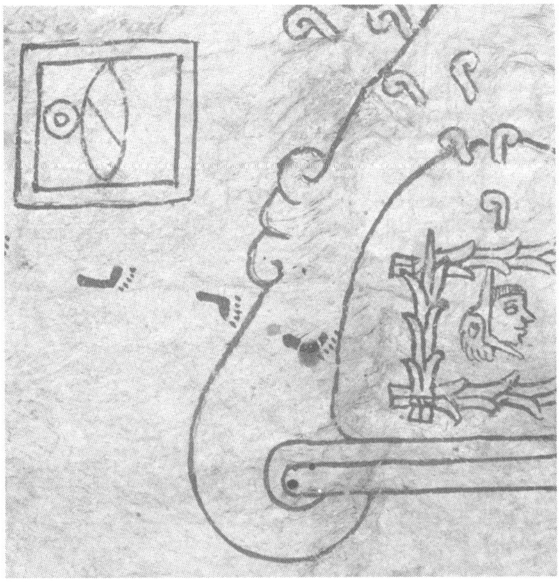

Figure 2.1. Detail of the Colhuacan glyph. Draft lines are not quite covered by the heavier dark overlay on the outer part of the date cartouche and on the left side of the place glyph, particularly where the three undulations appear. Codex Boturini, folio 1. CONACULTA-INAH-MEX; reproduced with permission of the Instituto Nacional de Antropología e Historia.

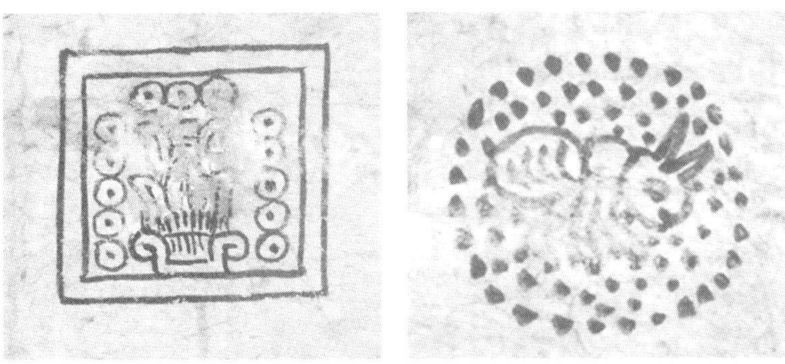

Figure 2.2. Details showing excesses of whitish base where corrections were made. Codex Boturini, folios 8 (left) and 16 (right). CONACULTA-INAH-MEX; reproduced with permission of the Instituto Nacional de Antropología e Historia.

proceeding to the red lines that connect the forms and promote reading clarity (figures 2.1 and 2.2). After applying an underlayer of opaque white gesso, the *tlacuilo* mapped out the pictorial forms of the manuscript, using a very faint black draft line. Once the final layout had been determined and corrections made, the *tlacuilo* committed to the composition by covering the draft line with a heavy application of opaque black pigment. In a few instances the draft line is visible in areas where the *tlacuilo* did not quite cover it completely. For example, the draft lines are visible in places on folio 1 beneath the glyphic form for Colhuacan, the Place of the Curved Hill (figure 2.1). On folio 8 (plate 2.8) the underdrawing is visible in the glyph for Atlitlalacyan as well as in the year-bearers 5 Flint and 6 House.

By sketching out the composition of the manuscript in faint lines, the artist could correct errors. For example, excesses of whitish base on the date 13 Reed on folio 8 and on the place sign for Azcapotzalco on folio 16 indicate areas of erasure and change (figure 2.2). The ghost lines of a set of dates in a vertical line beneath the place sign for Apazco on folio 9 are barely visible (figure 2.3). When the artist decided to move or omit them, the unused lines were covered with the whitish base. An error visible beneath the white base can be seen at the bottom of the place sign Coatlicamac on folio 5, where a black line that appears to be part of the underdrawing extends beyond the darker final version to the left and right (figure 2.4).

The *tlacuilo*'s process suggests that he worked on the manuscript as a whole rather than piece by piece. In contrast to the confident use of solid black lines, his use of red pigment in Codex Boturini is faint throughout, because it represents part of the original underdrawing. The artist presumably intended to paint over it in deep red for the final version. No underdrawing appears beneath the faint red lines, which are similar to the black underdrawing in width and lack of saturation. While the red pigment has faded to some degree throughout the manuscript, some places have faded to the extent that they are barely visible, such as on

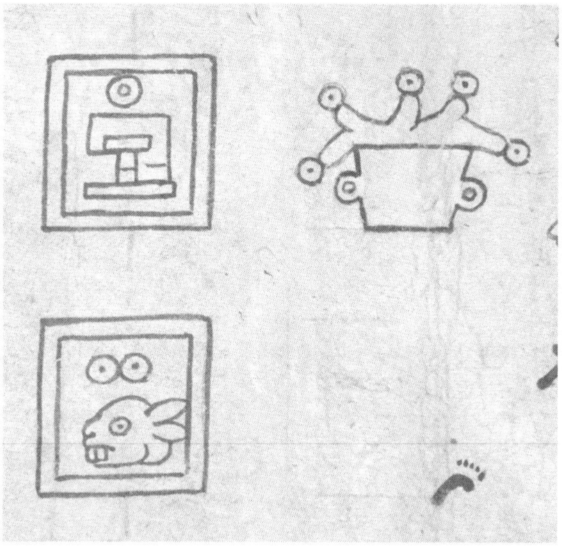

Figure 2.3. A set of ghost lines, just visible beneath the whitish base, marks a second vertical row of date cartouches. These appear to the right of the permanent row of date cartouches. The permanent glyph for Apazco is superimposed on top of the ghost lines. Codex Boturini, folio 9 (detail). CONACULTA-INAH-MEX; reproduced with permission of the Instituto Nacional de Antropología e Historia.

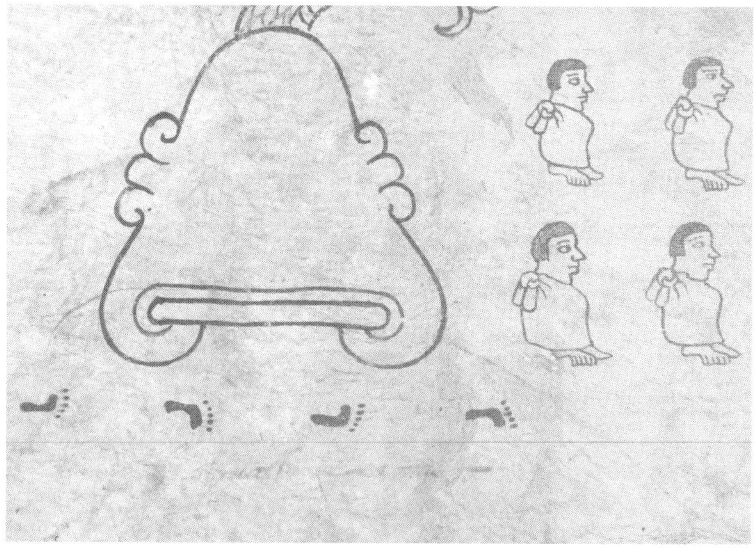

Figure 2.4. An error still visible beneath the white base occurs at the bottom of the Coatlicamac place sign, where a black line that appears to be part of the underdrawing extends beyond the darker final version to the left and right. Codex Boturini, folio 5 (detail). CONACULTA-INAH-MEX; reproduced with permission of the Instituto Nacional de Antropología e Historia.

folio 6 (figure 2.5).[31] Although the red has faded in some parts of manuscripts like Codex Borgia and Codex Vindobonensis, often leaving a faint "stain," overall the deep rich pigment has survived rather well. The red is so fugitive here that it was likely never intended to be the final version. The Boturini artist may have used a plant-based red, a diluted cochineal admixture, or perhaps even a clay-based pigment that would have been an inexpensive and readily available material for a draft. For the final layer of deep red the artist might have planned a cochineal pigment, which was highly prized for its intense bright red.[32]

Although the *tlacuilo* worked out the majority of his composition and committed to solid black overlay lines, the use of red pigment on the manuscript signals that the overall project was not completed. The use of pigment in Codex Boturini suggests that the *tlacuilo* worked out the full composition in draft, corrected mistakes and made final decisions, then proceeded to commit to the design with bold, highly pigmented frame lines. Since the designs in black appear complete and the red appears to be a draft, he probably worked his way systematically from one end to the other, rather than folio by folio. This process of beginning the composition with draft lines and later covering them with solid dark overlay occurs in other manuscripts as well.

In examining the original pre-Hispanic manuscript known as Codex Nuttall, Arthur Miller noted a similar process:

> The painting technique of the Nuttall obverse is remarkably like that of mural painting of the Postclassic period. This should not be surprising since Mixtec codices are foldable mural paintings which were hung on the walls of Mixtec houses. Upon a smooth prepared surface of lime stucco, a preliminary red line of the design was sketched, then the solid colors were blocked in from light to dark and, finally, the black outlines were applied. In the

> original codex (for example on page 28) I found some evidence of dark red and purple having been placed over the black outlines. This suggests that in some cases these two colors were applied last, after the black outlines.[33]

Miller's account of the production of Codex Nuttall's obverse describes a process similar to that employed by the Codex Boturini *tlacuilo*.

Notably, Miller points out that some of the flat washes of color were applied *after* the dark outlines were set in place. Though we cannot know for certain, the Codex Boturini *tlacuilo* may well have planned to continue with the addition of colored pigments. This seems likely, given the importance of color, aesthetically and symbolically, in pre-Hispanic art and in the extant pre-Hispanic manuscripts.[34] In three-dimensional works and in painted manuscripts, indigenous painters regularly used black pigment to frame figures and forms, filling them afterward with flat washes of color. Though the Florentine Codex was produced in the colonial period and reflects the introduction of European values, the descriptions of the *tlacuilo* imply that he was expected to mix and skillfully apply a variety of colors.[35]

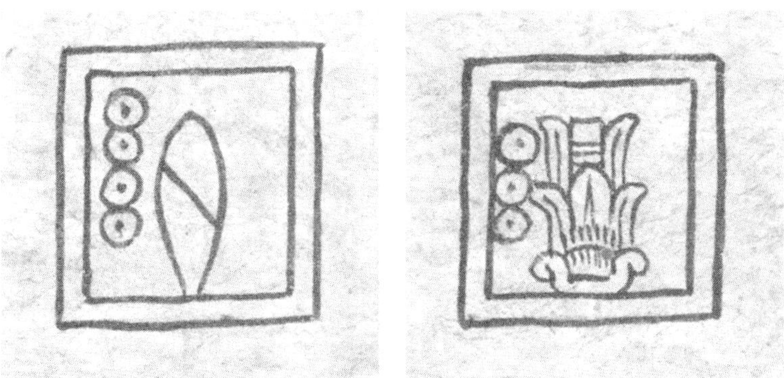

Figure 2.5. Compare the pale red draft line that connects 3 Reed to 4 Flint with the black draft line that is visible at the top of the 3 Reed cartouche. Codex Boturini, folio 6 (detail). CONACULTA-INAH-MEX; reproduced with permission of the Instituto Nacional de Antropología e Historia.

The erasures to the red pigment draft line offer insights into the kinds of decisions and changes that the *tlacuilo* was making. Just as the artist occasionally altered or corrected the composition worked out in pale black lines, he at times made changes in the use of the pale red lines. An area where the rejected red line is just visible beneath the white base occurs on folio 10. Close inspection of the original manuscript reveals a faint red line, now covered by a whitish streak, diagonally connecting the place sign for Tzompanco with the date 3 Flint (figure 2.6). Although the red is not always visible now, similar whitish streaks occur on folio 8, diagonally connecting the place sign for Atlitlalacyan with the date cartouche 10 Flint and the place sign Tlemaco with the date cartouche 7 Rabbit. White erasure lines on folio 9 diagonally connect Atotonilco with 12 Reed and Apazco with 4 Flint. On folio 11 they diagonally connect Xaltocan with 7 Flint. In each case the diagonal lines were replaced with simple horizontal and vertical lines that connect the dates in an unbroken sequence and footprints that connect the last date cartouche on the left with the new site (plates 2.8–11).

Though subtle, these changes reflect a problem that all *tlacuiloque* had to deal with when depicting the Mexica migration history. For the bulk of this history, they needed to record when the Mexica moved from one location to another and how long they stayed in each place. In doing so, they had to make an inherent decision. If the Mexica left in a given year and arrived at the new location in the same year, they had to choose whether to associate that year-bearer with the departure site or the new destination. The erasure marks in Codex Boturini suggest that the *tlacuilo* first tried using a red line to connect the place glyph with the first year-bearer to the right, which marked a complete year spent in that location. Though he began with this concept and tried it on folios 8–11, the erasures show that he ultimately rejected that format and chose instead to connect the year-bearers with a continuous red line. Rather than linking the place signs with the year-bearers to the right, which might not reflect the exact arrival date,

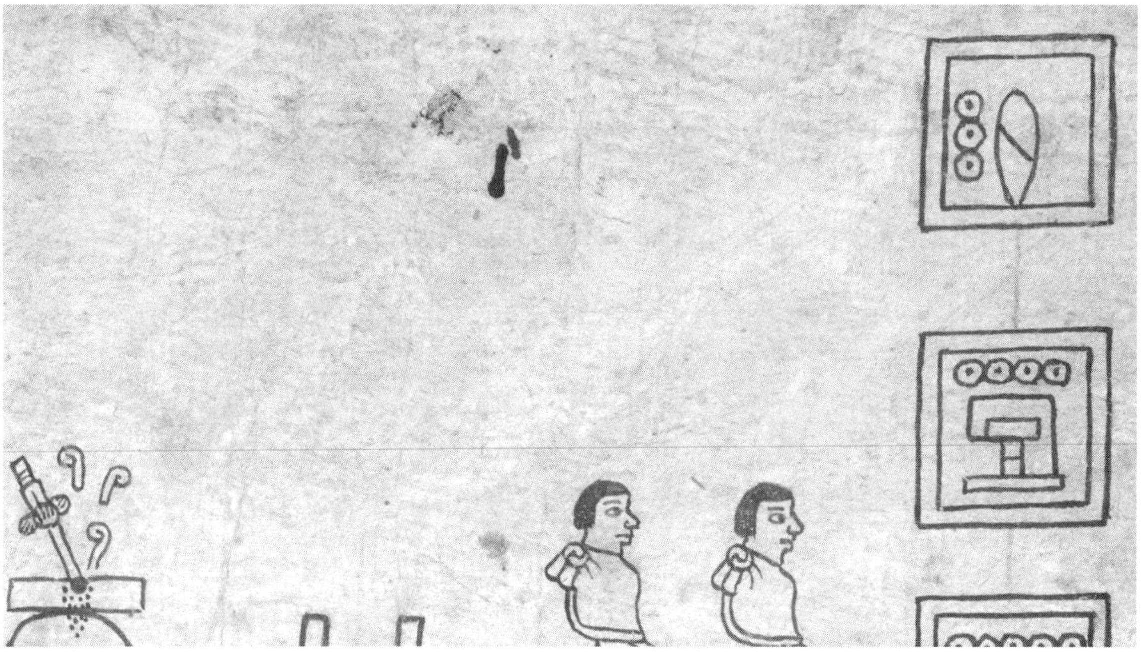

Figure 2.6. The *tlacuilo* used white base to "erase" the diagonal line connecting the date cartouche 3 Flint to the place glyph Tzompanco. Codex Boturini, folio 10 (detail). CONACULTA-INAH-MEX; reproduced with permission of the Instituto Nacional de Antropología e Historia.

the *tlacuilo* chose instead to emphasize the departure from the old site by using black footprints to connect the last year-bearer on the left with the new site to the right. The footprints thus reflect movement through space and a particular nuance of the relationship between time and space. This solution offered the most accurate visual rendering of the information that the *tlacuilo* wished to communicate. After folio 11 the diagonal erasure marks no longer appear.

We see the final system that the *tlacuilo* settled on so clearly demarcated in the bulk of Codex Boturini that we can assume that this is what he also intended in the earliest folios of the manuscript, which have a slightly different layout because they incorporate more events. Thus the Mexica departed from Aztlan in the year 1 Flint and arrived at Colhuacan in the same year (plate 2.1). Folios 2–5 contain no additional year-bearers, so we can assume that the events at the Place of the Broken Tree also occurred in the year 1 Flint. The sites of Cuextecatlichocayan and Coatlicamac prove a little more difficult to understand (plate 2.5). According to the later logic of the manuscript, because there is no year-bearer between the two sites and the footprints run continuously beneath the two signs, we must read the Mexica as departing from Cuextecatlichocayan in the year 1 Flint and arriving at Coatlicamac in the same year. The first year-bearer to the right of the glyphic place sign for Coatlicamac, 2 House, marks the first complete year spent in that location.

The 2 House sign on folio 6 (plate 2.6) also marks the first block of year-bearers in the manuscript and the first use of the pale red draft line to connect the date cartouches. As described above, the diagonal erasure marks occur early in the manuscript, immediately after the departure from Tula, on folios 8–11. As the *tlacuilo* began the alternating sequence of place signs and year-bearer blocks that make up the bulk of the manuscript, he presumably realized that confusion might arise in how to read the departures and arrivals. Notably, however, there are no erasure lines on folios 6–7, which show the Mexica departing from

Coatlicamac in the year 3 Flint and arriving at Tula, where they stayed from 4 House to 9 Reed. One possible explanation for this is that the *tlacuilo* had the manuscript opened up to work on about five to six folios at a time. This would be a manageable spread for a single artist to work with. The diagonal erasure marks are concentrated at the beginning of the manuscript, suggesting that the *tlacuilo* worked on the draft version of the manuscript sequentially, from beginning to end. However, perhaps he worked from right to left within this six-page spread.

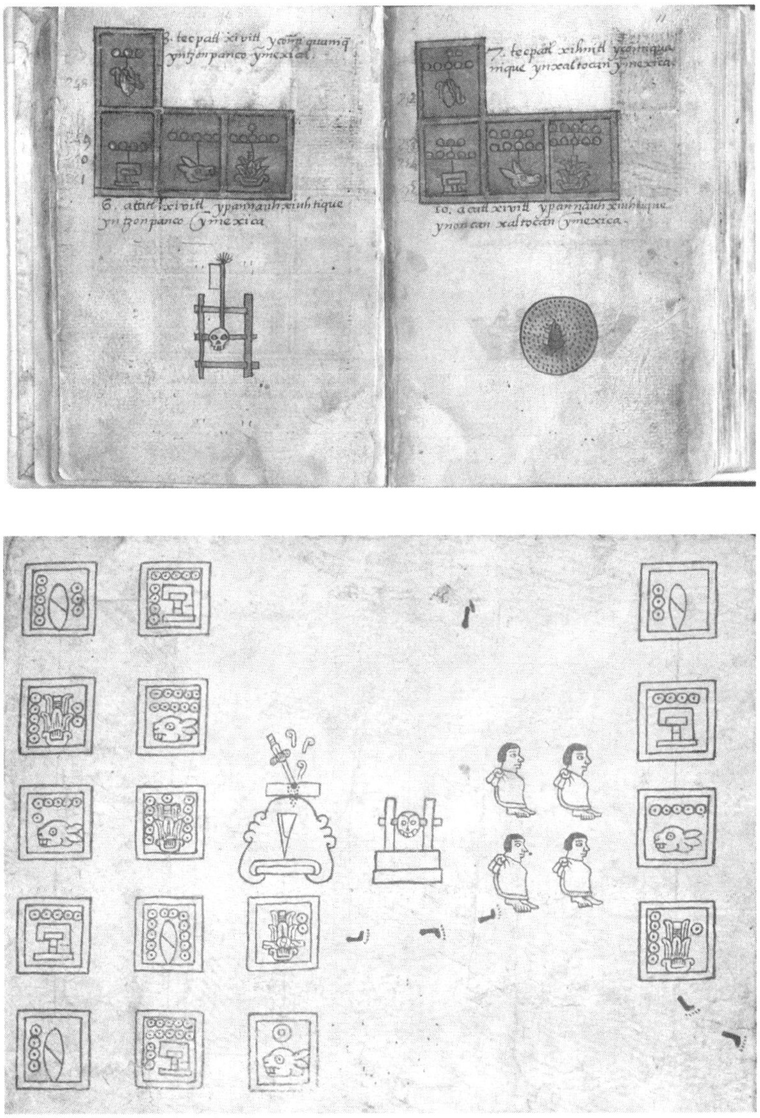

Figure 2.7. The stay at Tzompanco in Codex Aubin, folio 10v (top), and Codex Boturini, folio 10 (bottom). Codex Aubin, folio 10v. © The Trustees of the British Museum. All rights reserved. Codex Boturini, folio 10. CONACULTA-INAH-MEX; reproduced with permission of the Instituto Nacional de Antropología e Historia.

THE RELATIONSHIP TO CODEX AUBIN

Codex Boturini's physical traits reveal an artist dealing with a nuance of communication. The Codex Aubin manuscript shows that this *tlacuilo* dealt with the same kinds of considerations. Careful comparison between the two seems to indicate that the Codex Aubin *tlacuilo* worked directly from Codex Boturini. Codex Aubin records the same locations and almost exactly the same dates, so it is instructive to compare how the Codex Aubin *tlacuilo* solves this dilemma and the nature of the apparent discrepancies in dating between the two manuscripts. Like the Codex Boturini *tlacuilo*, the Codex Aubin *tlacuilo* valued clarity. Since he used a bound book format and alphabetic Nahuatl text in addition to pictographic forms, he had different tools and different constraints.

For the most part the Codex Aubin *tlacuilo* chose to group the year-bearers and associated text and glyphic forms on a single page or set of pages. For example, he records all of the information related to Tzompanco on folio 10v (figure 2.7). As with the other locations in Codex Aubin, he sets off the first year of the year-bearer block and adds an accompanying alphabetic text that states that in the year 3 Flint "at once the Mexica moved to Tzompanco." Immediately below, the *tlacuilo* records the additional years that document the stay, 4 House through 6 Reed. Beneath the block of year-bearers, the Nahuatl text reads: "In this <year>, the Mexica had been in Tzompanco for four years." Beneath the alphabetic text, the *tlacuilo* includes a glyphic place sign for Tzompanco.

A comparison of the representation of the stay at Tzompanco in Codex Boturini and in Codex Aubin indicates a slightly different emphasis. In both cases the *tlacuiloque* group the year-bearers 3 Flint through 6 Reed, indicating a stay of four years at Tzompanco. The Codex Boturini *tlacuilo*, however, chose to use three small footprints to emphasize the departure from Apazco in the year 2 Reed, leaving open the possibility that the Mexica arrived at Tzompanco sometime that year. The continuous screenfold format that the *tlacuilo* uses and his final decisions on composition allow for a slight ambiguity that in the end may be more accurate than the arbitrary and more binding decision made by the Codex Aubin *tlacuilo*. Limited by the bound book format that prohibited the kind of seamless, continuous narrative of Codex Boturini, the Codex Aubin *tlacuilo* essentially chose to do what the Codex Boturini *tlacuilo* rejected in those diagonal erasure marks. In the alphabetic text he associates the first full year of the stay at Tzompanco with the arrival at Tzompanco. The Codex Aubin *tlacuilo* chose to emphasize the arrival rather than the departure.

Codex Boturini and Codex Aubin share so many elements in common that it seems likely that one relied upon the other or that they shared another third source in common. They list exactly the same stops along the migration route as well as the same migrating groups in the same order and group the year-bearers in similar ways for most of the manuscript (table 2.1). If the Codex Boturini *tlacuilo* wanted to copy the Codex Aubin, he would have left the diagonal marks that coincide with the emphasis on the arrival. So this scenario seems unlikely. Rather, I believe the direction of influence ran the other way. The Codex Aubin *tlacuilo* appears to have relied directly upon Codex Boturini or a nearly identical manuscript. The alphabetic text in Codex Aubin describes and at times amplifies the pictorial content of Codex Boturini, as might be expected from an oral recitation of the contents. If the Codex Aubin *tlacuilo* used Codex Boturini as a source, as I suspect, he struggled with how to interpret and record the initial comings and goings. The seeming discrepancies in dating that occur at the beginning of the two manuscripts document this.[36]

Like Codex Boturini, Codex Aubin records the passage from Aztlan to Colhuacan to the Place of the Broken Tree as taking place in the year 1 Flint.[37] However, the Codex Aubin *tlacuilo* has trouble interpreting the relationship between the year-bearers and the Cuextecatlichocayan departure. The site is not depicted in a glyphic form in Codex Aubin, but the text reads: "they came to leave from there to Cuextecatlichocayan and to Coatlicamac in the year 2 House." In contrast, according to the visual logic in Codex Boturini, the Mexica would have left Cuextecatlichocayan in the year 1 Flint and would have begun their stay at Coatlicamac in the year 1 Flint or 2 House, staying there until 3 Flint.

As in Codex Boturini, the Codex Aubin *tlacuilo* associates the block of year-bearers that begins with 2 House with the stay at Coatlicamac. Perhaps because the Codex Boturini footprints on folio 6 lead from 3 Flint to the site of Tula, the Codex Aubin *tlacuilo* interprets this year as the date of arrival at Tula. His block of year-bearers associated with Coatlicamac ends with 2 Reed. He includes 3 Flint in the block of years associated with the two-page spread that deals with Tula. Like Codex Boturini, the Codex Aubin *tlacuilo* ends the block associated with Tula in the year 9 Reed.

This means that when the *tlacuilo* records the next site (Atlitlalacyan) his year block begins, like Codex Boturini's, with 10 Flint. Perhaps because he now recognizes that in Codex Boturini the blocks to the right are associated with the place sign, he disregards the footprints and interprets the first year to the right of Tlemaco as simultaneously the last year at Atlitlalacyan. While Codex Boturini indicates that 6 House is the last year at Atlitlalacyan, the Codex Aubin date block associated with this site ends on 7 Rabbit, essentially adding one year to the stay. Codex Aubin lists the stay at Tlemaco as beginning in the year 8 Reed, one year later than the date in Codex Boturini, and ending in 12 Reed, the date that Codex Boturini lists as the first year of the stay at Atotonilco. This time both blocks signal a stay of five years, but the Codex Aubin has shifted the dates by one year. As a result the stay at Atotonilco must be recorded as taking place one year later than is recorded in Codex Boturini. At this point the Codex Aubin *tlacuilo* appears to make a decision to follow the Codex Boturini pattern so that the date blocks in both manuscripts reflect the same groupings. Though Codex Aubin begins the stay at Atotonilco one year later, in 13 Flint, the *tlacuilo* records the end date as 3 Reed, the same as the date in Codex Boturini.

Table 2.1.
Comparison of the Mexica Migration Itineraries in Codex Boturini and Codex Aubin

CODEX BOTURINI	CODEX AUBIN	NEW FIRE (2)
Aztlan [–1 Flint]	Aztlan [–1 Flint]	
	Quinehuayan [–1 Flint]* (1)	
Colhuacan [1 Flint (1168)–1 Flint (1168)]	Colhuacan [1 Flint–1 Flint]*	
Broken Tree [1 Flint–1 Flint]	Broken Tree [1 Flint–1 Flint]	
Cuextecatlichocayan [1 Flint–1 Flint]	Cuextecatlichocayan [2 House–2 House]*	
Coatlicamac [2 House–3 Flint]	Coatlicamac [2 House–2 Reed]	(3)
Tula [4 House–9 Reed]	Tula [3 Flint–9 Reed]	
Atlitlalacyan [10 Flint–6 House]	Atlitlalacyan [10 Flint–7 Rabbit]	
Tlemaco [7 Rabbit–11 Rabbit]	Tlemaco [8 Reed–12 Reed]	
Atotonilco [12 Reed–3 Reed]	Atotonilco [13 Flint–3 Reed]	
Apazco [4 Flint–2 Reed]	Apazco [4 Flint–2 Reed]	(4)
Tzompanco [3 Flint–6 Reed]	Tzompanco [3 Flint–6 Reed]	
Xaltocan [7 Flint–10 Reed]	Xaltocan [7 Flint–10 Reed]	
Acalhuacan [11 Flint–1 Reed]	Acalhuacan [11 Flint–1 Reed]	
Ehecatepec [2 Flint–5 Reed]	Ehecatepec [2 Flint–5 Reed]	
Tolpetlac [6 Flint–13 Reed]	Tolpetlac [6 Flint– 13 Reed]	
Cohuatitlan [1 Flint–7 Reed]	Cohuatitlan [1 Flint–7 Reed]	
Huixachtitlan [8 Flint–11 Reed]	Huixachtitlan [8 Flint–11 Reed]	
Tecpayocan [12 Flint–2 Reed]	Tecpayocan [12 Flint–2 Reed]	(5)
Pantitlan [3 Flint–6 Reed]	Pantitlan [3 Flint–6 Reed]	
Amallinalpan, border of Azcapotzalco [7 Flint–1 Reed]	Amallinalpan, border of Azcapotzalco [7 Flint–1 Reed]	
Pantitlan [2 Flint–5 Reed]	Pantitlan [2 Flint–5 Reed]	
Acolnahuac [6 Flint–9 Reed]	Acolnahuac [6 Flint–9 Reed]	
Popotlan [10 Flint–13 Reed]	Popotlan [10 Flint–13 Reed]	
Techcatitlan [1 Flint–4 Reed]	Techcatitlan [1 Flint–4 Reed]	
Atlacuihuayan (Tacubaya) [5 Flint–8 Reed]	Atlacuihuayan (Tacubaya) [5 Flint–8 Reed]	
Chapultepec [9 Flint–2 Reed]	Chapultepec [9 Flint–2 Reed]	(6)
Acocolco [2 Reed–2 Reed]	Acocolco [2 Reed–2 Reed]*	
Contitlan, border of Tizaapan–Colhuacan [3 Flint–6 Reed]	Contitlan, border of Tizaapan–Colhuacan [3 Flint–6 Reed]	

CODEX BOTURINI	CODEX AUBIN	NEW FIRE (2)
Colhuacan [3 Flint–6 Reed]	Tizaapan, border of Colhuacan [3 Flint–6 Reed]	
	Mexicatzinco [7 Flint–7 Flint]	
	Nexticpac [8 House–11 Flint]	
	Iztacalco [12 House–13 Rabbit]	
	Zoquipan/Temazcaltitlan [1 Reed–1 Reed]	
	Mexico Tenochtitlan [2 Flint–]	

Notes: Black bar indicates apparent discrepancy in the year dates for the stays at these locations. Shading indicates areas of diagonal erasure.

In the Codex Boturini column the years listed represent the years stayed at each site. Beginning with Coatlicamac, Codex Boturini visually leaves open the possibility that the Mexica first arrived at each site one year earlier (see chapter 2).

*Sites named in the alphabetic text of Codex Aubin but not depicted as a glyphic place sign.

(1) Quinehuayan and Colhuacan are conflated in Codex Aubin. Quinehuayan may be described as a location at Colhuacan.

(2) The dates of the New Fire Ceremony are the same in Codex Boturini and Codex Aubin.

(3) 2 Reed. Codex Aubin specifies the location as Coatepetl Hill at Coatlicamac.

(4) 2 Reed. Codex Aubin specifies the location as a hill called Huitzcol at Apazco.

(5) 2 Reed. Codex Aubin specifies the location as a hill called Tecpayo at Tecpayocan.

(6) 2 Reed. Codex Aubin specifies the location as Chapultepec and indicates that the ceremony was delayed because of capture by their enemies.

Thereafter Codex Aubin reproduces the same sets of date blocks associated with the same sites as those found in Codex Boturini. From Apazco to Colhuacan, where the Codex Boturini breaks off, they are identical. They conform to one another visually. The only difference is that Codex Aubin includes alphabetic text associated with the first year-bearer declaring that year as the point when the Mexica moved to the given site, while the visual rhetoric of Codex Boturini allows for the possibility that the Mexica spent part of the previous year at that site. I believe that the apparent discrepancies in the six early sites and the conformity in the remaining sites show the Codex Aubin *tlacuilo* struggling with how to record this information in the clearest and most accurate manner before settling into a pattern that reflects his solution.

CONNECTIONS TO CODEX MEXICANUS

Notably, the solutions that the Codex Boturini *tlacuilo* arrived at to produce a nuanced record of the departure and arrival dates of the Mexica are also employed in the Codex Mexicanus. As Navarrete has noted, though Codex Mexicanus is an indigenous paper manuscript, it is bound like a book: the *tlacuilo* "took great care to draw the time lines and the footprint lines on each page at exactly the same height as on the previous one, maintaining the illusion that the book was a continuous unit."[38] In the migration segment of this manuscript the year-bearers run in a continuous stream horizontally through the center of the folios. Thick red lines link events and figures to the date cartouches. On folios 18–19 the *tlacuilo* draws a thick red line that emerges above the glyph for 2

House and terminates at 4 Reed (figure 2.8). In the middle of this line is the place glyph for Tlatzallan, marking a stay of three years at that site.[39] A second short red line emerges from 4 Reed; directly above the cartouche is a figure and a set of footprints that end at the place glyph for Chicomoztoc. Just as in the Codex Boturini, the footprints emphasize the year of departure. The next thick red line emerges from 5 Flint and terminates at 13 Flint. The place glyph for Chicomoztoc marks the center of this line, indicating a stay of nine years at Chicomoztoc. Another short red line emerges from 13 Flint and connects to a figure and footprints, which end at the place glyph for Coatlicamac. This line indicates that they departed for Coatlicamac in the year 13 Flint. The next thick red line emerges from 1 House and terminates at 3 Reed (with the glyph for Coatlicamac in the center), indicating a total stay of three years. The format continues as the Mexica depart for the next stop, Matlauacallan, in the year 3 Reed.

To recap, we may thus read the narrative as stating that the travelers spent three years at Tlatzallan, from 2 House to 4 Reed. They left Tlatzallan in the year 4 Reed and traveled to Chicomoztoc, where they stayed nine years, from 5 Flint to 13 Flint. In 13 Flint they departed for Coatlicamac, where they stayed for three years, from 1 House to 3 Reed. In 3 Reed they departed for Matlauacallan and stayed there three years, from 4 Flint to 6 Rabbit; and so on.

Codex Mexicanus, a palimpsest produced by multiple *tlacuiloque* in several stages in the latter part of the sixteenth century, is a very different kind of manuscript from Codex Boturini. Yet the visual relationship between time and space, or chronotope as

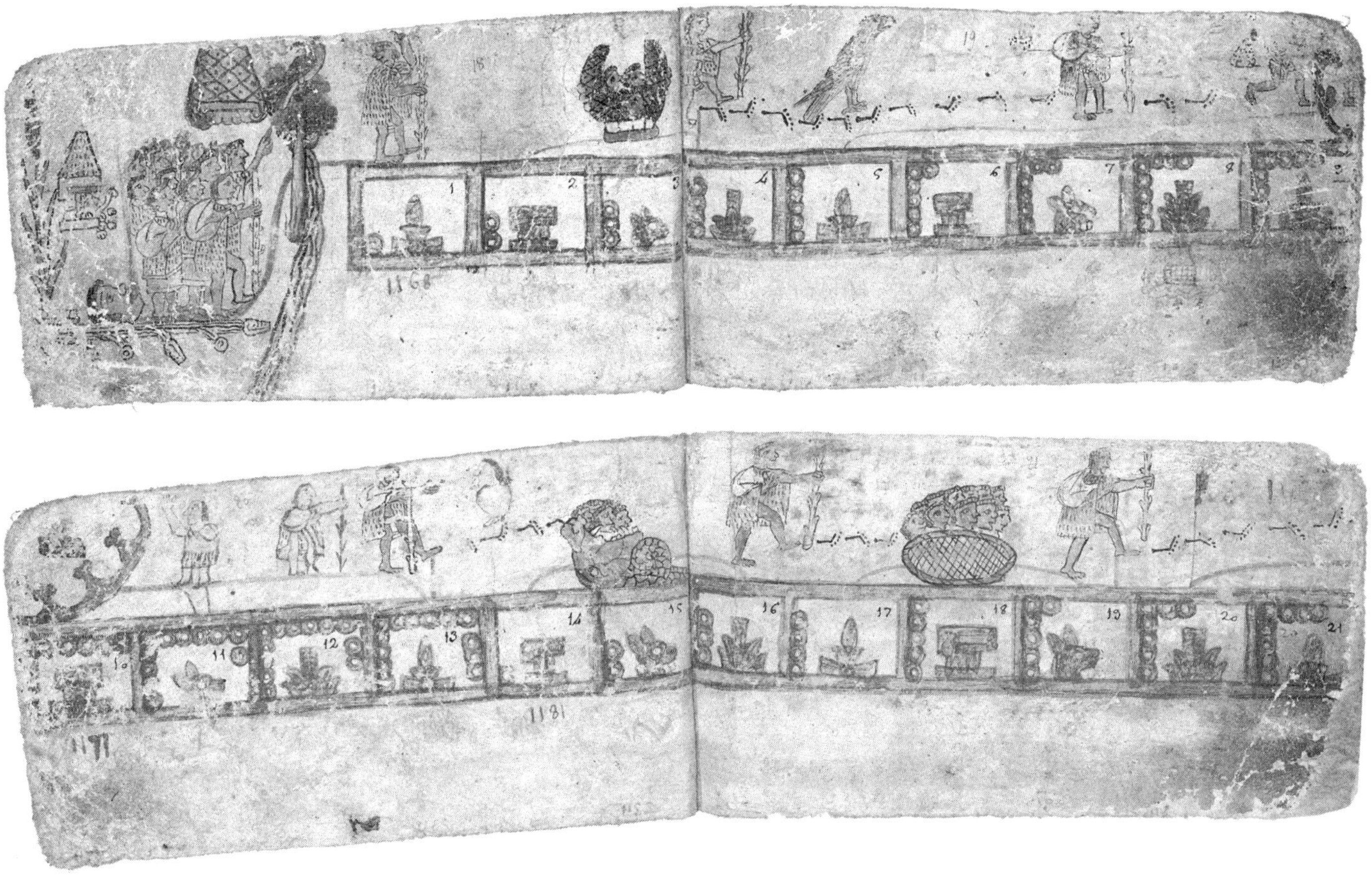

Figure 2.8. Codex Mexicanus, folios 18–19 and 20–21. Courtesy of the Bibliothèque Nationale de France.

Navarrete refers to it, functions in a similar manner. The *tlacuiloque* who worked on these manuscripts also used red and black pigment in similar ways. In Codex Boturini red connects the date cartouches and relates to the passage of time, while black is used for everything else. In Codex Mexicanus red pigment frames the date cartouches for most of the migration segment and is used for the lines indicating duration of time, while black is used to depict the footprints and the frame lines of figures and forms. Notably, the single figure on Codex Mexicanus folio 20 who faces left, rather than right, is attached to the date glyph 11 Rabbit by short black rather than red lines. These lines, one straight and one slightly curved, have no clear terminus and may serve to indicate the alternate journey taken by non-Mexica groups after Chicomoztoc. Like the tearful figure near the top of Codex Boturini folio 3, who is shown leaving the scene with a dotted black line and a footprint, the short black lines in Codex Mexicanus indicate that this individual is not a part of the Mexica chronology. While an in-depth examination of Codex Mexicanus is beyond the scope of this study, these basic observations confirm Navarrete's contention that "at least in the case of Mexica histories, the adoption of European forms and techniques was subordinated to the chronotope that gave them generic validity."[40]

THE GLOSSES

Although Codex Boturini is unfinished, sepia glosses were added at a later point. The sepia glosses are particularly difficult to study because they have faded considerably. The use of these glosses is not systematic: they are not integrated into the composition and thus appear to be a later addition. John Glass writes: "Delafield reports that, according to Bullock, the 24 glosses on the manuscript are by Boturini, an allegation that is presently unsubstantiated."[41] John Delafield Jr. included a lithographic facsimile of Codex Boturini in an 1839 book first published in Cincinnati, Ohio.[42] His lithograph was based on two copies of Codex Boturini that William Bullock had with him when he traveled to Cincinnati. As Glass notes, Bullock's alleged information has not been confirmed, but these data do suggest that the glosses were added prior to Bullock's acquisition of the manuscript. Patrick Johansson Keraudren has translated the legible Nahuatl glosses.[43] Most are place names, but there are a few short descriptive phrases. He describes the script as typical of the sixteenth century. Thus the glosses are probably by a sixteenth-century Nahua writer who was making notes on the manuscript sometime after its initial production.

Codex Boturini: A Paradigm for Depicting Mexica Identity

The narrative that the Codex Boturini *tlacuilo* composed so carefully articulated a story about Mexica identity. It defined the Mexica as the people of Aztlan, chosen and guided by Huitzilopochtli. In the Codex Boturini account the *tlacuilo* conveys that the Mexica merited their land, and their ultimate dominion and status in the Basin of Mexico, through their suffering, perseverance, and fierce spirit. As Elizabeth Hill Boone has elucidated, the migration journey is at once cyclical and transformational.[44] Aztlan and Tenochtitlan mirror one another at either end of the narrative. Colhuacan (the Place of the Bent Hill; sometimes described as Teocolhuacan, the ancient or deified Place of the Bent Hill) is the first stop after departure in Codex Boturini. The action at the end of the manuscript again takes place in Colhuacan and its vicinity just prior to the arrival at Tenochtitlan. Tenochtitlan does not appear in Codex Boturini, due to damage. Although the protagonists start and end in a version of the same place, they are transformed. They leave Aztlan as Aztecs but arrive and found their city as Mexica. They begin as people of rugged Chichimec heritage and end with increased connections to the prestigious Toltec lineage.[45] The second part of this chapter traces core elements of Codex Boturini's narrative that are used to define Mexica identity. Connections and discrepancies between the Codex Aubin and Codex Azcatitlan begin to elucidate how these manuscripts respond to the paradigm that Codex Boturini represents.

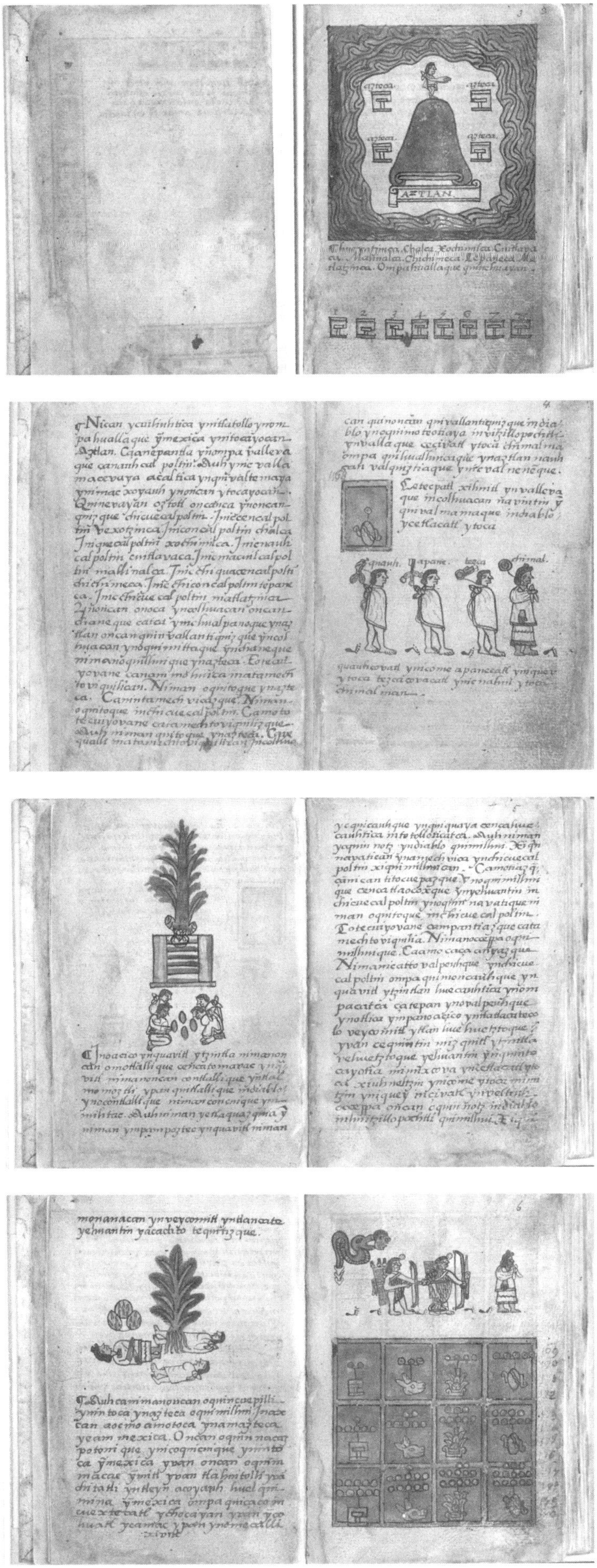

AZTLAN

In Mexica migration histories the process of shaping identity begins with Aztlan. Described as an ancient homeland and place of origin in many Nahua accounts, it is represented pictorially and prominently in Codex Boturini (plate 2.1), Codex Azcatitlan (figure 3.3), Codex Aubin (figure 2.9), Codex Mexicanus (figure 2.8), and Mapa Sigüenza. Most sources designate Aztlan as the place of origin exclusively of the Mexica.[46] The Codex Boturini, Codex Azcatitlan, and Codex Aubin all depict Aztlan as surrounded by water (an island), from which the inhabitants depart, arriving at Colhuacan in the year 1 Flint.

The most compact representation of the departure is in Codex Boturini, where a wavy oval line delineates the island and a larger wavy line surrounds it, marking a body of water (plate 2.1). A priest with darkened skin and long hair rows a boat away from the island, leading a male and a female named Chimalma to the opposite shore. On the island the primordial couple appear beneath a temple and six house forms, indicating that Aztlan was a settled place and referencing the different *calpulli* (neighborhood) groups that would migrate. All of the figures face right, signaling the direction of the narrative, which reads continuously from left to right. Footprints on the opposite shore guide the reader and indicate the path that the protagonists will follow to Colhuacan. A human head wearing the headdress of Huitzilopochtli (Hummingbird from the Left) appears surrounded by branches within a cave at Colhuacan. His speech scrolls summon the Aztecs. The date 1 Flint, set off in a square frame, indicates the auspicious date of departure.

While Codex Aubin relies on a scripted label to identify Aztlan, Codex Boturini and Codex Azcatitlan use a place sign composed of a reed and a flow of water. At the beginning of the twentieth century German scholar Eduard Seler provided the most convincing interpretation of this image as the combined representation of water (*atl*) and reed or sedge (*aztapilli*), which rendered the name Aztlan.[47]

Figure 2.9. Codex Aubin, folios 2v–6r. © The Trustees of the British Museum. All rights reserved.

Michel Graulich sided with Seler, as the prefix *az-* or *azta-* in Nahuatl carries the connotation of whiteness and some sixteenth-century texts describe Aztlan as "a place of whiteness."[48] For example, Durán writes that the name Aztlan "could mean 'Whiteness' or 'Place of the Herons.' Because of this the people originally were called Aztec, which means 'People of Whiteness.'"[49] The description of Aztlan as an island surrounded by water, and particularly the pictorial evidence in the Codex Mexicanus (figure 2.8), which has a very detailed depiction of reed and water, seems to support Seler's interpretation of Aztlan as a combination of water and reed.[50] The migration history in the Codex Mexicanus begins with a large group of figures departing along a path that leads from a tall reed (*aztapilli*) attached to water (*atl*), with a representation of teeth (*tlantli*) connecting the two (figure 2.8).[51] Codex Boturini and Codex Azcatitlan each depict the glyph for Aztlan atop a temple on the island.

CHICOMOZTOC, QUINEHUAYAN, AND COLHUACAN

Although Mexica narratives lay claim to Aztlan as a point of origin, they often closely link the departure from Aztlan with the sites of Chicomoztoc, Quinehuayan, and Colhuacan. These sites generally are depicted as coming after Aztlan. They are sometimes depicted separately but often elided, such that reference to one would have called to mind all of them for an audience used to hearing different versions of the migration account.[52] In Codex Boturini and Codex Azcatitlan the Mexica encounter the eight tribes with whom they begin the migration at Colhuacan (plate 2.2). Codex Aubin describes this part of the departure in script on folio 3v, where the departing groups are listed in the same order as in Codex Boturini and Codex Azcatitlan (figure 2.9):

> Here is written the history of the Mexica who came from a place called Aztlan. So from there in the middle of the water the four *calpulli* departed. And to do penance, they came in boats to put their fir branches there in the place called Quinehuayan. In that place there is a cave from where the eight *calpulli* left: the first *calpulli* of the Huexotzinca, the second *calpulli* of the Chalca, the third *calpulli* of the Xochimilca, the fourth *calpulli* of the Cuitlahuaca, the fifth *calpulli* of the Malinalca, the sixth *calpulli* of the Chichimeca, the seventh *calpulli* of the Tepaneca, the eighth *calpulli* of the Matlatzinca.
>
> When those who were inhabitants of Colhuacan remained there, they [the Aztecs] crossed over to here from Aztlan; there those of Colhuacan came out to receive them. When the inhabitants had seen them, then they said to the Aztecs: "Our lords, where are you going? We are willing to accompany you."
>
> Then the Aztecs said: "Where are we going to take you?"
>
> Then the eight *calpulli* said: "It does not matter, our lords, so we shall accompany you."
>
> And then the Aztecs said: "So be it, accompany us!"[53]

According to this passage, the Aztecs depart from Aztlan for Quinehuayan, where the cave from which the eight tribes depart is located. The description echoes the concept of Chicomoztoc (Place of the Seven Caves). The concept of caves as sacred places of emergence is ubiquitous in Mesoamerica and extends as far back as the Olmec culture.[54] The text mentions Colhuacan next, although its relationship to Quinehuayan is not explained. Perhaps Colhuacan is conceptualized as a location within Quinehuayan, as implied by some other texts. Codex Azcatitlan generally offers a pictorially expanded version of the Codex Boturini content (see chapter 3); the *tlacuilo* depicts both Colhuacan and Chicomoztoc after Aztlan.

While scripted sources on Mexica origin and migration describe various combinations of and relationships among Aztlan, Chicomoztoc, Quinehuayan, and Colhuacan, the pictorial sources are more straightforward about privileging Aztlan. This may mean that the fine distinctions among these sites, once articulated in the oral tradition, were elided or lost as the pictorial and oral traditions gave way to alphabetic writing. The Codex Aubin, Codex Boturini, and Mapa Sigüenza depict Aztlan but omit Chicomoztoc. Codex Azcatitlan and Codex Mexicanus place the departure from Aztlan before the emergence from Chicomoztoc, thereby privileging it.

CALPULLI LEADERS AND GOD-BEARERS

In Codex Boturini the Aztecs meet up with eight other groups at Colhuacan. A figure with a speech scroll, the group leader, is attached to each of the *calpulli* designations that are lined up vertically on folio 2 (plate 2.2). They are led by four god-bearers (from left to right): Chimalma, Apanecatl, Cuauhcoatl, and Tezcacoatl.[55] The horizontal presentation of the four god-bearers and the row of footprints beneath them signal the direction that all of the groups will take and that the god-bearers lead the assembled groups. The god-bearers carry the *tlaquimilolli* (sacred bundles) on their backs.

In contrast to the economy of Codex Boturini, Codex Aubin names the eight *calpulli* more than once. First they are listed in alphabetic text, just below the square representation of Aztlan on folio 3r, and are pictorially represented by eight house forms at the bottom of the page, each topped by the numerals one through eight (figure 2.9). On the following page, folio 3v, they are repeated in the text as listed above. Notably, the toponyms for the eight *calpulli* are not depicted. While much of Codex Boturini's iconographic content is represented in Codex Aubin, the *tlacuilo* makes decisions to carry some of the information in the scripted record.

As the text continues to describe the departure, the Christian perspective of the Codex Aubin *tlacuilo* becomes apparent:

> From Colhuacan they left carrying the devil who they worshipped as a god, the Huitzilopochtli. When they came they brought a woman by the name of Chimalma from there, from Aztlan. They divided into four as they walked.
>
> In the year 1 Flint they departed from Colhuacan. Four of them bore the devil on their back: a person by the name of Quauhcohuatl, a second <by the name of> Apanecatl, a third by the name of Tezcacohuacatl, a fourth by the name of Chimalma.[56]

The importance of Huitzilopochtli is made clear in this passage, but he is described with the Spanish loanword *diablo* (devil). Huitzilopochtli only appears pictorially once or twice in the Aubin migration history, always in the form of a *tlaquimilolli*. On folio 4r the *tlacuilo* shows Chimalma carrying a *tlaquimilolli*, and on folio 4v it appears discreetly placed on the steps of a small altar beneath a tree (figure 2.9). Perhaps the Christian *tlacuilo* felt that representation of Huitzilopochtli within the colonial confines of alphabetic text allowed for greater control and positioning of this powerful god (e.g., framing Huitzilopochtli within the text as a "devil").

THE SEPARATION: FROM AZTEC TO MEXICA

Following the departure of the Aztecs and the eight *calpulli* from Colhuacan, Codex Boturini folios 3–4 (plates 2.3–2.4), Codex Aubin folios 4v–6r (figure 2.9), and Codex Azcatitlan folios 3v–5r (figure 2.10) depict a series of scenes that mark the transition of the Aztecs to the Mexica. In this series of images (and script in the Codex Aubin) Huitzilopochtli singles out the Aztecs, separating them from the other tribes. As he proffers a new identity and a new name, "Mexica," he establishes an exchange relationship with his people. The Mexica are provided the tools that they need to survive and promised great success and prosperity in the future, even as they are instructed in the practice of sacrifice required by their god.

Huitzilopochtli instigates the separation of the Mexica from the other groups and plays an important role in the early part of the migration history. He is described in the Florentine Codex as the most venerated and most important god:

> First Chapter, which telleth of the highest of the gods whom they worshipped and to whom they offered sacrifices in ancient times.

> Uitzilopochtli (Hummingbird from the Left) was only a common man, just a man, a sorcerer, an omen of evil, a madman, a deceiver, a creator of war, a war-lord, an instigator of war.
>
> For it was said of him that he brought hunger and plague—that is, war. And when a feast day was celebrated, captives were slain; ceremonially bathed slaves were offered up. The merchants bathed them.[57]

This description makes clear the importance of this god in Mexica culture, his description as a hummingbird, his association with warfare, and his need for sacrifice, all elements that are established in the Mexica migration stories.

Representation of the god varies in the different codices. As noted, Codex Aubin exhibits a colonial Christian perspective in omitting figural representations of the god. Instead the god's role is acknowledged in the alphabetic text, where he is defined as a "devil." Codex Boturini limits representation of the god to the early plates of the manuscript, where his role is most influential to the narrative (plates 2.1–2.4). Sahagún's text describes Huitzilopochtli as "a common man, just a man." The images of the god in Codex Boturini reflect this definition in that almost all representations of the god show the head of a human figure wearing a hummingbird headdress and not a hummingbird per se. On folio 4, however, he appears as an eagle (plate 2.4). Codex Azcatitlan depicts the god often throughout the migration history. Huitzilopochtli typically appears in this codex as a human figure in a hummingbird costume as well, although some representations like the one on folio 4v (figure 2.10) show hybrid creatures. When shown emerging from the *tlaquimilolli*, he appears as a bird (figure 3.2). The god-bearers carry Huitzilopochtli throughout the narrative, and the pictorial images illustrate how "in some places they stayed and built themselves a temple; they erected a temple for their god Huitzilopochtli."[58]

Codex Boturini folio 3 (plate 2.3) begins with the image of a broken tree, shown separated at its middle. The tree sprouts twelve leafy branches from its top. The lower part of the tree depicts roots, typical of pre-Hispanic representations of trees and plants. Two arms protrude from either side of the lower part of the tree, giving it an anthropomorphic quality. Five black dots are connected to the lower part of the tree with a dark line. Visually and narratively, the broken tree foreshadows the break that the Aztecs make from the other *calpulli* who began the migration together.

Immediately adjacent to the roots of the tree, Huitzilopochtli sits atop a small altar. The proximity to the tree implies his role in the break or separation that is about to occur. The footprints lead past the tree and Huitzilopochtli to five male figures seated around a tripod vessel, eating from a woven basket. The next grouping shows six figures clustered around Huitzilopochtli. The speech scrolls that emanate from all of the figures indicate a discussion. The god's instructions regarding the break from the other tribes elicit tears from these figures. The sixth figure, added to this group since the previous cluster, wears a mantle with a border that differs from the others, but the significance is unclear.

The action decreed by the god is carried out above these figures. The figure to the left bears the reed-water glyph, indicating that he represents the Aztecs. He advises a figure connected to the Cuitlahuaca group of the decision. The speech scrolls signal the conversation, and the tear in the Cuitlahuaca figure's eye is its result. A footstep emerging from the dotted line connecting this figure with his tribal sign leads up and off of the codex page, literally removing the Cuitlahuaca and the other groups from the picture. Perhaps simply as a stylistic decision, the Cuitlahuaca are central in the depiction of the non-Aztec groups. The footsteps on Codex Boturini folio 2 (plate 2.2) lead to and from the Cuitlahuaca sign, and the Cuitlahuaca figure on folio 3 (plate 2.3) is singled out to receive the news of the separation. A semicircular sign with circular motifs inside appears above the Cuitlahuaca sign, representing the night sky when the conversation took place.[59]

Chimalpahin's "Mexican History or Chronicle" offers a version of the event similar to the depiction in Codex Boturini:

> And when they reached the foot of a tree, they thereupon seated themselves at its base. A very thick tree stood there, a cypress. They then erected an earthen altar there and upon it set the portent Huitzilopochtli. When they had set him down and a few days had passed, they presented him their travel ration. They would have eaten, [but] then they heard someone talk to them. He spoke from the top of the cypress. He said to them: You who are here, leave [lest the tree] fall on you; tomorrow the cypress will fall. They then left what they were eating; it was a long time [before] they swallowed [food]. They then left, they abandoned the cypress. It came to pass that at dawn it was uprooted; the cypress tree broke over them. Still the Azteca Mexitin spent four more years there when they settled and rested there at the foot of the cypress.[60]

In this version Huitzilopochtli forewarns the Aztecs as he guides and protects them. The indication that they spent "four more years" suggests a total of five in this location and may explain the five dots connected to the tree.[61] However, the visual logic of Codex Boturini indicates that all events between the departure from Aztlan and the stay at Coatlicamac took place in one year. The five dots may refer to smaller units of time, like *veintenas* (twenty-day "months"), *treicenas* (thirteen-day periods), or days. In Chimalpahin's version of events the narrative passes immediately to Huitzilopochtli's demands for tribute in the form of human sacrifice. Juan de Torquemada's account also aligns closely with the pictorial imagery in Codex Boturini and emphasizes that the process is painful because they have familial relationships to the other tribes: "Therefore the Mexicas did it although it was painful to leave the others, being all brothers and family members."[62] The departure represents a crucial point in the narrative because it is the moment when the Aztecs, under the guidance of Huitzilopochtli, begin to establish and develop their identity as the Mexica.

On Codex Boturini folio 4 (plate 2.4), the four god-bearers lead the Mexica to the next event, wherein they begin the practice of human sacrifice dictated by their god and make offerings to him to ensure their survival. Tezcacoatl carries Huitzilopochtli; the god continues to advise the leaders, as indicated by the speech scrolls emanating from him. The right half of the plate shows three figures stretched across plants in preparation for sacrifice. The central figure is stretched across a leafy bush, with two flanking figures lying on barrel cacti. The sacrificed figures wear animal-skin clothing, identifying them as members of noncivilized nomadic groups. The figures at left have name signs: a circular mosaic motif and a fish. The Aztec who announced the separation to the Cuitlahuaca appears again, this time engaged in the act of sacrifice. His victims are decorated with black paint (around the eyes of the figures at left and mouth of the figure at right).

Chimalpahin's narrative, after the account of the broken tree quoted above, follows a similar trajectory:

> And it has already been said that the Azteca were at the foot of the tree for a long time. Later, as they continued on their way, they came to the devils of the barrel cactus; they lay beside it. And at the foot of the mesquites lay some seven of those whom they named Mimixcoa. One man was named Xiuhneltzin; the second was named Mimichtzin; the third was a woman, their elder sister, named Teoxahual; and there were four more devils whose names are not known. There Huitzilopochtli spoke to the aforesaid god-carriers, the god-carriers of this false god. . . . It has already been said that there Huitzilopochtli spoke to the Azteca god-carriers. He said to them: Take those who are by the barrel cactus. They will be the first to pay tribute.[63]

Just as this is the first representation of sacrifice in the Codex Boturini, Chimalpahin's narrative emphasizes that it is at this point that Huitzilopochtli introduces the concept of human sacrifice as a tribute to be paid to the god. Presumably, the figures sacrificed in the Codex Boturini are the three Mimixcoa named in Chimalpahin's narrative.[64]

Chimalpahin's account emphasizes that Huitzilopochtli is behind the Mexica practice of human sacrifice. He describes the Mexica relationship to the god as follows:

> And in their keeping was he to whom they supplicated, whom they considered a god, he whom they named the portent Huitzilopochtli. He spoke; he conversed with the Azteca; he lived among them and was their friend. Hence, therefore, perished so many hundreds of thousands of people's spirits and souls that he carried away to Mictlan. . . .
>
> And thus the devil knew perfectly well how the Mexica would therefore be great examples; that they would be terrified, awe-stricken here and everywhere, and that he would carry off all, countless hundreds of thousands, of the spirits and souls [of] these Mexica to Mictlan when he took over their [way of] being, their customs, as is here laid out and disposed.[65]

Chimalpahin's account stresses the quantity of sacrifice required by Huitzilopochtli, thereby identifying the god as a fierce and deadly force. The fierceness is attributed to the god rather than specifically to the Mexica, who are presented as fearful minions. This emphasis may be a result of Chimalpahin's attempts to present a favorable view of the Mexica to seventeenth-century Christian readers by framing sacrifice as an imperative of the "devil" who "took over their [way of] being," rather than as an inherent quality of the Mexica.

Narratively, that first sacrifice establishes an exchange relationship with Huitzilopochtli that only comes to an end during the conquest. In exchange for their loyalty and sacrificial offerings, particularly the offering of human sacrifice, Huitzilopochtli guides, supports, and privileges his chosen people. It is only at this point that the "Aztecs" become "Mexica." On Codex Boturini folio 4 (above the sacrificial victims) a figure with a bow and arrow appears with speech scrolls indicating that he speaks to the eagle that approaches with the *xiuhmamalhuaztli* (the instrument used to light New Fire) in his clutches.[66] Dotted lines connect the eagle, the figure, and a net basket. This scene is paralleled in Chimalpahin's description of the moment when Huitzilopochtli shares with his people the benefits of the divine contract:

> And as the ancient ones said, when they emerged from Aztlan the name of the Azteca was not yet Mexitin. They all considered themselves Azteca. But we say that it was later that they took their name, that they considered themselves Mexitin. And thus were they given their name: as the ancient ones have said, it was Huitzilopochtli who gave them the name. And then and there he changed the Aztecas' name for them. He said to them: Now no longer is your name Azteca: you are now Mexitin. There they also applied feathers to their ears when they took their name as Mexitin. Hence they are now called Mexica. And he then also gave them the arrow and the bow and the net carrying bag. Whatever went [flying] above, the Mexitin could shoot easily.[67]

The reed-water glyph related to Aztlan no longer appears in the manuscript. Instead the figure holding the bow wears feathers in his hair, indicating his status change. Now a Mexica, he receives the bow and arrow mentioned in the text and is linked to the net carrying bag by a dotted line. He now has the tools to survive and to mark the years. In this image Huitzilopochtli takes the form of an eagle, rather than a human in a hummingbird headdress.

The migration histories typically only present the eagle as a symbol related to the foundation.[68] The presence of the eagle here references the promise that Huitzilopochtli makes to the Mexica, as his chosen people:

> And [do] this: go, look for the tuna cactus. There you will see that upon it stands an eagle. There it eats; there it suns itself. And now your hearts are content. . . . And there is where we are to remain, where we shall be on guard, where we shall await and contend against various peoples [in battle with] our breasts and our heads, our arrows and our shields. Thus shall we find all who lie surrounding us, all whom we shall conquer, whom we shall capture.[69]

As Huitzilopochtli cements their relationship, he takes the form of the omen that will signal fulfillment of his promise. Similarly, Huitzilopochtli is linked to the omen in Codex Azcatitlan. Rather than an eagle on the nopal cactus on folio 12r (figure 3.6), the *tlacuilo* depicts the head of a Huitzilopochtli impersonator wearing the hummingbird headdress. The god is there for the Mexica at the beginning and the end of the journey. In the early part of the narrative the Mexica gain a separate identity as the chosen people who will be led to success if they follow the commands and dictates of their god Huitzilopochtli. Read as a whole, Codex Boturini folio 4 (plate 2.4) shows the god-bearers receiving the words of Huitzilopochtli, enacting human sacrifice at his bidding, and receiving in return a new Mexica identity that comes with all the divine support, guidance, and promised privileges. This episode marks the start of an ongoing relationship that gives meaning to traditions (human sacrifice, the ritual veneration of Huitzilopochtli, the binding of the years) that would last through the time of conquest.[70]

Codex Aubin folios 4v–6r (figure 2.9) depict the same events in abbreviated form. The first image depicts the tree that will break atop an altar, four figures gathered to eat, and a *tlaquimilolli* that rests where the base of the tree and the top of the altar meet. The Nahuatl script contextualizes the images:

> And when they arrived at the foot of the tree, then they settled there. The tree was very wide. Then they formed an altar there on which they put the devil. When they had made the altar, then they had their provisions. But just as they were ready to eat, then the tree broke on top of them.[71]

In the pictorial representation the tree has not yet split, the bundle at the top of the temple stairs represents the god Huitzilopochtli, and the figures may represent the god-bearers shown earlier on folio 4r. The text continues on Codex Aubin folios 5r and 5v (figure 2.9) and begins to take on a dialogic format again. The text closely describes the pictorial imagery found in Codex Boturini folios 3 and 4 (plates 2.3–2.4):

> Then, as a result, they left what they were eating, they were with their heads bowed for a long time. And then, the devil called them and said to them: "Send the eight *calpulli* who accompany you, and say to them: 'We will not continue ahead, we will go in another direction.'"
>
> When they had told them this, the eight *calpulli* became very sad. When they had been sent, then the eight *calpulli* said: "Our lords, where shall we go? Since we accompany you."
>
> Then again, they said to them: "Do not go."
>
> Then first the eight *calpulli* departed. They abandoned them [the Aztecs] there at the foot of the tree; they remained there for a long time. Afterward when they left on the path, the "owl men" came to descend on them. Among the bisnagas (barrel cacti) they were falling, and some of them were falling at the foot of the mesquites.
>
> These were called *mimixcoa*: the first by the name of Xiuhneltzin, the second by the name of Mimichtzin, the third, a woman, their older sister.
>
> Again, there the devil Huitzilopochtli called them; he said to them:
>
> "Take what is among the bisnagas. They will be the first tribute."
>
> And at once, there, he changed the name of the Aztecs. He said to them: "From now on, your name is no longer *Aztec*, you are now *Mexica*."
>
> There he painted their ears black; in this way the Mexica took their name. And there they were given the arrow and the bow and the little net.

> Whatever flew overhead, the Mexica shot them well with bows and arrows.[72]

The Codex Aubin *tlacuilo* represents these events with two images. Folio 5v (figure 2.9) presents a reduced version of the events on Codex Boturini folio 4 (plate 2.4). Perhaps as a result of his Christian sensibilities, the Codex Aubin *tlacuilo* does not depict the act of sacrifice but rather its aftermath. Three figures, two males at right and one female at left, lie beneath the barrel cacti over which they were sacrificed. The Aubin *tlacuilo* exhibits less interest in or perhaps understanding of the details of costume and dress. Unlike the Codex Boturini imagery, the victims do not wear animal-skin clothing or body paint. A tree with roots appears to sprout from the uppermost male figure. Just as the eagle in Codex Boturini references the omen that relates to the promise made to the Mexica at this time regarding their future territory, the tree growing from the sacrificed figure may portend the nopal cactus that will grow from the sacrificed heart of Copil.[73] On folio 6r, in the aftermath of the sacrifice, the Mexica are shown with the bow and arrow, the net bag, and the feathers in their hair. The text states that they bound their years for the first time at Coatlicamac, a location represented by the serpent. The head with a tear adjacent to the serpent designates Cuextecatlichocayan. Although the *tlacuilo* pictorially depicts the component parts of this narrative differently than in the Codex Boturini, he chooses to convey the most essential elements. The reduction of imagery in Codex Aubin results from a new reliance on alphabetic text to convey detail in the narrative.

Codex Azcatitlan does not depict the separation from the other groups in the same way. Instead, an alternate version of separation is depicted on folios 3v–4r (figure 2.10). At far left a male in animal-skin clothing begins the migration. Robert Barlow reads the fish that names him as "Michin."[74] The house with two darts on top, identified as Tlacochcalco on the previous page, appears again to the left of the figure. This figure gestures along the direction of the path that leads to two warriors that face each other between the twin peaks of Tepemaxalco. Two additional males progress along the path as a female carrying a child turns toward the viewer, arresting the visual flow. The other figures gathered beneath the mountain peaks establish themselves by building houses, rolling tortillas, and gathering water, taking care of the most basic necessities of life: food, water, and shelter. The second gloss, *ymauh* (their water), emphasizes what must have been a key determinant for places they could stay—fresh water.

The figure identified by the fish (*michin*) may reference the site of Michoacan and an event that Durán describes at the beginning of his migration account:

> The Aztecs passed through the land of the Chichimecs, seeing this new country and the plains of Cíbola but nothing in that land pleased them, and finally they came to rest in the province that is now called Mechoacan, "Land of Those Who Have Fish," in a place called Patzcuaro. And before we continue, I wish to tell how that town and the rest of the province were founded, according to their account.
>
> It should be noted that the Aztecs[,] and those of the province of Malinalco, were of the same group or faction; they were related and all spoke the same language. When they had reached Patzcuaro and saw that it was so peaceful and pleasant, the priests consulted their god. They begged him, if this were not the land that had been promised them, that at least he allow them to leave part of their group there.

Durán's account goes on to describe how the Mexica abandoned some of their party there. While a group of men and women bathed in the lake, the Mexica stole their clothing and departed along the path designated by their god. "Naked and forsaken and not knowing where to go, they [the abandoned] decided to stay there and settle the land."[75]

The abandonment of these people has a divine parallel in Huitzilopochtli's abandonment of his sister Malinalxochitl, an event that immediately follows the occurrence at Michoacan in Durán's narrative.[76] Malinalxochitl is described as a cunning and dangerous sorcerer. The Mexica "had endured her because she was the sister of Huitzilopochtli, but finally they asked the god to get rid of her." When Huitzilopochtli obliges, they abandon her in her sleep. The abandoned party took an alternate path and settled the town now known as Malinalco. Durán links all of these stories by explaining: "It should be noted that the Aztecs and those who are now called the Tarascans of Mechoacan, and those of the province of Malinalco, were of the same group or faction; they were related and all spoke the same language." Such a claim links the Mexica at once to the realm of the gods and to the Tarascan kingdom of Michoacan in the north and northwest. The Mexica may have sought to highlight this connection as Patzcuaro had once been inhabited by Toltecs. However, the connection to Tepemaxalco and its presence at the beginning of the migration history is unclear.[77]

Whether the scene at Tepemaxalco in the Codex Azcatitlan reflects these legends or not, it illustrates the manner in which the Mexica settled and left behind members of their party along the journey. As José de Acosta, a Spanish Jesuit missionary, wrote:

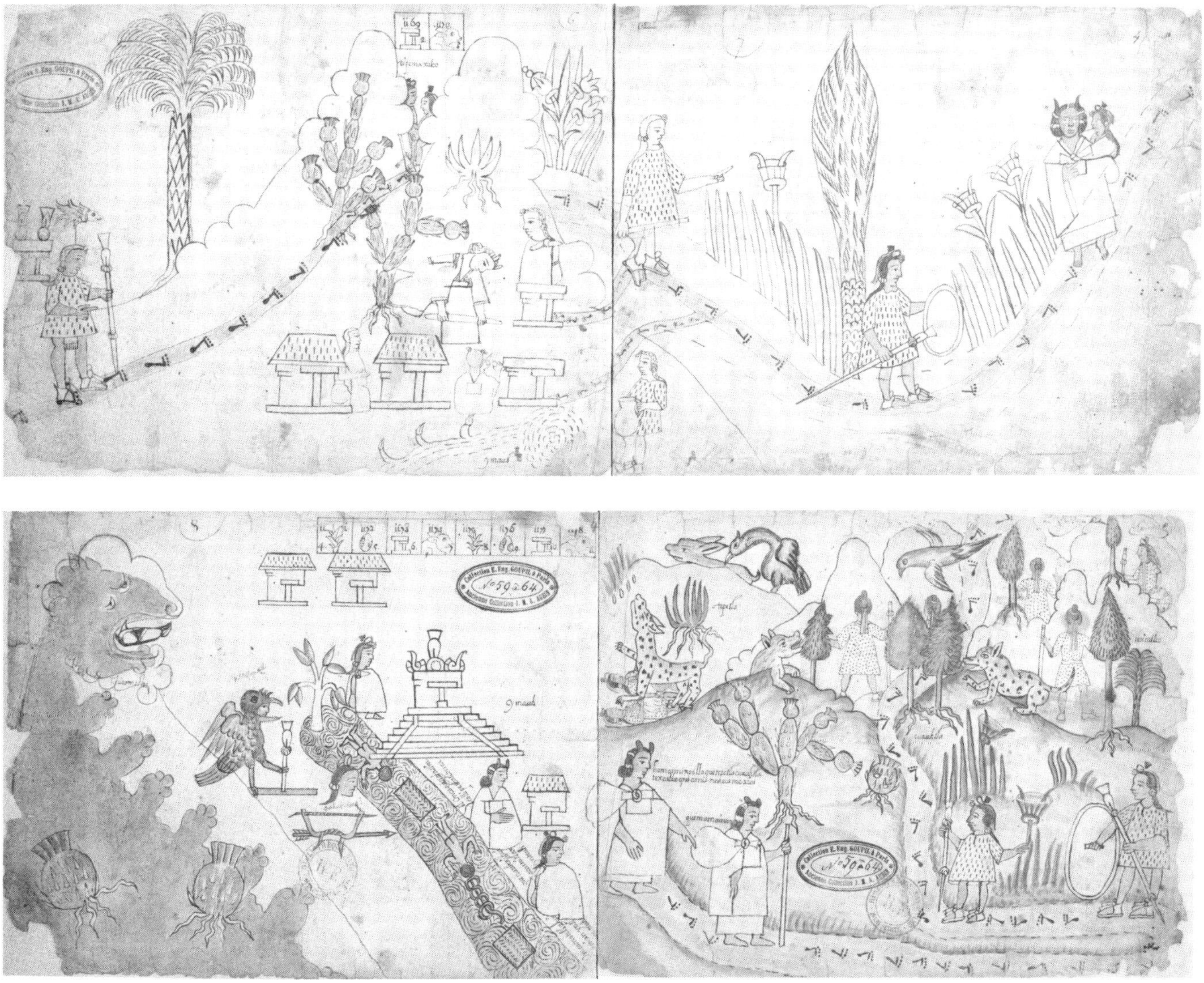

Figure 2.10. Codex Azcatitlan, folios 3v–5r. Courtesy of the Bibliothèque Nationale de France.

> The cause of so long a journey was that their gods (who were undoubtedly demons that spoke visibly with them) had persuaded them to go seeking new lands with such and such characteristics; and so they moved along, exploring the land and looking for the signs that their idols had given them, and where they found good places they settled them one after another and sowed and reaped. And as they found better places they would abandon those already settled, but leaving some folk there still, mostly the old and sick and folk who were exhausted, and also leaving fine buildings, traces of which can be found today along the route that they took.[78]

Such stops are shown repeatedly in the migration narratives of all three codices.

The equivalent of the sacrifice scenes appear in Codex Azcatitlan on folio 4v (figure 2.10). To the right of Chicomoztoc a spring flows from the base of a tree. The *tlacuilo* partially pigments the sacred spring, indicating that it flows in two colors, and depicts sacrificed bodies and reed mats floating in the water.[79] On the left side of the stream the *tlacuilo* depicts Huitzilopochtli as a hybrid human-hummingbird holding the fire drill, a human head wearing the down ball that identifies him as Mexica, and a bow and arrow. To the right a male, a female, and a priest sit near a temple and some houses. The text says that "there they have been bewitched for four years. There they will leave for Cintocoyan. Their god left them the human entrails on the mat."[80] As in Codex Boturini, Huitzilopochtli introduces the newly minted Mexica to the practice of human sacrifice and the New Fire ceremony, while providing them with their new identity and the bow and arrow that they need to survive. Here the sanctified spring may denote the omen of the promised land. In many migration accounts the sacred waters are as much an omen of the foundation as the eagle on the nopal cactus. In Codex Aubin's foundation scene, for example, the *tlacuilo* depicts two individuals submerged in the water beneath the nopal (figure 2.11).

Codex Azcatitlan's beautifully colored folio 5r (figure 2.10) shows the continuation of the journey. No equivalent scene exists in Codex Boturini or Codex Aubin. This likely represents the kind of "scenic" description often heard in an oral account. The landscape illustrates the nature of the terrain and the rigors of the journey, rather than specific areas of settlement. Contrasting with the concise imagery of Codex Boturini, Codex Aubin, and pre-Columbian art in general, the *tlacuilo* fills the whole plate with an elaborate landscape of hills, animals, birds, cacti, trees, and plants, rendering a landscape that recedes into the distance. As discussed in chapter 3, he draws on European stylistic techniques in the formation and positioning of the figures and in his use of color, shading, and perspective. Winding through the hilly landscape, the Mexica pass through mountains, forests, and rocky cliffs. A jaguar devours two male figures, emphasizing the danger of the journey. Two female *teomamaque* (god-bearers) in the left foreground bring up the rear. Nahuatl glosses identify the *teomamaque* and explain: "Here they were lost among the mountains, in the forests, in rocky spots, the Mexica followed their path wherever it led."

Chimalpahin's account describes a setting similar to the one depicted on Codex Azcatitlan folio 5r:

> And there at Quinehuayan, what was named Chicomoztoc was a crag hollowed [with] caves in seven places. They were on a mountain slope. It was from there that the Mexitin issued. They brought their women with them, so that they came issuing from Chicomoztoc in pairs. And it was a very terrifying place there. Countless fierce animals were there; bears, jaguars, mountain lions, snakes were on guard. And there were many pisonias and century plants and much grass. The seven caves are very far away; no one knows definitely where Chicomoztoc was. So those who were called the ancient Teochichimeca who emerged said when they moved from there. When they set out, everywhere there were forests, mountain ranges, gorges, many ferro-cacti, much reed-grass,

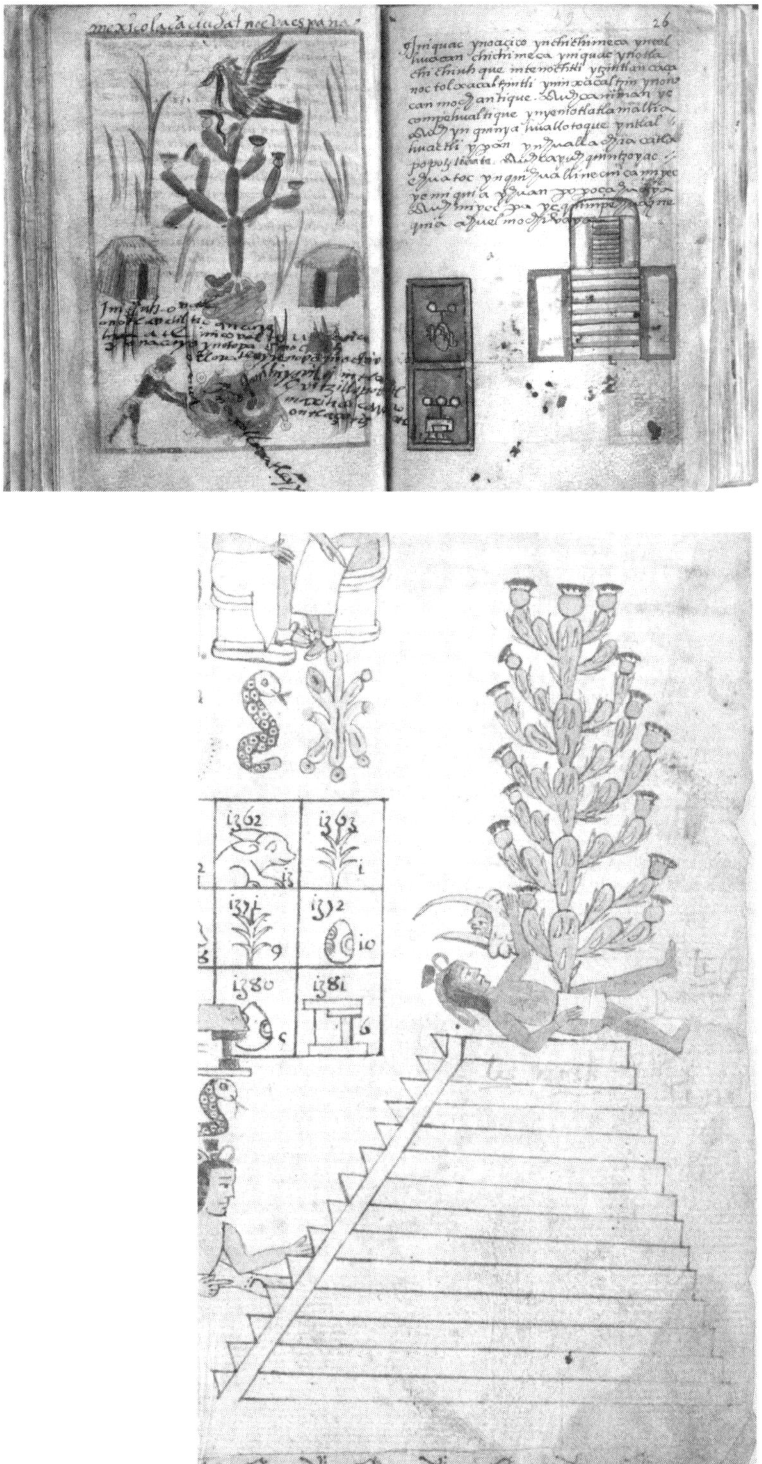

Figure 2.11. Foundation of Tenochtitlan in Codex Aubin, folio 25v (top), and Codex Azcatitlan, folio 12r (bottom). Codex Aubin, folio 25v. © The Trustees of the British Museum. All rights reserved. Codex Azcatitlan, folio 12r. Courtesy of the Bibliothèque Nationale de France.

> many pisonias, many century plants, much grass, many dry sticks in all places as they traveled hither barefoot. With their arrows they shot deer, rabbits, fierce animals, snakes, and birds. They ate them as they went and wore their skins as capes. And [so] there would be sustenance as they needed it, as will appear later on. They carried along the bundle in their keeping, which they worshipped and which spoke to them as they went.[81]

Just as in Chimalpahin's passage, the rugged landscape scene follows the emergence from Chicomoztoc. Like the dialogic exchanges in Codex Aubin, Chimalpahin's description and the *tlacuilo*'s work on folio 5r help the audience to engage with the narrative. As Tom Cummins notes, the use of perspective and the figure with his back to us take on a deictic function.[82] Like the recorded oral accounts that often begin with *nican* (here), the *tlacuilo* invites viewers into the narrative as they visually follow the winding path and figures into the picture plane.

CULTURAL MARKERS ALONG THE JOURNEY

While the three manuscripts emphasize the defining of the Mexica at their earliest stages of origin and beginning of the journey, Codex Boturini and Codex Aubin also record the development of other culturally important practices. The *tlacuiloque* depict the invention at Cohuatitlan of the intoxicating beverage called *octli*, made from the maguey plant (Boturini, folio 13; Aubin, folios 13r–13v), the discovery of the important weapon called an atlatl or spearthrower (Boturini, folio 18; Aubin, folio 18r), and ritual practices such as the celebration of the New Fire ceremony that came at the end of every 52-year cycle (the locations of these ceremonies are registered in table 2.1).[83]

THE ARRIVAL AT CHAPULTEPEC

The arrival at Chapultepec and events leading up to the foundation of Mexico Tenochtitlan and Tlatelolco further solidify the identity of the Mexica. On folios 18–22 of Codex Boturini the Mexica are shown fighting to establish themselves in the Basin of

Mexico, intermarrying with the prestigious Colhua people, and demonstrating their valor as allies of Coxcox, the ruler of Colhuacan (plates 2.18–2.22). Codex Boturini breaks off before the foundation scene, but the missing pages probably paralleled Codex Aubin's content.

Folio 18 of Codex Boturini depicts the arrival at Chapultepec, the Hill of the Grasshopper (plate 2.18). The glyph is oversized, marking the importance of the arrival in the Basin of Mexico. A spring flows from beneath the hill, referencing the site's importance as a source of fresh water. After a twenty-year stay, the Mexica celebrate New Fire and then suffer defeat during a battle that takes place at nearby Acocolco, a site represented by a curving flow of water. Two males and two females wear rough clothing in the swampy environment, with tears signaling their distress. To the right two warriors bring the captured Mexica ruler Huitzilihuitl (who has a hummingbird name glyph) and his daughter Chimalaxoch—*chimal[li]* (shield) + *a[tl]* (water) + *xoch[itl]* (flower)—before the Colhua *tlatoani* (ruler; plural *tlatoque*) Coxcox (his name sign has a pheasant with long feathers) (plate 2.20). Coxcox's high status is signaled by the *xiuhhuitzolli* (turquoise diadem) and elaborately bordered *tilmatli* (cape) that he wears and by his *petlatl icpalli* (high-backed reed throne). The glyph for Colhuacan identifies the *tlatoani*'s territory. Just as the Mexica arrive at Colhuacan right after leaving Aztlan, the appearance of Colhuacan at the end signals that they are about to arrive at the island city where they will found their new home.

From the year 3 Flint on, Codex Boturini depicts the Mexica in the region of Colhuacan. There they intermarry with the Colhua at Contitlan (Place of the Jar), represented by a couple in a house with a *contli* (jar), and procreate, represented by the small house form with an embracing couple inside. The footsteps that lead away may indicate the progeny that they leave behind in this location. The remaining images show the Mexica allying with Coxcox, who asks them to fight Xochimilco and to bring back the ears of the captives that they take as proof of their exploits. These episodes of the narrative emphasized their struggles prior to the foundation, their fierceness as warriors, and the elite bloodlines that they married into.

The people of Colhuacan (a town located in the southern part of today's Mexico City) were believed to have the most direct Toltec ancestry. The Mexica capitalized on Toltec prestige by intermarrying with the Colhua and electing Acamapichtli, son of the ruler of Colhuacan, as their king in 1375. By linking themselves to Colhuacan bloodlines, the Mexica established a claim to Toltec heritage and began promoting themselves as "Colhua-Mexica"; the Mexica are sometimes referred to in the literature by this name.[84] The Toltecs had migrated into the basin and neighboring areas after the collapse of Tula, their capital, around the end of the twelfth century.[85] The modern city of Tula lies sixty-five kilometers north of Mexico City in the Mexican state of Hidalgo and was the site of a complex Mesoamerican culture in the Early Postclassic period.[86] The Mexica regarded them as a refined and civilized culture renowned for their artistic and cultural achievements.[87]

The Codex Aubin script describes the events depicted in Codex Boturini and continues through to the foundation of Tenochtitlan (folios 18v–26r). As with the beginning of the migration history, the script at the end of Codex Aubin becomes more extensive and more dialogic from the arrival at Chapultepec to the foundation. The Codex Aubin script emphasizes the fierceness of the Mexica, describing how they fulfilled the impossible task set by Coxcox, instilling fear in the Colhua:

> Then they counted their captives before Lord Coxcoxtli. Then the Mexica said: "Our captives are enough, because there are 3,200 that we have taken."
>
> And then [Coxcoxtli] warned their fathers, then he said to them: "The Mexica are inhuman. How did they do what I asked them to do? Since I was only mocking them."
>
> The Mexica frightened many of (the Colhua).[88]

The text goes on to state that they secretly kept four of their captives and sacrificed them. This act of sacrifice, made before the altar of Huitzilopochtli, causes Coxcox to respond angrily: "Who are these barbarians? Cast them out!"[89] Like the separation from the eight tribes at the beginning of the narrative, the act of human sacrifice socially separates the Mexica from others with whom they have started to develop familial relationships and causes them to take their own path. In doing so, they demonstrate their allegiance to Huitzilopochtli, even in the face of adversity, and merit the fulfillment of the god's promise to them.

THE FOUNDATION AND THE END OF THE MIGRATION HISTORY

Codex Boturini breaks off before the foundation scene, but the completion of the journey is registered in Codex Aubin and Codex Azcatitlan. Since Codex Boturini and Codex Aubin parallel each other so closely, the representation in Codex Aubin probably indicates the content of Boturini's lost material. Codex Aubin describes a few additional stops that take place over the course of about seven years before the Mexica finally encounter the sacred waters, precious feathers, and the eagle on the nopal cactus that mark their arrival. The foundation scene in Codex Aubin describes and pictorially represents the moment when Huitzilopochtli's promise is fulfilled (folio 25v; figure 2.11). The text states:

> Axolohua and also the one called Quauhcohuatl, both went, they went in search, they went to enter among the reeds. There is a prickly pear <nopal> on which is perched an eagle. At the foot is its nest, its bed, all the different fine feathers; of the red bird, of the blue bird; all the precious feathers.
>
> And then comes along a man called Quauhcohuatl. Then he tells them, he says to them: "The water that we have come to see is like blue ink."
>
> But there they submerged Axolohua. And when they had submerged Axolohua, right away Quauhcohuatl returned. So he went to say to his companions: "There died Axolohua. Since they submerged him there where we saw among the reeds a prickly pear on which is perched an eagle, and his nest is there at the foot [of the prickly pear], his bed <is> entirely of different precious feathers, and the water like blue ink. There they submerged Axolohua."
>
> Quauhcohuatl informed them of this. Only on the next day, Axolohua came out. Then he says to his companions: "Since I went to see Tlaloc, because he called me, he said: 'My son Huitzilopochtli has arrived, since his house shall be here. Since he shall dedicate it here because we shall live united on the earth.'"
>
> And when they were informed, then they went to look, to see the prickly pear. When they had seen it, then they sweep. At the foot of the prickly pear they shaped an altar.
>
> [To make the] base [of the altar], they were rejoicing; there they found a captain of Colhuacan, then they brought him. When he had been brought, still alive, they put him in their altar; they made the captain called Chichilquahuitl, the captain of Colhuacan, as the heart [of the altar].
>
> The year in which they made their altar is the year 2 Flint.[90]

The Codex Aubin scribe links the foundation with acts of sacrifice. Axolohua is sacrificed in the water (but emerges alive after an encounter with Tlaloc), and a captain of Colhuacan is sacrificed to place a heart offering on the altar. The dual sacrifices and the pairing of water (abode of Tlaloc) and the eagle on the nopal cactus (a symbol linked to Huitzilopochtli) prefigure for Codex Aubin's audience the later large-scale sacrifices to Tlaloc and Huitzilopochtli that occurred on this site at the Templo Mayor. The precious feathers augur the future wealth of the Mexica *tlatoque*.

Codex Azcatitlan also depicts the nopal cactus and the reed-filled waters that mark the foundation site, but they are depicted as part of two separate scenes. On folio 12r the *tlacuilo* depicts the nopal springing from the sacrificed heart of Copil (figure 2.11).

Durán describes Huitzilopochtli recalling the events that lead up to the sighting of the nopal:

> You will remember how I commanded you to slay my nephew Copil, ordering you to remove his heart and fling it among the reeds, among the rushes. This you have done. Know now that his heart fell upon a stone and from this sprang a prickly pear cactus. This cactus is so tall and splendid that an eagle makes his nest in it. Each day the eagle in his nest feeds here, eating the finest and most beautiful birds he can find.[91]

According to scripted accounts, the sacrifice of Copil occurred several years earlier while the Mexica were staying at Chapultepec. As the warrior son of the sorceress Malinalxochitl, Copil bore a grudge against the Mexica and had caused them difficulties in the Basin of Mexico. On folio 12r the sacrificed figure of Copil and the nopal appear atop a temple, perhaps a reference to the future Templo Mayor. By depicting the omen in this way, the Tlatelolca *tlacuilo* diminishes the connections to the Tenochca Mexica, whose name derived from the symbol *tetl* (rock) and *nochtli* (prickly pear). The *tlacuilo* omits the rock. As described earlier, Huitzilopochtli takes the place of the eagle. The nopal cactus functions as an important marker of the foundation but not as the denouement of the migration history. Rather, the following set of images on folios 12v–13r functions as the end of the migration history. The *tlacuilo* depicts the installation of Tenochca and Tlatelolca *tlatoque*, as overseen by the Tepanec lord Tezozomoc. The cultivation of the reed-filled waters, a subject also addressed in Codex Aubin, fills the central area. Like the rich feathers described in Codex Aubin and in Durán's account, an anachronistic Spanish colonial lockplate references the promise of wealth and prosperity. The significance of this image is addressed further in chapters 3 and 5.

Conclusion

Before the conquest, migration history served to explain who the Mexica people were and how they differed from other Mesoamerican peoples. They linked themselves to the greater Mesoamerican tradition by including historically important stops, such as the Toltec-related Teocolhuacan/Colhuacan, the inheritor of Tula's accomplishments, or Chicomoztoc, the Postclassic continuation of the cave-related place of emergence, which many other groups closely linked to their own early histories. But they separated themselves from all others by claiming Aztlan as their specific place of origin. Their history depicts their leaving from Colhuacan with other migratory groups but highlights the point at which the Mexica separate from the crowd and make their own journey. The Mexica further distinguish their particular migration story by emphasizing the role of their tutelary god Huitzilopochtli: he guides them throughout the journey, creates a new identity for them when they change their name from "Azteca" to "Mexica," and introduces ritual practices, including human sacrifice. The hardships they suffered, the battles they fought, and the cultural practices that they enacted (such as the celebration of the end of a 52-year calendar cycle with the New Fire ceremony and the implementation of the use of maguey) further shaped a cohesive view of Mexica identity within the broader Mesoamerican world.

After the defeat of Azcapotzalco and formation of the Triple Alliance, promoting a strong, independent, and cohesive sense of Mexica identity would have been a potent political tool in a culturally diverse region. This narrative stood to combat the political factionalism that often divided rulers and territories.[92] In one sense it offered a unifying vision. The many stops include locations that later became subject to the Triple Alliance. The migration story shows the Mexica inhabiting these locations and leaving ancestors behind, drawing diverse dynastic and cultural traditions together. In another more direct sense the migration history established the supremacy of the Mexica and of Tenochtitlan within the establishment of the Triple Alliance.

The history linked them with the bloodlines of the Colhua (inheritors of prestigious Toltec heritage) and the Chichimecs, both desirable ancestral connections. Although the Mexica are chosen through divine intervention to occupy and rule this territory, they also earn their position by enduring great hardships as they loyally fulfill Huitzilopochtli's demands. As Elizabeth Hill Boone posits, the peregrination itself transforms the Mexica: "the migration story is not the journey of a people from one physical space to another; rather, the message is the transition of the Mexica from a small and relatively insignificant band to the people destined to rule the world as it was then known."[93]

Codex Boturini gives us a sense of how this grand narrative functioned on a more intimate scale. Perhaps working in the pre-Hispanic period or shortly thereafter, the *tlacuilo* mapped out his composition. His erasure marks indicate that he was not making an identical copy of another manuscript. Rather, he worked out an original composition, taking care to ensure that it communicated the essential components of a core narrative that circulated in the Basin of Mexico region. Perhaps he was innovating the use of date blocks, as Robertson suspected, from a manuscript with a continuous flow of year-bearers. Or maybe he originated his composition directly from an oral account. Following pre-Hispanic models, the indigenous *tlacuilo* prepared his surface and then proceeded to draft the composition from beginning to end. Mistakes were corrected at the draft stage by erasing errant lines with white base. Once the final layout was determined, the *tlacuilo* applied a heavy black line. In the second stage of production, he drafted the red lines used to connect the years. Erasures at this stage indicate the *tlacuilo*'s decision-making process. He settled on an approach that emphasized the departure from each site rather than the arrival. He opted to use a single unbroken red line that emphasized the continuous flow of time.

For unknown reasons, the *tlacuilo*'s work was interrupted. He never finalized the red lines or added pigment. The manuscript remained incomplete. The concisely rendered images that do exist reflect a visual minimalism that promotes clarity over diversity of representation. Codex Boturini relies on pre-Hispanic methods to date events and to name places and people, suggesting a *tlacuilo* and an audience familiar with pre-Hispanic pictorial and oral methods of communication. Comparison with the corpus of Mexica migration accounts shows that the Codex Boturini *tlacuilo* used glyphic images to anchor the most significant aspects of the narrative. Perhaps Codex Boturini was performed in a ritual or ceremonial context, as suggested by Elizabeth Hill Boone.[94] It may have been the basis for some of the *cantares mexicanos* (Mexican song-poems). Different orators surely elaborated this account to individuals or small groups, presenting the images and giving the story their own twist. The scripted account found in Codex Aubin probably reflects one such reading. The dialogues would have entertained and informed the audience, linking past and present. Whether experienced before or after the conquest, the migration narrative in Codex Boturini offered viewers a record of what it meant to be Mexica, what it meant to be the chosen people of Huitzilopochtli, and what the rights and obligations of that relationship entailed. Whoever retained custody of the manuscript after work ceased did not add to it beyond the glosses. As detailed in the epilogue, the manuscript suffered damage at a later point, and some of the final folios were lost between 1804 and 1824. Audiences in the sixteenth to eighteenth centuries would have seen the manuscript with the ending intact.

In Codex Aubin and Codex Azcatitlan Mexica identity is reframed or recast to suit the needs of the individual *tlacuiloque* or their patrons. In Codex Aubin the *tlacuilo* manifests his Christian perspective by selectively registering content in script, glyph, or both media. In a tacit acknowledgment of the power of images, he depicts Huitzilopochtli only twice, in the form of a sacred bundle, and opts to describe the deity in text as a "devil." Though he records the Mexica migration narrative with care, his Christian lens positions this history as part of a distant non-Christian past. Chapter 6 picks up this thread and explores the *tlacuilo*'s methods and motivations, arguing that they are part of a strategy of preservation that responds to his social context. Codex Azcatitlan modifies the core narrative to emphasize and highlight the Tlatelolca role in the Mexica migration. Rather than presenting the omen of the eagle on a nopal cactus as the terminus of the migration history, he presents the establishment of Tenochtitlan and Tlatelolco, through the seating of their *tlatoque*, as the final foundation scene. Thus the migration leads up to and culminates in the establishment of Mexica political power in the Basin of Mexico. Rather than depicting an eagle on a nopal that grows from a stone, a visual referent closely tied to Tenochtitlan and the Tenochca-Mexica, he references the heart sacrifice of Copil. He may set up this narrative angle by referencing the abandonment of Copil's mother, Malinalxochitl, at the beginning of the migration. Chapters 3, 4, and 5 further explore how the *tlacuilo* manifests his Tlatelolca perspective and how the migration narrative informs and structures the second half of the manuscript.

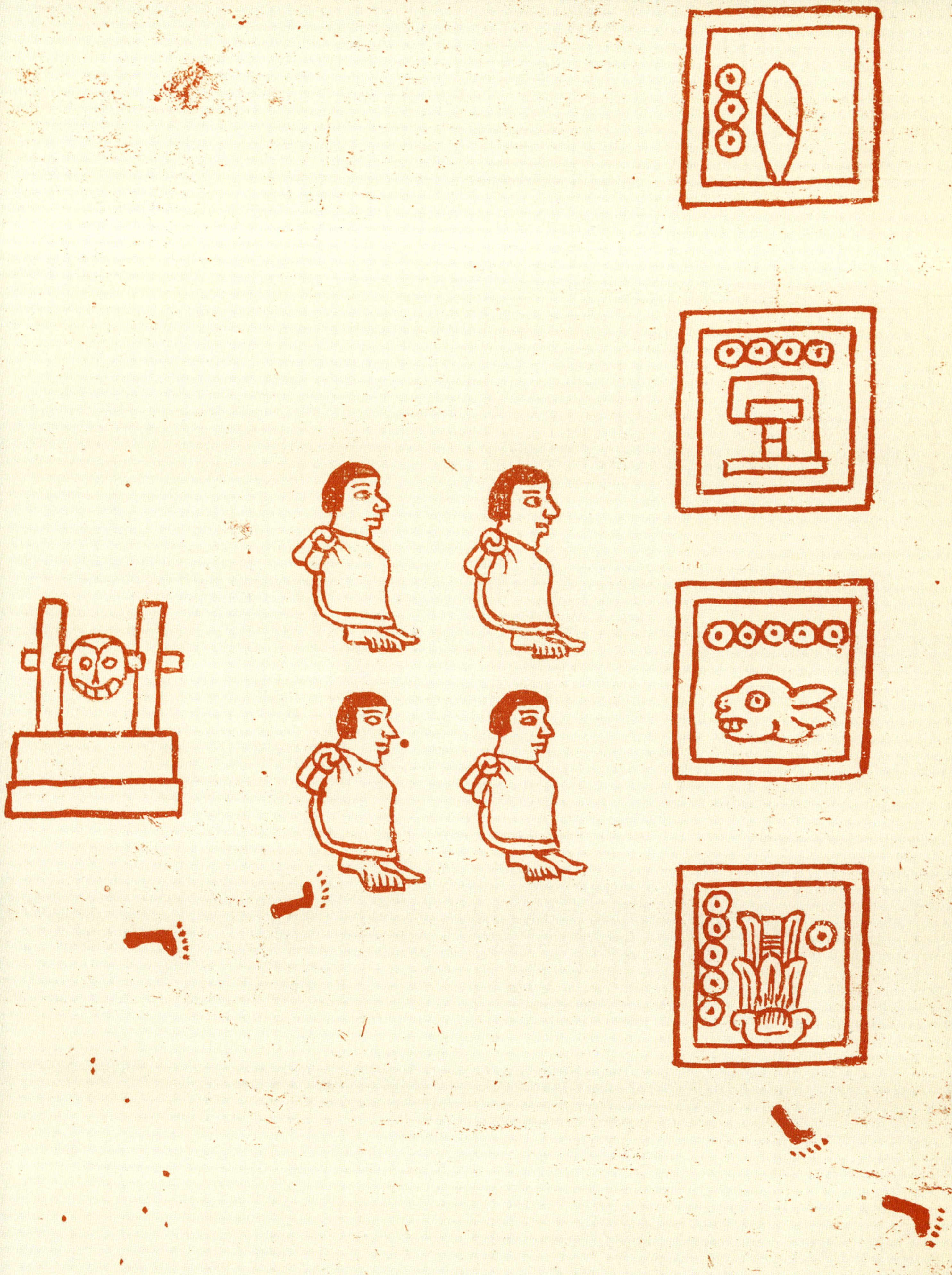

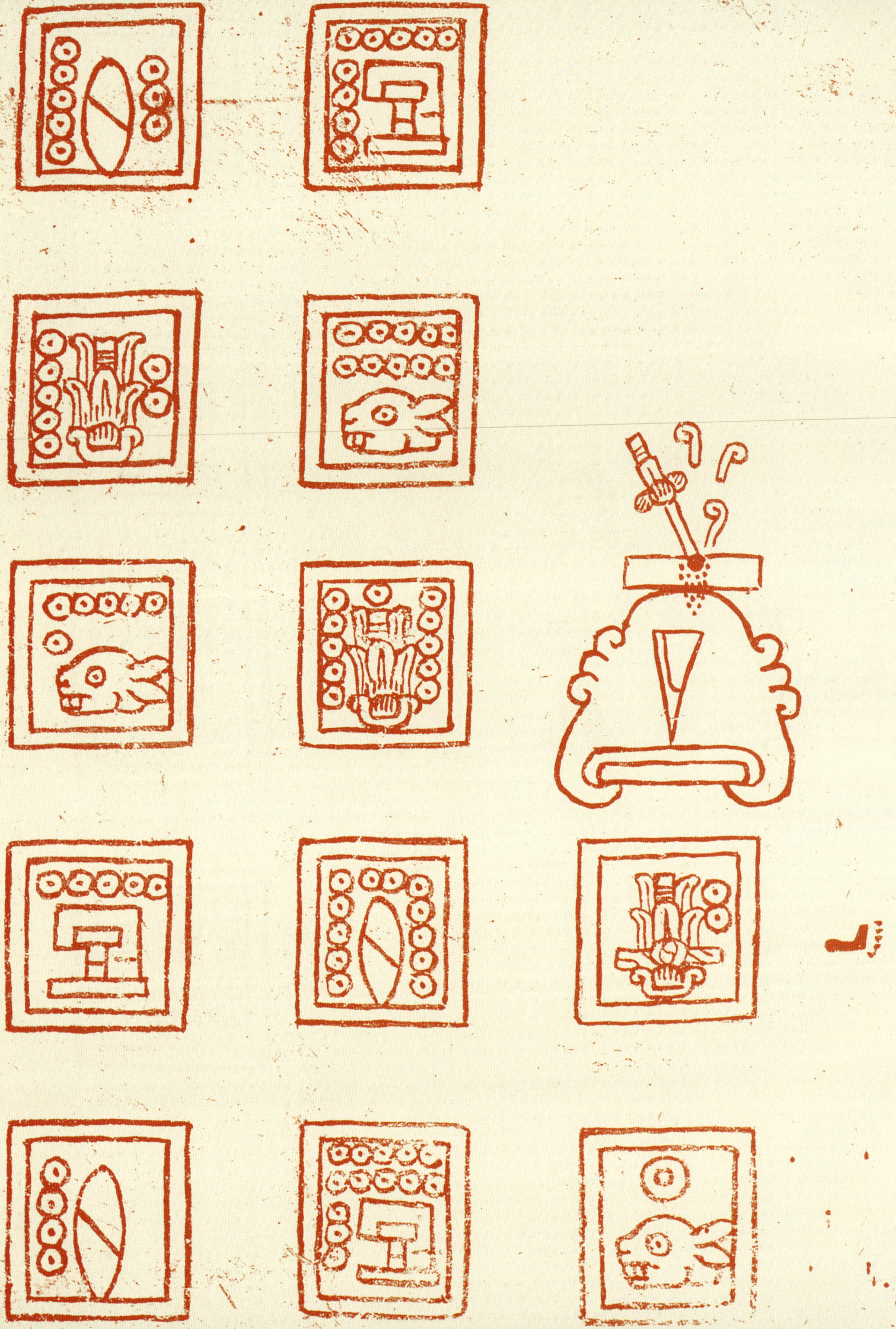

PLATES

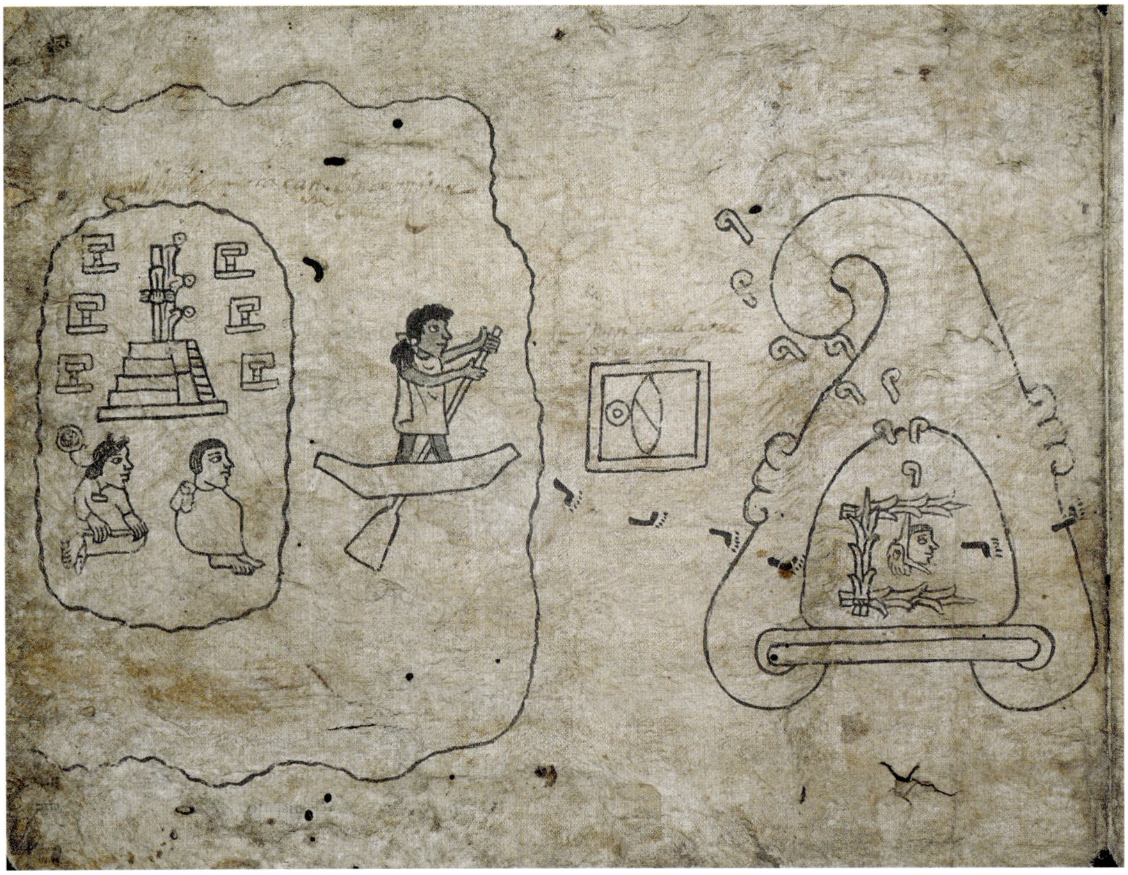

Plate 2.1. Codex Boturini, folio 1.

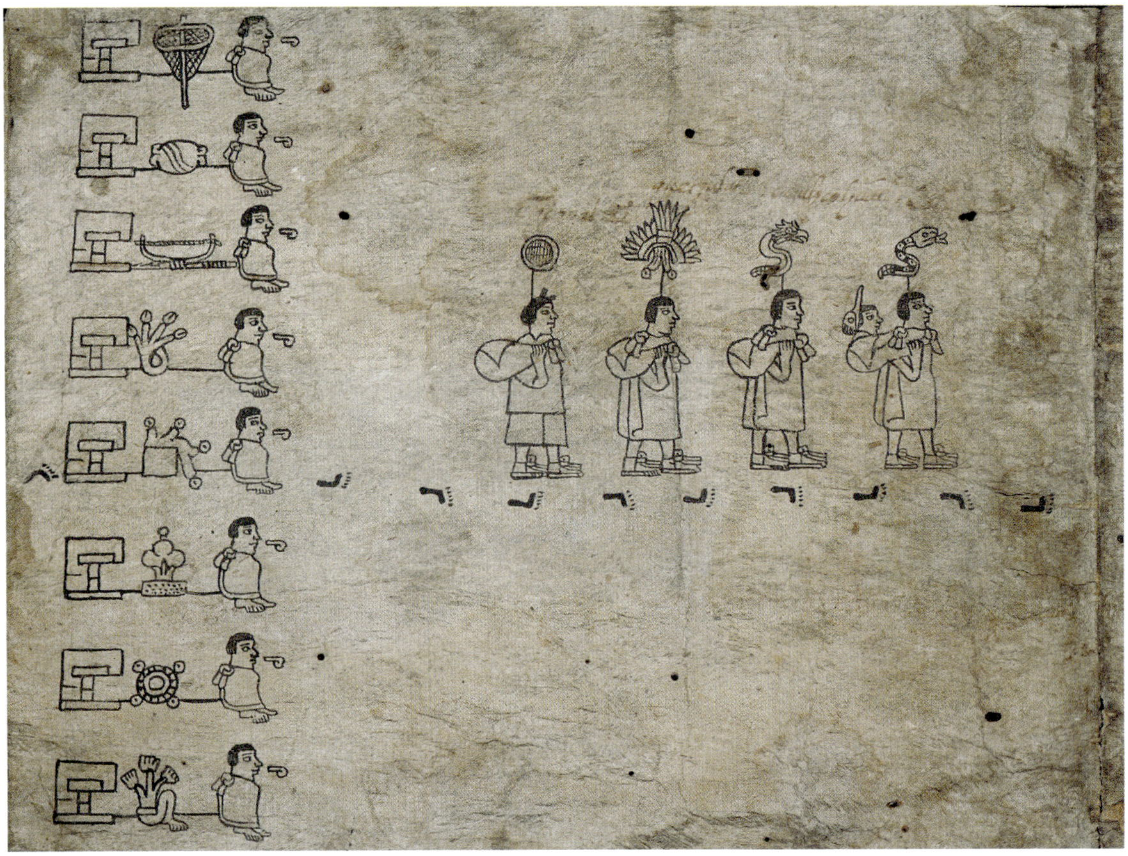

Plate 2.2. Codex Boturini, folio 2.

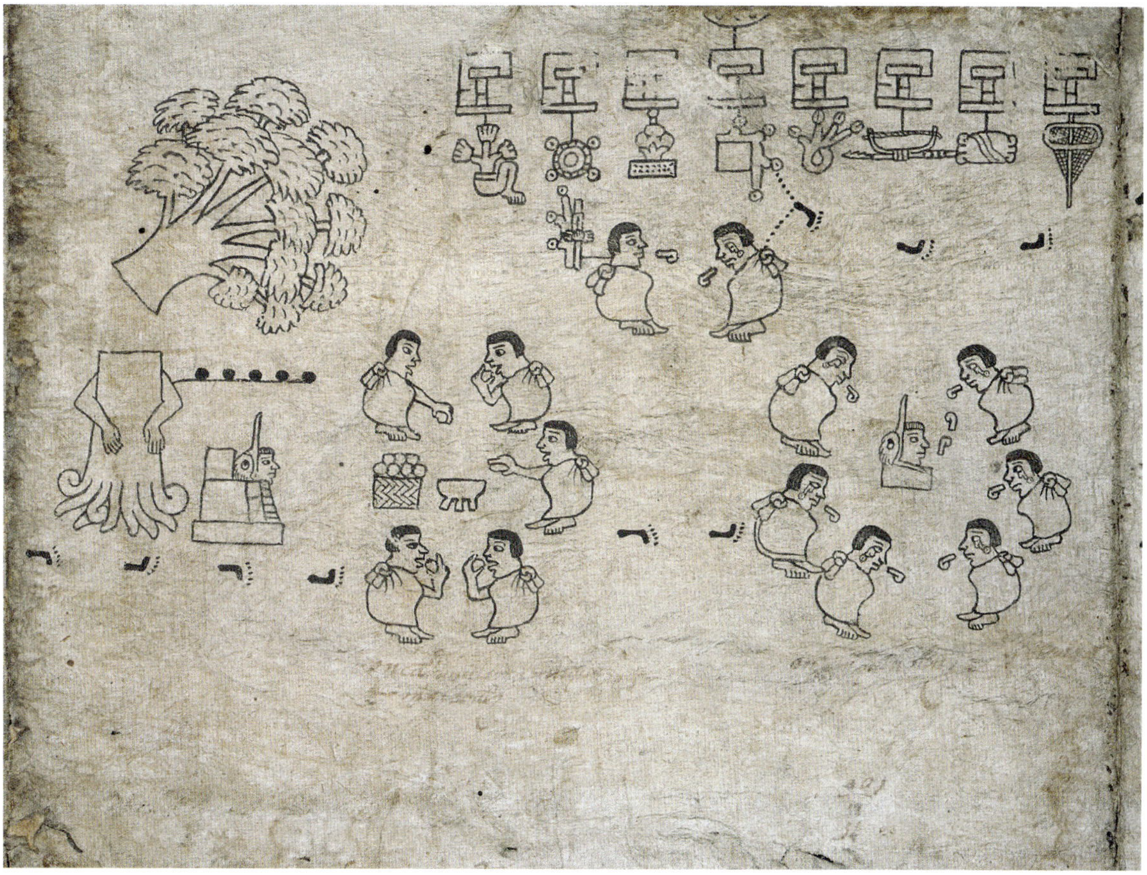

Plate 2.3. Codex Boturini, folio 3.

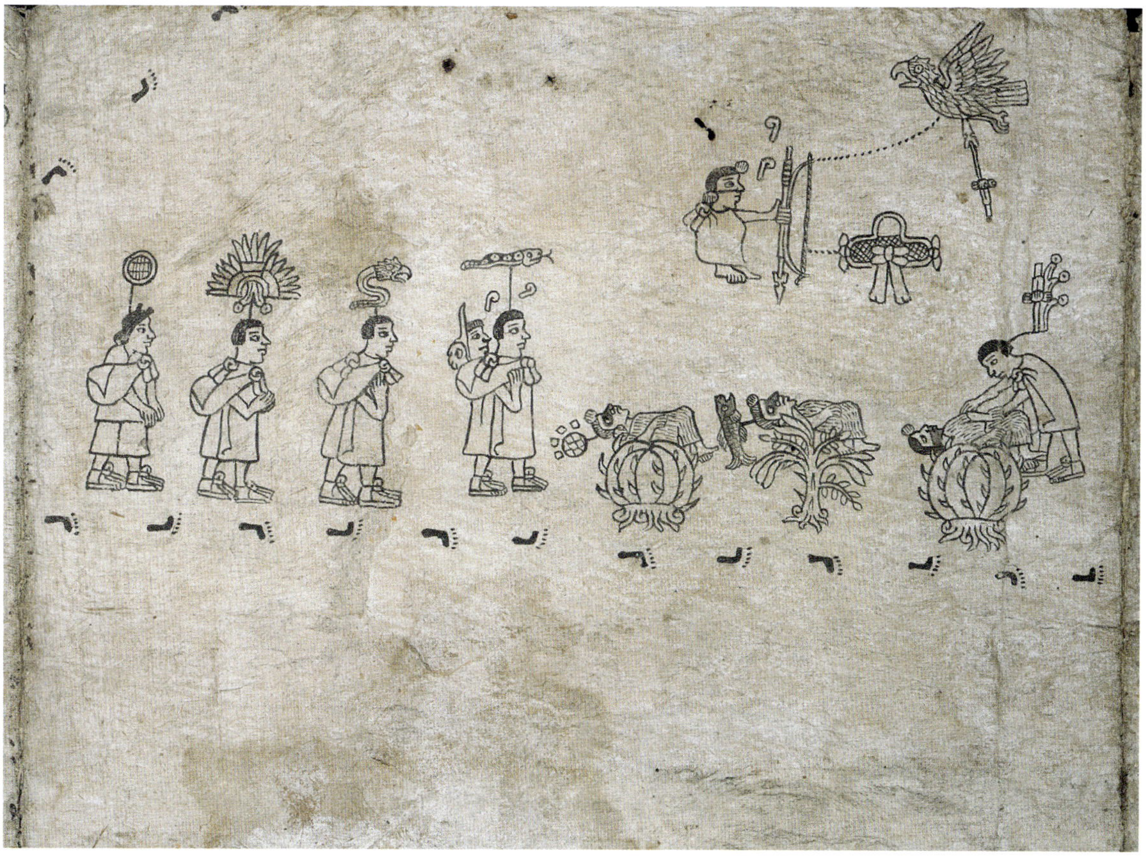

Plate 2.4. Codex Boturini, folio 4.

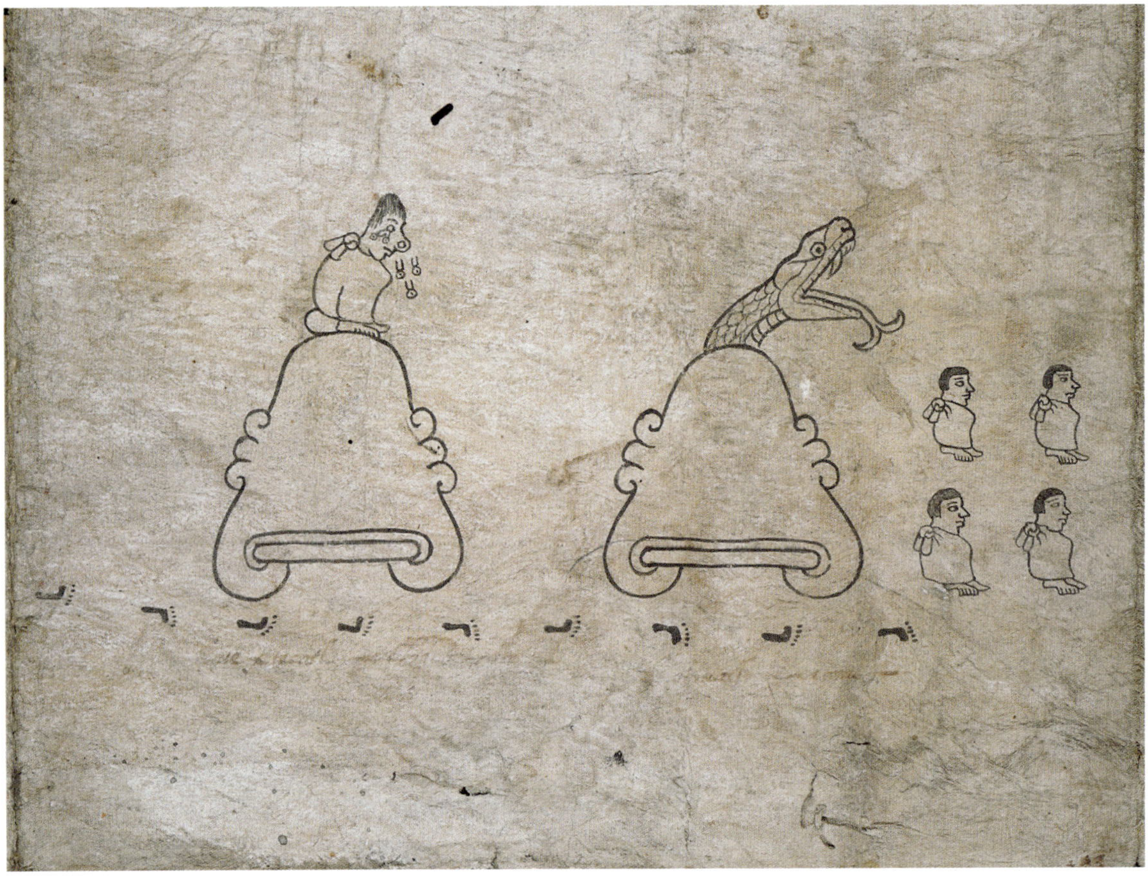

Plate 2.5. Codex Boturini, folio 5.

Plate 2.6. Codex Boturini, folio 6.

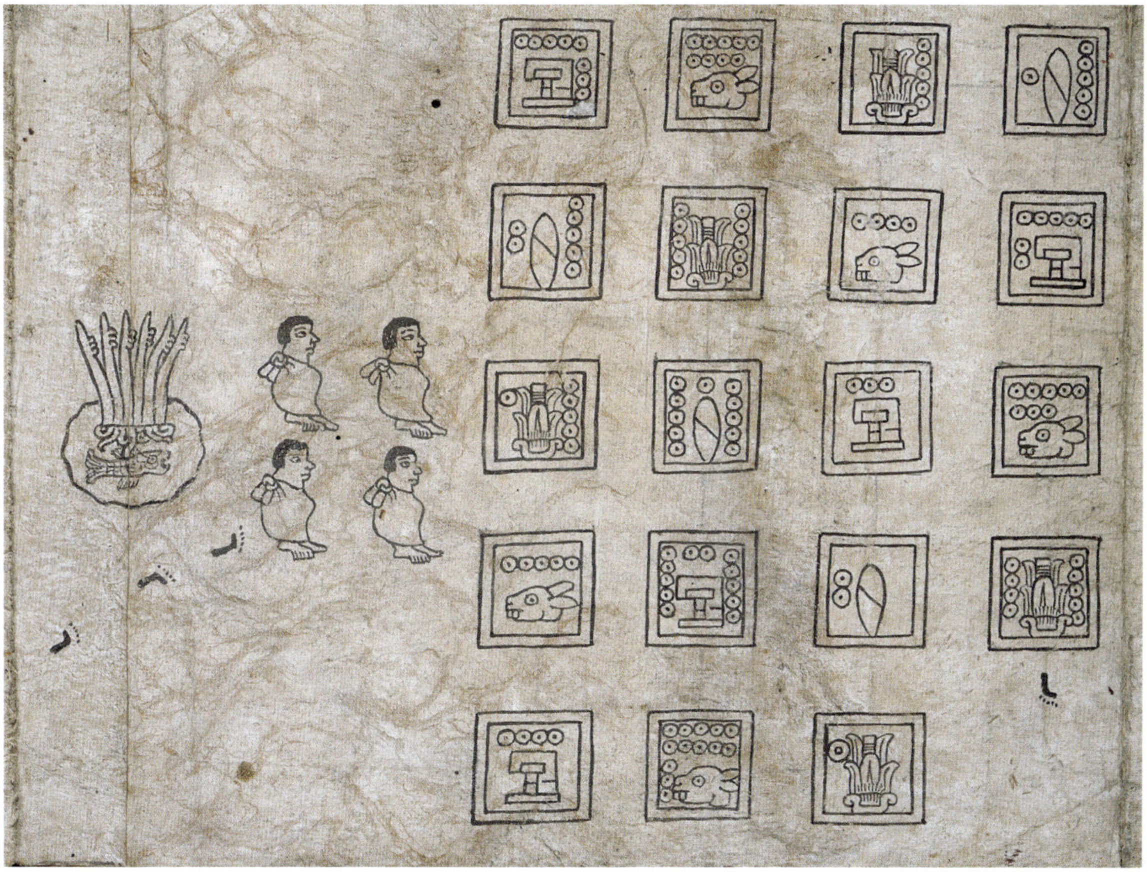

Plate 2.7. Codex Boturini, folio 7.

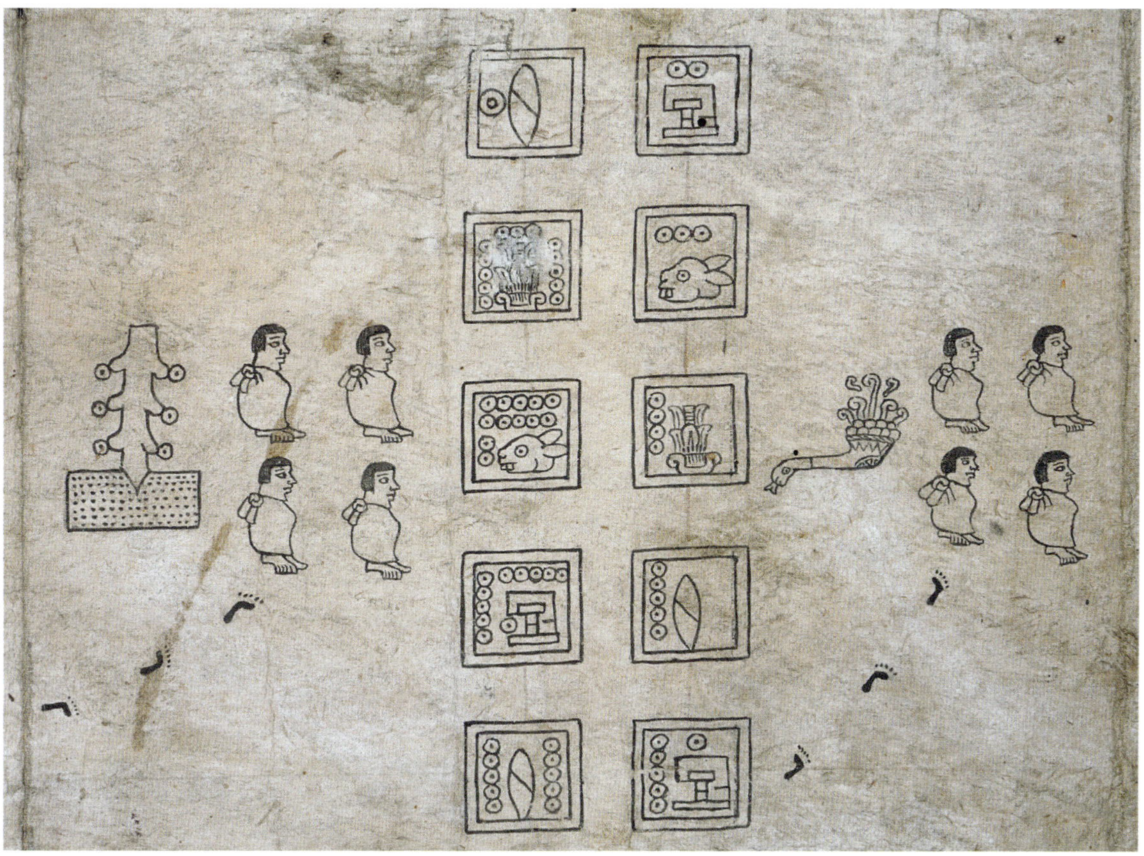

Plate 2.8. Codex Boturini, folio 8.

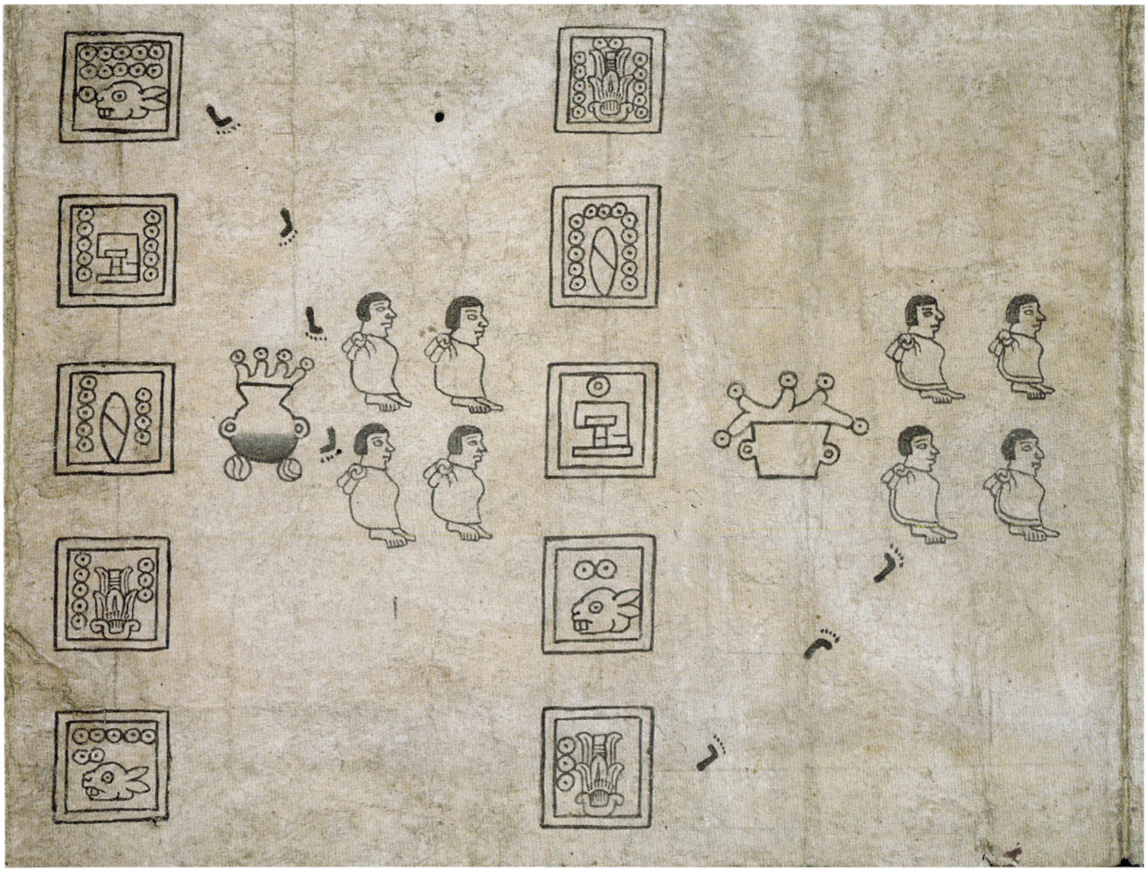

Plate 2.9. Codex Boturini, folio 9.

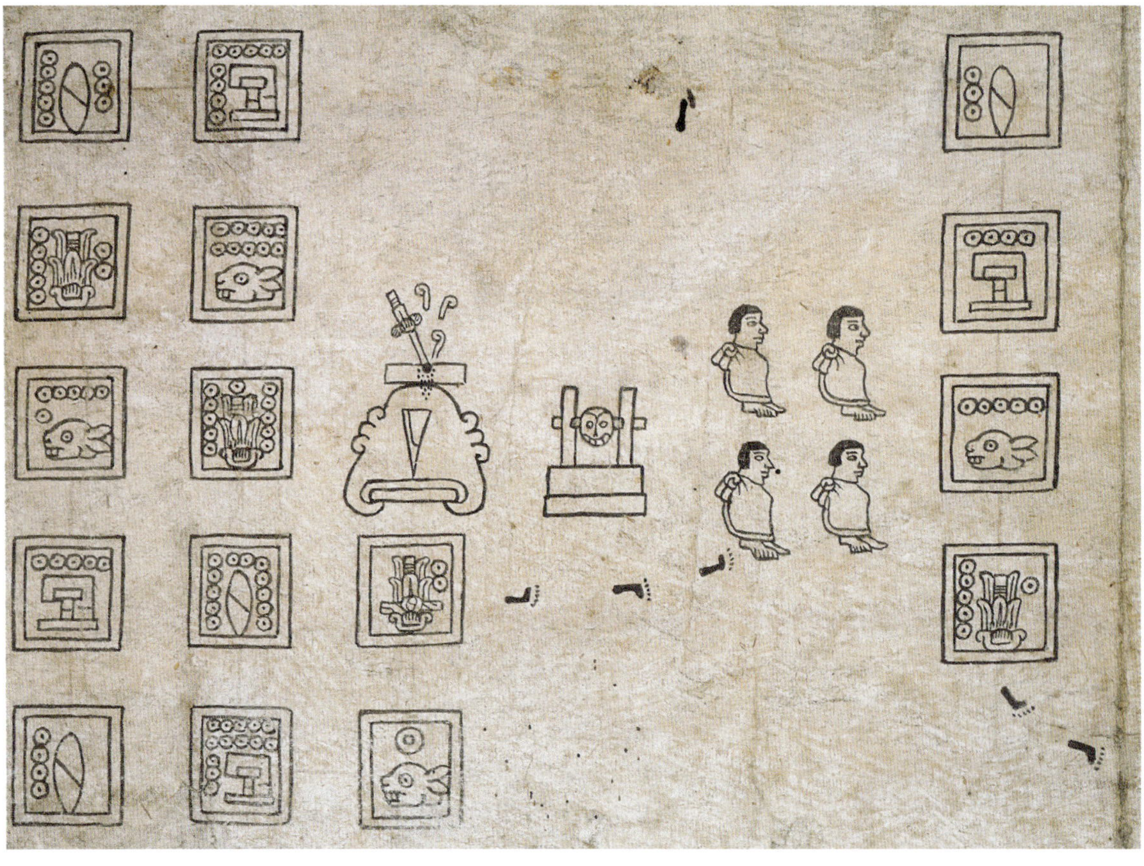

Plate 2.10. Codex Boturini, folio 10.

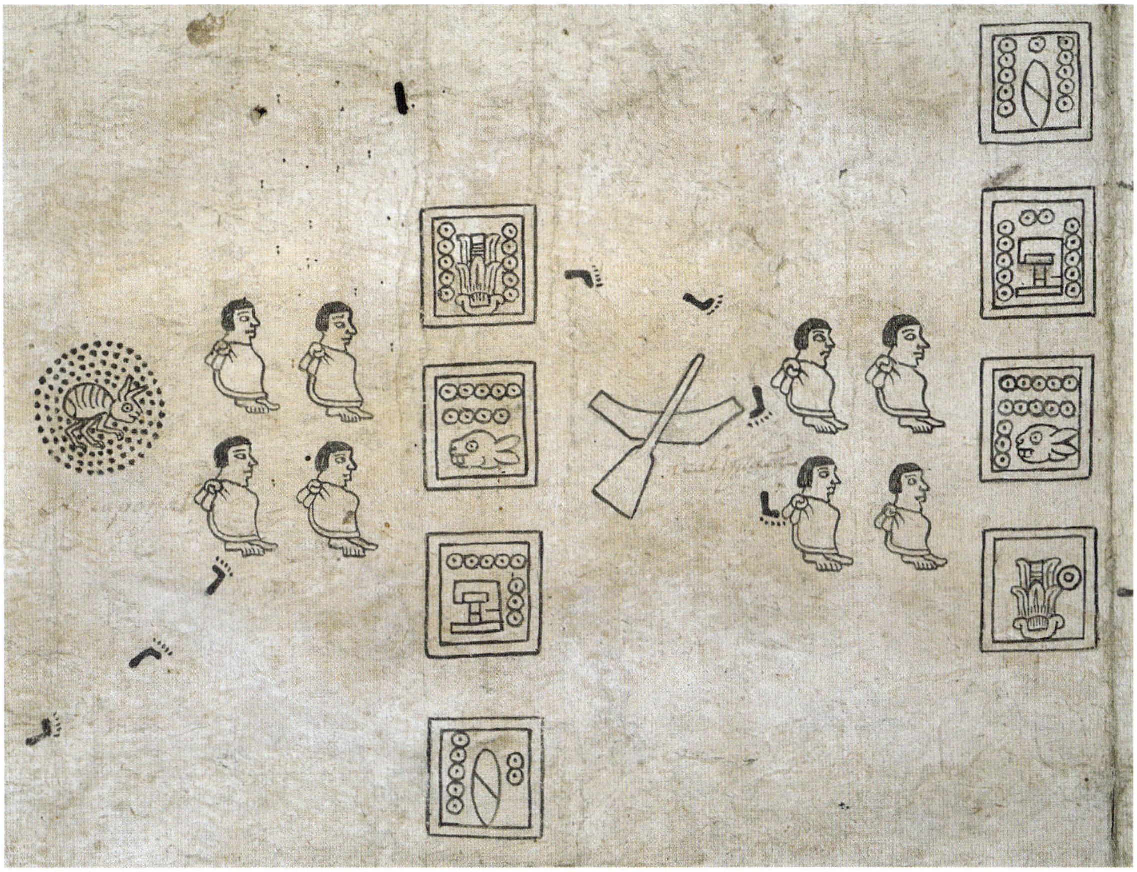

Plate 2.11. Codex Boturini, folio 11.

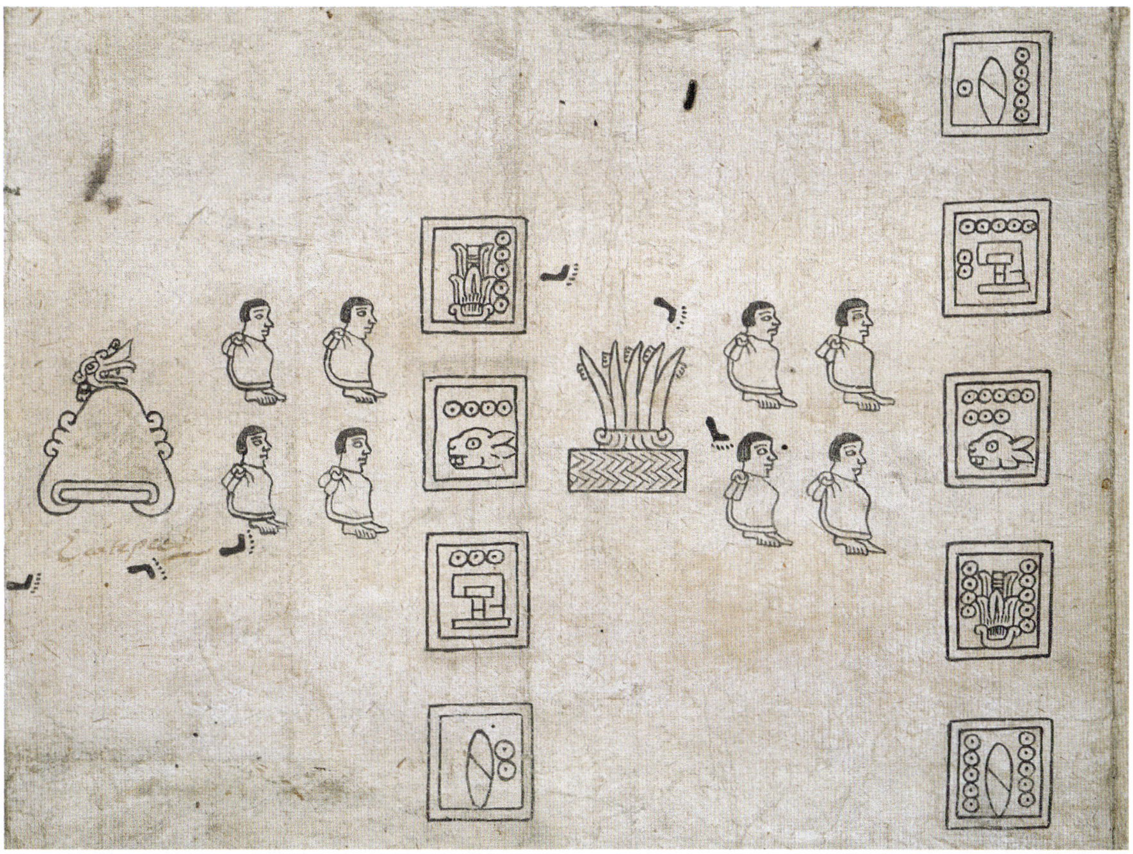

Plate 2.12. Codex Boturini, folio 12.

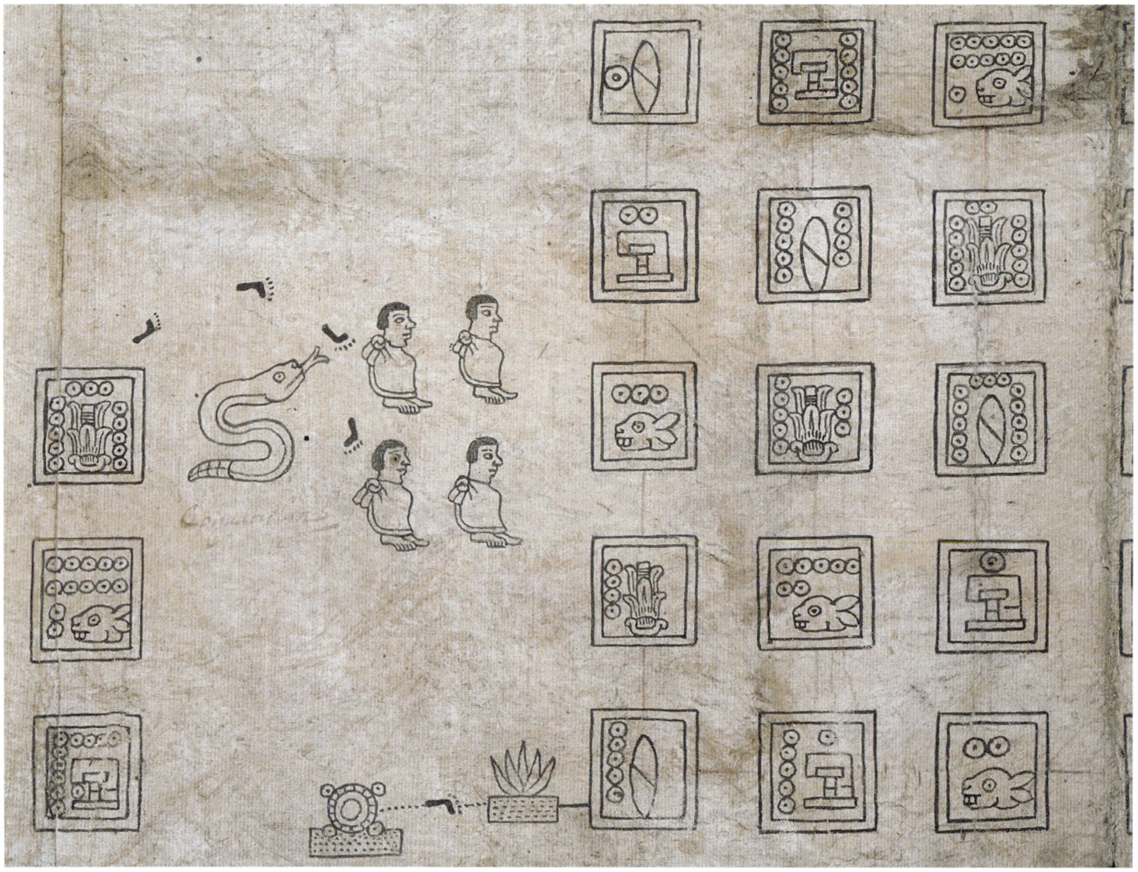

Plate 2.13. Codex Boturini, folio 13.

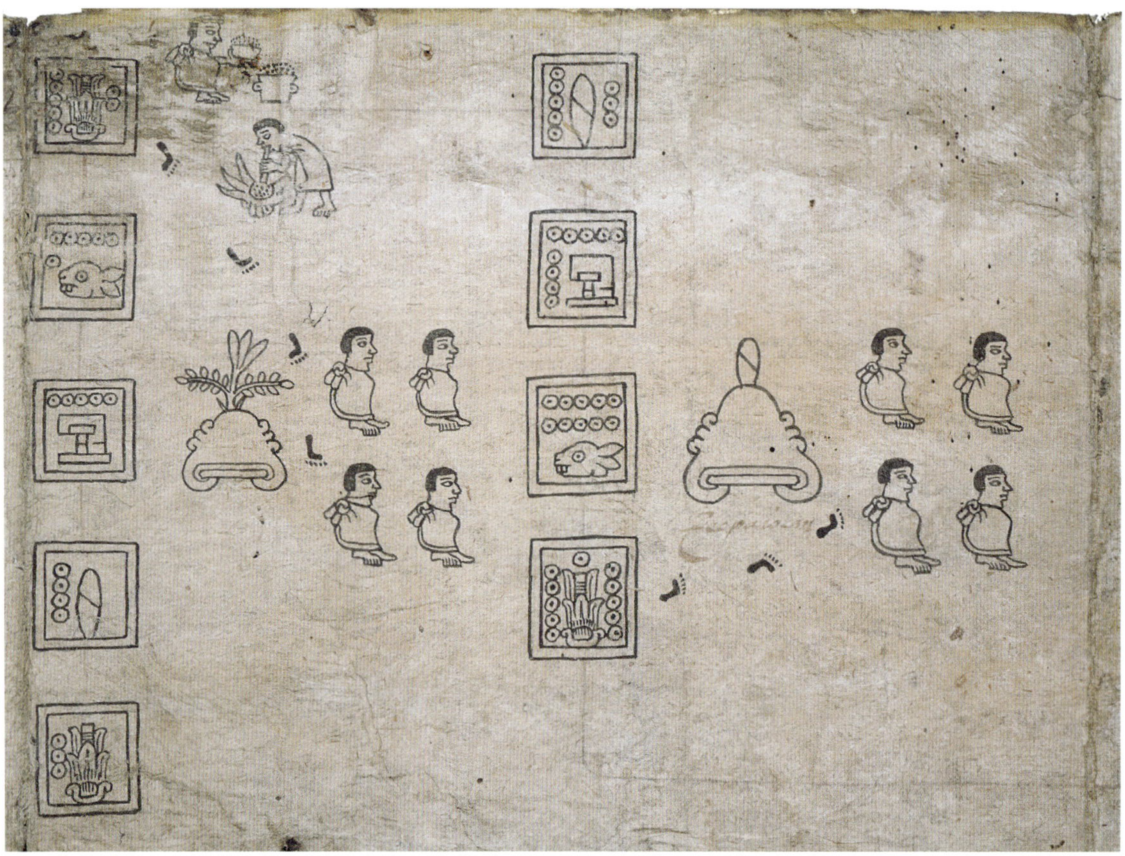

Plate 2.14. Codex Boturini, folio 14.

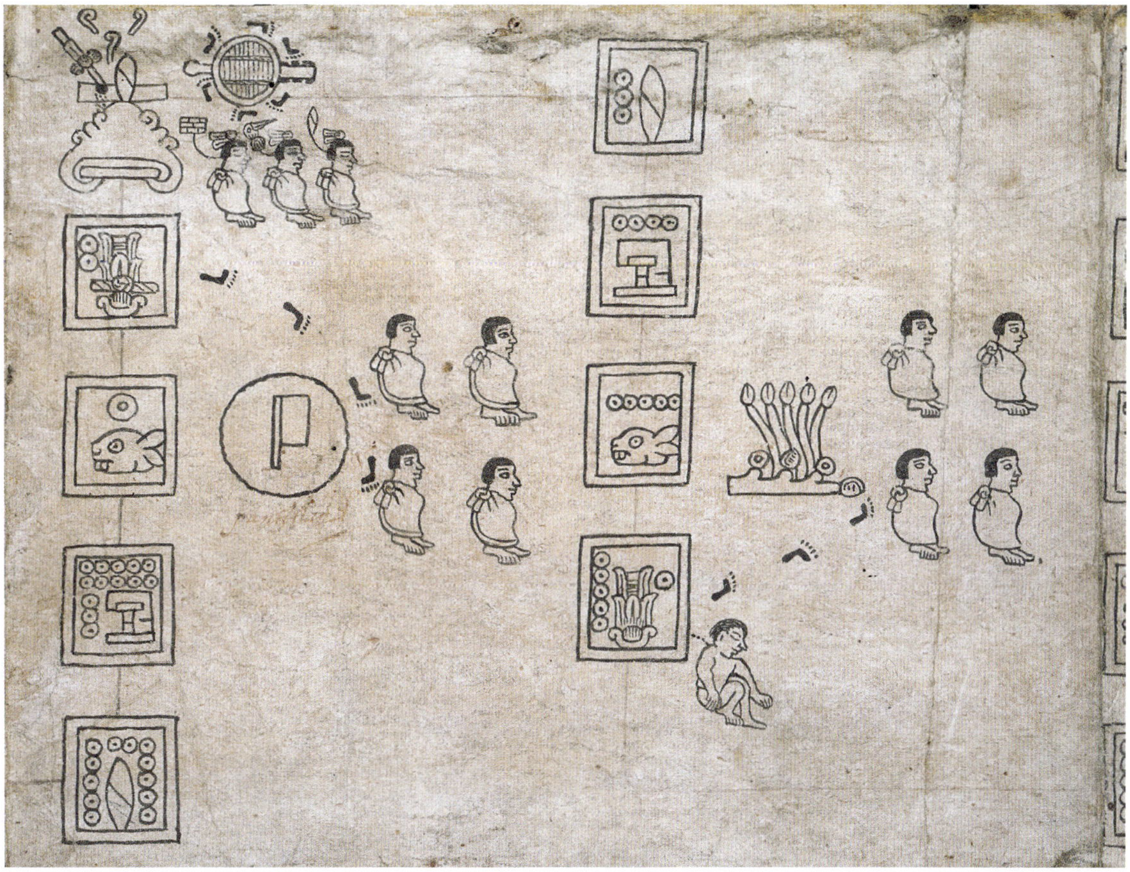

Plate 2.15. Codex Boturini, folio 15.

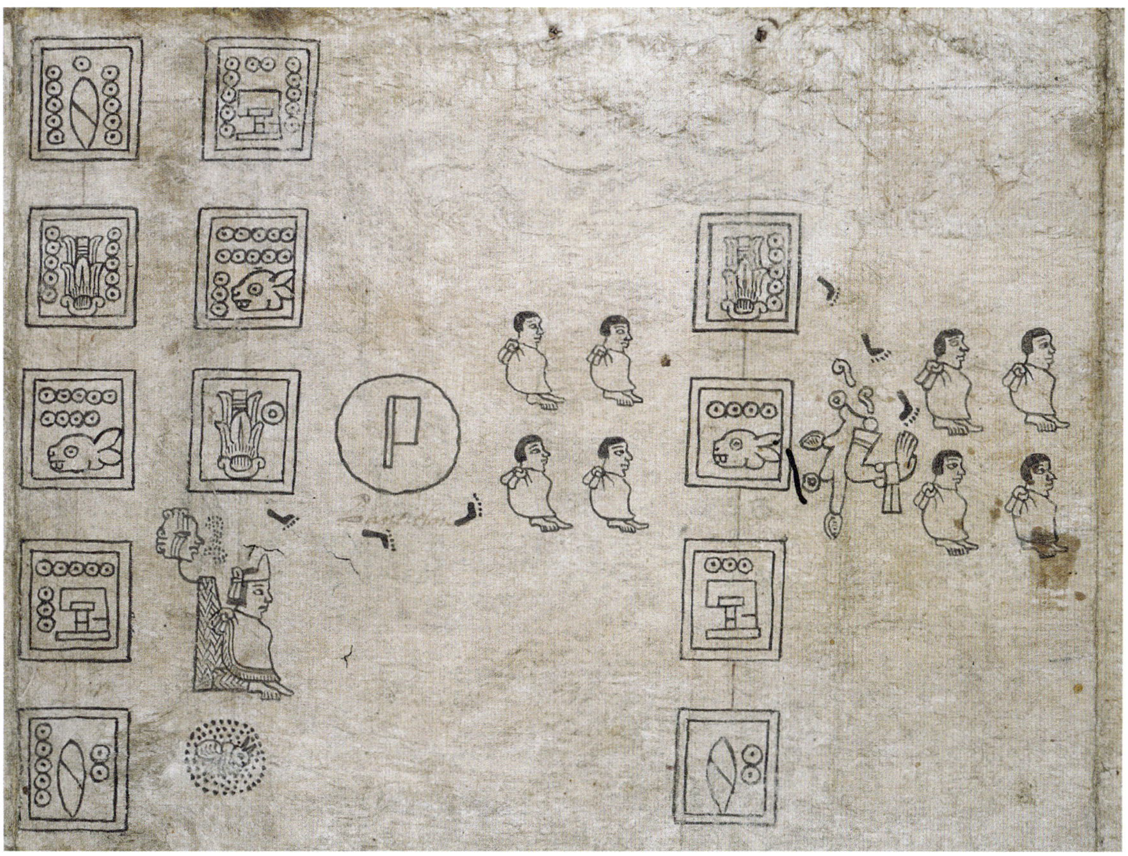

Plate 2.16. Codex Boturini, folio 16.

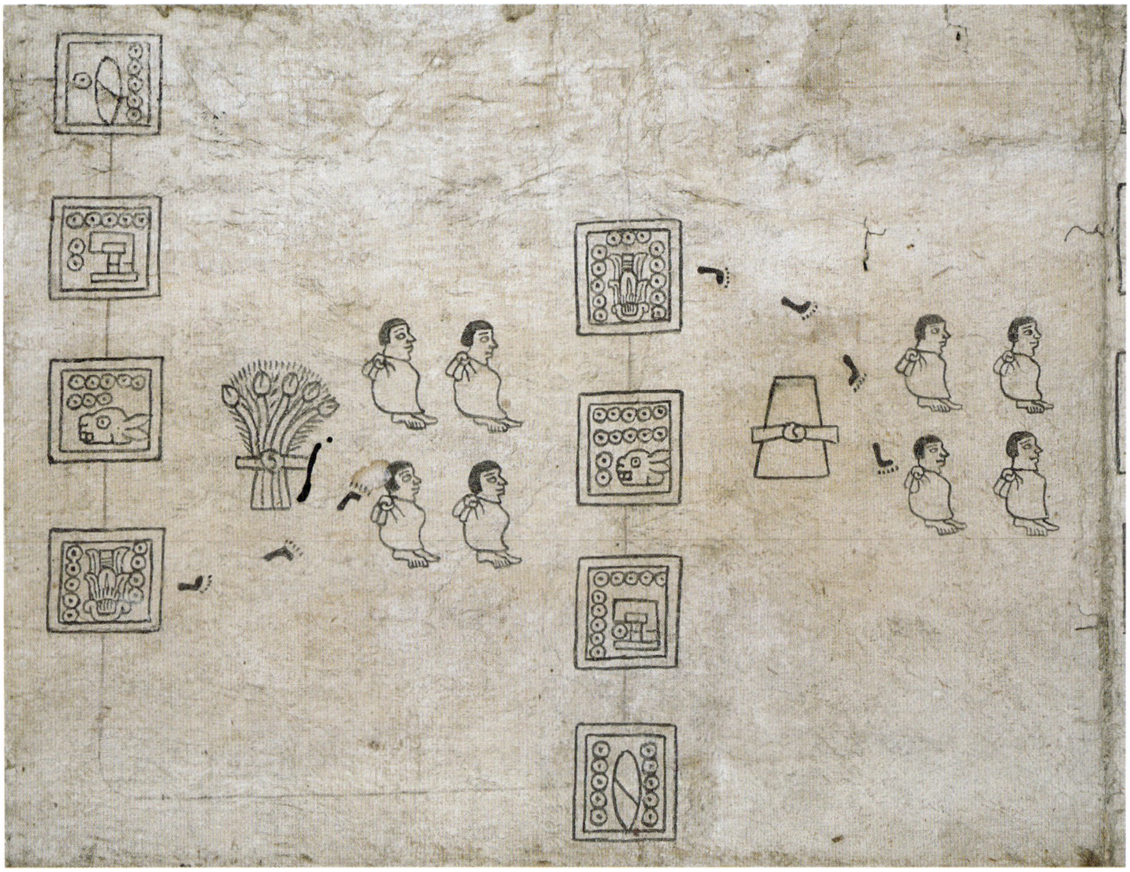

Plate 2.17. Codex Boturini, folio 17.

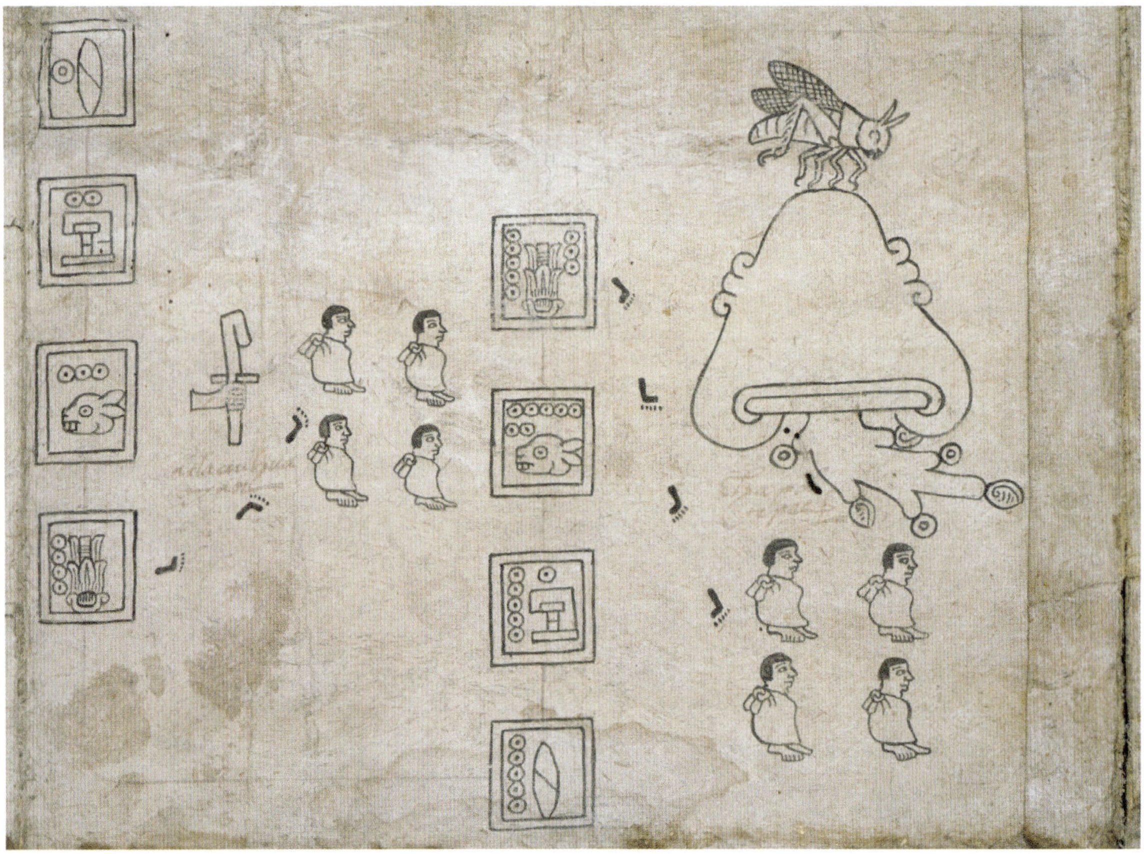

Plate 2.18. Codex Boturini, folio 18.

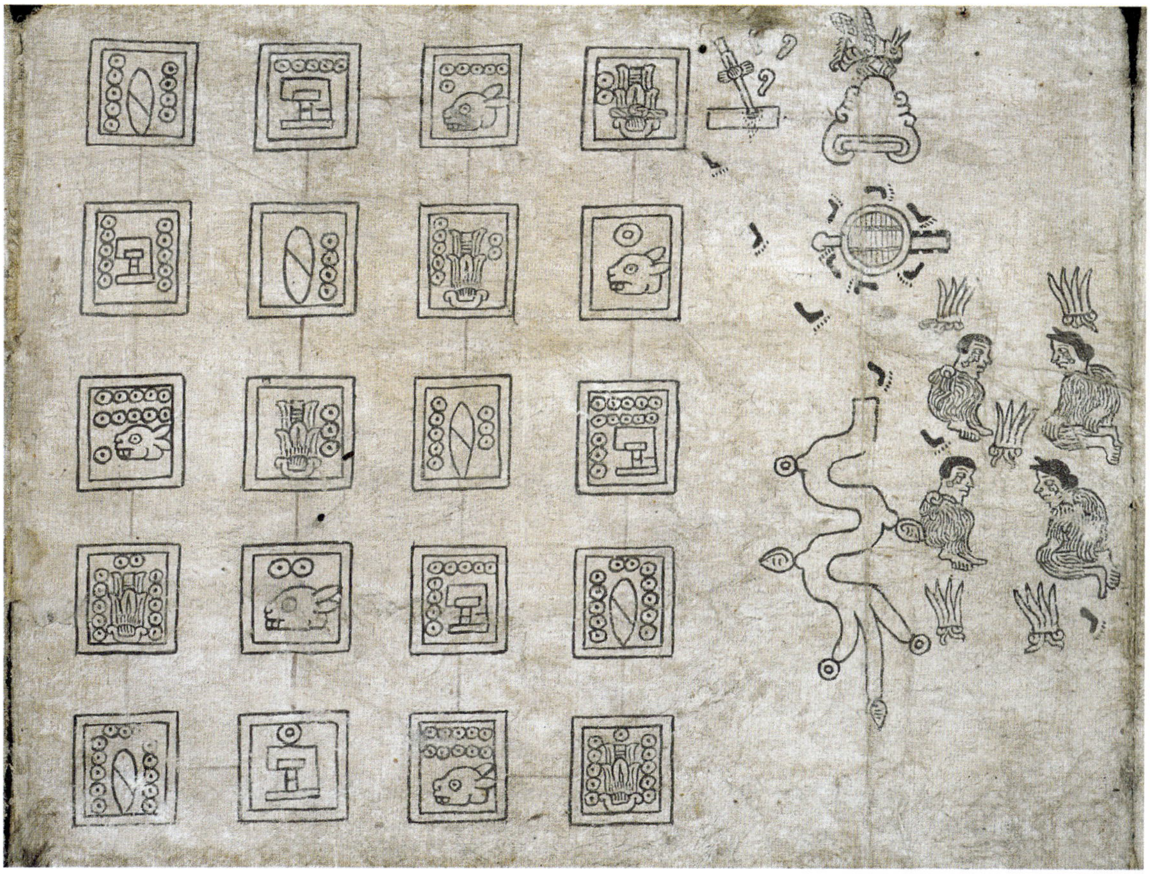

Plate 2.19. Codex Boturini, folio 19.

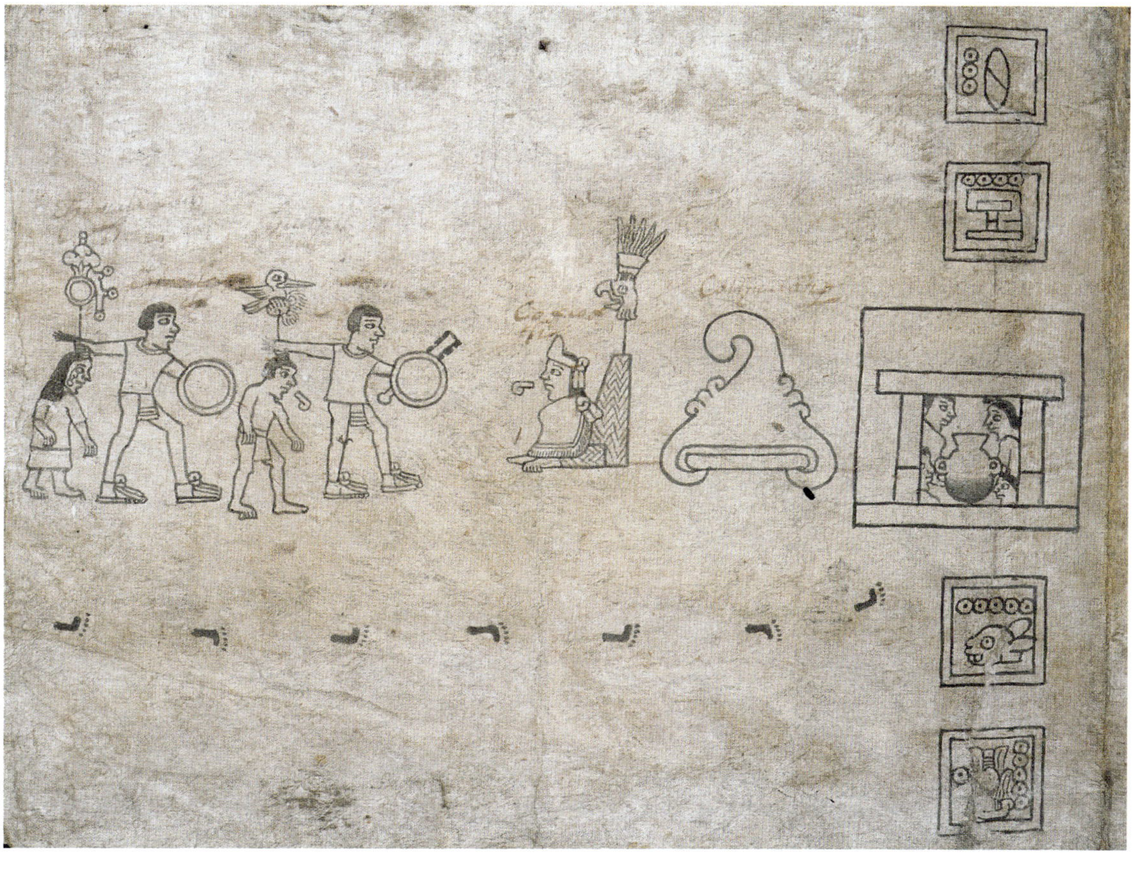

Plate 2.20. Codex Boturini, folio 20.

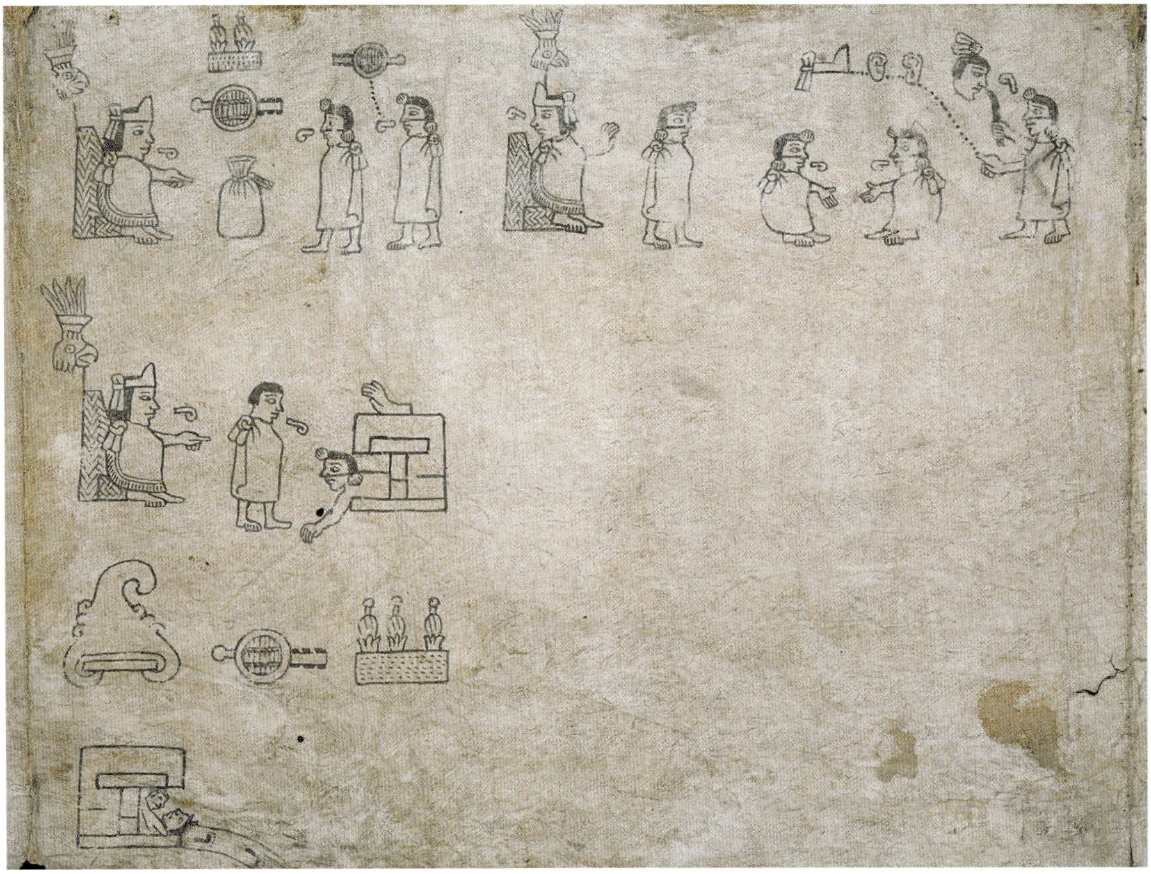

Plate 2.21. Codex Boturini, folio 21.

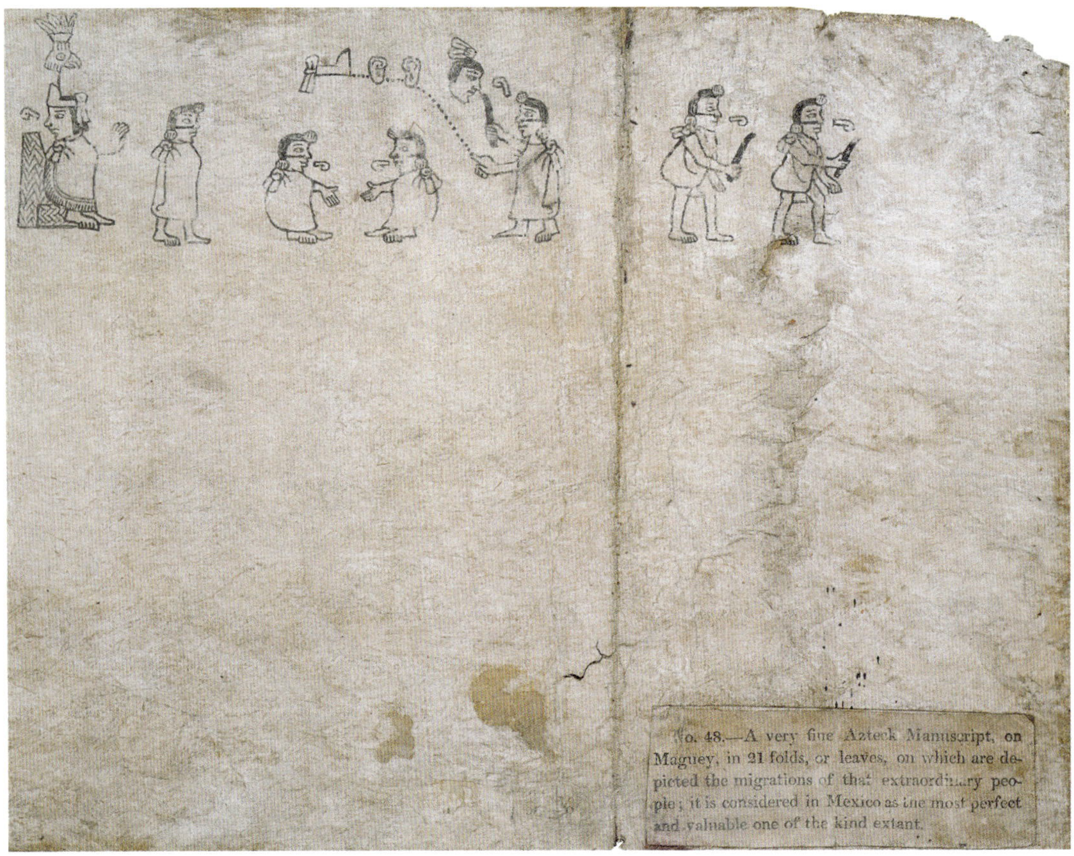

Plate 2.22. Codex Boturini, folio 22.

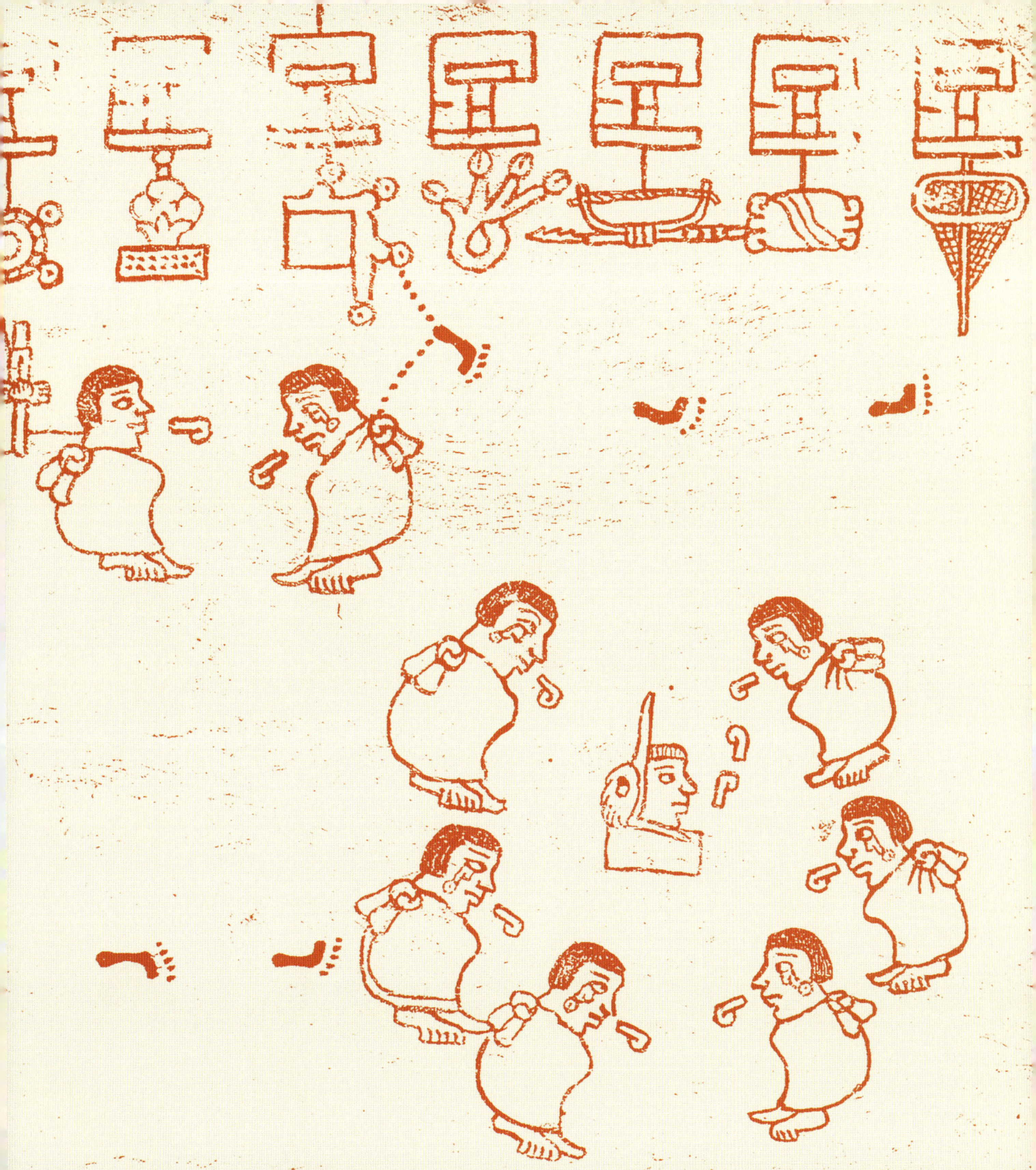

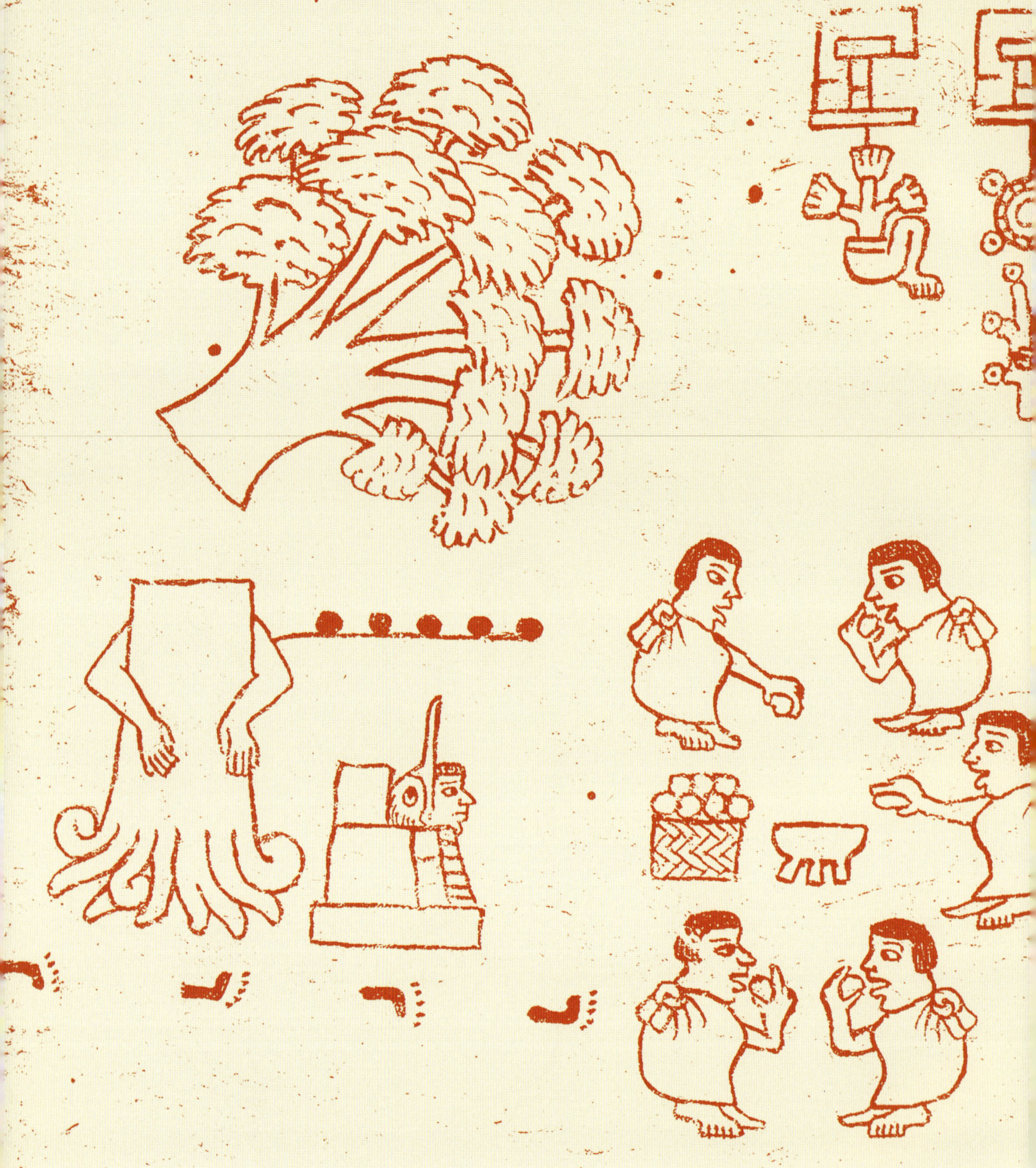

CHAPTER 3

MASTER AND APPRENTICE

The Multiple Artistic Hands in Codex Azcatitlan

UNLIKE CODEX BOTURINI and Codex Aubin, Codex Azcatitlan is truly collaborative. Throughout a significant portion of the manuscript, at least two indigenous *tlacuiloque* worked together to record their history in a primarily pictographic endeavor. On many pages of the migration history we see these hands engaging with each other and integrating their forms in a shared composition. Although the content of Codex Azcatitlan aligns closely with that of Codex Boturini and Codex Aubin, the degree of experimentation with introduced European artistic techniques is unparalleled. Visual analysis reveals both a senior or master artist who directs the project and ensures that indigenous paradigms form an armature for the narrative and a junior or apprentice artist who adjusts his forms from page to page, systematically and exuberantly redefining what it means to participate in the visual arts tradition in New Spain. Though more conservative in his methods, the master artist also actively adopts European Renaissance techniques that complement indigenous ways of recording knowledge.

A better understanding of how the artistic hands work, and how they integrate, aids analysis of the narrative content. This chapter identifies and characterizes the different artistic hands and provides an overview of the master artist's layout of the manuscript. In the migration history we find the master artist painting the most important scenes in the narrative: those that occur at the beginning and end. An analysis of the opening and closing scenes shows the master artist adapting Codex Boturini's migration narrative to forthrightly advance Tlatelolca interests. In between he allowed the apprentice artist, in gradations, to take over the task of recording the litany of stops along the migration route. In the second half of the manuscript the master artist employed different formats to mark shifts in time and narrative content. As an examination of Acamapichtli's reign demonstrates, the imperial history employs a Tenochca foundation, but the content recorded therein is by no means Tenochca-centric. While the basic structure of the conquest and postconquest histories is described here, a fuller analysis of the narrative and pictorial content is given in chapters 4 and 5.

Although scholarly interest in Codex Azcatitlan has escalated in the last few decades, very few studies discuss the multiple artistic hands that appear in this manuscript. In the mid-twentieth century Robert Barlow wrote the first detailed study of Codex Azcatitlan and suggested that two artists worked on the manuscript. The first, a skilled painter, produced the beginning of the manuscript, all of the imperial history, and all of the colonial history.[1] The second, an apprentice, produced the bulk of the migration narrative, from after the stop at Coatlicamac to just before the establishment at Tenochtitlan.[2] Ten years later, in his groundbreaking study *Mexican Manuscript Painting of the Early Colonial Period*, Donald Robertson offered a conflicting view. In his brief comments on the Codex Azcatitlan he suggested that more than one artist worked on the final colonial segment: "In this work, more than one artist seems to have alternated with the main master of the codex."[3]

In 1995 the Bibliothèque Nationale de France and the Société des Américanistes collaborated on the publication of a color facsimile of the manuscript that brought Codex Azcatitlan to a much wider scholarly audience.[4] Since then, several authors, including Elizabeth Hill Boone, Federico Navarrete, and Maria Castañeda de la Paz, have studied the narrative and historical content. Less attention has been paid to the stylistic aspects of the manuscript. Historian Federico Navarrete examined some of the stylistic choices of these *tlacuiloque* in a 2004 article, noting the use of European conventions to depict landscape, three-dimensional buildings, groups of people, and elaborate drawings of sacrificial victims. Although Navarrete noted the visual heterogeneity of Codex Azcatitlan, he argued that it "is a highly coherent document, since its *tlacuilome* [*tlacuiloque*] followed a carefully defined narrative program, which determined the different techniques, styles, and European motifs that they employed in each particular scene."[5] Focusing on the coherency of the manuscript allowed Navarrete to make important points about the complexity of Codex Azcatitlan. While I concur that Codex Azcatitlan is a highly unified document, I also believe that we can gain greater understanding of the manuscript by exploring the origin and function of its visual heterogeneity. The differences in painting style and the variable degrees of detail and care that Navarrete points out are the result of more than one artist's work and lead to Codex Azcatitlan's visual inconsistency.

"Artist A" and "Artist B"

As Barlow described, two distinct artistic hands are evident. Unusual or atypical figures and forms, however, occur at many points in the manuscript. These may represent additional hands, as Robertson believed, or may be interpreted as experimentation by one of the two primary artists. In some instances more than one artist seems to have worked on the same figure, perhaps in a training capacity. Both Barlow and Robertson recognized the presence of a more skilled master artist. For convenience, I call this *tlacuilo* "Artist A." Artist A oversees the project and guides the work of at least one "apprentice" artist whom I call "Artist B." Artist A's hand is skilled and confident, resulting in uniform images. Though Artist A adheres to many pre-Hispanic visual conventions, his work, like that of his apprentice, is informed by European artistic principles. Artist A paints the most important segments of the manuscript and maintains control over the compositional layout, gradually allowing the apprentice to take on increasing responsibility throughout the migration segment. The apprentice follows the model that Artist A sets, structuring the narrative imagery according to indigenous paradigms but expanding and enriching the content with visual detail.

It is perhaps easiest to begin to identify the different artists' hands by their representation of the human figure. Artist A typically produces compact human figures with a solid, confidently rendered exterior form line (figure 3.1). The majority of his figures are rendered in profile, and they are usually facing right to facilitate the left-to-right reading direction of the manuscript. His faces are characterized by an angular profile. The line indents very slightly beneath the lips to indicate the space below the mouth and then protrudes very slightly to signal the small angular chin. He uses straight or slightly curved eyebrows, and his pupils always touch the line below the eyebrow that represents the epicanthic fold. Female figures have a similar face. The hairstyle shows the two braid ends rising in the front, a roll of hair at the base of the neck, and two bands or ribbons that are sometimes painted red and sometimes left uncolored.

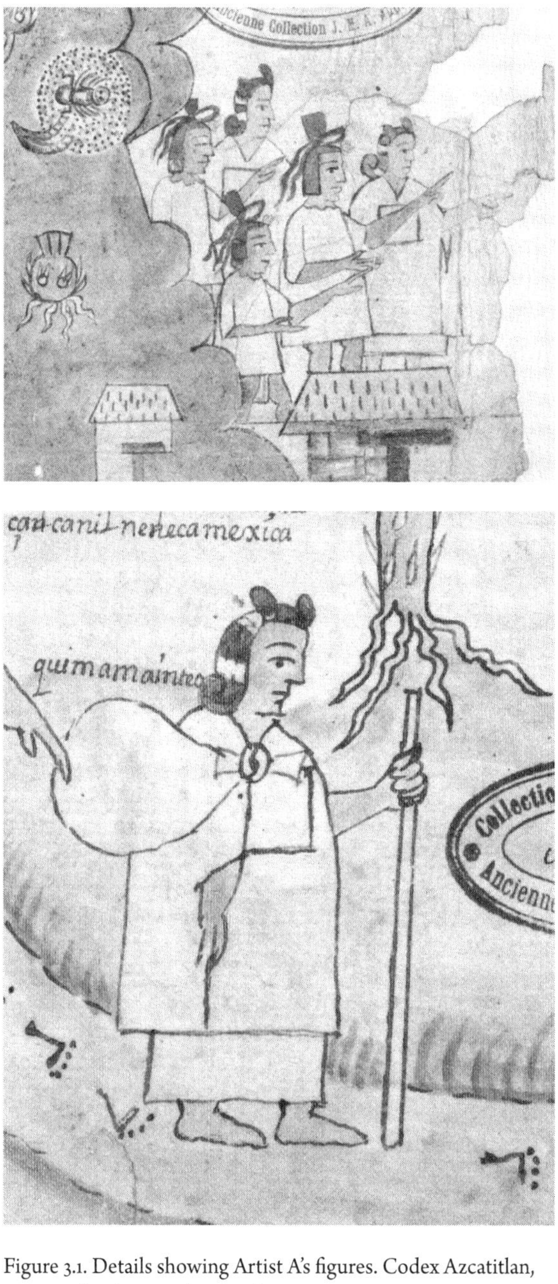

Figure 3.1. Details showing Artist A's figures. Codex Azcatitlan, folios 1v (top) and 5r (bottom). Courtesy of the Bibliothèque Nationale de France.

The next decidedly distinct artistic hand is introduced on folios 5v–6r (figure 3.2). Artist B builds up the exterior form of his figures using broken lines of uneven saturation and width. The lines used to define the body curve more than Artist A's, articulating to a greater degree thighs, knees, calves, ankles, and even toes. Many of his figures show the use of gray shadowing within the body to create contour and a sense of volume. While Artist A consistently uses a form line to define the exterior boundaries of the hair, Artist B tends to use multiple wavy lines. The effect is wavy or more textured hair. By folios 6v–7r Artist B shifts to more distinct hairstyles, showing men with either short haircuts that are cropped at neck length or long hair that is tied at the nape of the neck and has a prominent forelock (figure 3.2, center). Similarly, Artist B begins to depict women with their characteristic upturned braids, which take on a distinctive crescent shape. Both the eyebrow and the epicanthic fold on Artist B's faces arch considerably. The pupil often does not touch the line of the epicanthic fold, creating a wide-eyed look. His noses are long and come to a sharp point (figure 3.2). Unlike Artist A, he often depicts ears.

Artist B does all faces in profile until folio 9r. The figure standing on the path at the lower center of the page faces forward. A seated male further along the path turns his head to stare out of the picture plane. In both figures the heavily arched epicanthic folds

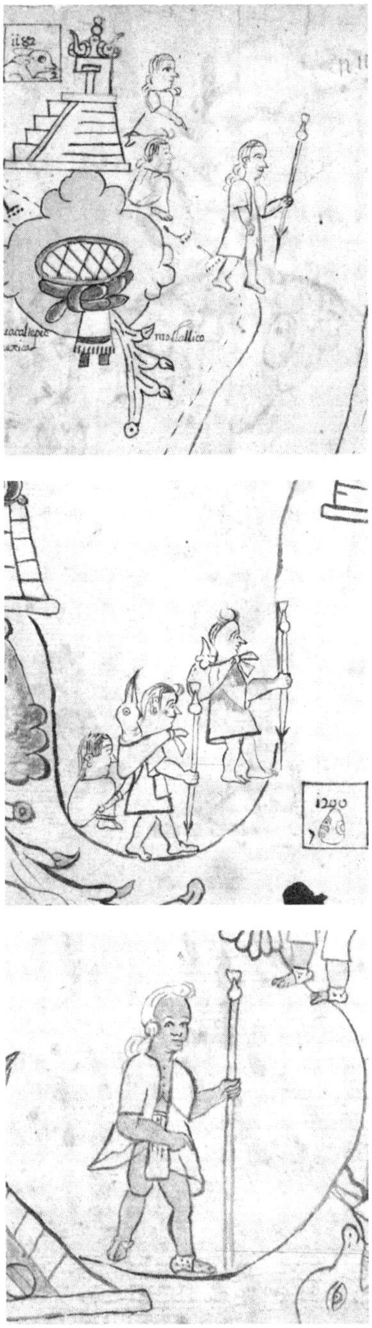

Figure 3.2. Details showing Artist B's figures. Codex Azcatitlan, folios 5v (top), 6v (center), and 9r (bottom). Courtesy of the Bibliothèque Nationale de France.

represent the frontal version of what the artist has been showing in profile. As the artist breaks away from the strict profile heads, he allows his figures to break through the picture plane and engage with the viewer.

As the primary artist who painted the bulk of the manuscript, Artist A established the content and organization of Codex Azcatitlan. His hand predominates at the beginning and end of the migration narrative, throughout the imperial history, and in the conquest and postconquest segments. His distinctive human figures occur throughout the manuscript, and his strong, confident form line characterizes his date glyphs, place glyphs, and architectural structures. The grids that enclose the date glyphs and many of his forms look as if they were rendered with the aid of a straight-edge tool. For example, on folios 1v–2r the rigid lines that delineate house and temple structures, the priest's boat and paddle, and the rectangle that forms the island of Aztlan create a crisp order that is typical of many of his compositions and anchors the winding narrative of the peregrination (figure 3.3). Artist A uses these rigid lines consistently in the imperial and postconquest histories as well, rendering things like thrones, buildings, boats, and platforms. Artist A confidently renders organic forms and is responsible for the more scenic landscapes, such as those on folios 3v–4r and on folio 5r (figure 2.10). The most pigmented images in Codex Azcatitlan generally belong to Artist A. He demonstrates a skillful use of color in forms like his Huitzilopochtli impersonators (folios 1v, 2v, 4v, 6r), the rugged landscape of folio 5r, and the image of Acamapichtli on his throne (folio 13v). Artist A uses unbounded and layered colors to contribute to a sense of spatial depth and to create the appearance of mass and volume by modeling forms.

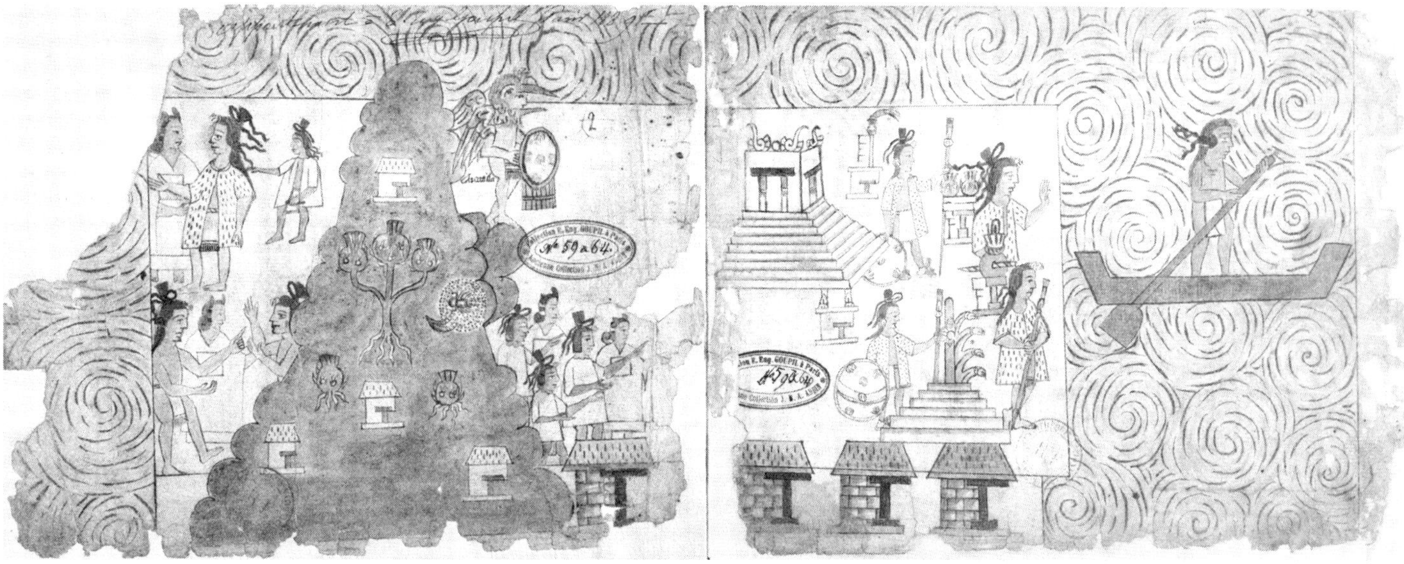

Figure 3.3. Codex Azcatitlan, folios 1v–2r. Courtesy of the Bibliothèque Nationale de France.

An Overview of the Structure

The structure created by Artist A relies upon and reinforces indigenous models. There are three distinct overall shifts in Codex Azcatitlan's compositional layout. The migration segment is organized as an annals history with blocks of year-bearers. The composition is further ordered by the place glyphs that represent stops along the peregrination and places that were passed through. An undulating path flows horizontally through the plates, generally guiding the reader from left to right. In the imperial history each two-page layout represents the reign of a Tenochca ruler. The lower part of each composition features the ruler seated on a throne at far left and identified by a name glyph. In many instances his mummy bundle appears at far right. Various kinds of information are recorded in between, including battles and conquests, temple expansions, New Fire ceremonies, pest invasions, and so forth. Although the organizational structure is based on the lineage of Tenochca rulers, the content and information on these pages is not exclusively Tenochca and relates to the Tlatelolca and to rulers of neighboring territories. For the most part the *tlacuilo* did not complete the upper portion of the compositions, but the images that do exist often tend to elaborate and expand upon events that run along the lower part of the plate.

As Navarrete has noted, the final sections of the manuscript that deal with the conquest and early colonial history "present a clear stylistic and narrative contrast to the previous two parts of the Codex . . . the *tlacuilome* of the Azcatitlan had no established visual narrative conventions to follow, and so they were free to experiment."[6] This final section of the manuscript still flows chronologically, but the compositions are organized by important events rather than by places or the lives of political leaders. The conquest pages are laid out in what would have been four two-page compositions (before the missing pages were removed). The postconquest history reads roughly in vertical columns of information, from left to right. Artist A's hand throughout the manuscript and his decision to respect established indigenous paradigms result in an overall consistency.

THE YEAR-BEARERS

Narratively and compositionally, the beginning and the end of the Mexica migration receive the most attention, while the stops along the journey form a rhythmic pattern of dates and places. The *tlacuilo* records each year of the migration but groups the year-bearers that signal how long the Mexica stopped in a given place. For example, on folio 5v the Mexica stop for two years at Coatlicamac, represented by the open mouth of a serpent, before proceeding to Huacaltepec, located near the top of folio 5v, where they stay another two years (figure 3.4). Next they proceed to stay three years at Huixachtitlan, designated by the plants that top the large mountain glyph at center. The last stop, located to the far right of folio 6r, records a lengthy stay of nine years at Coatepec. Though Codex Azcatitlan is more visually complex than pictorial manuscripts like Codex Boturini and Codex Aubin, the dates and places still anchor the narrative.

Elizabeth Hill Boone has described the continuous year-count annals format as highly codified, to the extent that it became a diagnostic of Tenochca control. She writes:

> The manuscript painters of the empire embraced the pan-Mexican tradition of recording history, but as is shown below, the dominant group of the Triple Alliance—the Culhua-Mexica or Tenochca of Tenochtitlan—additionally developed a particular kind of royal history, the continuous year-count annals, which, in its conception of time and its structuring of events, became diagnostic of Tenochca control.[7]

Beginning on folio 2v, Artist A adopts this structure and starts recording the years. Grouped blocks of year-bearers mark the amount of time the Mexica stayed in various locations along the journey. The grouping of year-bearers allows more space for pictorial content, which Artists A and B fully exploit. As Boone has stated, the clustering of years is used in similar ways in Codex Boturini, Codex Azcatitlan, Codex Aubin, and two annals cognate with Aubin (Fonds Mexicain 40 and 85, Bibliothèque Nationale de France).[8] However, while the Codex Mexicanus, Codex Boturini, and Codex Aubin *tlacuiloque* grappled with the problem of how best to communicate when the Mexica left a location and when they arrived at the next stop (as discussed in chapter 2), Artist A does not or had not yet engaged with this problem. The viewer is left to assume, for example, that on folio 5v (figure 3.4) the Mexica arrived in

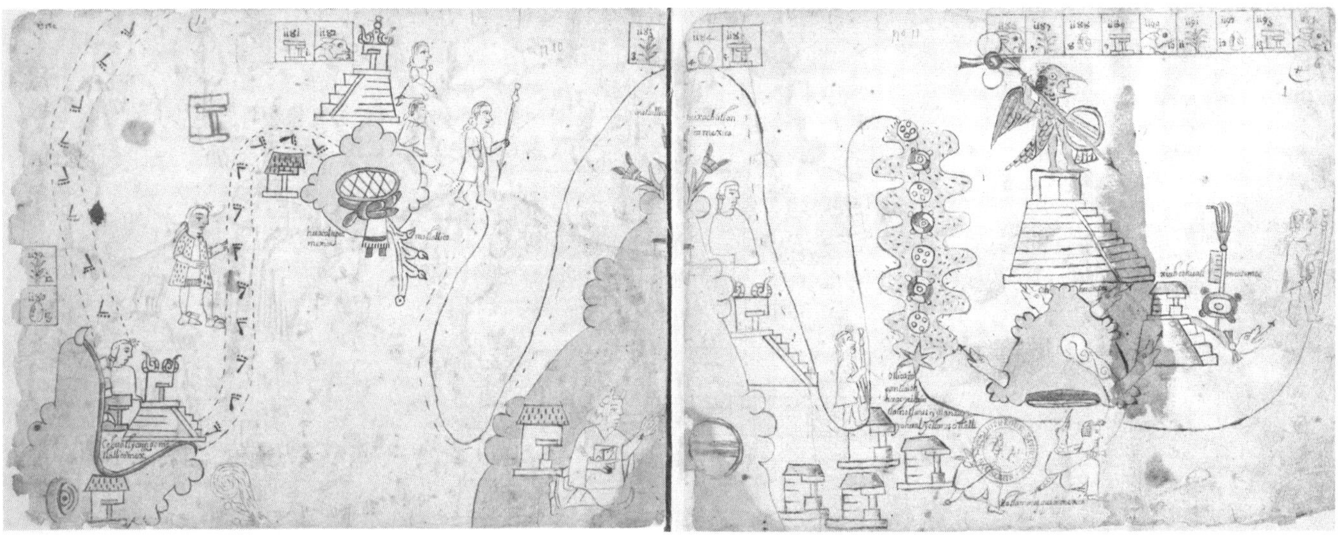

Figure 3.4. Codex Azcatitlan, folios 5v–6r. Courtesy of the Bibliothèque Nationale de France.

Coatlicamac in the year 12 Reed and departed from there in 13 Flint, arriving at the next destination, Huacaltepec, in the year 1 House. The possibility that they may have arrived in 13 Flint, the same year they departed, is not entertained. The path of the Mexica runs continuously through and around the various place glyphs but does not intersect with the date glyphs as deliberately as in Codex Boturini.

Artist A paints the Codex Azcatitlan year-bearer glyphs (House, Rabbit, Reed, and Flint) and their Arabic numeral glosses uniformly throughout the migration history. They form an integral part of the compositions. In examining the original Codex Azcatitlan manuscript, I have noted that the Rabbit glyphs are in a slightly different tint than those depicting House, Reed, and Flint. This suggests that after the artist mapped out the date blocks he filled in all of the House glyphs at once: all of the Rabbits at once and so forth rather than consecutively alternating among House, Rabbit, Reed, and Flint. This repetition surely contributed to the uniformity of the glyphs. He clearly diverted himself in this mundane task by varying the placement of the Rabbit's pupil (figure 3.5). Throughout the migration sequence the creature's eyes are open, shut, gazing upward, downward, backward, forward, and centered. In finished and unfinished examples on folios 6r, 8v, 9v, and 12r Artist A allows certain forms to penetrate the date block, creating the illusion that the forms overlap the date cartouches (see, for example, figures 3.4, 3.5, and 3.6). This indicates that the *tlacuilo* probably filled in the date glyphs after the basic composition of the page was established or at least at the same time. There are 213 years in all, depicting a journey that takes place between 1168 and 1381. No years appear to be missing, so if there is a plate missing between 4v–5r, as Michel Graulich has suggested, it probably would have had extensive pictorial content, like that found on folio 5r.[9]

The *tlacuilo*, presumably Artist A, added the Arabic numerals last. The numbers are clear and legible; his only omission is a zero on the cartouche for the year 1240. The numerals occasionally overlie the glyphs (e.g., 1274 and 1287). In those places where the figures and forms overlap with the date cartouches, the Arabic numerals were clearly added after the composition was worked out. They either work around the overlapped forms, as on folio 8v, or overlie the figure when there is not enough room to do that, as on folio 12r, where the numbers overlap the left arm of the figure standing between the date blocks (figure 3.6). In two instances numerals appear in the alphabetic glosses (on folios 13v and 15r). The numbers are formed in the same way as those in the date cartouches, indicating that one scribe produced both the glosses and the numeric inscriptions. The

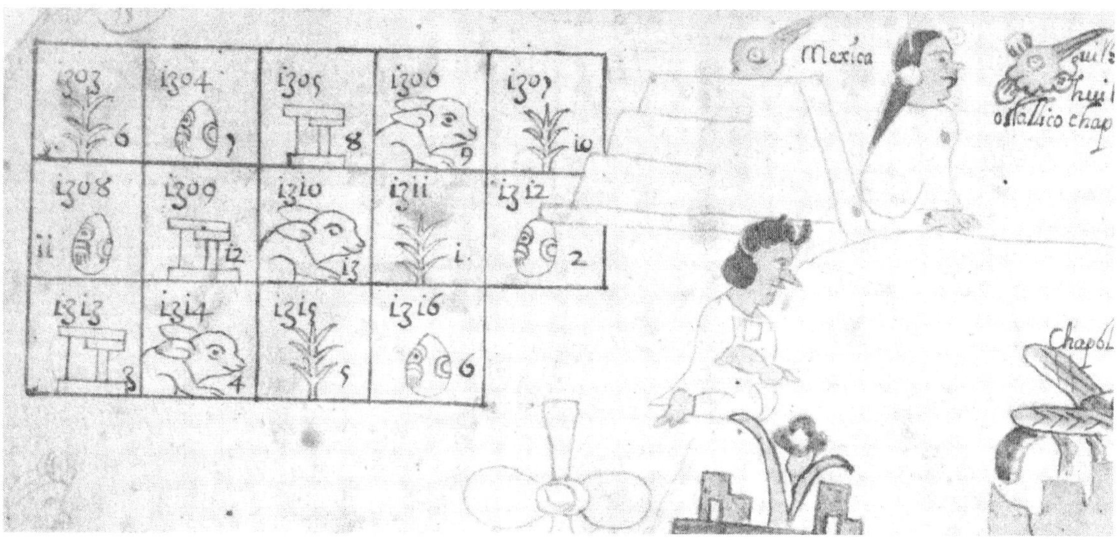

Figure 3.5. Codex Azcatitlan, folio 9v (detail). Courtesy of the Bibliothèque Nationale de France.

Codex Boturini and Codex Aubin *tlacuiloque* used the pre-Hispanic dot numbering in their year-bearers and had to design their cartouches to accommodate as many as thirteen dots. By using Arabic numerals in the date cartouches, the *tlacuilo* uses far less space and has more room for his pictorial content.

The Arabic numeral years and the alphabetic glosses relate to the most significant structural components of the migration sequence, time, and place. The Arabic numeral years "translate" the indigenous year count and the majority of the alphabetic glosses "translate" information that is also glyphically rendered (see appendix 1). In this way the *tlacuilo* emphasizes the same key information that is registered in Codex Boturini and Codex Aubin: where the Mexica traveled and how long they stayed in each location. On the few occasions when the glosser is not naming places and people he elaborates on glyphs or images that may have been more difficult for his Nahuatl-speaking audience to understand, as they grew increasingly distant from and less familiar with the oral and pictorial traditions of the pre-Hispanic past. Finally, the majority of the glosses appear in the migration segment. Only a few glosses appear in the imperial segment, and none are present in the colonial section. The glosses, like the images, are incomplete.

THE INITIAL FOLIOS—ARTIST A

The initial plates of Codex Azcatitlan appear to be the work of Artist A and give a sense of how the artist worked and in what ways he adhered to pre-Hispanic conventions while experimenting with introduced European techniques. The very first plate in Codex Azcatitlan is folio 1r, which shows three indigenous rulers seated on European-style thrones (figure 3.7). They wear indigenous dress and *xiuhhuitzolli*, indicating that they are rulers. Each holds a staff of office pointing in the direction that the throne faces. The images are unfinished; the bottoms of the thrones are not articulated, the bottom of the staff at far right has not been completed, and the color use is limited. Artist A applies a solid wash of dark color within the form line that articulates a blunt-cut hairstyle arranged in the *temillotl* (pillar of stone) associated with warriors. He uses warmer tones to indicate skin tone, a light red on the staffs, and a brighter red on the lips and the ribbon that adorns the *temillotl.*

Folio 1r demonstrates some of Artist A's interests in introduced European techniques (figure 3.7). As described above, Artist A uses a straight-edge tool to produce architectural forms. Although the results are awkward, he attempts to use perspective on the stairs and European-style thrones to create a sense

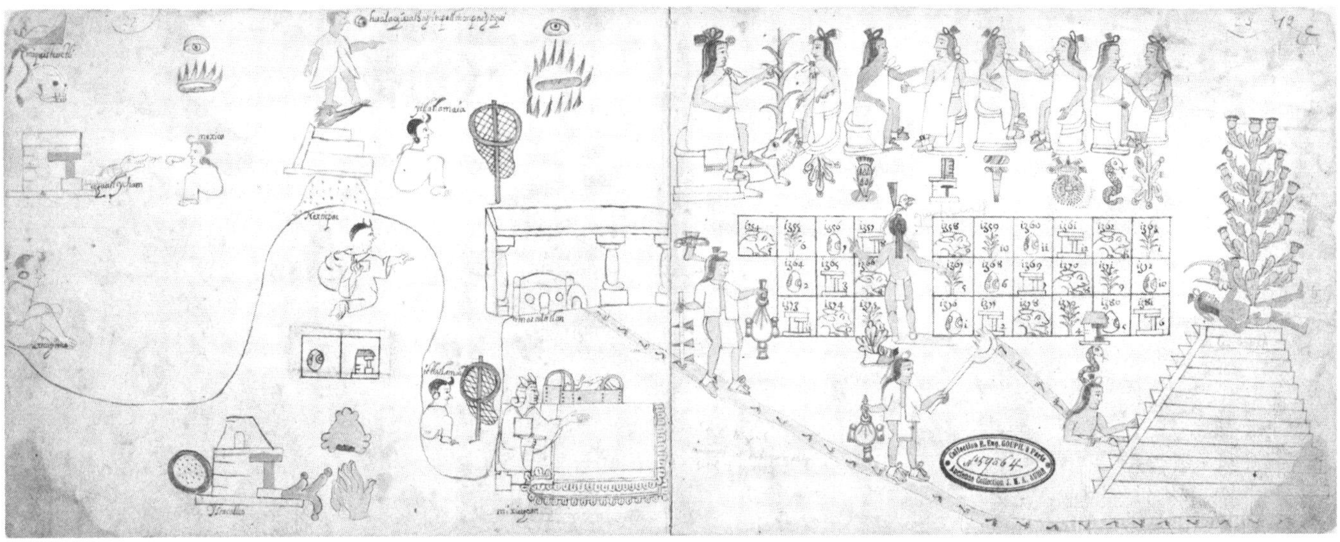

Figure 3.6. Codex Azcatitlan, folios 11v–12r. Courtesy of the Bibliothèque Nationale de France.

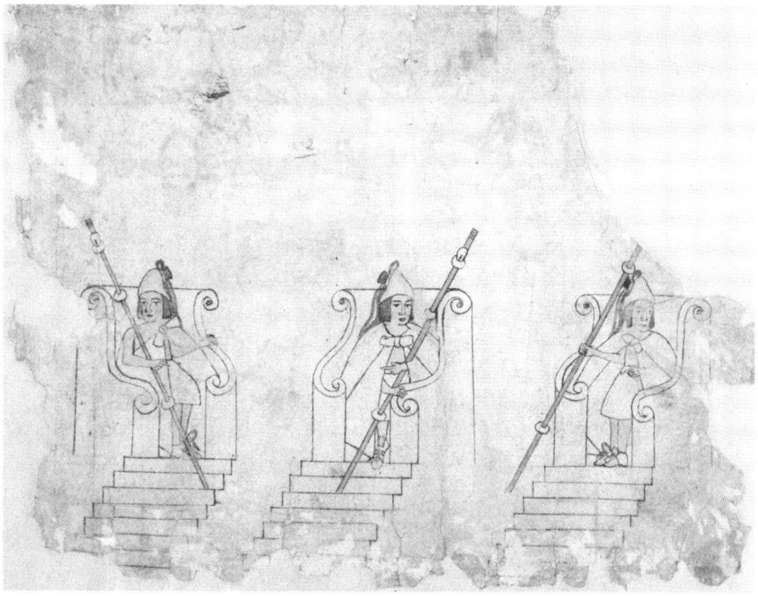

Figure 3.7. Codex Azcatitlan, folio 1r. Courtesy of the Bibliothèque Nationale de France.

of recession into space. Rather than depicting the figures in strict profile, as seen in Codex Boturini, he produces frontally facing figures. Artist A breaks with the indigenous tradition of using flat washes of color within hard boundary lines by using color to model his forms. In these figures he begins to use light and shadow to define the eye area and the nose and uses a pale wash of pink on the cheeks.

Although folio 1r reflects a significant amount of European influence, indigenous components that convey key information are retained. The turquoise diadems, staffs, and *temillotl* hairstyle all signal the status of these individuals as rulers and warriors. This is reinforced by their thrones, even if they are European in style. In Mesoamerican manuscripts produced by indigenous artists after the conquest, rulers are often shown occupying the seat of office. The three figures are rendered equally and appear without name glyphs on the first page, which indicates that they are to be understood as the three rulers of the Triple Alliance. Located here at the beginning of the manuscript, they recall the invocations to the three rulers of the Triple Alliance that begin many of the *cantares mexicanos*. This association may have been apparent to Artist A's intended audience and may signal one of the additional sources that the *tlacuilo* used as he expanded Codex Boturini's content. According to John Bierhorst, indigenous songs accompanied by dance were performed throughout the sixteenth century, despite explicit attempts by Spanish authorities to terminate the practice. The practice began to die out around the 1590s, but manuscripts recording the songs were still in circulation and were used as source material by authors like Chimalpahin through the middle of the seventeenth century.[10]

Thereafter Artist A paints four (or five if a page is missing between folios 4v and 5r) additional scenes that are designed as compositions that read across two facing pages. Narratively these initial pages correspond to folios 1–4 of Codex Boturini, conveying essential features in expanded form. Codex Boturini places Aztlan and Colhuacan on folio 1 and then details several important events (plate 2.1). Although Codex Azcatitlan represents Aztlan, Colhuacan, and Chicomoztoc on separate pages, Michel Oudijk has noted that "we can see that Aztlan, (Teo)Colhuacan/Colhuacatepec, and Chicomoztoc are so closely related that they should be regarded as one and the same place whose name can be interchanged according to the needs of a *tlacuilo*, or scribe."[11] In Codex Azcatitlan the same eight groups are depicted departing in the same order. The same four god-bearers lead, along with additional figures that are associated with the tribes listed above. On Codex Boturini folio 4

Huitzilopochtli provides the Mexica with support in the form of a *xiuhmamalhuaztli*,a bow and arrow, and a basket, while a sacrifice is offered below. Similar themes are depicted on Codex Azcatitlan folio 4v (figure 2.10). Huitzilopochtli appears with a fire drill, a bow and arrow, and sacrificial victims. The separation of the Mexica from the other tribes and the site of Cuextecatlichocayan, an event and location recorded on Codex Boturini folio 3, are not depicted in Codex Azcatitlan but may have been shown on a missing page. Artist A further expands on Codex Boturini's content by depicting two very scenic compositions (folios 3v–4r and 5r) that articulate how the Mexica traveled (with their children and god-bundles, stopping at places where fresh water was available), what they did when they arrived at a destination (building houses and temples, cooking food), and how difficult the journey was (they got lost, it was rocky, animals attacked them).

This prelude, laid out by Artist A, articulates some of the most important religious content and sets the stage for the more abbreviated images that document the migratory destinations that follow. Thereafter, for example, a single house glyph or set of house glyphs indicates settlement at a site with fresh water. While the toponym was required, the addition of other figures and elements was optional. Aside from differing dates that must derive from the collating of information from an additional source, Artist A does not so much contradict Codex Boturini as expand upon it. This expanded content reflects artistic experimentation, the visual rendering of details that might have been described in an oral account (as on folio 1r), and the desire to articulate political and social identity. While Codex Boturini records a narrative of Mexica identity, Artist A makes clear from the very start of his manuscript that the Tlatelolca as well as the Tenochca lay claim to this heritage. He articulates this most clearly in the scene depicting the departure from Aztlan and again at the end of the peregrination.

FOLIOS 1V–2R: THE DEPARTURE FROM AZTLAN—ARTISTIC EXPERIMENTATION

On folios 1v–2r Artist A negotiates between retaining pictographic components that carry important pre-Hispanic information and experimenting with introduced European stylistic conventions (figure 3.3). To begin to understand how Codex Azcatitlan functions visually, it is helpful to compare the opening pages to those in Codex Boturini (cf. plate 2.1 and figure 3.3). In many ways they are similar. The initial plates of both manuscripts feature the departure from Aztlan. Like the *tlacuilo* of the Codex Boturini, Artist A begins by depicting the island as if we are looking down on it from above. As in Codex Boturini, many forms are flat and stylized, like the priest's canoe and paddle, the large hill glyph that dominates the left side of the composition, the house glyphs, and the temple at lower right with the reed-water glyph. In both Codex Azcatitlan and Codex Boturini the Aztecs leave the island city of Aztlan, led by their priest who canoes across the water. In both manuscripts the priest's darkened skin signals his identity.[12] In Codex Boturini a compact composition shows that the departure takes place in the year 1 Flint and that the hummingbird deity Huitzilopochtli guides the participants. In Codex Boturini a deity impersonator depicted in the cave at Colhuacan represents Huitzilopochtli and speech scrolls signal his communication and leadership. Codex Azcatitlan significantly expands the visual content and is laid out to accommodate its bound book format, so it depicts the year and the stop at Colhuacan on the following folios, 2v–3r. However, Artist A makes sure to represent Huitzilopochtli at the initial departure. The deity impersonator appears on folio 1v, perched on top of the hill. The deity impersonator wears the head and wings of a hummingbird and carries a warrior's shield. Both images identify the site as Aztlan by depicting a small temple topped by a glyph that is made up of a reed and flowing water.[13] Codex Boturini depicts a male and female figure and six house glyphs to represent the groups that departed. A set of four house glyphs is repeated in various forms in Codex Azcatitlan, and the scene is filled with figures.

Though Codex Azcatitlan and Codex Boturini essentially record the same core components of the narrative, they differ substantially in style and composition. Following pre-Hispanic stylistic conventions, the Codex Boturini *tlacuilo* renders his images in two dimensions with heavy frame lines outlining the forms. The forms generally do not overlap, and he makes no attempt to depict landscape or perspective. Stylized renderings privilege clarity and consistency over innovation. In contrast, Codex Azcatitlan's Artist A experiments with two- and three-dimensional forms. For example, the larger temple on folio 2r is rendered in three dimensions, while the smaller one with the reed-water glyph is two-dimensional. Though Artist A tends to use frame lines as well, he includes more visual details such as in the clothing and dress. Artist A expands the visual representation to include numerous figures and structures, which he then attempts to locate in space. The clustered figures, for example, are overlapped and stacked to create a sense of depth. At times the results are awkward. For example, the shield of the figure associated with the banner glyph appears to occupy the space directly beneath the large three-dimensional temple. While the Codex Boturini *tlacuilo* uses conventionalized positions and gestures to depict the figures in strict profile or a combination of profile head and partially frontal body, Artist A experiments with a more plastic rendering of the body and tries a variety of poses. Two of the figures in folios 1v–2r have crossed legs, and the male at far left lifts one foot off the ground. Artist A paints most of his heads in profile but experiments with some three-quarter and frontal views. On folio 1r and folios 2v–3r the artist tackles new problems, such as how to render the noses on frontally facing figures.

In this important departure scene Artist A sets a precedent that will be followed throughout the migration segment. The essential components of the narrative are recorded and then expanded upon visually. For example, each repetition of the house forms conveys slightly different information. On the *altepetl* mountain they may serve to remind us, like the house glyphs in Codex Boturini, that several different groups migrated. On the lower right of the island in Codex Azcatitlan the houses take on more detail, showing that they are built up of mud brick or stone and have thatch roofs. The four house forms are repeated once again above these. This time each is associated with a human figure and identified with a glyph.

Like the repetition of house forms, the multiplication of human figures adds information and enlivens the narrative. To the left of the hill two groups of figures face each other. As in other sixteenth-century indigenous manuscripts such as the Florentine Codex and the Lienzo de Tlaxcala, the figures gesture toward each other, signaling communication. To the right of the hill the departure begins. All figures face right, and many point in the direction that the travelers will take. The leaders at far right are closest to the priest and wear the rough animal-skin cloaks that signal their rugged Chichimec ancestry. Pictorial detail was not required in the manuscripts in the pre-Hispanic period because a trained orator would present the material to an audience, elaborating and expanding verbally upon the core narrative recorded in the images. Overall Codex Azcatitlan still functions like this, but Artist A attempts to record some of this detail visually.

FOLIOS 1V–2R: THE DEPARTURE FROM AZTLAN, A PROJECTION OF TENOCHTITLAN-TLATELOLCO

While others have noted the Tlatelolca presence and perspective in Codex Azcatitlan, it is usually discussed as a component of the imperial history and as a secondary position woven into a Tenochca narrative or "hidden" code, as Navarrete puts it.[14] The visual and narrative analyses presented in this chapter and the two subsequent chapters build on these studies and lead to a conclusion that Artist A foregrounds the Tlatelolca presence such that, far from being hidden, it is writ large. Like the Annals of Tlatelolco, Codex Azcatitlan borrows Tenochca models and recognizes the complex and intertwined history of the Mexica descendants but is first and foremost a Tlatelolca document.

As such, the Tlatelolca presence is registered from start to finish in the manuscript and appears in the opening scene depicting the departure from Aztlan (figure 3.3). The *tlacuilo* presents the departure from Aztlan as an event that belongs to the historical narrative of descendants living in both Tlatelolco and Tenochtitlan. Boone has described Aztlan in these migration stories as a projection of Tenochtitlan, another island city surrounded by water.[15] The migration narratives are highly structured and symmetrical. Aztlan, an island city, prefigures and echoes the later development of Tenochtitlan, thereby emphasizing the cyclical nature of time. Colhuacan appears at both the beginning and end of the migration narrative. Aztlan is a projection of Tenochtitlan-Tlatelolco in Codex Azcatitlan. Just as the Tlatelolca would annex the smaller northern portion of the island in Lake Texcoco soon after settling, the first pages of Codex Azcatitlan divide Aztlan into two parts. The large hill that dominates folio 1v carries associations with Tlatelolco, while the four figures on folio 2r relate to the later quadripartite division of Tenochtitlan.

At first, the hill place glyph would not seem out of place here. It takes the overall form of a large *altepetl* place glyph similar to those found in other parts of the manuscript, albeit without the red and yellow bars at the base. The glyph has undulations typically grouped in threes, like that of Colhuacan on the next plate. Throughout the migration narratives, toponyms signal the various stops along the migration route. Why not mark the site of Aztlan at the beginning of the journey? Codex Aubin's departure scene on folio 3r shows a large hill glyph on the island with a European scroll and alphabetic letters that identify it as "Aztlan" (figure 2.9). The Codex Azcatitlan hill, however, is not glossed as Aztlan and does not carry the glyph associated with Aztlan. Rather, the reed-water glyph appears atop the small temple in the lower right part of the main rectangle.

The large hill glyph may be better understood as an oblique representation of Tlatelolco: *tla[lli]* (land) + *telol[li]* (hill) + *-co* (locative suffix). Tlatelolco means "in the little hill of land" or "in the place of the mound of earth." While the place glyph itself could be understood to be the mound of earth, the extension at upper right (on which a Huitzilopochtli impersonator perches) seems to function as the identifying modifier for the generic hill-shaped place glyph. If this is the case, the *tlacuilo* purposely opts against the typical spotted mound that is used to designate Tlatelolco in the rest of the manuscript. The allusion is subtle: this hill references but is not yet Tlatelolco. The hill simultaneously references Tlatelolco and forms a part of the landscape of Aztlan. The spotted mound that usually signifies Tlatelolco only appears for the first time on folio 13r, when the first leader of this newly separate entity takes the seat of office.

Similarly, the four figures on folio 2r represent migrating groups but also signal the later quadripartite division of the city of Tenochtitlan. Each figure is associated with a house topped by identifying glyphs. As Graulich notes, these same glyphs appear in a map of Mexico in the Codex Ixhuatepec.[16] There they are identified as Cihuatecpan (two jars); Chalman (the glyph for jade with a cord running through it); Tlacochcalco (two darts); and Tlacatecpan (a banner). As Pedro Carrasco notes, these four names correspond to the four *parcialidades* (neighborhoods) of Tenochtitlan before and after the conquest.

> Before the Spanish Conquest, Tenochtitlan was divided into four parcialidades or principal barrios, and this division continued throughout the colonial period. The boundaries between these parcialidades ran from north to south and from east to west so that each one occupied a quarter of the city, Atzacualco (San Sebastián) in the northeast, Cuepopan (Santa María) in the northwest,

> Moyotla (San Juan) in the southwest, and Teopan (San Pablo) in the southeast. The histories of the Mexica migration usually give the names of seven original calpulli. . . . Four of these can be identified with the four parcialidades: Tlacatecpan with Atzacualco, Tlacochcalco with Cuepopan, Cihuatecpan with Moyotla, and Chalman with Teopan.[17]

Because this island is a precursor, Artist A does not employ the typical toponym for Tenochtitlan, a nopal cactus and a stone. But he does make an association that will resonate with an indigenous audience familiar with the divisions of the capital city that existed before and after the conquest.

In addition to referencing the *parcialidades* of later Tenochtitlan, these four figures may locate the scene spatially. According to the associations above, the two figures on the left of folio 2r are associated with the north, while the two figures just behind the priest are associated with the south. This would correspond with a reading where the "place of the mound of earth" or future Tlatelolco is to the north of the future Tenochtitlan. This would also correspond with indigenous traditions of privileging east geographically and describing Aztlan as a location to the north, from which people migrated south. If the *tlacuilo* intended to signal directionality with precision, however, we would expect to see Cihuatecpan (southwest) on the lower register and Chalman (southeast) above.

Alternatively, the *tlacuilo* may have intended to associate the future Tlatelolco with the lower part of the rectangular island. Beneath the large rectangle, additional lines extend to the bottom of folios 1v–2r, adding mass to the island. The width of the lower portion is slightly diminished on the right side. Although the lower portion of the island is small, the large place glyph that dominates folio 1v sits squarely in this territory. It is unclear whether the addition was intended from the start or added to accommodate the composition as it evolved. The rooflines of the four large houses to the right of the hill partially camouflage the dividing line, perhaps suggesting the latter.

Immediately adjacent to the protruding mound of earth that associates the large place glyph with the future Tlatelolco the *tlacuilo* painted a circular glyphic sign featuring an insect surrounded by small dots. This glyphic element has been subject to various interpretations. Barlow follows the gloss above the glyph, "Ascatitla," and reads the site as Azcatitlan (Place of the Herons). Graulich suggests a more convincing reading of the glyph as Azcapotzalco: *azca[tl]* (ant) + *potzal[li]* (hill) + *-co* (locative suffix) (Place of the Anthill).[18] Graulich notes that the glyph appears again on folio 16v, where it is more easily recognizable as one of the early conquests in Itzcoatl's reign. While similar toponyms in Codex Azcatitlan represent both Xaltocan, in the Place of the Mound of Sand (folios 8r, 10r), and Azcapotzalco (folios 10r, 12r, 16v), the internal logic of the manuscript dictates that the insect in the Xaltocan glyphs is painted dark, while those of the Azcapotzalco glyphs remain light or accented with red, as on folio 1v.[19] The gloss "Ascatitla" appears just above this glyph, and the mound that extends from the hill. This gloss may represent an incomplete or altered translation of the glyph below, reading it as *azcatl* (ant) + *-ti-* (ligature) + *-tlan* (locative suffix).

Graulich was not sure of the significance of the corded hornlike form that emerges from this glyph. This ropelike form resembles those lines that link individuals in sixteenth-century genealogical charts. In this way it marks the Azcapotzalca origin or ancestry of this place, which I am reading here as at once Aztlan and Tlatelolco. In effect the gloss and glyphic element may serve to remind the viewer that when the Aztecs left Aztlan and arrived at Tenochtitlan-Tlatelolco they were granted use of their new island city by Tezozomoc, the Tepanec ruler of Azcapotzalco. Additionally, the first *tlatoani* of Tlatelolco, Cuacuapitzauac, was the son of Tezozomoc. Thus the *tlacuilo* directly references the Tepanec dynasty of the Tlatelolca rulers, a genealogical heritage cited to establish and enhance the prestige of Tlatelolca descendents.

Artist A makes it clear from the start that his history will highlight the role of both Tlatelolco and

Tepanec lineage within the Mexica migration narrative. In the postconquest context the Codex Azcatitlan *tlacuilo* had greater freedom to respond to the dominant Mexica-Tenochca history and counter or complement it with a Tlatelolca history (presumably of his own people), which had been suppressed since the time of Axayacatl. Michael E. Smith has noted the possible prominence of Tlatelolco during the period of control by Azcapotzalco and the historical erasure of this legacy: "After a dispute between the two kings, Axayacatl of Tenochtitlan fought and defeated Moquihuix of Tlatelolco in 1473, perhaps to better control the marketplace. As part of their rewriting of history to glorify themselves, the kings of Tenochtitlan tried to eliminate references to the early power and glory of Tlatelolco (just as they did with Azcapotzalco), making it difficult to reconstruct the city's early history."[20]

As the grip of Tenochca-Mexica dominance lessened after the conquest, descendants of the different *altepetl* began to reassert their unique roles in history and to make their respective cases to the Spanish government regarding land, rights, and privileges. In central Mexico one of the ardent supporters of the Azcapotzalca legacy was don Antonio Valeriano (d. 1605), who promoted the idea that the most important indigenous noble lineages all sprang from Azcapotzalco. As historian Peter Villella writes, Valeriano authored a 1561 petition on behalf of the Azcapotzalco cabildo (municipal council) that returned to thirteenth-century history to highlight the cabildo's illustrious past:

> This reflected Azcapotzalco's unique history; although the Spaniards had found it a mere tributary of Tlacopan, the altepetl had dominated Anahuac prior to the 1420s. Valeriano's account was one of decline and diminishment, contrasting this town's ancient greatness with its contemporary poverty.
>
> "Although at the present our pueblo is small," he began, "in the past . . . it surpassed [the other provinces] in antiquity and nobility." The elders told that Azcapotzalco had been founded fifteen centuries earlier, and that all the noble lineages of Anahuac had origins there. At the height of its empire, Azcapotzalco maintained tributaries throughout central Mexico, from Cuernavaca in the south to Xilotepec (today Jilótepec) in the north. The Mexica, insisted Valeriano, had been mere squatters in lands controlled by Azcapotzalco, and it was only out of pity that its lord had allowed them to settle Tenochtitlan and sustain themselves in the lake. The imperial order collapsed, however, when the ungrateful Mexica attacked Azcapotzalco, repaying this benevolence with betrayal and violence. Valeriano concluded by stating the purpose of his history: "So that our pueblo, which as we have shown was historically a provincial (independent province), should be named a city by Your Clemency." On the municipal coat of arms it proposed, the cabildo placed the image of a heart, to symbolize how, just as the heart is the origin of all life, Azcapotzalco was the origin of all nobility in "New Spain." The implications were subtle yet powerful: Justice and reason demanded that Spanish officials acknowledge and embrace the Azcapotzalca legacy, the most ancient in all the land.[21]

While this was just one of many such competing claims by different *altepetl*, Antonio Valeriano occupied influential roles in central Mexico and operated in spheres that may have intersected with Artist A. Given the focus on Tlatelolco, the *tlacuiloque* probably lived in this vicinity and may have had interactions with the Colegio de Santa Cruz at Tlatelolco. As Villella notes, Valeriano was an important figure there. "Although not of high noble birth, he won lasting fame as a prodigy at the College of Santa Cruz de Tlatelolco, where he taught Latin alongside don Pablo Nazareo, and helped lead the Franciscans' mid-century efforts to compile native artifacts and detail Nahua history and culture." In the 1550s and 1560s he sat with the Azcapotzalco cabildo. Later Valeriano entered the Tenochca nobility through marriage to the daughter of don Diego de Alvarado Huanitzin and became governor of Tenochtitlan between 1573 and 1599.[22] On folio 1v and in later parts of the manuscript Artist A's perspective reflects a growing interest in promoting Tepanec dynastic history, in this case as a tool for amplifying the glory of Tlatelolco.

Like Codex Boturini, Codex Azcatitlan (folio 2v) depicts Huitzilopochtli in a cave at Colhuacan. A human head appears within the hummingbird headdress in both. In Codex Boturini this is the first appearance of the god. In Codex Aubin the alphabetic text first mentions the god in relation to Colhuacan: "From Colhuacan they left carrying the devil who they worshipped as a god, the Huitzilopochtli."[23] Codex Azcatitlan differs from these two manuscripts by including an additional earlier representation of Huitzilopochtli. A male figure, dressed in a *maxtlatl* (loincloth) and carrying a shield decorated with five down balls, wears the headdress and wings of the hummingbird god.[24] The additional incarnation of the god that we see perched on the place glyph for Tlatelolco on folio 1v reinforces the idea that Huitzilopochtli was the god and protector of both the Tenochca and the Tlatelolca. The dual appearance of Huitzilopochtli in effect emphasizes that both were the "chosen people" of this tutelary god.

Additionally, the image of Huitzilopochtli on folio 1v, perched on the small mound, further reinforces a reading of this site as the future Tlatelolco. In many colonial manuscripts the toponym for Tlatelolco features an eagle on top of the monticule. Examples include the Florentine Codex (figure 4.5) and the *Ordenanza del Señor Cuauhtemoc*. Huitzilopochtli has associations with the eagle and is sometimes depicted in this form, as in Codex Boturini, folio 4 (plate 2.4). As discussed earlier, rather than depicting an eagle on a nopal cactus to signal the arrival in the Basin of Mexico on folio 12r, Artist A depicts Huitzilopochtli as a human head wearing a hummingbird headdress, just as on folio 1v.

The large hill on folio 1v functions as both a place glyph and a painted landscape. The barrel cacti, the Huitzilopochtli impersonator who rests on the protruding mound of earth, and the partial figures that are meant to be read as "behind" the hill all suggest a physical landscape that the figures move on and through. The *tlacuiloque* play with this intersection to varying degrees throughout the migration segment. At times the place glyphs are more traditional, fully encompassed by a solid dark form line with red and yellow bars at the base. At other moments they are more landscape-like. On folio 3v Tepemaxalco (Place of the Hills' Crotch) is identifiable by the mountain with two tall peaks (figure 2.10).[25] The path and figures that cross between the peaks and the flowering nopal cacti and agave depicted on the hills suggest a physical space.[26]

On a basic level the four house glyphs that appear on the hill signify settlements or groups that once occupied these lands. Such house glyphs are frequently found on or near toponyms throughout the migration sequence. Like the four house glyphs that run along the base of the island, these are unidentified. It is unlikely that the unidentified house glyphs represent the eight additional groups that would join the Mexica, as those groups are named on the following plates. Furthermore, most sources, such as Codex Aubin, indicate that the Mexica left Aztlan for Colhuacan and only then encountered the other groups that they would allow to join them. Like the four house glyphs identified with the *parcialidades* of Tenochtitlan, these represent both settlements at Aztlan and future divisions at Tlatelolco. As Barbara Mundy writes, however, while Tenochtitlan was divided into four *parcialidades*, Tlatelolco had no such equivalent: "Lacking the four-*parcialidad* division, Tlatelolco seems to have had two hierarchical levels: the first, the city of Santiago Tlatelolco (the complement to Mexico-Tenochtitlan), and the second, the *tlaxilacalli*." Perhaps the *tlacuilo* used these unidentified house glyphs to allude to the many *tlaxilacalli* that would later form the city of Santiago Tlatelolco.[27]

Finally, it is worth reiterating that the large hill place glyph representing the future Tlatelolco is not an afterthought. It dominates the departure scene depicted on folios 1v–2r and is fully integrated into the composition. The lines that form the rectangles denoting the island do not pass beneath the hill. The hill was drawn first or at the same time as the surrounding components. The *tlacuilo* designed the hill and the Huitzilopochtli impersonator to extend beyond the upper register of the island, towering above all other figures in the scene. Artist A not only includes Tlatelolco in this opening event but privileges it in the composition.

INTERACTIONS BETWEEN ARTISTS A AND B

The imperial history and early colonial history are primarily the work of Artist A, so most of the interactions between Artists A and B are found in the first segment of the manuscript, which depicts Mexica migration. Although Artist A determines the overall structure and organization of Codex Azcatitlan, he incorporates Artist B to a significant degree. In the migration segment he allows Artist B to participate and to take on increasing responsibility. At various points in the manuscript, including the imperial history, he allows Artist B to practice painting with color.

The first appearance by an apprentice artist occurs on folios 5v–6r (figure 3.4). On these folios Artist A collaborates with a second hand, Artist B. Artist A establishes the pattern for the folios at far left, beginning with the footprinted path that carries over from the previous page. He uses a dashed line that would have later been enhanced with color like the path on folio 5r. He uses an even, unbroken line to paint the first three place glyphs and contributes to the fourth by adding a fully pigmented image of a deity impersonator in the guise of Huitzilopochtli. He paints all of the date glyphs. For example, the House yearbearer is rendered in a manner similar to the houses associated with glyphic forms in the departure scene. At Coatlicamac Artist A paints all of the forms inside the serpent's mouth and the draft of a figure above that. At Huacaltepec he paints the place glyph and the temple above but allows Artist B to paint the peripheral figures along the path.

As Artist B takes over the path and the figures along it, the footprints disappear and the two lines eventually merge into a single unbroken line. Some of the house forms at the bottom of folio 6r appear to be the work of Artist B, who starts to experiment with shading here and on the cape of the final figure at far right. The uneven quality of the line that defines the hill of Coatepec indicates that Artist A allowed the apprentice to take on greater responsibility at this point.

Starting on folio 6r, Artist A paints only the date glyphs, leaving the place glyphs and most peripheral figures and forms to the apprentice. Artist A takes over again on folio 12r (figure 3.6) when the Mexica arrive at Tenochtitlan. On folios 5v through 11v it is difficult to determine if one or more apprentices participate. The features of the figures seem to indicate Artist B, but there is a lot of experimentation in the rendering of the bodies. If it is a single apprentice at work, he seems to be more adventurous than Artist A as he explores the possibilities of action scenes showing battle, sacrificial victims falling from temples, and drumming, among other subjects.

As Artist B works, he seems to receive some instruction from Artist A. For example, Artist B's first figures on 5v (figure 3.2) have loose, wavy hair. The two figures at left follow pre-Hispanic conventions by depicting the female kneeling and the male with knees drawn up beneath his cape, but the female and the standing male at right have similar hair. Perhaps Artist A, more familiar with indigenous paradigms, instructed his apprentice that hairstyles could signal important information about gender and status. Thereafter Artist B's Mexica males have a forelock and their hair is worn tied back (figure 3.2). Artist B's females are shown with a crescent at the forehead, meant to represent the upturned braids of the traditional female hairstyle.

While Artist A is especially interested in experimenting with depth and spatial recession, Artist B actively explores various techniques to model figures and forms. On folio 6v (figure 3.2) Artist B applies shading to both the female figure and the adjacent place glyph. While Artist A uses color pigment and shading at times to model faces and the landscape settings in plates 5r and 22v, he never applies shading

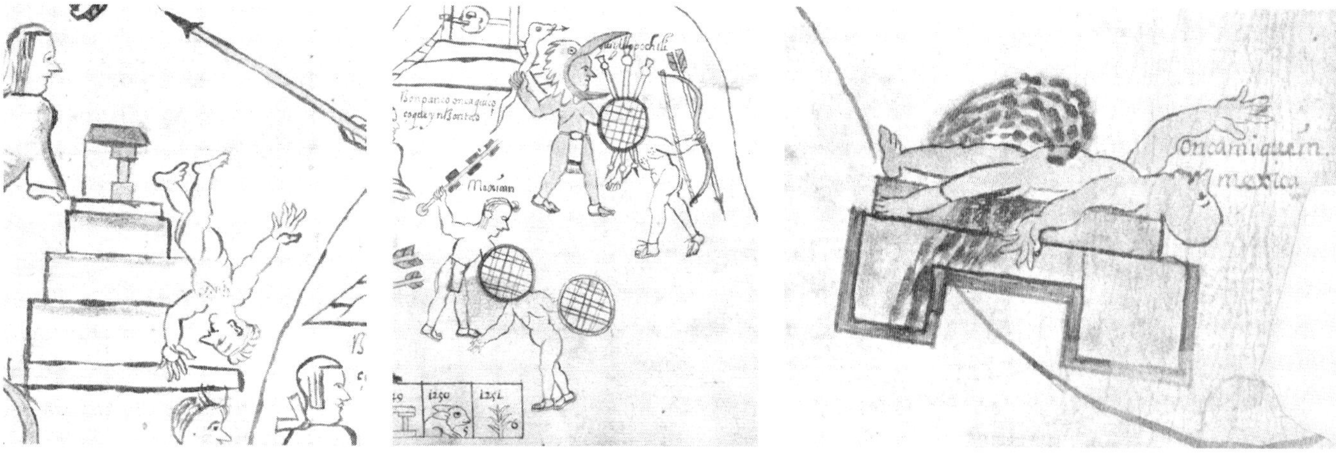

Figure 3.8. Codex Azcatitlan, folios 8r (left and center) and 10r (right) (details). Courtesy of the Bibliothèque Nationale de France.

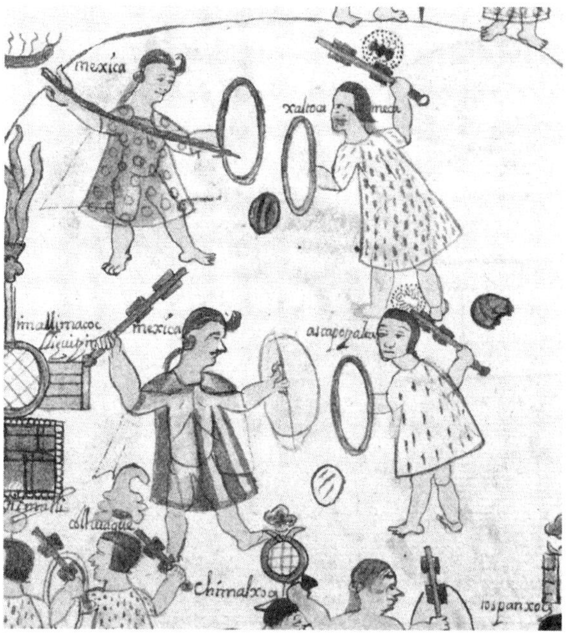

Figure 3.9. Codex Azcatitlan, folio 10r (detail). Courtesy of the Bibliothèque Nationale de France.

to place glyphs. On plate 8r Artist B moves beyond seated and walking figures to explore the body in a variety of poses (figure 3.8). As another strategy for articulating the body, Artist B experiments with defining pectoral muscles and body hair (figure 3.8). On plate 9r he depicts frontal faces for the first time (figure 3.2). On plate 10r he draws the nude body of the figure first before covering it with clothing (figure 3.9).

Artist A teaches Artist B how to work with the date cartouches. One set of unglossed date glyphs, produced by the apprentice artist, appears at the center of folio 11v (figure 3.6). Faint shadow lines show an initial attempt to create cartouches. The uneven lines and inconsistent size were rejected and "erased" with gesso, much like Artist A's error beneath the glyph for Tlatelolco on folio 13r. Perhaps as part of a learning exercise, the cartouches were redrawn, approximating the size and straight lines of the other year-bearers. The Flint and House signs approximate Artist A's, but the apprentice adds a thatched roof to the house glyph and neither glyph is neatly centered. Ultimately they are rejected; Artist A's year-bearers neatly bypass this error and flow continuously through the House, Rabbit, Reed, Flint sequence, eventually receiving Arabic numeral years. Artist A also teaches Artist B to create images that integrate with the date blocks (figure 3.5).

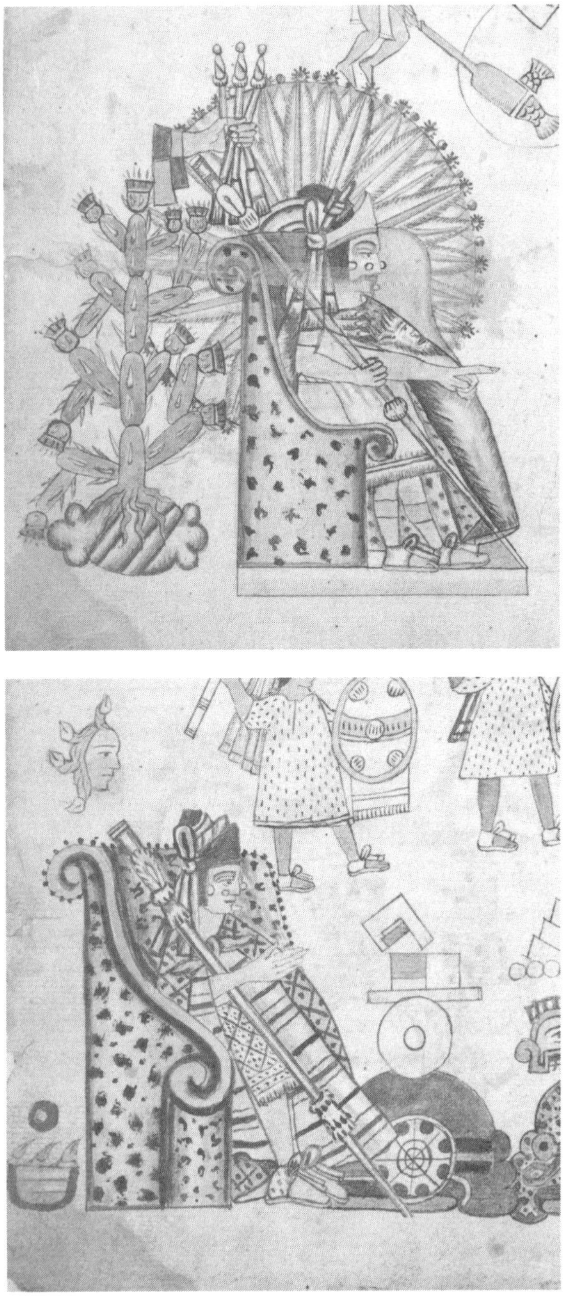

Figure 3.10. Codex Azcatitlan, folios 13v and 18v (details). Courtesy of the Bibliothèque Nationale de France.

Artist A uses color skillfully and allows Artist B to practice painting with color at times. Only two ruler images in the imperial history are fully pigmented (figure 3.10). Artist A paints Acamapichtli on plate 13v, while Artist B emulates his painting techniques on the figure of Axayacatl on plate 18v. Artist B uses a heavier hand to apply the paint, as seen with the jaguar spots on the throne. His brushstrokes are more uneven, and the shape of the *temillotl* does not correspond to that of the other rulers. Artist B departs from pre-Hispanic tradition by painting the diadem of his ruler black. As no blue is used in the manuscript, Artist A leaves Acamapichtli's diadem unpainted.

FOLIOS 12V–13R: SEPARATION OF THE TLATELOLCA FROM THE TENOCHCA

Folios 12v–13r represent the midpoint of the extant manuscript and the pendant to the scene depicting the departure from Aztlan (figure 3.11). Although Artist A depicts the nopal cactus growing from the sacrificed heart of Copil on folio 12r, the journey does not end there (figure 3.6). The path and the gestures of the figures lead the viewer to the final scene of the migration on folios 12v–13r. Artist A's last date cartouche appears on folio 12v (figure 3.11). It is a Rabbit year, and the Arabic numerals have not been added. According to the list of Tlatelolca rulers in the Annals of Tlatelolco, the Tlatelolca separated from the Tenochca in the thirteenth year after they arrived. Their first ruler, Cuacuapitzauac (pictured here on the right), took the throne in the year 1 Rabbit (1350).[28] For the Tlatelolca the migration ends when they make their last trek to the northern part of the island for the installation of the first Tlatelolca *tlatoani*. On folios 12v–13r a row of footprints along the bottom of the image marks that final journey and the house glyphs signify the dual settlements of Tenochtitlan and Tlatelolco. The composition consists of three parts. On the left a Mexica ruler is installed, on the right the first Tlatelolca ruler is installed, and in the middle six men are shown hunting the fish, frogs, ducks, and birds of the rich lacustrine environment surrounding the island.

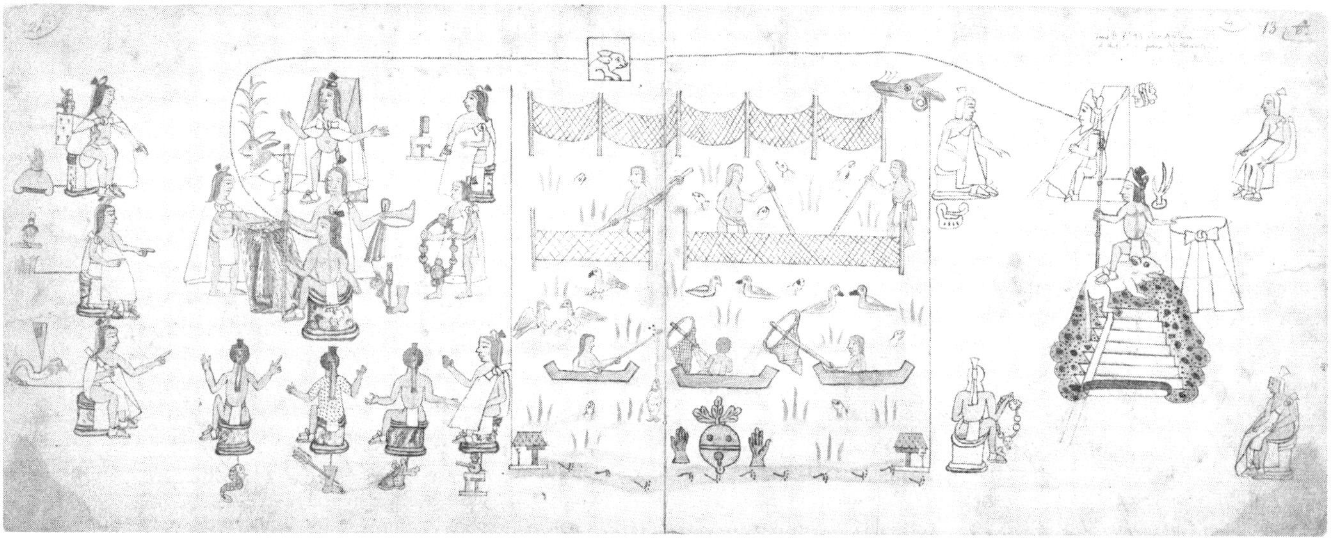

Figure 3.11. Codex Azcatitlan, folios 12v–13r. Courtesy of the Bibliothèque Nationale de France.

On the right side of the composition Artist A paints the figure of Cuacuapitzauac, the first ruler of Tlatelolco, surrounded by five additional figures. The glyph with a thin branch next to his head names him, and he sits atop the place glyph for Tlatelolco (Place of the Monticule). Barlow interprets the animal above the place glyph as a poorly drawn *ocelotl*, which provides an alternate name, Ocelopan Tlatelolco (Place of the Ocelot).[29] On the front of the place glyph Artist A depicts a temple. The image references the early stages of the temple at Tlatelolco and may refer to rites of investiture that took place at the temple site. In comparison to the Mexica ruler on folio 12v, Cuacuapitzauac appears further along in the installation process. He already wears the *xiuhhuitzolli* and holds his royal mantle in one hand and the staff of office in the other. Tezozomoc, who is identified by his glyph of a stone with a face on it, appears just above the figure of Cuacuapitzauac. Tezozomoc, the Tepanec leader of Azcapotzalco, installed his son as the ruler at Tlatelolco.[30] Four additional figures surround Cuacuapitzauac, and the figure at lower left presents a golden necklace. Like Cuacuapitzauac, the four figures that face him wear the *temillotl* hairstyle of accomplished warriors. The figure opposite Tezozomoc is adjacent to the glyph for Coyoacan, the second most important Tepanec city. Below his feet is a glyph that consists of a diadem and a speech scroll.

As with the figure who oversees the Mexica installation on the left, Artist A signals Tezozomoc's elevated status by depicting him on a large throne. His son Cuacuapitzauac is seated on a place glyph, and the remaining figures in the installation scenes are seated on oval backless seats.[31] A row of tiny dots runs across the top of the page, through the date cartouche, from Tezozomoc's mouth to that of the newly installed Mexica ruler. While both Mexico-Tenochtitlan and Tlatelolco were subject to Tezozomoc, Tezozomoc's relationship to the Tlatelolca ruler was one of direct family. The direct line of communication between Tezozomoc and the newly installed Mexica ruler suggests Tezozomoc's oversight.

Although Acamapichtli's name glyph is not shown, Barlow and Graulich interpret the left side of the composition as a depiction of his installation as the first *tlatoani* of Mexico-Tenochtitlan. He is seated at the center of the composition and has one hand on the staff that is being presented to him. While Cuacuapitzauac has already received the diadem, mantle, and staff, Acamapichtli is shown in the act of receiving these items. A figure on the left hands him the mantle. The figure directly above him hands him the staff and is about to place the diadem on his head. A figure to the right presents a golden necklace. Nine additional figures witness the installation, surrounding the central figures. Each of these nine figures has a name glyph with a red line that connects the glyph to the individual. Five of the named figures can be found on the preceding page, including the figure whose glyph is made up of a Reed and a Rabbit. Artist A sets him off on folio 12r by depicting him as the largest figure on the page. On folio 12v he oversees the installation of the ruler from the top center of the composition. He does not wear a diadem, but he sits on a throne similar in style to that of Tezozomoc.

Artist A separates the coronation events with two vertical lines that set off a watery scene. Nets have been erected in the lake surrounding the island, and six male figures use spears, boats, a fishing pole, and nets to hunt the avian and aquatic creatures that Artist A disburses evenly throughout the composition. As in the landscape in folio 5r, strokes of unbounded color contribute to the sense of spatial depth, suggesting the green reeds that grew in the marshy waters. The lower center of the composition has two hands that flank a circular golden lockplate that is adorned with a foliate design on top.

Artist A's compositions allow for connections between the scenes depicting the departure from Aztlan and the founding of Tenochtitlan-Tlatelolco. These two episodes, at either end of the migration, mirror each other and reflect pre-Hispanic notions of time in which temporal cycles begin and end in the same place. In central Mexican indigenous accounts of the migration written in the sixteenth and seventeenth centuries the eagle on the nopal cactus is an important sign that the Mexica have arrived at their promised destination, but so too are the reedy waters and sacred springs. For example, in Chimalpahin the promised land is "where the blue and yellow waters mingle." Codex Aubin describes waters "like blue ink," and Durán describes a spring "where the red and blue waters flowed."[32] In addition to depicting the eagle on the nopal cactus in his foundation image, the Codex Aubin *tlacuilo* painted a reedy environment, a sacred pool, and two house forms (figure 2.11). Rather than depicting the eagle on the nopal cactus, a sign that evoked Tenochca identity, Artist A opted to show the cactus emerging from the sacrificed heart of Copil. Instead of foregrounding this foundation symbol, he emphasized the sacred waters on folios 12v–13r, showing them tamed, bountiful, and evenly shared by both Tenochca and Tlatelolca. Just as Artist A's image of the departure from Aztlan prefigures the end of the migration journey, the hands and lockplate signal the present moment (when they receive the bounty promised them by Huitzilopochtli) and a future moment when that bounty is returned, a subject discussed in greater depth in chapter 5.

The Imperial History

While folios 12v–13r mark the end of the migration segment, they also function as a hinge, connecting the content of the first half of the manuscript to the elite history of the second half. Within the framework of the year-count annals, both the Mexica migration history and the imperial ruler history had established indigenous paradigms. Though no pre-Hispanic manuscripts from central Mexico survive, several postconquest examples have similar content.

Federico Navarrete has discussed the compositional shift that takes place in the transition from migration to imperial history. After pointing out the basic template of Codex Azcatitlan's imperial history, he writes: "The exact same conventions representing the crowning and death of each *tlatoani* and the conquests of the Mexica are employed in Codex Mexicanus, and in the Telleriano-Remensis and Vaticano-Ríos." Codex Aubin and Codex Mendoza employ a similar format.[33]

After folios 12v–13r Artist A adopts a new structure for the imperial history that resembles the structure found in other manuscripts painted by indigenous artists (figure 3.12). Boone describes the imperial segment of Codex Azcatitlan as follows:

> A mutation of the Codex Mendoza's structure, one further removed from the annals form, appears in Codex Azcatitlan, where, after the founding of Tenochtitlan, the successive reigns of the Mexica rulers span facing pages. The ruler's enthronement on the left opens each reign, and events in each reign are gathered in what seems to be roughly chronological order, but no hard dates are added. Like the Codex Mendoza, it is a history organized by reigns, except that the Codex Azcatitlan includes a broader range of events (paralleling the range of events pictured in the annals) and omits the years entirely. It is hard to say whether this organization of Mexica history reflects a preconquest form.[34]

As Boone notes, Codex Azcatitlan follows an organizational format similar to that of another annals history, Codex Mendoza, in which the years of the rulers' reigns are listed in a strip and the rulers' accessions and conquests are associated with that date range but not with individual dates. In Codex Azcatitlan the ruler's reign drives the organization and composition of the page. Although there are no hard dates, the compositions are incomplete: Artist A probably intended to add them. The date cartouches require little space, generally measuring around 14 to 16 mm high. The imperial history pages have ample room either at the very bottom of the folio or in the space above. On many of Codex Azcatitlan's folios the figures, forms, or date glyphs extend to the very edge of the paper. On folio 7r, for example, the *tlacuilo* opts for date glyphs that are 14 mm high and just 3 mm from the edge of the page. The *tlacuilo* likely planned to include date glyphs at the bottom of the record of imperial history.

Some of the incomplete figures and forms in the imperial segment also provide evidence that Artist A intended to add date glyphs. In each of the ruler compositions the place glyphs and figures are organized along a straight line. In some cases, like folios 15v–16r, this very faint organizational line is still visible. While most of the forms appear above this line, some elements dip just below. For example, the body of the captive on folios 15v–16r rests along the line, but his clothing and toes dip just below (figure 3.13). If the artist planned to include date cartouches below, he may have wanted the forms that dip below this line to overlap and integrate with the date cartouches, as we see him working in the migration sequence. Artist A also leaves parts of the lower composition unfinished, perhaps as another strategy to facilitate this overlapping. On folios 13v, 14v, and 20v the enthroned rulers have staffs that have been drafted completely, that end above the bottom line, and that end in a sharp point.

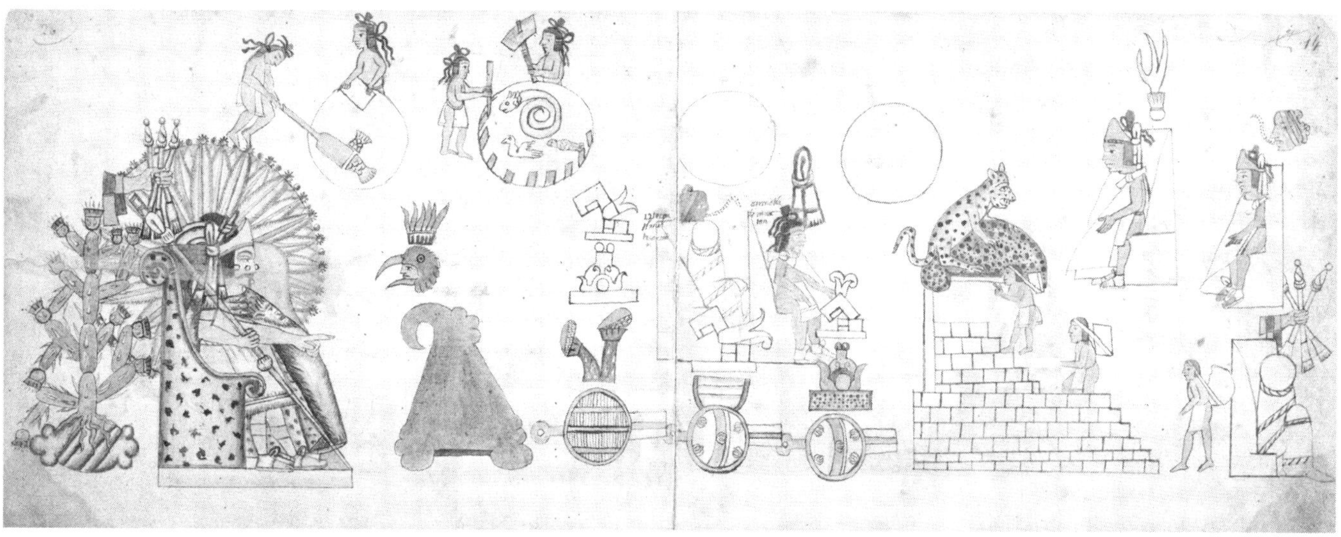

Figure 3.12. Codex Azcatitlan, folios 13v–14r. Courtesy of the Bibliothèque Nationale de France.

The remaining six rulers hold staffs that are unfinished or open ended at the lower end. A few other unfinished lower compositions include the forearm and hand of the deceased figure to the right of Huitzilihuitl on folio 14v, the deer head to the right of Tizoc on folio 19v, and the lower part of the fifth place glyph to the right of Ahuitzotl on folio 20v (figure 3.13). While there is sufficient space for the date glyphs at the bottom of the pages throughout the imperial history, the space is a little tighter on folios 18v–19r. These plates depict the reign of Axayacatl. He only reigned for a little over a decade. So if his date cartouches started at the far left, they would not extend past the second place glyph to the right of the ruler.

Of those few glosses in the imperial section, two list specific dates. Next to the image of a mummy bundle with Tezozomoc's name glyph, the glosser tells us on folios 13v–14r that *12 tecpatl mic tecocomoc* (in 12 Flint Tezozomoc died) (figure 3.12). The gloss immediately to the right, above the throne of a male figure

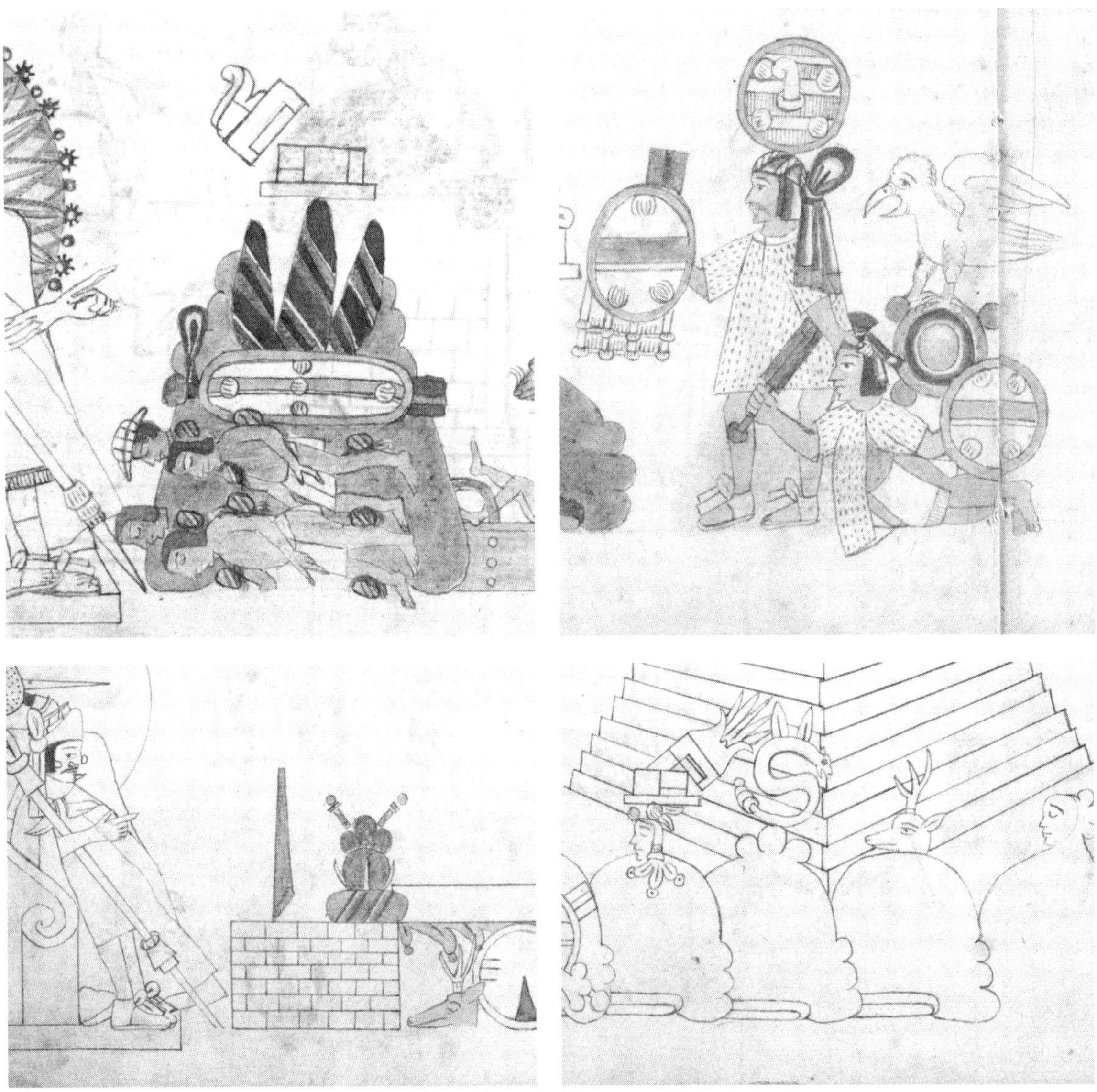

Figure 3.13. Details from the imperial history showing areas where the tlacuilo may have planned to integrate the composition with date blocks. Codex Azcatitlan, folios 14v (top left), 15v–16r (top right), 19v (bottom left), and 20v (bottom right). Courtesy of the Bibliothèque Nationale de France.

with Maxtla's name glyph, reads *ommotlali Maxton* (Maxton was installed). The third and last alphabetic gloss on folio 15r reads 5 *tochi in mic matlato* (in 5 Tochtli Maxtlaton died). All of these glosses relate to Tepanec history. Strictly speaking, the events referenced are incongruent with the dates of the Mexica ruler reigns in which they are contained. It is possible that these glosses reflect errors on the part of the *tlacuilo*, as others have suggested. However, when taken in the context of the pictorial composition, the glosses may, alternatively, be read as providing context for the primary narrative in a way that parallels imperial histories recorded in other indigenous accounts.

The first two glosses appear on folios 13v–14r, which show Acamapichtli's reign, which began in 1376 and ended upon his death in 1395.[35] On the far left of the page the ruler appears enthroned. The large nopal on a stone appears behind the ruler, signifying his rule over Tenochtitlan. Just above his head the glyph of a hand holding a bunch of reeds or darts signifies the ruler's name, Acamapichtli. The ruler faces right and points in that direction, guiding the viewer through the image. The Mexica ruler on his throne is the first and largest figure in the composition, signaling his importance. To the far right of the composition his mummy bundle appears on a throne, with his name glyph identifying him. In this format, which organizes the composition, the beginning and end of the Mexica ruler's reign forms the armature of the composition. From Acamapichtli to Moteuczoma II, all of the two-page compositions begin with the large enthroned figure of the ruler. Most end with the enthroned mummy bundle, facing right and leading the viewer to the next plate.[36]

The bottom ground line, discussed earlier, serves as a secondary organizational tool. Key events are anchored along this ground line and elaborated on in the space above. The first place glyph to the right of the ruler shows Colhuacan, the place of the bent hill. The glyph may or may not represent a conquest that the Mexica participated in.[37] In contrast to the next three place glyphs, there is no burning temple above Colhuacan to identify it as a conquest. Above the place glyph for Colhuacan Artist A paints an image of Huitzilopochtli, incarnated as a human head wearing the costume of the hummingbird god. A crown of quetzal feathers appears above the deity.

Because there is no burning temple, the image may relate to accounts of Acamapichtli's reign found in Tezozomoc, Chimalpahin, and Durán. In the "Mexican History or Chronicle" Chimalpahin describes how they decide to go to Colhuacan to set up a new ruler after the death of the Mexica leader Tenochtzin:

> Let us go to find the child who issued from the warrior Opochtli. For he is our Mexica Chichimeca child. He will want us, he will guard the Mexica Tenochca altepetl. And he comes into being from ancestry on both sides; he was born the grandson of Culhuaque lords and rulers and of us Mexica Chichimeca. And [let us do] this, Mexica: let us go.[38]

After they find Acamapichtli, they humbly ask the ruler Teuhctlamacazqui Nauhyotl, who responds to them:

> It is well, Mexica. What am I to say here in Culhuacan, but [that] truly he is your child, your grandson. Let him go. Take him.... And heed this: Let him govern the commoners, vassals of the All Pervasive, the Night and the Wind, Yaotzin Tezcatlipoca. And let him guard the offering priest Huitzilopochtli.[39]

The glyph of Colhuacan to the right of Acamapichtli in the Codex Azcatitlan may reference background information on the establishment of his reign. The devil that appears on his cloak signals Acamapichtli's role as a speaker for the deity Tezcatlipoca.[40] The ruler's role as a guardian of the offering priest Huitzilopochtli is signaled by the image of Huitzilopochtli above the hill of Colhuacan. The human head wearing the hummingbird headdress shows that this is a priest incarnating the deity. After importuning Acamapichtli and warning him that they are not on their own lands but are on "Azcapotzalcan islands," the text goes on to name descendants of the Mexica ruler:

> The sons of Tlatolçacatzin were great, brave warriors who bound quetzal feathers to their heads. These indeed were grandsons of the aforementioned rulers Acamapichtli and Tlacacuitlahuatzin.
>
> And here are called by name all those said to be and known as old noblemen, grandsons of the late lord ruler, Huehue Acamapichtli: as many of his children as are known by name and who issued from him, whom [he] begot.[41]

Although Codex Azcatitlan does not elaborate on the children of Acamapichtli, the crown of feathers may stand in for the "great, brave warriors who bound quetzal feathers to their heads."[42]

To the right of Colhuacan Artist A paints three sets of shields and obsidian blade weapons, signifying battles that the Mexica participated in. The broken smoking temples and place glyphs identify the conquered areas as, from left to right, Mixquic, Cuitlahuac, and Xochimilco. As Barlow points out, the glyph for Xochimilco also appears above that of Mixquic, perhaps to indicate that Mixquic was a part of this ancient principality.[43] These glyphs have a shield and weapons beneath them but do not have an *altepetl* place glyph because they were battles fought with Tlatelolco on behalf of the Tepanecs of Azcapotzalco.

Next a significant amount of the ground line is used to depict the construction of a large stone temple or palace at Tlatelolco. Artist A shows three indigenous workers carrying stones in tumplines as they erect the building. The image is incomplete: only the hands of the uppermost figure have been painted in. An *ocelotl* on top of a monticule tops the structure, indicating that it was built at Ocelopan Tlatelolco. Four enthroned figures appear in the register above. Just to the right of the glyph for Tlatelolco and closest to it Artist A paints Cuacuapitzauac, the first ruler of Tlatelolco. After Acamapichtli, he is the second largest figure in this composition. He is named by the glyph showing a thin branch above his head. This large figure of the Tlatelolca ruler, in close proximity to the construction of the building, forms a unit of information. The three additional figures are smaller and provide genealogical and family history information related to Cuacuapitzauac.

Behind Cuacuapitzauac Artist A paints the Tlatelolca ruler's father Tezozomoc, whose glyph is the stone with a face on it. Through this figure Artist A documents that Cuacuapitzauac was the son of the powerful Tepanec ruler of Azcapotzalco. In the middle of folios 13v–14r, facing Cuacuapitzauac, Artist A paints an enthroned mummy bundle with Tezozomoc's name glyph and the gloss: *12 tecpatl mic tecocomoc* (in 12 Flint Tezozomoc died). Just in front of the mummy bundle is an image of Maxtla, identified by the loincloth that records his name glyphically. The image is accompanied by the gloss *ommotlali Maxton* (Maxton was installed). If we read this as additional genealogical information that relates to the Tlatelolca ruler, it is not an error or a chronological mistake. Rather, these figures signal the information that Cuacuapitzauac was the brother of the famous Maxtla, who would later usurp the throne of Azcapotzalco from his brother Tayatzin upon Tezozomoc's death.[44] Perhaps these figures were glossed precisely because they refer to events that happened later and not within Acamapichtli's reign. As in the migration segment, the glosses clarify images that might elicit confusion.

In the uppermost register of the composition Artist A drafts four circles. The first two appear on folio 13v and show the fencing and building of lacustrine environments for fish, fowl, and water creatures. The second two circles on folio 14r are unfinished and have not been elaborated. These show the development of aquatic food resources but may also relate specifically to Tepanec demands. As Frances Berdan and Patricia Anawalt have noted:

> During Acamapichtli's reign, the Mexica served essentially as vassals to the Tepanec ruler, Tezozomoc. They paid tribute in lake products, a tribute

> reportedly made especially difficult because of Tezozomoc's outrageous demands: at one point he required his Mexica subjects to supply him with a raft planted with all kinds of vegetables, along with a duck and a heron, both in the process of hatching their eggs.[45]

These images also continue the development of lacustrine food sources depicted in the central part of the previous plates.

If the figures surrounding Cuacuapitzauac are read as conveying background contextual or genealogical information about him, the whole right side of the composition (except for Acamapichtli's mummy bundle) relates to Tlatelolca history, while the whole left side of the composition pertains to Tenochca history. The three battles referenced in the center of the composition along the ground line pertain to both, as both sides participated under the auspices of Azcapotzalco and both rulers claimed the conquests. The upper register also pertained to both: they developed lakeside farming and aquaculture and paid tribute with the fruits of these labors to the Tepanecs of Azcapotzalco. The binary emphasis on the history of Mexico-Tenochtitlan and Tlatelolco echoes the composition on the previous plates, 12v and 13r.

This reading of the composition and content on plates 13v–14r indicates that time is no longer structured by a strictly chronological format. By using the armature of the ruler's reign to structure the composition, the *tlacuilo* maintains an overall chronology, but within that he is free to make references to the past and future. The place sign Colhuacan may reference Acamapichtli's origins and the events of his investiture, while the feather crown may reference the nobility of his future progeny. Likewise, the smaller figures surrounding Cuacuapitzauac provide background information on this Tlatelolca ruler by referencing future events. This reading also suggests an interest in family relationships and genealogy that is commonly found in pictorial and alphabetic imperial histories.

CONQUEST AND POSTCONQUEST HISTORY

The conquest (figures 4.1–4.3, 4.8) and postconquest (figures 5.1, 5.5) segments of Codex Azcatitlan contain neither date glyphs nor glosses. However, like the imperial history, most compositions reserve space that may have been intended for date glyphs. Folio 22v, depicting Cortés and his indigenous allies, leaves a significant portion of the upper page blank (figure 4.1). Artist A fills folio 23r completely but may have left space on the missing plate that came before it (figure 4.2). The battle scene on folio 23r clearly carried over onto the opposite folio. Folio 23v leaves ample space at the top of the composition (figure 4.3). Folio 24r reserves space to the left of the women escaping Tenochtitlan by boat (figure 4.8). The final three folios (24v, 25r, and 25v) again leave space at the top of the page (figures 5.1, 5.5). Some images at the top of folios 24v and 25r are incomplete. As in the imperial history, the *tlacuilo* most likely intended eventually to integrate these forms with a row of year-bearers. The circular glyphic form on 24v is unfinished at the top, and the candles surrounding the deceased figure on 25r have not been completed (figure 5.1).

If the date glyphs were incorporated into the manuscript as described, each shift in year-bearer format would further highlight the narrative shifts. Blocked date cartouches characterize the migration sequence. Date cartouches at the bottom of the page would anchor the dates of each ruler's reign. Upper page date cartouches would signal events related to the conquest and postconquest period.

Conclusion

No early provenance information exists for Codex Azcatitlan, so analysis of the artists' hands, their structure, and their working methods can help to build a picture of the circumstances of production. These *tlacuiloque* chose to record canonical events of preconquest and postconquest Mexica life from a Tlatelolca perspective, indicating that they claimed this heritage or worked for a Tlatelolca patron. Analysis of Codex Azcatitlan's facture suggests a hierarchical learning environment. Taken as a whole, Codex Azcatitlan shows an apprentice artist (Artist B) learning to paint under his master (Artist A) and learning to work within indigenous paradigms. At the same time, these *tlacuiloque* are not tethered to a static view of the past. Often, and in different ways, the master artist and his apprentice engage with their changing environment and the new possibilities that are introduced with exposure to Renaissance image making. The pedagogical nature of this relationship and the access to indigenous and European models might suggest a formal educational environment, like that of the Colegio de Santa Cruz in Tlatelolco. The frequent depictions of Huitzilopochtli and the less than favorable representation of the Spanish in the conquest and postconquest sections, however, suggest that this was not made for Spanish consumption.

Who did these *tlacuiloque* imagine as their audience and how did they anticipate that the manuscript would be used? Despite the expensive European paper, the bound book format, the European stylistic influence, and the expansion of some content into scenic depictions, the images still employ an underlying glyphic structure like that of Codex Boturini, which was meant to be elaborated orally. Perhaps they envisioned an accompanying script that was lost or never written. While the Nahuatl glosses clarify certain passages, they do not reflect the thrust of the narrative and do not extend much past the migration history. As it exists today, the manuscript seems to court an indigenous Tlatelolca audience that was literate and able to read Arabic numerals and Nahuatl script and/or familiar with pre-Hispanic pictographic and narrative conventions.

Artist A took the Codex Boturini migration history as a paradigm and freely manipulated the content to suit his needs. He drew out and emphasized the Tlatelolca role in this history, while remaining true to the core Mexica narrative. When the *tlacuiloque* expand upon Codex Boturini's paradigm, it is usually the result of three defining trends: (1) the stylistic and aesthetic explorations of the *tlacuiloque*; (2) a more lengthy visual record that includes information that previously would have been part of an oral tradition alone; and (3) the introduction of Tlatelolca history and interests. The master artist does not just copy the Codex Boturini narrative but he reinvents it. As discussed in chapter 5, he uses the conceptual and spiritual framework of the narrative to shape his manuscript as a whole.

CHAPTER 4

DON MARTÍN ECATZIN

Codex Azcatitlan's Cosmic Hero

AS DEMONSTRATED IN CHAPTER 3, the master *tlacuilo* at work on Codex Azcatitlan systematically articulated his narrative from a Tlatelolca viewpoint.[1] In the migration narrative he relied on and retained a traditional account of the peregrination derived from Codex Boturini but added visual elements to clarify and reinforce the idea that this was an Aztec and Mexica account shared by both the Tenochca and the Tlatelolca. The account begins with a representation of Aztlan, reimagined as the future Tenochtitlan-Tlatelolco, and ends with the separation of the Tlatelolca from the Tenochca. For the dynastic history, he anchored Tepanec and Tlatelolca history within a Tenochca framework. Although each two-page spread begins with the reign of a Mexica ruler, the incomplete contents of each reign include dynastic information related to other groups. For the conquest and postconquest history, well-established paradigms did not yet exist, allowing the *tlacuilo* greater freedom to innovate. This chapter examines Codex Azcatitlan's four images of the conquest, folios 22v–24r. Through images that are both scenic and symbolic, the *tlacuilo* constructs a narrative that privileges indigenous strength over suffering and places the actions of the Tlatelolca war hero Ecatl (at times referred to as don Martín, his Christian name, or Ecatzin, a reverential form) in a cosmic context.

The images found in Codex Azcatitlan have much in common with Tlatelolca narratives recorded in Nahuatl script in the Annals of Tlatelolco and in book 12 of the Florentine Codex. The Annals of Tlatelolco, archived in the Bibliothèque Nationale de France, consists of two manuscripts. The older manuscript is catalogued as Manuscrit Mexicain 22 (MS 22). A later version, Manuscrit Mexicain 22bis (MS 22bis), copies the former and adds additional commentary. Lockhart dates MS 22 to around 1545 and MS 22bis to a later period, perhaps in the seventeenth century.[2] Here "Annals of Tlatelolco" refers to content found in both MS 22 and MS 22bis. I distinguish between the two where relevant. The Annals of Tlatelolco includes "Document 1—The Genealogy of the Tlatoque of Tlatelolco"; "Document 2—The Genealogy of the Tlatoque of Tenochtitlan"; "Document 3—The Genealogy of the Tlatoque of Azcapotzalco"; "Document 4—Supplement to the Genealogy of the Tlatoque of Azcapotzalco"; and "Document 5—The History of the People of Tlatelolco."[3] Along with other correlations, the account of Cuauhtemoc's death (found at the end of document 1 in MS 22bis) aligns closely with the pictorial representation of this event in Codex Azcatitlan. There are also parallels between the Tlatelolca accounts of the conquest in book 12 of Sahagún's Florentine Codex and related images in Codex Azcatitlan. Tlatelolca survivors of the conquest first shared their memories of the conquest with Franciscan Friar Bernardino de Sahagún's collaborators around 1553 to 1555. Later copies of this history were paired with images and Spanish text between 1575 and 1580.[4]

Some themes emerge in the pages of Codex Azcatitlan's conquest and postconquest history. First, the *tlacuilo* highlights indigenous successes and downplays the losses. In the brief conquest history he highlights the two times when Mexica warriors successfully drove the Spanish from Tenochtitlan-Tlatelolco. Rather than foregrounding the carnage of the massacre during the feast of Toxcatl on folio 23r, the *tlacuilo*'s composition focuses on the retaliation that would lead to the Spaniards' substantial losses on the Noche Triste. On folio 23v he records the last great rout of the Spaniards that took place in Tlatelolco before Cuauhtemoc's surrender. Although Codex Azcatitlan's conquest history is a version of the vanquished, the *tlacuilo* downplays the more devastating losses that the Mexica endured, which are frequently described in visceral terms in other pictorial and written sources. Second, the *tlacuilo* records the heroic and treasonous deeds of several individuals. In the conquest history the *tlacuilo* elevates the role of Ecatl alongside Cuauhtemoc, who was likely depicted on many of the missing folios. Third, his images allude to a larger cosmic frame that connects the events of the conquest and postconquest history with the earlier parts of the manuscript.

Folios 22v–24r

1519–1521: EVENTS OF THE CONQUEST

The *tlacuilo* depicted the events of the conquest using four two-page layouts. Because two pages are missing from this part of the manuscript, each composition exists only partially. The conquest history contains no identifying name glyphs and no glosses. The paintings, though well developed, are unfinished. The images from folios 22v–24r record events that took place between 1519 and 1521. Folio 22v marks a formal shift from the visual layout of the ruler history but a thematic transition, in that it records an event that occurred during Moteuczoma's reign. The *tlacuilo* did not paint Moteuczoma's mummy bundle on folio 22r because he had not yet died. Folios 22v–24r continue to depict events that occurred during Moteuczoma's reign, but a new compositional format reflects the temporal and social disruption that occurred with the encounter between the indigenous and the Spanish.

Folio 22v

1519: CORTÉS GREETS MOTEUCZOMA

Folio 22v depicts Cortés and his party in a moment of encounter (figure 4.1). The golden-haired Cortés has removed his hat and reaches his hand out in greeting. Malinche, Cortés's indigenous consort and translator (sometimes referred to as doña Marina or Malintzin), stands just before him. She points to Cortés, indicating that she is actively translating for him and is in dialogue with the figure on the opposite page, now missing. Surrounding Cortés are eight Spanish conquistadors in armor, wielding shields and weapons; one African slave; a small horse; the Spanish banner; and three Indian allies bearing food and other supplies with a tumpline. This image most likely represents Cortés and his party greeting Moteuczoma and his entourage for the first time on November 8, 1519.[5]

The encounter took place on the southern Ixtapalapa causeway near the canal and bridge of Xoloco. Moteuczoma arrived on a feathered litter, descending in the midst of a crowd of rulers to greet Cortés. In the Florentine Codex account these are Moteuczoma's last free moments. He is immediately imprisoned by the Spaniards and begins to lose the respect of his people.[6] Diego Durán states that many indigenous accounts describe the immediate shackling of Moteuczoma after he and Cortés had visited a small nearby shrine to the goddess Toci: "But according to traditions and to paintings kept by certain elders, it is said that Moteuczoma left the sanctuary with his feet in chains. And I saw this in a painting that belonged to an ancient chieftain from the province of Tezcoco."[7]

The composition on folio 22v closely resembles an illustration found on folio 415 of Durán's *History of the Indies of New Spain*, a manuscript that was written in 1581 and is now located in the Biblioteca Nacional de España, Madrid. Many of the "illustrations" in this book were cut and pasted from indigenous pictorial manuscripts, so the provenance of the image is unknown. In the Durán image Cortés and an African man tending his horse occupy the central part and dominate the composition. To the right Moteuczoma offers Cortés a jade necklace. To the left a group of tightly packed Spaniards stands behind the horse. The artist's painting engages with European stylistic

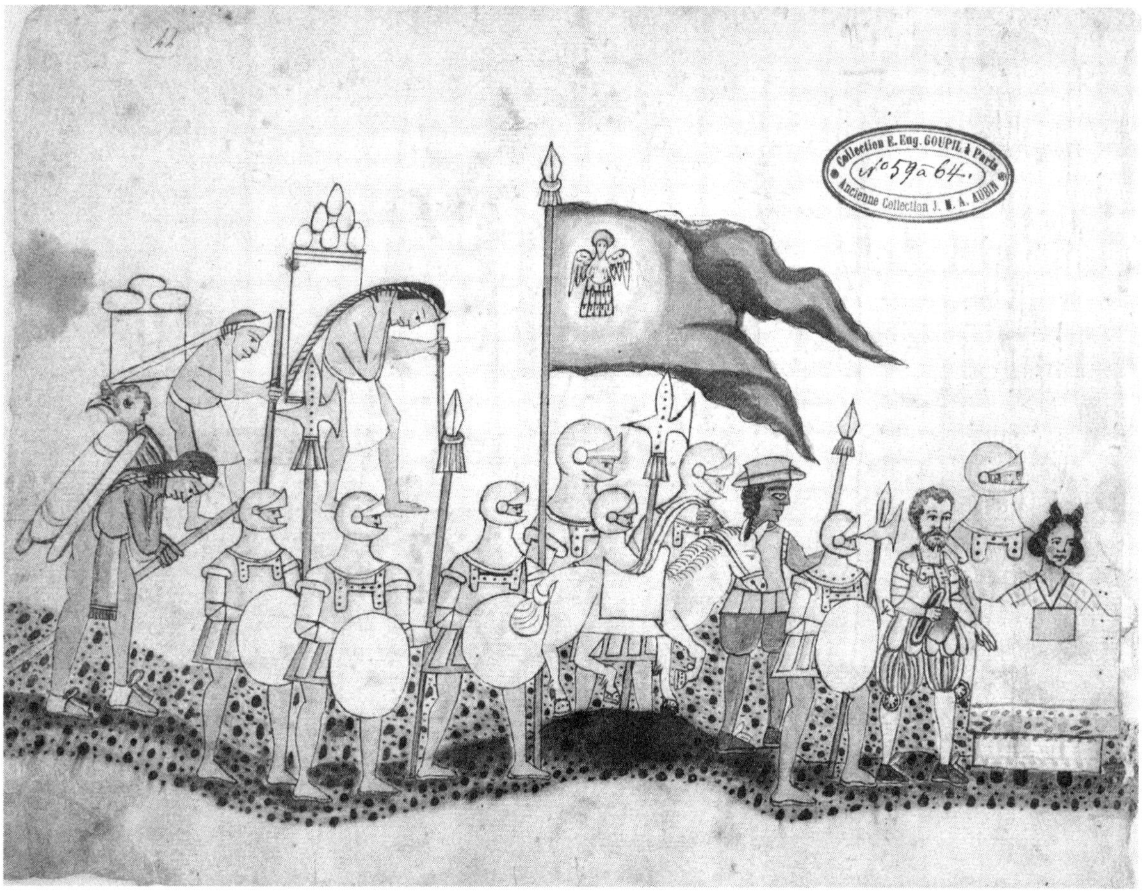

Figure 4.1. Cortés's troops meet Moteuczoma. Codex Azcatitlan, folio 22v. Courtesy of the Bibliothèque Nationale de France.

traditions, and he places his figures in a landscape setting. His focus on the three central figures and their pigmentation, however, suggests an indigenous perspective. Through composition and color use the artist highlights the blond hair and European dress of Cortés, the dark-skinned African, and the horse, all three new and remarkable to the indigenous people when the Spaniards first arrived.

The Codex Azcatitlan *tlacuilo* presents an expanded version of this same composition, with a few key additions. On folio 22v indigenous allies appear. Malinche stands by Cortés's side and like him is set off from the others by her forward-facing stance. Indigenous allies appear at the rear, carrying food and supplies. While the African man's spear and the peak of the mountain mark the center of the Durán composition, a large red Spanish banner fills the central area of folio 22v, where the mountain landscape is replaced with the spotted ground of the causeway. A similarly expanded folio depicting Moteuczoma and his entourage presumably would have appeared opposite the representation of Cortés. The nature of the relationship between these two images is unclear.

Folio 23r

1520: MASSACRE DURING THE FEAST OF TOXCATL

Folio 23r features the right half of a scene representing the massacre that took place during the feast of Toxcatl in late May or June of 1520 (figure 4.2). At this time Cortés had departed for the coast to meet Pánfilo de Narváez, who had come from Cuba with orders to arrest him. As the Annals of Tlatelolco author writes: "Then the Captain left for the seashore; he left behind don Pedro de Alvarado, Tonatiuh [the Sun]." According to this account, Alvarado "ordered" them to celebrate their god but then betrayed them by attacking the unarmed celebrants on the second day of their festivities.[8] As in the pages of the ruler sequence, where many discrete events are summarized, the Codex Azcatitlan *tlacuilo* condenses or collapses time in order to record multiple narrative moments associated with this event. The images simultaneously record the initial Spanish attack that abruptly and violently halted the music and dance just as it was beginning to gain momentum and the aftermath of the attack, when the Mexica burned the bodies of the victims and took up arms against the Spaniards.

Folio 23r depicts the temple courtyard where the attack took place. The Templo Mayor, represented as a large temple with an open superstructure, dominates the right side of the composition, while an arcaded structure at the top represents one of the four sides of the plaza. The columns and arches of the structure in the background represent an introduced viceregal architecture that did not exist at the time of the massacre but that helped the *tlacuilo*'s contemporaries situate the events of the past in the main square that had come to be called the Plaza Mayor (principal plaza).[9] This space represents the main plaza where the Templo Mayor stood. A 1563 map of the Plaza Mayor, here oriented to show west at the top, represents the space as the Codex Azcatitlan *tlacuilo* might have experienced it (figure 4.2). In this orientation the Templo Mayor (not pictured) would have been located below the cathedral, labeled on the map as the "Yglesia Mayor" (principal church). The arcade appears at top left. The Nahuatl text of the Florentine Codex indicates that the Feast of Huitzilopochtli (the part of the festival of Toxcatl that was happening the morning of the massacre) occurred in the "place called the Temple Courtyard."[10] This account indicates that the Spaniards arrived in battle dress in the midst of the music and dancing and "came to block everywhere the ways leading out and in, [called] Quauhquiauac, Tecpantzinco, Acatl yiacapan, and Tezcacoac."[11]

Folio 23r depicts a moment after Pedro de Alvarado's men blocked off the courtyard and attacked those participating in the rituals. The imagery on folio 23r echoes the Nahuatl account in the twentieth chapter of Florentine Codex book 12:

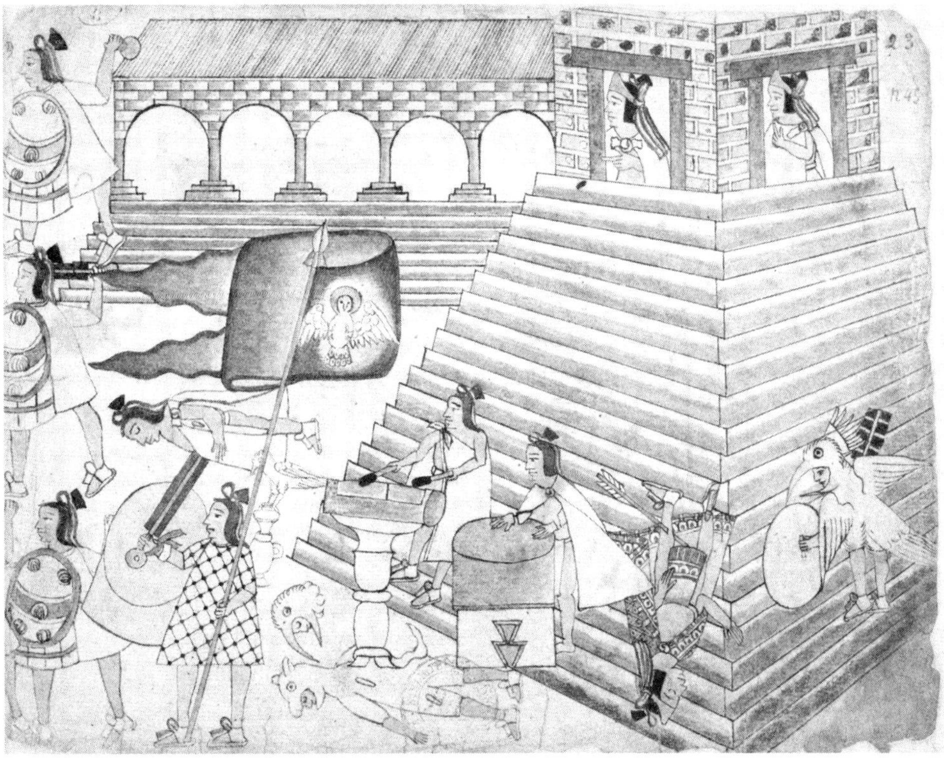

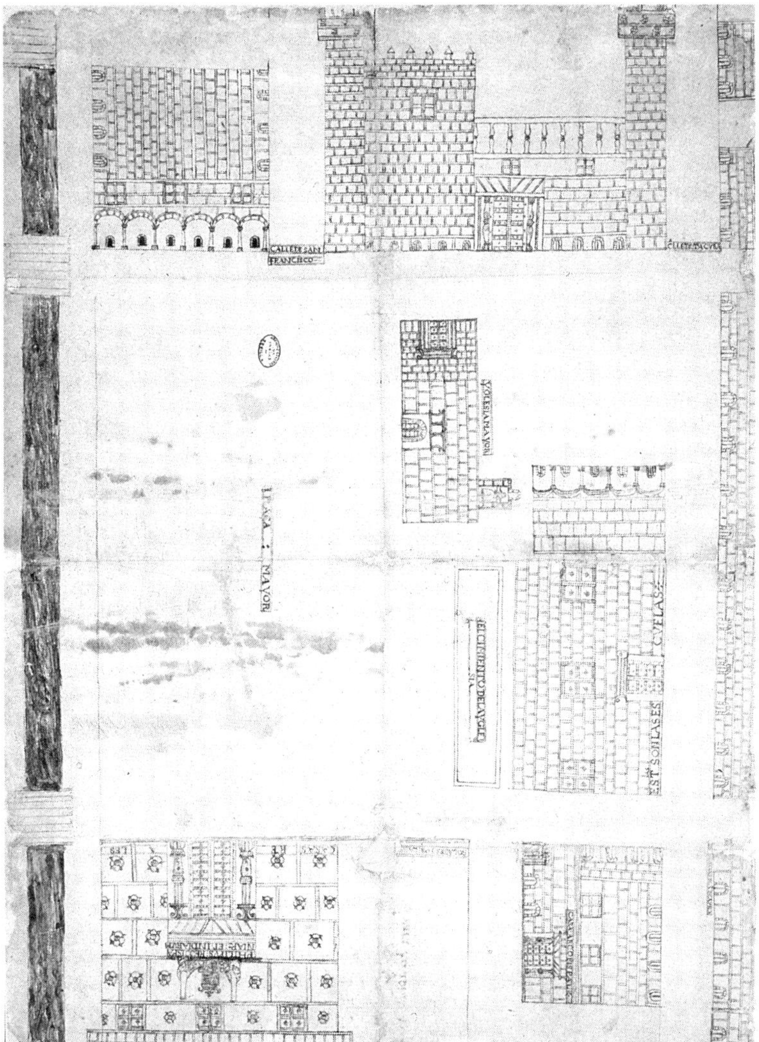

Figure 4.2. Codex Azcatitlan, folio 23r. Courtesy of the Bibliothèque Nationale de France. Map of the Plaza Mayor of Mexico City, ca. 1563. The top is oriented to the west. Spain, Ministerio de Educación, Cultura y Deporte, Archivo General de Indias, 3.

> And when this had been done, thereupon they entered the temple courtyard to slay them. Those whose task it was to slay them went only afoot, each with his leather shield, some, each one, with his iron-studded shield, and each with his iron sword. Thereupon they surrounded the dancers. Thereupon they went among the drums. Then they struck the drummer's arms; they severed both his hands; then they struck his neck. Far off did his neck [and head] go to fall. Then they all pierced the people with iron lances and they struck them each with iron swords.[12]

As in the Annals of Tlatelolco, the violence begins with the attack on the drummers and the severing of their hands. The drummers on folio 23r represent the onset of the attack. The *tlacuilo* depicts the drummer to the right with both hands severed. The drummer to the left continues to play. Both have their eyes open and are shown alive, suggesting that the violence has just occurred. Sahagún's informant next describes a scene of bloody carnage and trailing entrails, something not pictured in Codex Azcatitlan. Along with the attack on the musicians and dancers, the Annals of Tlatelolco describes the death of visiting nobles:

> When Tonatiuh gave the order, Moteucçoma was already being detained, along with Itzquauhtzin, the Tlacochcalcatl in Tlatelolco. At this time they hanged the nobleman of Acolhuacan, Neçahualquentzin, at the wall near the water. The second who died was the ruler of Nauhtla, named Cohualpopocatzin. They shot him with arrows; when they had shot him, he was burned while alive.
>
> As to how the Tenochca <stood guard or were in charge> at Quauhquiahuac, on one side were the houses of the Tenochca, on the other side the houses of the Tlatelolca.[13]

On folio 23r two *tlatoque* view the activities from the top of the temple, while a third deceased *tlatoani* lies upside down on the temple steps with an arrow wound to the leg. The Spanish attack the Tenochca and the Tlatelolca as well as visiting elites in the passage above. The attack occurs in part because the leaders of Tenochtitlan and Tlatelolco have been imprisoned. The Annals of Tlatelolco describes the unimpeded attack as going on for three hours.[14]

The twenty-first chapter of Florentine Codex book 12 next recounts the aftermath of the attack. After describing continued Spanish attacks and the shackling of Moteuczoma, the narrative describes the treatment of the dead:

> And thereupon there was the bringing forth, the taking out, the identification of each of the brave warriors who had died. And their mothers, their fathers raised a cry of weeping; there was weeping for them; there was weeping. First they had taken them, each one, to their homes; then they took them forth to the temple courtyard; they brought them together. There they burned them together, in a place apart, where it is called Quauhxicalco. But some burned only at the various young men's houses.[15]

Between the standard bearer and the drummers, on folio 23r, are three deceased figures, all rendered horizontally and with closed eyes. A fallen figure with the *temillotl* hairstyle appears just beneath the banner. Below him lies a decapitated head, still wearing its hummingbird headdress, and another figure in animal costume. Compositionally, these figures fill in the empty space between the upright warriors and drummers. The frame lines on these figures are not as dark as those defining the drummers and architecture and seem to adapt to the existing composition, suggesting that they were a later addition. There are no weapons in the vicinity of these figures, who appear to represent the unarmed costumed dancers or participants in the festival, now deceased. The Florentine Codex describes in great detail the production of a representation of the deity Huitzilopochtli during the feast. The two figures on folio 23r in hummingbird dress wear ritual costumes appropriate for the veneration of this deity.

Between the deceased figures and overlapping the uppermost one is the image of a bird and a tall ceramic vessel. The lines of these forms are of equal saturation as the three surrounding deceased figures. This may be a glyphic representation of Quauhxicalco: *cuauh[tl]* (eagle) + *xical[li]* (vessel) + *-co* (locative suffix). Book 2 of the Florentine Codex makes four mentions of Quauhxicalco and one Uey Quauhxicalco located within the temple square.[16] Correspondingly, excavations have so far revealed five *cuauhxicalco* (round circular stones used for cremation), including one at the foot of the Templo Mayor. These figures likely represent the treatment of the dead, as described above.

Folio 23r shows armed Mexica warriors, indicating a subsequent moment after the attack became known and the Mexica responded. On the left side of the folio three armed Mexica warriors carry shields with down balls. The limbs of the opponent fighting with the warrior on the lower part of the page are visible, as is the hand of the uppermost warrior's opponent. The middle figure holds an obsidian blade weapon. The upper warrior also holds a weapon, but only the handle has been painted. The composition privileges the Mexica warriors, depicting them whole, while the opponents would have been bisected, to varying degrees, by the book's seam. Another warrior stands just behind the front lines of this battle. In one hand he holds the captured standard of the Spanish, indicating that the Mexica have regained the upper hand. He is not engaged in active combat and holds both his shield and obsidian-blade weapon in the other hand. This figure wears a net cape, indicating that he was a dancer who took up arms in the aftermath. The Annals of Tlatelolco explains: "While dancing they went bare [of weapons], with only their net cloaks, their turquoise [ornaments], their lip plugs."[17] In the rush to retaliate, he still wears his ritual clothing, rather than the quilted armor of the Mexica warriors. Likewise, a ritual participant, still dressed in the hummingbird costume of Huitzilopochtli, guards the steps of the temple with shield and weapon in hand.

While the *tlacuilo* registered indigenous deaths that took place during the massacre, he focused on the later retaliation, making it the central component of his two-page composition. The large red Spanish banner, a motif introduced in the previous composition, appears here in the hands of an indigenous warrior. It signals the indigenous triumph that led to the imprisonment of the Spaniards and their subsequent losses as they tried to escape the city on the Noche Triste. The individual behind the massacre was Pedro de Alvarado. On folio 23r the *tlacuilo* demonstrates that his betrayal is avenged. The Florentine Codex characterizes the moment when the Mexica rallied to battle with the Spaniards after the massacre as "how the war first began."[18] When the Spaniards were subsequently placed under siege in the palace of Axayacatl and expelled from the city on the Noche Triste, the Mexica triumphed.

The highest-ranking Tenochca and Tlatelolca leaders were imprisoned when the massacre occurred. As early as November 1519, when the Spanish arrived in the capital, Cortés kept Moteuczoma and Itzquauhtzin under house arrest. This meant that leadership during the retaliation came from elsewhere. The Codex Aubin account of the massacre names four protagonists along with an unnamed "man who was the image of the devil" and an "incenser, who came from Acatliyacapan."[19] The named individuals are Tonatiuh (Pedro de Alvarado), Hernando Cortés, a "brave, young soldier" named Quatlazol, and the "general Ecatzin." Though Codex Aubin is a Tenochca account, it accords Ecatl an important role. In a brief dialogue between Ecatl and Moteuczoma, the general warns the *tlatoani* that the Spanish are plotting an ambush like the one that occurred in Cholula. This account notes the Tlatelolca warrior's important role in the event and presumably his presence during the retaliation. Ecatl may or may not have been pictured on the page opposite folio 23r, but the *tlacuilo* depicted him facing off against Alvarado on the following page, folio 23v.

Folio 23v

1521: THE ROUT OF THE SPANIARDS AT TLATELOLCO

On folio 23v the *tlacuilo* records the most important indigenous victory during the siege of Tenochtitlan (figure 4.3). He references this victory through two iconic events, the near-capture of Hernando Cortés and the capture of the Spanish banner by the Tlatelolca warrior Ecatl. These events took place on the same day in the heart of Tlatelolco, when the Mexica warriors forced a Spanish retreat, taking and sacrificing many captives in the process. In spatial terms they represent attacks that occurred against the Spanish avant-garde and the rear guard. The Annals of Tlatelolco would have us believe that "the Tlatelolca were exclusively responsible for it."[20] The Florentine Codex describes Ecatl as the head of this tremendous force. On folio 23v Hernando Cortés and Pedro de Alvarado, two of the most powerful Spanish conquistadors, are shown in subjugation. The subject matter and the focus on Tlatelolca involvement are in keeping with the rest of the manuscript.

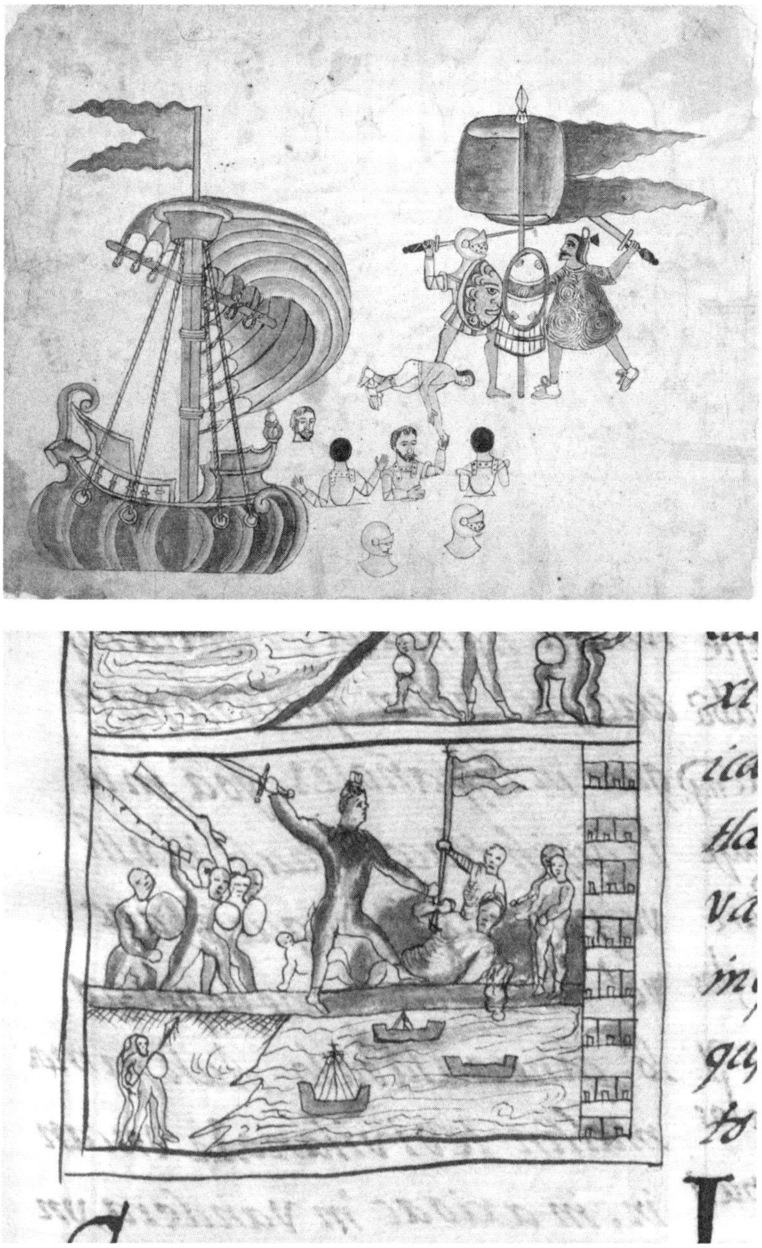

Figure 4.3. Ecatl capturing the Spanish banner in Codex Azcatitlan, folio 23v, courtesy of the Bibliothèque Nationale de France, and Florentine Codex, book 12, ch. 34, fol. 473r, ca. 1575–1577, Florence, The Biblioteca Medicea Laurenziana, MS Med. Palat. 220, folio 473r. Reproduced with permission of MiBACT. Further reproduction by any means is prohibited.

The left side of folio 23v depicts a brigantine with a Spanish flag. Although the water has not been painted, we can read the brigantine as floating on a body of water. Six Spaniards dressed in armor are shown partially submerged. An indigenous man helps the central figure out of the water. Two figures on foot are engaged in combat above. To the left a Spaniard holds a sword and a shield decorated with an anthropomorphized solar motif. To the right an indigenous warrior holds a Spanish sword and a shield decorated with five down balls that identify him as Mexica. A large, richly pigmented Spanish banner appears behind his shield, suggesting that the Mexica have once again gained control, as in the scene of the massacre during the feast of Toxcatl.

The presence of the brigantine indicates that this is not the Noche Triste, when the Spaniards were escaping from Tenochtitlan on foot.[21] Rather, this scene shows one of the conquest battles of 1521, when Cortés returned to Tenochtitlan after building several ships in Texcoco. Barlow identified the Spanish figure with the solar shield as Pedro de Alvarado, noting that the indigenous called him Tonatiuh (Sun).[22] Barlow described the scene as alluding to an episode that occurred on a bridge in San Martín Atezcapan (located south of the garden of Santiago Tlatelolco), explaining that Cortés was about to perish and that the event was recorded later in the church of Santiago.[23]

Several sixteenth-century sources describe this event. It takes place in the late summer of 1521, toward the end of the conquest, when pitched battles were occurring along the causeways that led to the city.

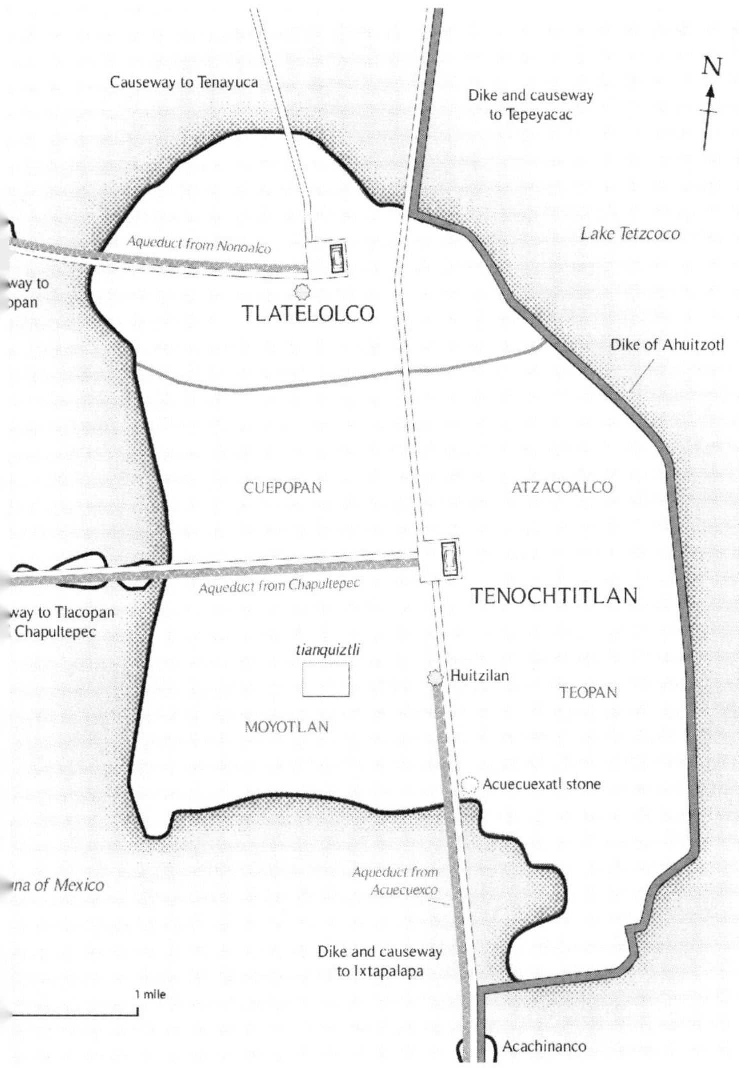

Figure 4.4. Map of pre-Hispanic Tenochtitlan and Tlatelolco by Olga Vanegas. Reproduced from Barbara Mundy, *The Death of Aztec Tenochtitlan, the Life of Mexico City*, fig. 1.10, p. 16.

The Spanish had completed construction of their thirteen brigantines in Texcoco earlier in the summer, in May 1521. As the Spanish conquistador Bernal Díaz del Castillo recounts, Cortés "ordered them to put in each brigantine a royal banner and another banner with the name given to each brigantine."[24] A large, carefully painted brigantine dominates the left side of folio 23v; it is shown at full sail and with the Spanish banner flying. With the arrival of the ships and the May 13 destruction of the aqueduct that conveyed fresh water to the island from Chapultepec, the siege began in earnest.[25] Cortés divided the ships among his captains, sending four to Pedro de Alvarado in Tacuba (where Bernal Díaz was stationed), six to Cristóbal de Olid (where Cortés battled with him from Coyoacan), and two to Gonzalo de Sandoval on the causeway of Tepeyacac. The thirteenth boat was considered unfit and was decommissioned.[26]

From these different stations the Spaniards worked to gain control of the causeways. In an effort to inhibit Spanish access, the Mexica removed the bridges that spanned the gaps in the causeways. On a near daily basis Cortés's men attempted to gain ground by placing temporary bridges or by filling the gaps. Just as quickly, Cuauhtemoc's troops removed the bridges. By the end of the summer additional indigenous allies had joined Cortés, and he advanced into the city from the south. The fighting moved to Tlatelolco in the northern part of the island (figure 4.4).

Cortés set his sights on the northern Tacuba causeway that Pedro de Alvarado's camp was controlling. Additional forces were brought to Tacuba. The Spanish began advancing along the causeway, one bridge at a time. With the center of Tlatelolco looming close, Alvarado pushed on over the final bridges. Cortés and his group, who defended the rear guard, wished to join the avant-garde fighting near Alvarado and crossed over a poorly filled bridge. When the Mexica mounted their attack and the Spanish fled, the bridge failed and many Spanish and indigenous allies were taken prisoner.[27] According to Cortés, as the Spaniards were being forced into the canal, he leaped into the water to help save some of the drowning men. He was captured and then freed with the assistance of one of his captains, who did not survive the attack.[28] Bernal Díaz del Castillo identifies the man who pulled Cortés out of the water as a Spaniard named Cristóbal de Olea who worked with the aid of another soldier named Lerma. A group of soldiers was pulling Cortés from the mud when Cristóbal de Olid, the "maestre de campo, came in haste, and they took Cortés by the arms and helped him get out of the water and mud, and they brought him a horse on which he escaped death."[29] Durán identifies Cortés's rescuer as a "Biscayan page," who was subsequently torn to pieces by indigenous combatants.[30]

Although the Spanish accounts vary somewhat, they generally indicate a misstep on the part of Alvarado. Cortés suggests that Alvarado's men did a poor job of filling in the gap, causing it to fail.[31] López de Gómara is more openly critical, writing that Alvarado "wanted to make a name for himself as captain" and that after the devastating Spanish loss "Alvarado was cured of his madness in not believing Cortés, who had always told him never to advance without first securing his way of retreat."[32] Durán implies that Alvarado's rashness led him into a Mexica ambush: "Cortés had ordered that no one move or attack until he commanded and the trumpet was sounded. But don Pedro de Alvarado, whose heart rebelled against the contempt and scorn shown him by the Indians, did not wait for the signal."[33] Díaz del Castillo remains loyal to Alvarado, his captain, and pins the blame on Cortés.[34]

Folio 23v depicts either a single scene centered around Alvarado's camp or two separate incidents. The Spanish sources concur that Alvarado and Cortés were battling at some distance from each other on the causeway and could not see each other. María Castañeda de la Paz and Michel Oudijk have argued that two scenes are represented: the rescue of Cortés and a battle with Alvarado that resulted in the loss of the Spanish banner.[35] This is quite likely, as the rout of the Spanish and temporary capture of Cortés was a noteworthy event that features prominently in many sixteenth-century sources. Although the figures in the water on folio 23v are not particularly expressive, the varying degrees of submersion, the closed eyes of one helmeted Spaniard, and the upraised arms of another signal distress. The figure being rescued is depicted frontally and is surrounded by the others, indicating his importance.

While the Spanish accounts cited above describe Cortés being rescued by a Spaniard, folio 23v depicts an indigenous man pulling him from the water. Alva Ixtlilxochitl claims that it was his great-great grandfather Ixtlilxochitl (the king of Texcoco) who had sided with Cortés:

> Ixtlilxochitl, who got there just in time, ordered his soldiers to stop the enemy. He quickly reached Cortés and offered his hand and pulled him out of the water as one of the enemy warriors was about to cut off his head. Ixtlilxochitl cut off the attacker's arms. Though this is attributed to certain Spaniards, it is actually quite the opposite, since it could be seen painted on the main door of the monastery church at Santiago Tlatelulco. But now a certain friar, who must have been one of Olea's relatives, had it repainted, making Olea the one to cut the arms of Cortés's attackers, while Ixtlilxochitl pulled him out of the water. In any case, Ixtlilxochitl saved Cortés.[36]

If the Codex Azcatitlan *tlacuiloque* painted their manuscript before the Church of Santiago in Tlatelolco was rebuilt and consecrated under Fray Juan de Torquemada in 1610, they may have encountered a similar composition on a regular basis.

The second event featured on folio 23v, the capture of the Spanish banner, is described in detail in the Florentine Codex. In the thirty-fourth and thirty-fifth chapters the scribes and *tlacuiloque* record the battle in Tlatelolco and Ecatl's capture of the Spanish banner. The Tlatololca leader carried the titles *tlacatecatl* (military governor) and *tlapanecatl*. At the end of chapter 34 the Nahuatl text of the Florentine Codex describes the Spanish filling in the gaps in the canal and widening the road before entering the city in formation: "They came very slowly, with the standard leading them, playing wind instruments and beating drums." The scribe later describes the beginning of the ambush against the Spaniards:

> When they got to Tlilhuacan [which is now San Martín], the [Tlatelolca] warriors crouched far down and hid themselves, hugging the ground, waiting for the war cry, when there would be shouting and cries of encouragement. When the cry went up, "O Mexica, up and at them!" the [Tlatelolca captain] Tlappanecatl Ecatzin, a warrior of Otomí rank, faced [the Spaniards] and threw himself at them, saying, "O Tlatelolca warriors, up and at them, who are these barbarians? Come running!" Then he went and threw a Spaniard down, knocking him to the ground; the one he threw down was the one who came first, who came leading them. And when he had thrown him down, he dragged the Spaniard off.[37]

The *tlacuilo* states that Ecatl defeated "the one who came first, who came leading them"; as the passage quoted earlier makes clear, the Spanish came "with the standard leading them." Furthermore, the corresponding image that appears at the end of chapter 34 depicts this (figure 4.3). Ecatl and his fallen Spanish foe appear larger than the other figures. As they fight along the road, with the canal beneath them and the city structures in a stylized column to the right, the Tlatelolca warrior subdues his enemy with a European sword while he grasps the Spanish banner with its Christian cross.

This passage states that Ecatl "dragged the Spaniard off" (temporarily or permanently, we cannot be sure), making it unclear whether his opponent was Alvarado. Alva Ixtlilxochitl's text belies this, stating that both of the standard bearer's arms were cut off.[38] The depiction on folio 23v may be a symbolic rather than literal representation of the capture of the flag from Alvarado's troops. Indigenous and Spanish sources do indicate, though, that captains served as standard bearers at times. An image at the end of chapter 32 may support Codex Azcatitlan's visual claim that a banner was taken from Alvarado (figure 4.5). That chapter describes the Spanish entry into Tlatelolco and the onset of fighting there two or three days before the rout. The glyph for Tlatelolco, depicted as a spotted hill glyph with an eagle on top, identifies where the fighting took place and the place of origin of the warriors. Three brave Tlatelolca warriors are named in the text: Tzoyectzin, Temoctzin, and Tzilacatzin.[39] Holding indigenous and European weapons, they combat the Spaniards. The Spaniard at lower right holding the banner wears elaborate plumes that indicate his high status. His horse and the ally beside him turn away from the fighting as they retreat. The text explains that the Spaniards, tired of fighting that day, returned to their camp. The plumes suggest that this figure is a captain, probably Alvarado at this stage and location of the fighting. In the context of his account of the final siege of Tenochtitlan-Tlatelolco, Díaz del Castillo comments sympathetically on those responsible for the flag, including his captain, Alvarado: "Well, I want to talk about our captain, standard-bearer, and other flag bearers, who were covered with wounds and their banners ragged; and I say that every day we had need of a new standard-bearer, because we all came out in such a condition that they could not go back to the fight carrying the flags again."[40]

Durán's native informants state that

> the men of Tlatelolco did everything in their power to defend themselves and killed numerous enemy Indians and some Spaniards, among them a lieutenant from whom they snatched the banner, tearing it to pieces in front of the entire army. This took place in a barrio now called San Martín. In another document I read that they destroyed four Spanish flags and killed a captain by the name of Guzmán and that the Tlatelolcas won much glory in this battle.[41]

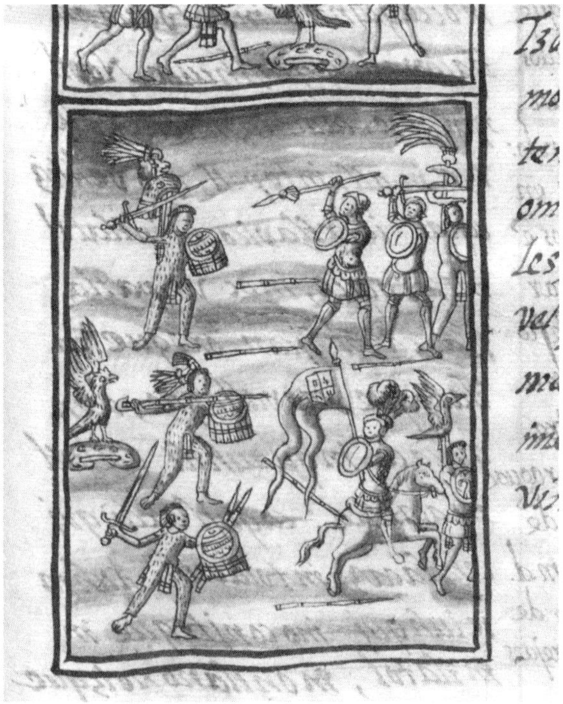

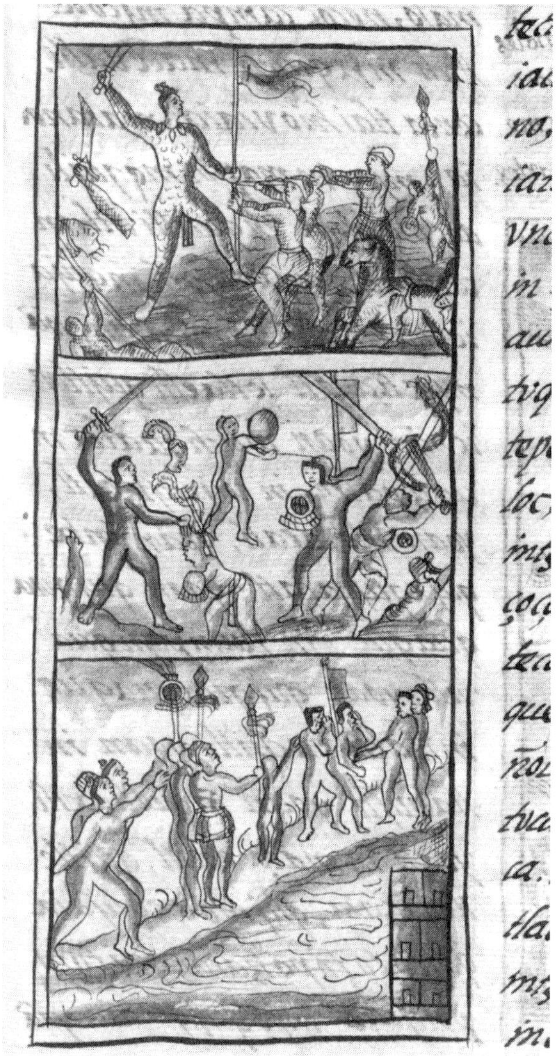

Top: Figure 4.5. Tlatelolca warriors battling the Spanish in Florentine Codex, book 12, ch. 32, fol. 468r, ca. 1575–1577. Florence, The Biblioteca Medicea Laurenziana, MS Med. Palat. 220, folio 468r. Reproduced with permission of MiBACT. Further reproduction by any means is prohibited.

Right: Figure 4.6. Events surrounding Ecatl's capture of the Spanish banner in Florentine Codex, book 12, ch. 35, fol. 474r, ca. 1575–1577. Florence, The Biblioteca Medicea Laurenziana, MS Med. Palat. 220, folio 474r. Reproduced with permission of MiBACT. Further reproduction by any means is prohibited.

These texts and images convey that the banners carried by captains and others were particularly important to the indigenous warriors and were a target during battle.

While Florentine Codex chapter 34 in book 12 alludes to the banner being taken by Ecatl, it is mentioned again more directly in chapter 35, which describes the capture of the banner at San Martín. The text further describes the capture and sacrifice of Spanish prisoners, recounting how the Spaniards and their allies were forced into the water, making the road very slippery. "This was where the banner was captured; that is where it was taken. It was the Tlatelolca who captured it, at the place now called San Martín."[42] The Spanish text clarifies that San Martín was a church. The position of Ecatl in the accompanying image is similar (figure 4.6). Larger than the others, he is shown capturing the standard in the midst of fierce battle and dismembered body parts.[43]

The Annals of Tlatelolco mentions Ecatl's capture of the flag twice. The colonial history found in Document 1 includes an account of when Ecatl was found, together with the indigenous noble Temilotl, stowing away on Cortés's ship bound for Castille in 1528. In this text he is called the "tlacatecatl, tlapanecatl

Ecatzin Popocatzin." The seaman who finds Ecatl identifies the stowaway to Cortés as the one "who seized the banner."[44] In the account of the conquest in Document 5 MS 22 tells us:

> Then they reached the temple courtyard; the fighting lasted four days.
>
> And when they reached Yacacolco here, Spaniards were captured on the Tlilhuacan road, as well as all the people from the various altepetl. Two thousand died there, and the Tlatelolca were exclusively responsible for it.
>
> At this time we Tlatelolca set up skull racks; skull racks were in three places. One was in the temple courtyard at Tlillan, where the heads of our lords [the Spaniards] were strung; the second place was in Yacacolco, where the heads of our lords were strung, along with the heads of two horses; the third place was in Çacatla, facing the Cihuateocalli [Woman-Temple]. It was the exclusive accomplishment of the Tlatelolca.[45]

MS 22bis has an added line, just after the reference to Tlillan: "and there they placed the banner that the tlapanecatl, tlacatecatl Ecatzin Popocatzin captured."[46] The insertion occurs just after the mention of Tlillan, indicating that this is where the banner was displayed. Torquemada mentions a temple in Tlatelolco called Tlillan that existed at the time of the war of 1473.[47] The paleography of the Nahuatl text of the Florentine Codex records the site of the capture of the flag as "tlalhoacan"; in Spanish it is written "Tliloacan."[48] These three designations reference the same area. On the Tlilhuacan road Ecatzin captured the banner that was later displayed in the nearby temple of Tlillan. In "Los barrios antiguos de Tenochtitlan y Tlatelolco" Alfonso Caso states that Tlilhuacan, Yacacolco, and Atezcapan were probably all on modern Tlatelolco's Calle de González Bocanegra.[49] This would correspond with the Florentine Codex's Spanish references to the church of San Martín that might have been built adjacent to or on top of the former temple, in the barrio of San Martín Atezcapan (which included part of today's Calle de González Bocanegra). This location also would have been near the terminus of the causeway to Tacuba, where the fighting was taking place.

The Florentine Codex artist depicts a horizontal row of buildings on the right side of his image of Ecatl taking the banner, specifically to locate this event at the causeway's terminus (figure 4.3). After the Tlatelolca leader captures the banner, chapter 35 describes many captives being taken and states that those who escaped were chased "as far as Colhuacatonco, at the edge of the canal." Then, as depicted in the third image (figure 4.6, bottom) associated with this chapter, "they took the captives to Yacacolco, hurrying them along, going along herding their captives together. Some went weeping, some singing, some went shouting while hitting their hands against their mouths." There they were sacrificed on an altar platform and their heads mounted on a *tzompantli* (skull rack).[50] The herding of the captives is shown in the third image (figure 4.6, bottom), where a partial vertical row of structures at the lower right again orients the viewer spatially.

Unlike the images in the Florentine Codex, the Codex Azcatitlan *tlacuilo* depicts the figure of Ecatl without providing much detail regarding warrior rank and costume. Throughout Codex Azcatitlan most of the warriors engaged in battle and taking prisoners are simply shown in quilted armor, represented as a tunic with dashed lines worn over a *maxtlatl*. There is some variation in headgear. Most wear the *temillotl* hairstyle; others of elite status wear their hair down with a cloth cap tied closely about the head (e.g., on folios 15v and 18v). On folios 15v and 18v, where Axayacatl and Chimalpopoca appear engaged in battle, they wear this headgear; their status as *tlatoani* is further identified by the red ribbons at the back of their heads. Aside from this, the *tlacuilo* primarily distinguishes elite warriors by depicting them in sandals. Both indigenous figures on folio 23v wear this elite footwear.

While Ecatl wears a tunic similar to that of the other warriors in Codex Azcatitlan, his is decorated with a swirling water motif that sets him apart (figure 4.7). Half is painted red and half is unpainted or

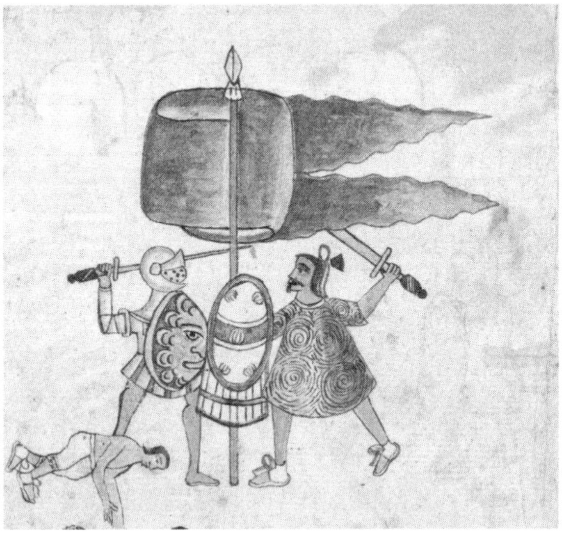

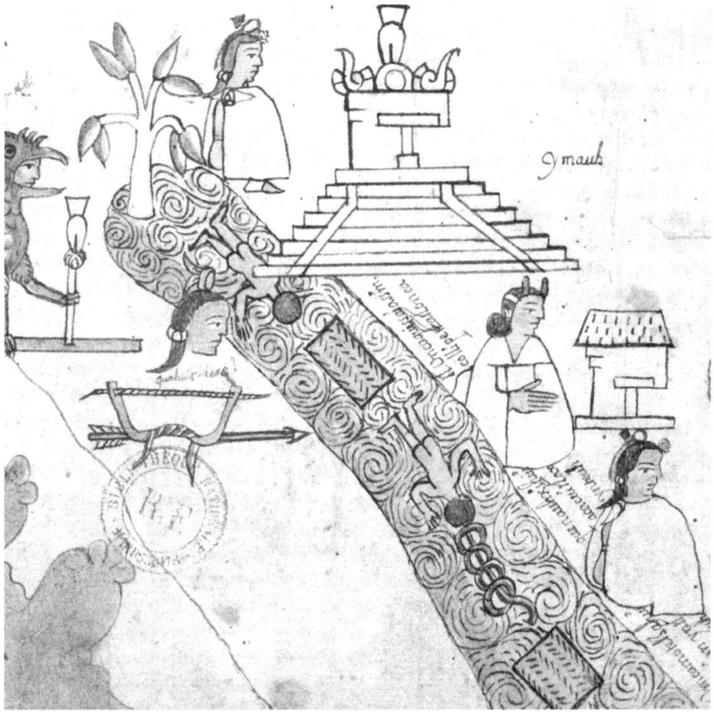

Figure 4.7. Codex Azcatitlan, folio 23v (detail), and Codex Azcatitlan, folio 4v (detail). Courtesy of the Bibliothèque Nationale de France.

shows vestiges of a faint yellowish pigment. In Codex Azcatitlan this faint color often appears in areas where blue is intended. For example, Moteuczoma's *xiuhhuitzolli* on folio 21v exhibits a faint yellow rather than blue. Although the *tlacuilo* has not yet painted in the water below, he carefully decorates and pigments the swirling water on the tunic. These swirls recall the turbulent water that surrounds Aztlan on folios 1v–2r and make an even more direct visual reference to the sacred waters that flow from the base of a tree beside the toponym for Chicomoztoc on folio 4v (figure 4.7). The water on the tunic recalls both the turbulent sacred waters associated with these sites of origin and the spring that signaled to the Mexica, even before the eagle on the nopal cactus, that they had arrived at their promised land. As Durán writes: "Thus again they found the spring they had seen the day before. But the water on that day had been clear and transparent, and it now flowed out in two streams, one red like blood, the other so blue and thick it filled the people with awe."[51] Codex Aubin describes this sacred spring as "like blue ink."[52]

As described in chapter 2, these sacred waters are linked to the idea of sacrifice. On folio 4v two sacrificial victims and their entrails float in the water. As established at the beginning of the migration histories, Huitzilopochtli's guidance and support was part of an exchange relationship. Sacrifice was required to maintain this relationship and to keep the Fifth World in motion. Here Ecatl takes the lead in defending Tenochtitlan-Tlatelolco, the reimagined Aztlan, from invading enemy forces. The Tlatelolca-led attack on the Spanish leads to a mass sacrifice that is described in both Spanish and indigenous sources.[53] It seems likely that this sacrifice, so closely tied to the rout, would have been depicted on the missing opposite page.

The shield that this warrior carries also references a cosmic template. Commonly referred to as an *ihuiteteyo chimalli*, this shield features varying numbers of down balls. On folio 23v five down balls are arranged in a quincunx pattern. Used by warriors of different ranks, including *tlatoque* at times, the shield signals Mexica identity. Recently Justyna Olko has refined our understanding of the down ball shield. She argues that the term *ihuiteteyo chimalli*, derived from the *Primeros memoriales*, means "the shield with the feather border" and does not accurately reflect the design:

> It seems more probable that the term properly designating this shield design was the *tehuehuelli chimalli* (morphology unclear). It also appears in the *Primeros Memoriales* in reference to a shield design very similar to the one described as *ihuiteteyo* [fol. 261r] . . . and is carried by Huitzilopochtli, which is fully congruent with the basic association of this shield in Mexica manuscripts. The *tehuehuelli chimalli*, carried by the effigy of Huitzilopochtli in the feast of Toxcatl, is described as made of reeds and decorated in four places with eagle down (FC XII, 52). Its symbolic dimension is also confirmed by its frequent appearance as part of the Mexica symbol of war and conquest, combining a war club or a spear-thrower with a shield.[54]

The shield design reflects Mexica identity, specifically as the people of Huitzilopochtli. As described in the analysis of folios 1v–2r, Codex Azcatitlan reinforces the idea that both the Tenochca and the Tlatelolca are the people of Huitzilopochtli. On folio 1v the figure of Huitzilopochtli is dressed as a warrior and carries a shield of similar design.

While the *tehuehuelli* shields could feature differing numbers of down balls, here and throughout Codex Azcatitlan the *tlacuiloque* frequently painted five balls in a quincunx pattern, referencing space and time, creation and destruction. Spatially, the four cardinal directions and fifth vertical direction connected the earthly and spiritual realms. Temporally, the quincunx referenced the four previous Suns or Eras and the Fifth World in which the Mexica believed themselves to be living. The *tlacuilo* reinterprets Ecatl's capture of the Spanish banner through a cosmic template. On folio 23v Ecatl defends the sacred waters of Tenochtitlan-Tlatelolco, and the Fifth Era or Sun, as he battles the coming Era, the next Sun, in the form of Alvarado.

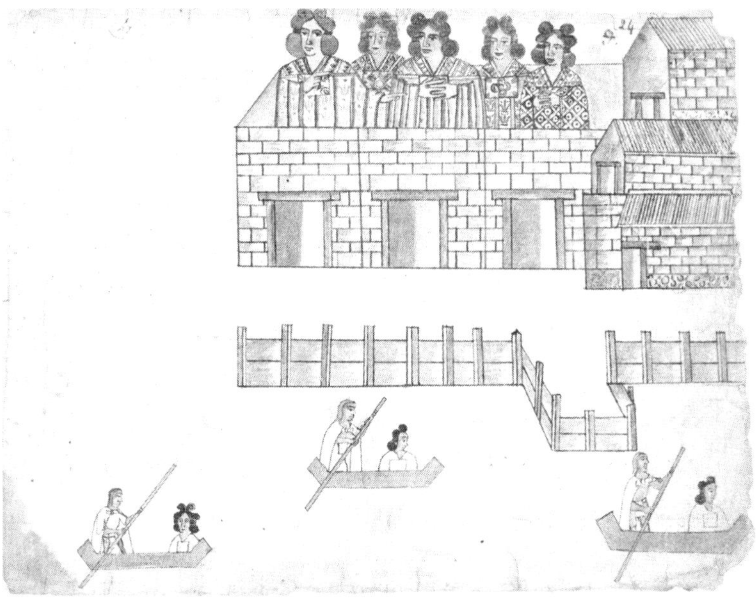

Figure 4.8. Codex Azcatitlan, folio 24r. Courtesy of the Bibliothèque Nationale de France.

Folio 24r

1521: THE EVACUATION OF TLATELOLCO

Folio 24r depicts the right half of a scene that shows the evacuation by boat of Cuauhtemoc's wife Tecuichpotzin and her entourage on August 13, 1521 (figure 4.8). At the upper right five women stand on the rooftops of a set of buildings. Beneath them is a wooden fence. In the area below the fence, toward the bottom of the page, three canoes appear. In each a man paddles or punts the canoe with a seated female passenger. Most of the figures in the canoes face right, indicating that the boats are moving in that direction. Although the women on the ramparts all look to the left, the figure at far left points to the right with both hands. The positioning of figures throughout the page suggests that help is coming from the left and that the women are escaping to the right.

The woman gesturing at the far left directs attention to the woman at the far right who wears a black and red mantle. The women and their identity are the focus of the scene, so the *tlacuilo* depicts them with a greater level of detail than in other images of women in the codex. The women's clothing indicates that they are of high status. They wear elaborate coiffures and elegantly decorated *huipilme* (blouses; singular *huipilli*). Although none of the women are identified glyphically, the woman at far right wears a *huipilli* that incorporates the design of a *xiuhtlalpiltilmatli* (turquoise-tied mantle), a royal mantle that was worn by Mexica kings and emphasized Toltec ancestry.[55] Moteuczoma Xocoyotl wears one on folio 21v. The *xiuhtlalpiltilmatli* design appears on the lower half of her *huipilli*, suggesting that she is a royal wife.

The reverse of this scene, folio 24v, depicts postconquest events, so the royal woman must depict Tecuichpotzin (later known by her baptismal name, Isabel Moctezoma). She was the daughter of Moteuczoma Xocoyotl and his principal wife, Teotlalco, and was married to Atlixcatzin at a tender age.[56] After the death of her husband and her father in 1520, she was married to her uncle, Cuitlahua. He became *tlatoani* after Moteuczoma's death but ruled just a few months before his own death from smallpox. Tecuichpotzin was then married to the next Mexica ruler, eighteen-year old Cuauhtemoc. The visage of the royal woman on folio 24r is slightly less full and her stature slightly shorter than that of the women surrounding her, perhaps indicating her youth.

This scene reflects a period after the arrival of Cortés in 1519 (folio 22v), the massacre during the festival of Toxcatl in May 1520 (folio 23r), and the siege of Tenochtitlan-Tlatelolco in August 1521 (folio 23v), but before some of the earliest events of the postconquest period in 1521 (folio 24v). As such, we can read it as an episode related to the end of the conquest. The *tlacuilo* shows us the end of the conquest when Cuauhtemoc surrendered and his family was evacuated (figure 4.8). A related image can be found in cell 48 of the Lienzo de Tlaxcala. There Tecuichpotzin appears in Tlatelolco, near the home of Aztahuatzin in Amaxac, the site of the surrender. She is set off from the other ladies by the glyphs that record her name: *tecu[l]* (the head of an old woman) + *ich[catl]* (cotton flower) + *poch[tli]* (smoke). The text in this cell reads: "Here ended the Mexica."

According to Cortés, the conquest ended lakeside when Cuauhtemoc was captured in a canoe:

> Then the brigantines swept into that inner lake and broke through the fleet of canoes; but the warriors in them no longer dared fight. God willed that Garci Holguín, a captain of one of the brigantines, should pursue a canoe which appeared to be carrying persons of rank; and as there were two or three crossbowmen in the bows who were preparing to fire, the occupants of the canoe signaled to the brigantine not to shoot, because the lord of the city was with them. When they heard this our men leapt aboard and captured Guatimucín [Cuauhtemoc] and the lord of Tacuba and the other chieftains with them. These they then brought to the roof close to the lake where I was standing, and, as I had no desire to treat Guatimucín harshly, I asked him to be seated, whereupon he came up to me and, speaking in his language, said that he had done all he was bound to do to defend his own person and his people, so that now they were reduced to this sad state, and I might do with him as I pleased. Then he placed his hand upon a dagger of mine and asked me to kill him with it; but I reassured him saying that he need fear nothing. Thus, with this lord a prisoner, it pleased God that the war should cease, and the day it ended was Tuesday, the feast of Saint Hippolytus, the thirteenth of August, in the year 1521.[57]

Earlier in this letter, as Cortés describes the devastating conditions of the city preceding that moment, he indicates that Cuauhtemoc had been living in the boat: "I also ordered the alguacil mayor to make ready the brigantines, so that they might sail into a large lake between the houses, where all the canoes had gathered; for they now had so few houses left that the lord of the city lived in a canoe with certain of his chieftains, not knowing where else to go."[58] The relative calm on folio 24r may reflect the evacuation from the city immediately following Cuauhtemoc's capture. Notably, this image of dignified women, well dressed and coiffed, belies the piled corpses and utter devastation that Cortés describes.

Conclusion

The colonial history recorded in Codex Azcatitlan presents an indigenous perspective. What emerges from these pages is a narrative that celebrates indigenous victories and dignifies indigenous losses. The bodies of the victims of the massacre during the feast of Toxcatl have been recovered and are neatly stacked, awaiting cremation, even as the Mexica warriors enact their vengeance center stage. Tecuichpotzin and her attendants appear regal in defeat, an image that fit the *tlacuilo*'s vision, if not the actual circumstances of that grisly day. The *tlacuilo* addresses his indigenous audience without the burden of trying to appeal to a Spanish audience. In four scenes of the conquest, half are devoted to events that led to the two most devastating Spanish losses. The large, red Spanish banner, adorned with a haloed dove to signify the holy spirit, functions less as a symbol of Christianity than as a leitmotif used to illustrate shifting power relations. Even the indigenous foes are given due respect. Flanking Cortés's party on folio 22v are the indigenous allies that made his victory possible. On folio 23v Cortés faces imminent death, except for the helping hand of an indigenous man.

Codex Azcatitlan's conquest history, however, is not only a record of indigenous strength. It is also a story by, for, and about indigenous individuals. The *tlacuilo* highlights what would have been perceived as strange and new in 1519, by detailing the blond hair of Hernando Cortés and the dark skin of the African man who attends his horse. Women of importance are recorded in this history. When viewed from the *tlacuilo*'s colonial present, both Malinche and Tecuichpotzin had unusual and exceptional roles that were inconsistent with the norms of pre-Hispanic society and would transcend the conquest. Malinche, a former slave from the Maya region, in her role as translator would regularly engage in direct dialogue with Moteuczoma, the highest-ranking political official in the Nahua domain. In addition to serving as Cortés's primary translator during and after the conquest, she had a child by him in 1523. Tecuichpotzin, wife of the last two preconquest Mexica rulers, survived the conquest and continued to play an influential role in colonial society. She too had a child with Cortés around 1528. In the conquest history, allies and foes are paired and pitted against one another. Cortés and his allies confront Moteuczoma. Mexica forces, perhaps led by Ecatl, battle Alvarado and his troops after the massacre, avenging the death of individuals like Cohualpopocatzin. Ecatl faces off with Alvarado directly, even as Ixtlilxochitl pulls Cortés from the water. While little can be said of Cuauhtemoc, he probably would have figured prominently in several of the missing pages, perhaps appearing among the nobles who attended Moteuczoma when he greeted Cortés or sacrificing the Spanish captives taken on the causeway. His death is so carefully recorded in the postconquest history that he probably would have appeared ceding to Cortés, opposite the evacuation of his wife. Based on the extant images, the *tlacuilo* singles out Ecatl as one of the most heroic figures of the conquest. He is depicted as a powerful warrior, whose feats in battle are elevated to a cosmic level.

The image of Ecatl and Alvarado locked in combat also reveals something about how the *tlacuilo* works. Folio 23v presents detailed, dimensional, and articulated images and objects within a space, such that they construct a scenic environment. Though the background has not been painted, the proximity of the figures indicates that these two events share a spatial setting made up of the surface of the causeway and the watery canal. On a more finished page Cortés and his party stand on the spotted ground. The representation of the massacre during the feast of Toxcatl situates figures on the temple steps and on the ground of the plaza. They are integrated together and cohere to create a single scenic image. However, these scenes are frequently made up of components that carry additional meaning and signify outside of this initial context. The capture of the banner and the rescue of Cortés overlap and appear to function as one scene, even though two temporal and spatial moments are depicted. Likewise, the scenic representation of the massacre and its aftermath combines multiple narrative and temporal moments to signify the different aspects and details of something conceived of as a single event.

The collapsing of the temporal occurs on a grander scale at times. When the *tlacuilo* references his contemporary moment by including an arcaded wall in the massacre scene, he navigates and makes connections between the pre-Hispanic past and his colonial present. The Codex Azcatitlan's viewers may have also drawn connections between the *tlacuilo*'s composition of Cortés being pulled from the water and the painting depicting this in the Church of Santiago Tlatelolco. Like the imagined dialogues that enliven the Annals of Tlatelolco and the Codex Aubin, these connections orient viewers and make real a vision of the past. The image of Ecatl defeating Alvarado places these events of the past in a cosmic context, where the past, present, and future overlie one another through the ceaseless cycles of time. The *tlacuilo* presents this cosmic template in the postconquest history as well.

CHAPTER 5

TRAITORS, INTRIGUE, AND THE COSMIC CYCLE IN CODEX AZCATITLAN

ON FOLIOS 24V–25R of Codex Azcatitlan the *tlacuilo* recorded postconquest information that pertains to the years 1521–1527 (figure 5.1). As he began to record a greater number of events in this section of the manuscript, he condensed his content, arranging it to read generally in vertical columns from left to right and from top to bottom. As in the earlier parts of the manuscript, most of the horses and human figures face and gesture to the right, reinforcing the reading order. Sometimes recorded events took place over a longer period and thus do not necessarily relate to only one year. As described in chapter 3, these pages leave room at the top for date glyphs. Thus some of the images in the upper register are incomplete because the *tlacuilo* intended to merge the imagery with the date cartouches. Based on interpretation of events recorded here, only two to three date cartouches would have been needed on each plate.

This formatting represents a shift from the two-page scenic imagery of the conquest history. While the images in the conquest history function in a primarily pictographic manner, closer to European traditions of image making, the postconquest history returns to the strategy used earlier in the manuscript, making greater use of ideograms and phonetic referents. As in the depiction of the massacre during the festival of Toxcatl, or the capture of the Spanish banner, these images continue to function not as the record of a specific moment but as a synopsis of a given event that may compress time by representing an ongoing event or a series or collection of events. While they are pictorially more detailed than the kind of images we see in Codex Boturini, they still function as prompts to be elucidated more fully through oral traditions.

In comparison to entries for the same period in Codex Aubin, these pages offer a decidedly different focus. While the Codex Aubin account of the conquest is centered on the role of Moteuczoma and his death, Codex Azcatitlan focuses to an equal or greater degree on the martial leadership of Ecatl and Cuauhtemoc.[1] Moteuczoma's death is omitted, along with Cuitlahua's brief reign. By contrast, the unjust murder of Cuauhtemoc during the Honduran expedition is a major focus of the postconquest material. This attention to Cuauhtemoc is congruent with the *tlacuilo*'s Tlatelolca perspective. Although Cuauhtemoc is typically thought of as the last great Tenochca ruler, he also descended from Tlatelolca lines. Document 1 of the Annals of Tlatelolco, for example, lists Cuauhtemoc as a Tlatelolca rather than a Tenochca ruler. As Kevin Terraciano has pointed out, this surprising frame has some basis in truth: "According to the Nahua historian Chimalpahin, and one of his annals sources, Quauhtemoctzin was the only son of a high-ranking noblewoman from Tlatelolco named Tecapantzin, who married the tlatoani of Tenochtitlan, Ahuitzotzin, a brother of two Tenochca rulers, Axayacatl and Tizoc."[2] Document 2 of the Annals of Tlatelolco, a genealogy of the rulers of Tenochtitlan, conforms to this idea as well by ending the list of Tenochca rulers with Moteuczoma II.

The Codex Aubin annals offer very brief, one-line entries for the years following the conquest, becoming more detailed only in the 1560s. In contrast, Codex Azcatitlan, though unfinished, offers a relatively detailed account of events that took place during and immediately after Cortés's 1524–1526 Honduran expedition. Though likely painted much later, the annals of Codex Azcatitlan terminate in 1527. My proposal that the postconquest history in Codex Azcatitlan dates to this period differs from earlier studies and is based on new and expanded readings of many images. Where relevant, I have taken interpretations proposed by earlier scholars as a point of departure, primarily Barlow, Graulich, Castañeda de la Paz, and Oudijk.[3] While Castañeda de la Paz and Oudijk have explored the possibility of a narrative that ends in the late 1560s, this reading suggests a much earlier terminus.

Folio 24v

1521–1522: DESTRUCTION OF TENOCHTITLAN-TLATELOLCO, LEAVING THE CITY, AND THE POSTCONQUEST RETURN OF INDIGENOUS RULE

Folio 24v begins with a brief visual reference to the destruction so efficaciously belied on the previous folio (figure 5.1). Just below the upper edge of the page, at far left, is a group of dismembered bones. Two large bones, a foot, a hand, and a segment of spine surround a cranium. This image calls to mind one of the most famous passages recorded in the Annals of Tlatelolco.[4] As the MS 22bis scribe copies that part of the text that addresses the devastation of Tenochtitlan in the final days of the conquest, he adds an additional commentary: "And on the roads lay shattered bones and scattered hair; the houses were unroofed, red [with blood]; worms crawled on the roads; and the walls of the houses were slippery with brains. And the water seemed red, as though it were dyed, and thus we drank it. We drank salt water, and we hammered on the adobe."[5] The pile of bones compactly references the devastating effects of the conquest on Tenochtitlan-Tlatelolco in August 1521.

The next set of images represents the departure from Tlatelolco and the resettlement of the city's ruling elite. A circular form appears at the top of the page. The top of the circle is left open, and a path or flow emanates from an opening below to the base of a hill place glyph. The circular glyph resembles the toponym that identifies the location of Cuauhtemoc's surrender to Cortés in cell 48 of the Lienzo de Tlaxcala (figure 5.2). The Annals of Tlatelolco describes the surrender as taking place at Amaxac.[6] The Florentine Codex places the surrender in the district of Amaxac on the rooftop of a Tlatelolca leader named Aztahuatzin.[7] It also explains that people went to Amaxac, where the road forks, after the surrender to depart the city.[8]

Etymologically, Amaxac means "where the waters or springs divide." Codex Mendoza represents another Amaxac, an *altepetl* of eastern Guerrero, as a phonetic glyph consisting of a pair of spread legs with water emerging: *atl* (water) + *maxac* (between my legs, in the crotch). The Codex Azcatitlan and Lienzo de Tlaxcala glyphs, however, more closely resemble another toponym in Codex Mendoza that represents Ameyalco (Place of the Springs), where a flow of water emerges from a white disk (figure 5.2).[9] In Lienzo de Tlaxcala cell 48 the springs that flow from the white disk separate or divide at the bottom and flow in different directions, perhaps indicating Amaxac (Where the Waters Divide) (figure 5.2).

Alternatively, this glyph may identify the home of Aztahuatzin, a Tlatelolca noble who is identified with the honorific *–tzin*. In the Lienzo de Tlaxcala the glyph marking the site of surrender appears on a house structure, supporting this interpretation. Pilar Máynez interprets this name to mean "venerable owner of the white feather or of the heron."[10] In this case the small tufts at the top of the circle in the Lienza de Tlaxcala cell 48 may represent heron feathers and the aquatic components the bird's habitat.

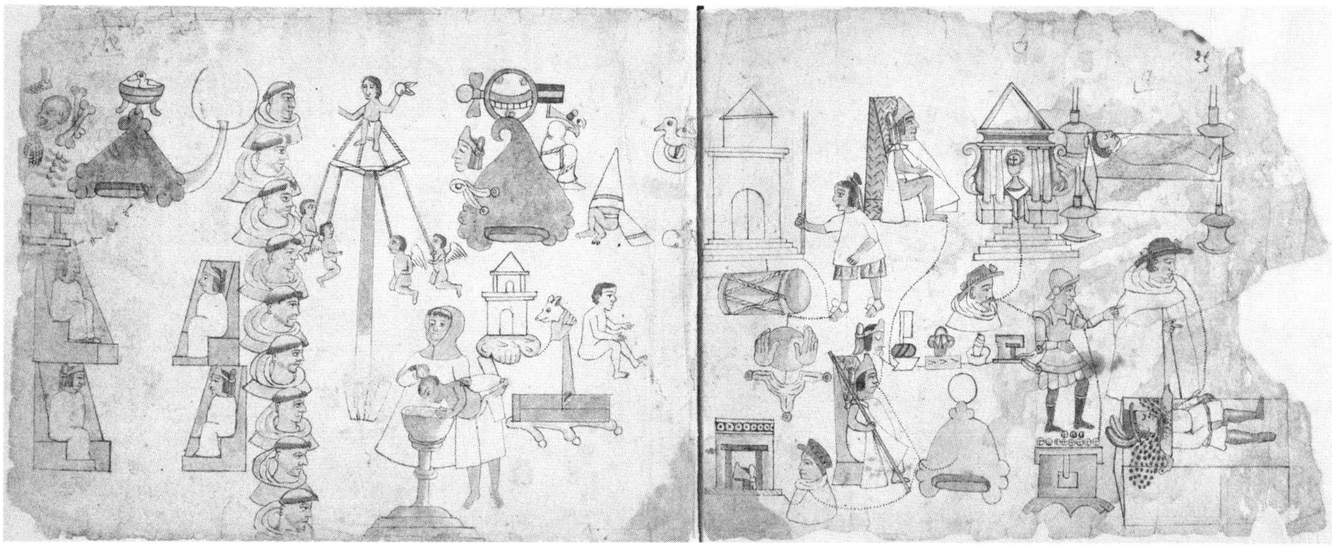

Figure 5.1 Codex Azcatitlan, folios 24v–25r. Courtesy of the Bibliothèque Nationale de France.

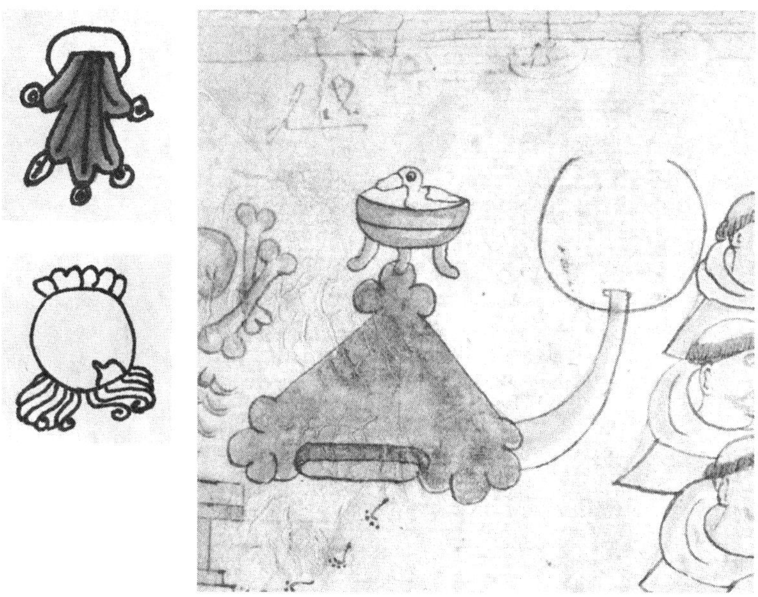

Figure 5.2. Left: Codex Azcatitlan, folio 24v (detail). Courtesy of the Bibliothèque Nationale de France. Far left, top: Codex Mendoza, folio 32r (detail), the glyph for Ameyalco. Courtesy of Joseph Leonard Herren. Far left, bottom: Lienzo de Tlaxcala, cell 48 (detail), the glyph associated with the site of Cuauhtemoc's surrender. Courtesy of Joseph Leonard Herren.

The Codex Azcatitlan *tlacuilo* may have intended to add a similar component; the open top area of the glyph most likely represents an unfinished area that the artist meant to integrate later with a date glyph. As with other areas intended to be blue, the flow from the disk is faintly pigmented with an earth tone, similar to the color of the baptismal water on the same page. This glyph leads to and perhaps identifies the *altepetl* form. At the top of the hill glyph is the image of a duck, similar to those found on folios 12v–13r, contained within a three-footed ceramic vessel. This image may represent a calendar month.

In several of the indigenous accounts the events of the conquest are described and dated within the context of the eighteen lunar months and five *nemontemi* (unlucky days) that together constituted the 365-day calendar. Attention to the ritual significance of these months even dictated the actions and responses of the warriors during the conquest. For example, in the Annals of Tlatelolco, toward the end of the siege, Cortés sent a message back to the Tlatelolca camp, asking Cuauhtemoc and the other leaders to surrender. Upon consultation with the ritual calendar,

> [t]he Teohua, learned with papers, cutter of papers, said, "My lords, listen to what we will say. In only four days, eighty will have passed [since the fighting began]. Perhaps it is the order of Huitzilopochtli that [nothing should be done when that term] is not yet fulfilled. Perhaps you will see [what should be done] secretly <have it revealed to you>. Let us wait out the eighty days, for there are only four more." But when the time came, it was not approved <by the god>. The war began again.[11]

According to the Annals of Tlatelolco, without the support of Huitzilopochtli, the war ensued and quickly terminated with the Tlatelolca warriors Coyohuehuetzin, Topantemoctzin, and Temilotzin delivering Cuauhtemoctzin by boat to Cortés for the surrender. The Annals of Tlatelolco further notes: "When we dispersed and the altepetl was lost, it was Three House year. We dispersed in [the month of] Nexochimaco, on a day One Serpent." Great warriors left the city wearing rags and settled wherever they could.[12]

Sahagún refers to this same month, during which the dead were honored, as "Tlaxochimaco" and tells us: "On the night before this feast, all busied themselves in killing fowls and dogs in order to eat them, and in making tamales and other things concerned with food."[13] Perhaps the image of a duck in a ceramic bowl references this part of the monthly calendar (the night before Tlaxochimaco started) rather than a place name. Although the last holdouts in Tlatelolco were starving and certainly not carrying out a regular feasting ritual, a glyphic reference to this traditional practice would be one way of signaling the end of the conquest from an indigenous perspective. On the last night of Huey Tecuilhuitl, when it became clear that Huitzilopochtli had not approved their petition, the immediately ensuing surrender of Cuauhtemoc and evacuation of the city became inevitable. Another example of a calendar reference more specific than the year occurs on Codex Azcatitlan folio 18v, where the day 5 Rain is noted above the toponym for Tlatelolco: there it specifies the day the Tenochca defeated the Tlatelolca in 1473 during Axayacatl's reign.

The Annals of Tlatelolco does not end with the departure from the city. It goes on to describe the torture and death of indigenous nobles as the Spanish searched for gold and for the "appurtenances of the demon" Huitzilopochtli, followed by a brief account of how life went on:

> After this, the people began to come back to settle here in Tlatelolco, in the year of Four Rabbit. Then Temilotzin came and settled in Capoltitlan, and don Juan Huehuetzin came to settle in Aticpac, but Coyohuehuetzin and Topantemoctzin died in Quauhtitlan. When we came to settle here in Tlatelolco, we were still all alone.[14]

The Annals of Tlatelolco concludes with a few sentences about the following events. While the Spaniards were still in Coyoacan, they began to distribute the *altepetl* (setting up the *encomiendas*). The Tenochtitlan rulers were released and then went to Azcapotzalco to consult about a military expedition in Metztitlan. The final line reads: "Then the Captain proclaimed war in Oaxaca; they had gone to Acolhuacan. Then Metztitlan, then Michoacan, then." MS 22bis fills in the abrupt ending with "then Honduras, Guatemala, and Tehuantepec." Lockhart tells us that the MS 22bis scribe also notes that this is the end of the document being copied: "('there ends the reading of this document as it was done')."[15]

On the far left of folio 24v, beneath the toponym, footsteps signal movement to another location where settlement occurs, as referenced by the house glyph. The *tlacuilo* depicts four *tlatoque* seated on thrones. The four enthroned rulers probably represent the return of indigenous power (though limited within the new Spanish structure). In the new Spanish order, the indigenous government was known as a cabildo and the leader took the title *gobernador* rather than *tlatoani*.[16] On folio 24v the new leaders are still represented as *tlatoque*, wearing the *xiuhhuitzolli* and seated on a *petlatl icpalli*. Though no glosses or glyphs identify these figures, they may represent the three (former) rulers of the Triple Alliance and the new leader of Tlatelolco.

This reading is feasible because the Codex Azcatitlan *tlacuilo* works from a Tlatelolca perspective and because Tlatelolco had regained political ground in the wake of the conquest.[17] After the defeat of the Tlatelolca *tlatoani* Moquihuix in the war of 1473, Tlatelolco had been subjected to Tenochtitlan and the Tlatelolca were no longer allowed to have a *huey tlatoani*. After Moquihuix, those occupying the highest office were *cuauhtlatoque* (eagle rulers or interim rulers; singular: *cuauhtlatoani*). Although the political reality was surely complicated in the immediate aftermath of the conquest, all of the highest leaders were now ostensibly on a more equal footing as they sought rights and privileges from the Spanish government. The four primary rulers of central Mexico were known as Cuauhtemoc of Tenochtitlan (baptized "don Hernando"); Coanacoch of Texcoco (baptized "don Pedro Alvarado"); Tetlepanquetzal of Tlacopan (baptized "don Pedro Cortés"); and Temilotl of Tlatelolco (baptized "don Pedro"). As the former head of the Triple Alliance, Cuauhtemoc may be set apart. The *tlacuilo* represents the *tlatoani* at top left slightly differently. His throne is slightly bigger, the division between the legs suggests that his body is turned slightly toward the viewer, and his shoes are visible. These differences may reflect stylistic experimentation on the part of the artist or an attempt to distinguish Cuauhtemoc slightly from the others. Largely similar in depiction, these four *tlatoque* echo the three unnamed rulers of the Triple Alliance at the start of Codex Azcatitlan.

1523–1524: ARRIVAL OF THE CLERGY

The next segment depicts nine tonsured friars, a baptism, and a *palo volador* (or flying pole dance). The vertical row of nine friars visually separates this segment and signals the introduction and enforcement of Christianity in the years following the conquest. As Durán tells us in the last chapter of his *History*, the religious instruction of the indigenous was begun in the aftermath of the conquest by a cleric of dubious morality that Cortés had brought with him.[18] In his fourth letter to the Spanish king, Cortés requests that additional religious representatives be sent.[19] In 1523 a group of Franciscans, including Fray Pedro de Gante, arrived. In 1524 the famous group of twelve Franciscans known as the "Twelve Apostles" came.[20] Baptism and religious conversion began in earnest at that time. Folio 24v depicts a tenth friar baptizing an indigenous man over a font. The oddly drawn indigenous figure may be interpreted as having removed the top part of the white robe that he wears for the baptism, the collar and sleeves of which hang behind his back at the waist.

Above and between the friars, a *volador* performance is shown. The image in Codex Azcatitlan recalls the performance as it is practiced today. Four *voladores* (flyers) attach themselves with ropes to a small platform at the top of the pole. They slowly descend, while a fifth sits atop the platform and plays a drum or flute. The four dancers revolve around the pole thirteen times for a total of fifty-two revolutions.

As practiced today, the ceremony recalls the pre-Hispanic *toxiuhmolpilli* (binding of the years) that occurred at the end of a 52-year cycle. As art historian Annabeth Headrick has noted, "the fifty-two circumambulations indicate a strong calendrical association for the ritual and implicate the tree in creation symbolism." She also describes the *palo volador* as one of three Mexica "tree-raising ceremonies" that carried significant ritual and cosmic significance. The other two did not endure. The ceremony for the Tota (Our Father) tree was performed during the Feast of the Waters. The celebration of the *xocotl* (precious pine) took place during the Small Feast of the Dead and the Great Feast of the Dead.[21] These ceremonies were an integral part of annual ritual activities associated with sacrifice, making them a more immediate target of Spanish Catholics.

The fact that the *palo volador* tradition has endured suggests that Spanish friars did not directly associate the performance with sacrifice and pre-Hispanic ritual practices. On folio 24v the compositional integration of the *palo volador* scene with the depictions of friars and baptism suggests that the scenes are related and that the performance may have functioned as a celebration of the arrival of the friars or even of the sacrament itself.[22] The flyers wear bird wings that might be read as angels within a Christian setting. Friars aware of the calendric significance of the *palo volador* may have fostered the connections between the renewal implied by the completion of a 52-year cycle and the spiritual rebirth promised through the baptismal rite. The Codex Azcatitlan *tlacuilo* depicts the figure at the top of the pole holding a down ball, an emblem of Mexica culture, in his upraised hand. Taken together, the images mark the religious conversion of the Mexica and profound changes to ritual practice.

1522–1524: REBUILDING THE CITY

Immediately adjacent to the baptism, the *tlacuilo* depicts a two-story European style structure attached by a row of dotted lines to a hand holding an animal. Just below the hand are a *coa* (digging stick), wood, and water. These elements reference postconquest construction in the city. The image of a *coa* is paired with blocks of stone earlier in the manuscript to reference construction projects on folios 18r and 19v. Here the *tlacuilo* depicts the finished result of the construction, a two-story structure that uses the recently introduced arch and keystone technology on both levels. The form beneath the building resembles glyphic representations of plowed earth. However, instead of being contained within a neat rectangle, as in the toponym for Xochimilco, the glyph is defined by an uneven billowing line, evoking the disturbed earth or clouds of dust that accompany construction. As Barbara Mundy has noted, when Mexico-Tenochtitlan was rebuilt, only elite and civic structures like the *tecpan* (palace of indigenous government) or churches had two stories.[23] The *tecpan* structures are usually depicted with a row of *chalchiuhtlicue* (small circles that symbolize preciousness and mark the *tecpan*, as on the lower left of folio 25r), so this likely represents another type of structure, such as an elite residence. We can probably read this as a secular structure, because the *tlacuilo* does not depict a bell, cross, or other motif to designate a Christian function. An example of the *tlacuilo*'s depiction of a church can be found on folio 25r, where a chalice and wafer with a cross on it mark the Christian sacrament and the purpose of the structure.

The other type of construction referenced here by the wood and water relates to hydraulic work. The rectangular wood with water below resembles the wooden structures that appear in the water on folio 24r (figure 4.8). It also resembles the rectangle that appears atop a hill glyph on folio 17r, where the conquest of Xochimilco is followed by this image, a record of how the Tenochca *tlatoani* Itzcoatl ordered the Xochimilca to work on a southern causeway.[24] Taken together, this set of glyphs on folio 24v references the general rebuilding of the city and repair of the causeways that took place after the conquest. The unidentified glyph of the hand grasping a small animal head may relate to Tlacotl. After the conquest, when Cortés decided to establish his new capital city on the ruins of Tenochtitlan-Tlatelolco, he placed a Tenochca noble named Tlacotl in charge of the rebuilding and restored his former title of *cihuacoatl*.[25] In the high-ranking role of *cihuacoatl*, Tlacotl had advised Moteuczoma II, just as his grandfather Tlacaelel had advised his own brother, Moteuczoma I. Tlacotl, baptized don Juan Velázquez Tlacotzin, would oversee the tremendous labor force required to raze and rebuild the new capital until 1524, when Cortés brought Tlacotl and several other indigenous nobles on the Honduran expedition.[26]

1522–1524(?): BATTLE AT COLHUACAN

Above the images related to construction, a curved hill sign depicts Colhuacan. A shield and obsidian blade weapon top the *altepetl*, documenting a battle at this location. On either side of the hill are deceased figures. On the left the head of a *tlatoani* wearing a *xiuhhuitzolli* appears with his eyes closed, signaling death. Below is a glyph composed of an eye (*ixtli*) and water (*atl*). To the right a mummy bundle appears with a glyph for 2 Ehecatl (2 Wind). This set of glyphs may document one of the many postconquest conflicts. Its location on the page suggests an event that dates between 1522 and 1524.

Folios 24v–25r

1525–1526: DEATH OF CUAUHTEMOC, COANACOCH(?), TETLEPANQUETZAL, AND TLACOTL

The remaining images on folio 24v and all of the images on folio 25r relate to events that occurred during the years of Cortés's Honduran expedition. He had sent a conquistador named Cristóbal de Olid to conquer Honduras. During a refueling stop in Havana, however, Diego Velázquez, the governor of Cuba, convinced Olid to defect from Cortés and conquer the territory for himself. Cortés sent Francisco de las Casas after Olid but did not have confidence in his abilities. In October 1524 Cortés set out after Olid himself. To prevent rebellion in his absence, he brought a group of powerful indigenous nobles with him, many of whom had already been kept under his direct watch in Coyoacan. The group included Cuauhtemoc (ruler of Tenochtitlan), Coanacoch (ruler of Texcoco), Tetlepanquetzal (ruler of Tacuba), Oquitzin (ruler of Azcapotzalco), Temilotl (ruler of Tlatelolco), and other high officials such as the Tenochca *cihuacoatl* Tlacotl, Tlacatlec, and a figure known by variants such as "Cozte Mexi," "Mexicalcinco," and "Mexicatl Cozoololtic." Cortés departed for Honduras in October 1524 and returned in July 1526. During this period, several of the indigenous leaders were accused of a conspiracy and killed. At the same time, another plot unfolded in the Basin of Mexico as high-ranking Spaniards sought to undermine Cortés's authority.

On the upper right of folio 24v three small forms mark the ritual month of Tozoztontli, in which the death of Cuauhtemoc and the other lords occurred in the year 1525 (figure 5.3). The pierced bird in a jade ring represents this third month of the ritual calendar.[27] Susan Milbrath places this month in March or April, a period that corresponds with López de Gómara's assertion that the rulers were hung during Lent and Alva Ixtlilxochitl's dating of Shrove Tuesday (the day before Lent) in 1525.[28] The entries on this month in the Florentine Codex describe offerings of flayed skins and the first flowers of the season being brought to the pyramid named Yopico.[29] On folio 24v the conical cloth with the bent knees of a male figure below designates Yopitzinco.[30] The small horizontal mortuary bundle may represent the *malteutl* (god-captive) prepared during this month from a sacrificed captive's bundled and masked thigh bone.[31]

The pictorial account of Cuauhtemoc's death in Codex Azcatitlan has much in common with the narrative included in the Annals of Tlatelolco. The death of Cuauhtemoc is not included in Document 5, an annals history of the people of Tlatelolco.[32] The last lines of that document come from MS 22bis and simply reference how the "Capitán" and others went to Honduras, Guatemala, and Tehuantepec. In contrast, a dialogue-rich narration of Cuauhtemoc's death can be found in Document 1, the genealogy of the rulers of Tlatelolco. MS 22 begins Document 1 with the Mexica arrival at Chapultepec at the end of their migration, before the Tlatelolca had separated from the Tenochca. The *tlacuilo* names the Tlatelolca leaders and registers the installation of rulers and the length of their reigns. MS 22 ends with the fall of the last Tlatelolca *tlatoani*, Moquihuix, in the War of 1473.

At this point MS 22bis adds to the genealogy.[33] It begins by naming five "two-faced" Tlatelolca nobles, the "traitors" who brought Tlatelolco to a state of perdition. After naming them, the scribe reiterates: "These were the traitors. All were liars, men of two faces." The deception is illuminated through imagined dialogue between the traitors, the Tlatelolca ruler Moquihuix and the Tenochca ruler Axayacatl. Although the sovereignty of Tlatelolco ended at this time, the scribe notes: "They did not destroy it [Tlatelolco] completely."[34] The scribe then goes on to name the interim rulers (*cuauhtlatoque*) who governed Tlatelolco under the dominion of Tenochtitlan. Then the installation of Cuauhtemoc as *tlatoani* is presented as a resumption of the line of Tlatelolca rulers. The scribe states that Tenochtitlan had no *tlatoani*, only a dwarf named Mexicatl Cozoololtic and some of his friends.

A lengthy description of the betrayal and death of Cuauhtemoc through a series of dialogues follows. In this account Cuauhtemoc is presented not as a prisoner, kept under the watchful eye of Cortés, but as a dignified ruler who believes that he is on his way to Castile to meet the great *teotl* (god) who is *tlatoani* of Castile (the Spanish king). The dwarf Mexicatl is traveling with them; along the way, the huts of the Tenochca and the Tlatelolca are built in isolation from one another. Cuauhtemoc believes that his vassals in Acallan can help him and sends messengers ahead to contact them. Cuauhtemoc's vassals greet him warmly: the deferential lords shower him with lavish gifts and arrange a feast. After dinner and a speech by Cuauhtemoc exhorting the people to take care of the commoners, additional gifts are given and subsequently delivered to Cuauhtemoc's hut. The

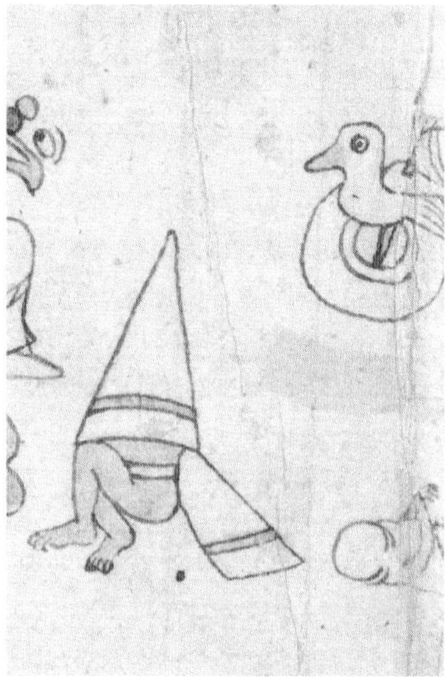

Figure 5.3. Codex Azcatitlan, folio 24v (detail). Courtesy of the Bibliothèque Nationale de France.

people of Acallan then bring out drums for the singing and dancing. Cuauhtemoc, Coanacoch (of Texcoco), and Tetlepanquetzal (of Tlacopan) dance the night away with the other lords. They do not bring their vassals. The magnanimous ruler Cuauhtemoc provides his vassals with food because they did not have any.

While the festivities are taking place, Mexicatl, who has not been invited, sits alone in his hut. He can hear the singing and drumming and see the beautiful green quetzal feathers from the isolation of his hut. The narrative implies that his jealousy provokes the betrayal. When Cortés's translator Malinche politely greets Mexicatl, he proceeds to tell her that he has overheard a plot to kill her and Cortés. As the three *tlatoque* finish another meal and retire from the festivities, they are immediately seized. Without any questioning, Cuauhtemoc is hanged from a ceiba tree, followed by Coanacoch and Tetlepanquetzal. The scribe tells us that from then on the Tlatelolca called Cozte Mexi a liar. Through Malinche, Cortés tells Cozte Mexi that they are going to Castile without him and that he should head straight back to Tenochtitlan. Malinche tells Cozte Mexi that the Capitán Marqués (Cortés) will find him when they return from Hueymollan Acallan.

The representation of Cuauhtemoc's death on Codex Azcatitlan folios 24v–25r reflects the larger narrative shifts of the MS 22bis account. MS 22bis offers a detailed account of this episode and focuses on the role of the Tenochca traitor who betrayed Cuauhtemoc. The act of betrayal is prompted by jealousy and is initiated during the dancing and singing after the feast. The three most important *tlatoque*, the existing representatives of the former Triple Alliance, are unjustly hung. On the right side of folio 24v the three glyphs discussed above represent the month when the deaths occurred. Just below this and to the right of the construction imagery the dwarf named Mexicatl Cozoololtic appears as a nude male figure. On folio 25v the first set of images connected with dotted lines shows an indigenous lord bringing the drums out of a two-story structure and beginning a musical performance at a site in Acallan. The second set of images connected by dots references the imminent deaths by hanging of the *tlatoque* at Hueymollan Acallan and Cortés's subsequent appointment of the Tlacatecatl Tlacotl as *gobernador* of Tenochtitlan.

In MS 22bis the traitor is described as a dwarf named "Mexicatl Cozoololtic" and later referred to as "Cozte Mexi." In Chimalpahin's records he is referred to as "Cotztemexi."[35] The unflattering designation "Cozoololtic," shortened in the other two appellations, indicates that Mexicatl's calves were as round as balls.[36] Mexicatl derives from the name of a Basin of Mexico site, Mexicatzinco. Alva Ixtlilxochitl says that Coztemexi "was a native of Iztapalapan or, according to others, Mexicalcinco."[37] Durán states that during the migration of the Mexica a *temazcalli* (steam bath) was built at a site that was later named Mexicatzinco.[38] The name of this figure seems to be made up of various combinations of the following: Coz[ooloTltic] + *te[mazcalli]* + Mexicat[zinco]. The nude figure with bent knees on folio 24v resembles (in positioning and bare legs) the figure identified with the migration stop at Mexicatzinco on folio 11v (figure 3.6). The bent knees in both suggest the phonetic element *-tzin*, as in the designation for Yopitzinco on folio 24v. The nudity of the figure also suggests an association with the *temazcalli*. While the figure's legs are not excessively distorted, they are less smoothly rendered than those of the other figures on folios 24v–25r, perhaps signaling the "calves as round as balls."

Throughout the postconquest pages of Codex Azcatitlan name glyphs are generally lacking and have not been added systematically. The *tlacuilo* may have intended to represent Mexicatl Cozoololtic by glyph only. Alternatively, the image may be intended to serve as both a name glyph and a pictorial representation. This would be unusual but not entirely without precedent in Codex Azcatitlan. On folio 11v the figure associated with the gloss Mexicatzinco apparently simultaneously references the name of the site and functions like the other participants in the migration, who appear seated at various points along the path (figure 5.4). Likewise, a woman on a bed and a child in a cradle on the same folio designate Mixiuhcan (Place of Childbirth) (figure 5.4). The two figures simultaneously represent the action that precipitated the naming of the site and name the site. The woman who has just given birth also functions as a migratory participant, gesturing in the direction of the path that the Mexica will follow. If the *tlacuilo* chose to represent the reviled Mexicatl Cozoololtic through his glyph, he may have capitalized on the added associations between nudity and captives. While prisoners in Codex Azcatitlan are shown being grasped by the forelock (folio 15v) or controlled by a rope about the neck (folio 18r), there is also a long-standing Mesoamerican tradition of depicting slaves and captives nude and in awkward positions.

As in the Annals of Tlatelolco narrative, the figure representing Mexicatl Cozoololtic is distanced from the festivities. He faces but is not a part of the scene with the drums on folio 25r. The host of this musical entertainment carries a staff and wears sandals that resemble those of the *tlatoque* in the ruler list. He does not, however, wear a *xiuhhuitzolli*, and his clothing is unusual.[39] This figure may represent the Maya king who governed the province of Acallan and provided Cortés and the lords with food and supplies.

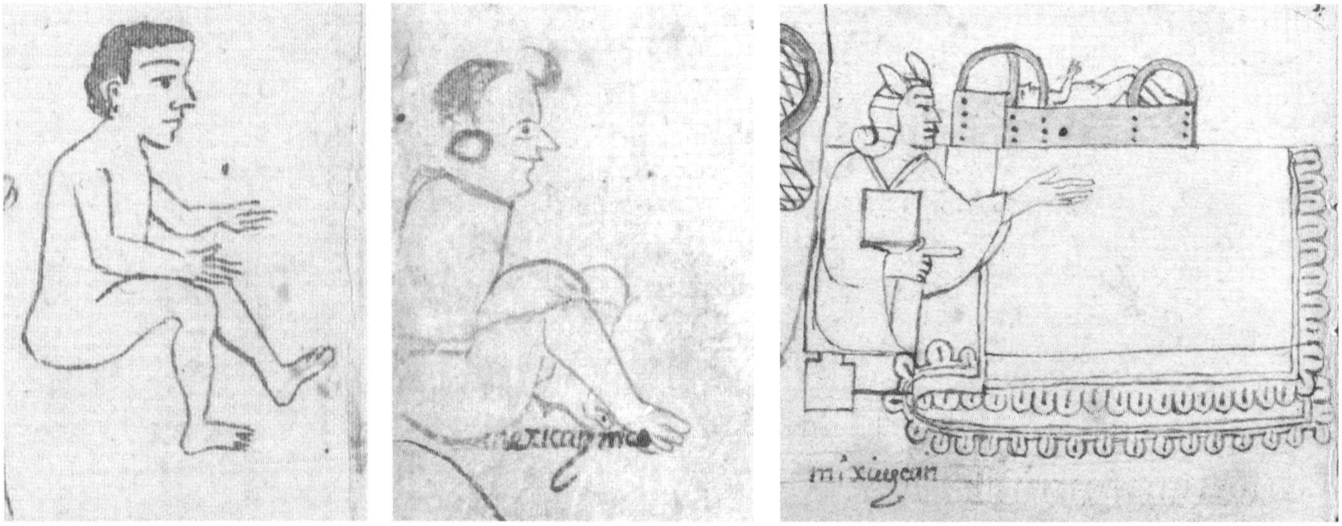

Figure 5.4. Codex Azcatitlan, folio 24v (detail), depicting Mexicatl Cozoololtic; folio 11v (detail), depicting Mexicatzinco; folio 11v (detail), depicting Mixiuhcan. Courtesy of the Bibliothèque Nationale de France.

A Chontal Maya account of Cuauhtemoc's death describes the Maya king Paxbolonacha as a generous host, but one obliged to share Cuauhtemoc's plot with Cortés.[40]

The two-story Renaissance-style structure from which this figure retrieves the drums represents an important civic or private structure. This was the Chontal Mayas' first encounter with the Spaniards, so no such buildings would have existed.[41] As in the massacre during the feast of Toxcatl scene (folio 23r), where the arcaded building appears in the background, this anachronism is meant as a communication device to facilitate the intended audience's understanding. Two-story private and civic structures with arched entries or arcades were built after the conquest (as documented on folio 24v) and signaled elite use. Such choices reveal the *tlacuilo*'s desire to communicate his history in a way that would be understood by his contemporaries, in this case a Nahuatl-speaking Tlatelolca audience living in the rebuilt city several decades after the conquest.

Drums just below the structure mark the performance, and a water glyph may indicate location. The *tlacuilo* positions the first drum below the church horizontally, like a *teponaztli* (slit-drum), but the crisscrossed ropes imply a vertical *huehuetl* drum. The second image shows a vantage point from above as two hands play on the skin of a vertical *huehuetl* drum. The glyph for water that flows in three directions may reference a more specific geographic location. Alva Ixtlilxochitl's account also describes the festivities that preceded Cuauhtemoc's death and their location near a river:

> They arrived early in the morning on the bank of the big river, the same one that lets out at Cohuatzacualco. When they arrived, they built some huts or lodgings made of straw so that Cortés and his men could stay in them. They built separate ones for their kings behind the main temple. The Spaniards were celebrating Carnival, just as the natives had seen them do in years past, which coincided with native celebrations. Following their ancient custom, the natives greatly rejoiced this day and night. It was common for our forces to celebrate when they reached a new place, but here the rejoicing was greater for the aforementioned reasons, and because they were nearing the end of the long journey. Cortés had told them that from Acalan they would turn back without going any farther.[42]

Alva Ixlilxochitl's account accords with the prominence of the all-night feasting and music described in MS 22bis. The next set of connected images documents the deadly aftermath of the festivities.

Dotted lines connect three figures who wear the *xiuhhuitzolli*. Two are represented in full length, seated on a *petlatl icpalli*, while a third image shows just the head of a *tlatoani* with a closed eye signifying death. As the former leader of the Triple Alliance, Cuauhtemoc was the most prestigious victim. His death is recorded in all accounts of this plot. Although name glyphs for the enthroned rulers had not yet been added, the staff carried by the lower enthroned figure sets him apart and may designate Cuauhtemoc. MS 22bis names Coanacoch of Texcoco and Tetlepanquetzal as additional victims.[43] Alva Ixtlilxochitl says that all three were hung but that Coanacoch was cut down when his brother Ixtlilxochitl threatened retaliation; in his account Coanacoch dies a few days later from "bloody diarrhea brought on by heartache and sadness."[44] Cortés claims that he hung Cuauhtemoc and Tetlepanquetzal but released the others.[45] To the right of the head with a closed eye is a glyph that names the Tepanec ruler Tetlepanquetzal: *tetl* (stone) + *pan[tli]* (flag) + *quetzal* (quetzal feather).[46] Because the two enthroned rulers are depicted alive, the head with a closed eye (wearing a *xiuhhuitzolli*) likely functions as a reference to the death of the rulers rather than as the representation of one individual. The upper enthroned figure may represent Tetlepanquetzal. In this case the head with the closed eye may represent the death of both Cuauhtemoc and Tetlepanquetzal. Alternatively, the upper enthroned figure may represent Coanacoch of Texcoco. As the Tepanec contingent was always the least powerful member of the Triple Alliance, the *tlacuilo* may have opted to name Tetlepanquetzal without depicting him in the limited compositional space.[47] In this reading the head with the closed eye would represent the death of all three rulers.

To the right of the glyph for Tetlepanquetzal are three other glyphs. The glyph for Xochimilco, *xochi[tl]* (flower) + *mil[pa]* (field) + *-co* (locative suffix) is well known and appears in other parts of Codex Azcatitlan. To the right of this are two glyphs that name Hueymollan Acallan, the same location cited in MS 22bis.[48] The image of a large *molcajete* (grinding bowl) represents Hueymollan: *huey* (large) + *mol[cajete]* (grinding bowl) + *-lan* (locative suffix). The image of *a[tl]* (water) + *cal[li]* + *-lan* (locative suffix) represents Acallan.[49] The possible significance of the Xochimilco glyph is discussed below.

The dotted line that extends from Cuauhtemoc leads to a place glyph with a circle on top. A similar toponym appears in Codex Mendoza on folio 51r, where it is identified as Tlatlauhquitepec. Just as Hueymollan Acallan marks the site of the death of the rulers, Tlatlauhquitepec marks the site of the death of Tlacotl. Chimalpahin's sources claim that Cortés appointed "Tlacotzin cihuacoatl" ruler as soon as Cuauhtemoc and Tetlepanquetzal were hung in Hueymollan and that Tlacotl died that same year in Seven House (1525):

> And the Marquis at once installed don Juan Velásquez Tlacotzin cihuacoatl as ruler. He was a grandson of Tlacaeleltzin cihuacoatl. He then would have ruled Tenochtitlan, but as the rulers were turning back and were already in Nochiztlan, the ruler, don Juan Velásquez Tlacotzin cihuacoatl, died. And then, in the said same year, Seven House, Motelchiuhtzin assumed the rulership. He was interim ruler of Tenochtitlan.
>
> And the ruler Quauhtemoctzin, son of Ahuitzotzin, had held the rulership of Tenochtitlan for only five years. And he left only a daughter, a noblewoman, who likewise has disappeared.
>
> There [in Huey Mollan] the Spaniards gave [Tlacotzin] their [type of] clothing and a sword, a dagger, and a white horse.[50]

This passage indicates that Tlacotl died "as the rulers were turning back": in other words, once they had already reached Honduras and were returning to Mexico. While Cortés departed from Trujillo for his return journey by brigantine, he had left troops behind in Naco under the command of Captain Luis Marín. This group returned overland; Tlacotl and Bernal Díaz del Castillo were among them. On the way, they caught up with Pedro de Alvarado's party, who had been sent to look for Cortés. As the groups joined and headed north, they lost some members of their party. As Díaz del Castillo writes: "From this place we marched to Soconusco and Teguantepec [Tehuantepec], where two of our countrymen, and the Mexican cazique Juan Velasquez, who had been commander-in-chief under Quauhtemoctzin, died on the road."[51] Chimalpahin's sources place the site of Tlacotl's death a bit farther along in the Mixteca Alta region, when they were "already in Nochiztlan [Place of Scarlet]."[52] Codex Azcatitlan seems to identify the same location. Tlatlauhquitepec (On the Red Hill), with its similar appellation, may refer to the same place.[53]

Chimalpahin describes Cortés providing the newly appointed Tlacotl with European clothes, weapons, and a horse, Spanish status symbols that reflected his new rank.[54] On folio 25r Tlacotl appears as the bust of a figure in Spanish dress. The Codex Azcatitlan *tlacuilo* takes several measures to undermine Tlacotl visually. Unlike the enthroned *tlatoque* above him, he is turned left, away from the forward flow of time. He is painted as a bust rather than as a full-length figure and positioned at the bottom of the page. His clothing aligns him more closely with the Spaniards than with the *tlatoque* that preceded him. The *tlacuilo* may accord him this diminished status because he ruled for such a brief time and with no real exercise of power.[55] As in the Chimalpahin passage, "[h]e then would have ruled Tenochtitlan" if he had not died. Similarly, although the Tenochca ruler Cuitlahua reigned briefly after Moteuczoma's death and before Cuauhtemoc's ascension, the Codex Azcatitlan *tlacuilo* does not bother to depict him.[56]

This series of connected images ends on the lower left of folio 25r with a house, adorned with small circles that signify preciousness and mark this space as a *tecpan* (royal house). A *xiuhhuitzolli* appears within it and a length of rope beneath it, which likely references the hangings at Hueymollan. The *xiuhhuitzolli*, representing rulership but not an individual ruler, may reflect the end of Tenochtitlan's royal line of pre-Hispanic *tlatoque*.

As demonstrated in other parts of the manuscript, sets of images that relate to or express a single event do not necessarily show a single moment in time or a neat progression from moment to moment. While they sometimes have scenic aspects, the images are more emblematic and symbolic. Despite the European stylistic influence, they are still designed for an oral function, much like those in Codex Boturini. Multiple temporal and geographic moves are linked together with the dotted lines in this last set of images. The rulers are alive; they die as the result of a traitorous act at Hueymollan Acallan. A new ruler of lesser status is installed by Cortés but dies on the return journey at Tlatlauhquitepec. These events lead to a *tecpan* that is for the moment empty. As Cortés was separated from this group and would not have been immediately aware of Tlacotl's death, the seat of power would remain vacant until Cortés was informed and appointed Motelchiuh as his replacement.

The *tlacuilo* uses subtle, understated methods to record the death of Cuauhtemoc and the other leaders. Rather than depicting the hanging (as, for example, on folio 90r of Codex Vaticanus A), he shows the leaders alive and documents the death through the empty *tecpan* with a rope underneath and perhaps through the glyph of a *tlatoani* head with a closed eye. This is similar to the way he references the carnage of the conquest with a small pile of bones rather than with a scene of bloodied and dismembered bodies. The *tlacuilo* continues to highlight indigenous strength while discreetly recording indigenous suffering and death.

At the core of this narrative, from the calendar month Tozoztontli to the empty *tecpan*, these related images convey a story of unwarranted betrayal and death, fueled by the jealousy of an ignominious rival. The impact of the betrayal was profound. With Cuauhtemoc's death, the Mexica lost the last pre-Hispanic *huey tlatoani* of Tenochtitlan or Tenochtitlan-Tlatelolco, as the *tlacuilo* might have viewed it. As the *tlacuilo* added the various components of this narrative, the visual signs that would cue an oral history, he placed a reference to Xochimilco just before the glyphs for Hueymollan Acallan. The location of this place name seems to signal that Coztemexi's lie was the most significant betrayal since the Xochimilca betrayal during the conquest in 1521.

Florentine Codex book 12 devotes chapter 33 to this event. It occurs just before the rout of Cortés and the taking of the banner described in chapters 34 and 35. Sahagún's Nahua informants explain that people of Xochimilco, Cuitlahuac, Mizquic, Colhuacan, Mexicatzinco, and Iztapalapan came to Cuauhtemoc offering to help fight against the Spaniards. Cuauhtemoc accepted their offer and provided them with warrior devices and shields as well as cacao. When the fighting resumed, the Xochimilca initiated the betrayal and led an attack against Cuauhtemoc's forces.

> But these Xochimilco people, though then they too set up a clamor and hurled themselves in their boats, did not help us at all, but started snatching people. They snatched the women and little children and also the old women; then they killed some of them there and they expired. The others they did not kill, but, uncontested, lowered them into the boats.[57]

Although many groups are described as participating in the plot, chapter 33 makes it clear that the Xochimilca lead the betrayal and are the primary offenders. In this passage they are described not as valiant, worthy foes but as attackers of women, children, and the elderly. According to the narrative, Cuauhtemoc quickly retaliates, killing the Xochimilca, taking captives, and freeing all of the hostages. Mayehuatzin, the ruler of Cuitlahuac, is presented as having been unaware of the scheme. He greets the captives by saying: "You wretches, did I invite you? What have you done?"[58] Upon Cuauhtemoc's invitation to "do his service," Mayehuatzin then sacrifices four of his own men. Cuauhtemoc sacrifices an additional four men and then orders that all remaining captives be sacrificed in the temples. By picturing Coztemexi and referencing Xochimilco, the Codex Azcatitlan *tlacuilo* identifies and names infamous traitors. This recalls the focus on traitors in the MS 22bis contributions to the "Genealogy of the Tlatoque of Tlatelolco" in the Annals of Tlatelolco. There the scribe calls out Tlatelolco's traitors, the "two-faced liars," and incorporates Coztemexi as a leading protagonist in the account of Cuauhtemoc's death.

Folio 25r

1524–1526: PLOT AGAINST CORTÉS

The theme of betrayal and death continues on the right side of folio 25r, where a plot against Cortés initiated in 1524 is documented.[59] Cortés departed for Honduras in October 1524.[60] Before leaving, he placed the *tesorero* (treasurer) Alonso de Estrada, the *contador* (accountant) Rodrigo de Albornoz, and *justicia mayor* (justice) Alonso Zuazo in charge. He took two other high-ranking Spanish officials on the journey to Honduras, the *factor* (tax collector) Gonzalo de Salazar and the *veedor* (auditor) Pedro Almíndez Chirino. All five of these individuals were appointees of the Crown, sent to assist and oversee Cortés, who had been granted the titles of governor and captain general of New Spain in 1522. Shortly after Cortés departed for Honduras, he received reports of escalating disagreements between Estrada and Albornoz. When a written reprimand failed to solve the problem, he sent Salazar and Chirino back to settle the matter. They were given "secret papers" that authorized Salazar and Chirino to take power if necessary. When they arrived in Mexico at the end of the year, Estrada and Albornoz had resolved their differences, but Salazar and Chirino deployed the secret papers immediately to seize power. A power struggle ensued that would persist until Cortés's return in June 1526.

Codex Azcatitlan folio 25r appears to reference some of the most notable events of the intrigues. The two deceased figures mark the two occasions on which individuals were killed. The deceased figure on the upper right surrounded by candles represents the 1525 torture and death of Cortés's cousin Rodrigo de Paz. The church represents the Church of San Francisco, where supporters of Cortés (including Rodrigo's brother Pedro) took refuge. This is also where funeral rites for the still-living Cortés were held as false rumors of his death began to circulate. In late 1525 or early 1526 Salazar violated the sanctuary by forcibly taking the supporters of Cortés that he identified as "traitors." When Fray Martín de Valencia excommunicated the whole town, the prisoners were returned. While Salazar was doing this, Chirino went to quell an indigenous uprising in Oaxaca, where he continued his practice of trying to extort gold and other treasures.[61] At the end of January 1526 a member of Cortés's party returned with new papers authorizing the arrest of Salazar and Chirino. They were imprisoned in wooden cages. During the week of Easter 1526, a locksmith who had been petitioned to create keys for the cages turned in a group plotting to free Salazar and Chirino. Estrada had the culprits arrested and seven ringleaders executed, including three *hidalgos* (members of the Spanish nobility), who were beheaded rather than hung because of their high station.

The *tlacuilo* depicts Salazar, Chirino, and Estrada on folio 25r. Salazar and Chirino are connected by a dotted line. At the far left Salazar is also connected to the Church of San Francisco and an adjacent image of the deceased Paz. Paz is surrounded by four large candles, the flames of which have not yet been painted.[62] Both he and Chirino were responsible for the torture and death of Paz. The figure in military dress represents Chirino, and the attached treasure chest relates to his attempts to seize gold and treasure of both indigenous peoples and Cortés. The treasure chest with coins above may also serve to identify Chirino in his role as *veedor*. As inspector, he was the royal official in charge of income paid in coin or precious metals.[63] The dotted line does not connect Salazar and Chirino to the next figure. However, Chirino's gesture leads the viewer to Estrada and the subsequent events resulting from Salazar's and Chirino's actions. Another dotted line connects Estrada to the executions that he ordered. The plumed hat of the executed *hidalgo* signals his high status.

Alva Ixtlilxochitl's account provides insight into why the juxtaposition of Cuauhtemoc's death and the plots against Cortés might have been relevant to an indigenous audience. The far right of folio 24v and all of folio 25r represent events that took place between 1524 and 1526. On the left are events that relate to the Honduran expedition. On the right are events that took place in central Mexico. In Alva Ixtlilxochitl's account the intrigues against Cortés are included to document abuses against the indigenous peoples, to demonstrate indigenous valor (he describes one group escaping from Chirino with their gold and riches), and as further proof that Cuauhtemoc's death was unjust:

> During the period that Alonso de Estrada was governor, he meted out punishments, chastened the Spaniards, and brought peace to Mexico. This clearly shows that Quauhtemoc and the rest of the lords died unjustly and that they were falsely accused; their vassals never rose up or took up arms against the Spaniards. Even though the vassals complained about the wrongs the Spaniards committed against them, their lords always replied that they should bear it with the love of God. They also said to follow the example of their kings and lords and consider their long and arduous journey, which was filled with hardships, and on which they were famished, sunburned, and frostbitten. Since their lords bore it with much patience, they should do the same. And so it is true, as I have said, that the hopeless and persecuted natives would not have left a single Spaniard alive if it had not been for the love of their lords. . . . But those

> who have written or said that Quauhtemoc and the others were killed because they wanted to kill the Spaniards say this only, as is well known, to cover up their misdeeds and treason. Perhaps we could believe them if there were a native history or native person who said this to be true, but there is no history or account that does. All the histories, accounts, and natives of New Spain agree that it was a false accusation and an act of great tyranny.[64]

Alva Ixtlilxochitl's account presents the indigenous peoples as fully capable of having staged an uprising; he suggests that only the discouragement of their lords kept them from doing so.[65] He argues that these lords could have killed the Spaniards easily and did not, which proved that the accusations against Cuauhtemoc and the others were fabricated. Since folio 25r juxtaposes Cuauhtemoc's death with these events, an oral presentation might have been accompanied by such rhetoric.

The death of Cortés's cousin Rodrigo de Paz also might have carried additional significance when juxtaposed with Cuauhtemoc's injustices. After having manipulated Paz in the course of their machinations, Salazar and Chirino leveled trumped-up charges of treason against him in August 1525.[66] As Cortés's mayordomo, Paz had been managing the conquistador's home and estate during the Honduran expedition. After taking possession of Cortés's property and looting it, Salazar and Chirino sought the additional wealth that they thought Paz had hidden from them. They tortured him by pouring boiling oil on his feet and then hung him so that he could not testify against them.[67] This punishment and the reasons behind it, enacted against Cortés's cousin and the keeper of his estate, probably seemed a fitting recompense for the torture and eventual death of Cuauhtemoc.

Shortly after the conquest Cuauhtemoc's feet were burned at Cortés's bidding to coerce a confession of hidden treasure. The Annals of Tlatelolco states that "they turned to the Tenochtitlan rulers and interrogated them. At this time they burned Quauhtemoctzin on the feet. And at dawn they brought them, tied to poles, and they came and tied them to poles at the home [palace] of Ahuitzotzin in Acatliyacapan."[68]

López de Gómara explains that they were seeking Moteuczoma's treasure: "The gold that our men had taken in Mexico was not all recovered; nor was a trace of Moctezuma's famous treasure ever found. The Spaniards were much annoyed at this, for they had thought, once Mexico had been taken, to find a great hoard, or at least as much as they had lost in the retreat." López de Gómara states that Cortés stopped Cuahtemoc's torture, "either because he thought it degrading and cruel, or because [Cuauhtemoc] had told him that, ten days before his capture, the devil had informed him he was going to be defeated, so he had thrown the [captured] guns, his gold and silver, precious stones, pearls, and rich jewels into the water."[69]

According to López de Gómara, one of Cortés's motives in torturing Cuauhtemoc was to combat rumors that he had kept the treasure for himself:

> In his residencia Cortés was charged with the crime of putting a great king to death in this shameful fashion, and with doing so from avarice and cruelty. Cortés defended himself by saying that he had acted at the request of Julián de Alderete, the King's treasurer; also, to bring the truth to light, for everyone was saying that he had kept all the treasure of Moctezuma for himself and had not wanted to torture [Cuauhtemoc], lest this fact be laid bare. Many, acting on Cuauhtemoc's words, sought the treasure in the lake and on land, but it was never found. And truly it was a remarkable thing that he could have hidden such a quantity of gold and silver and not reveal it.[70]

These persistent rumors that Cortés had somehow recovered Moteuczoma's treasure and kept it for himself had led to the later torture and death of Paz.

Folio 25v

The images depicted on the final page, folio 25v, can be dated with less certainty (figure 5.5). Given the sequence of dating on the preceding two pages, readers might expect to find events related to 1527 or 1528. On the leftmost side of the page the *tlacuilo* records an astronomical or weather-related event, with a mummy bundle and a glyph composed of a tree and water beneath. The figures on horseback and the indigenous lord depicted on the upper register of folio 25v record the October 1527 arrival of the first bishop in New Spain, Fray Julián Garcés. As we have seen on folios 24v–25r, the chronological reading order of these pages proceeds more or less from left to right and from top to bottom. Thus the final set of images in the manuscript is located on the lower half of folio 25v. They represent further acts of torture undertaken by a Spaniard in an effort to recover the lost treasure of Moteuczoma.

Folio 25v

1527(?): A NATURAL EVENT

The upper part of folio 25v has sustained substantial damage, complicating an interpretation of the first vertical column of information. At the top a partial image of what appears to be a cloud with lightning survives. Alternatively, the image may represent a

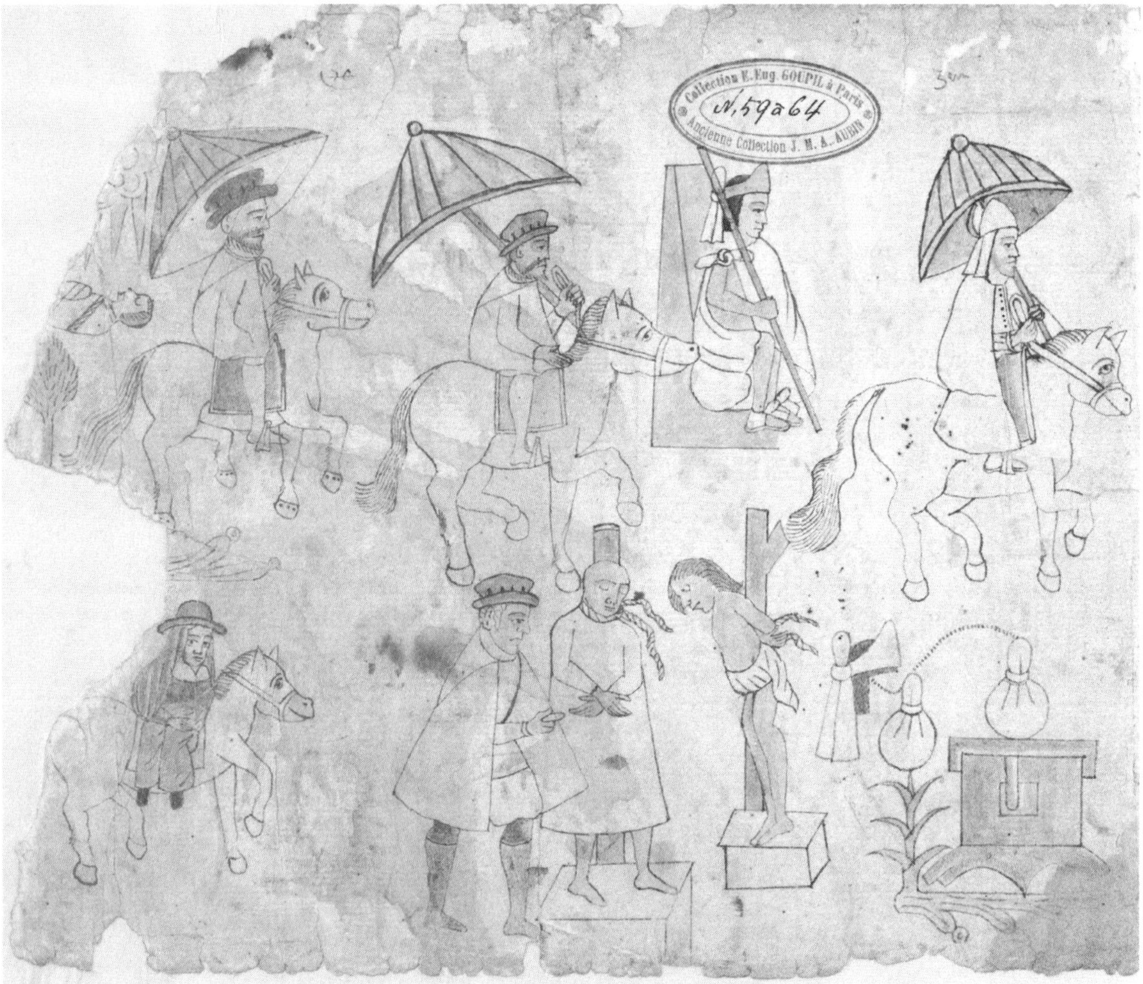

Figure 5.5. Codex Azcatitlan, folio 25v. Courtesy of the Bibliothèque Nationale de France.

comet, solar eclipse, or other natural event. Below this motif the *tlacuilo* painted a partially bundled human figure with a stone on his chest. The unwrapped head has a closed eye, signaling death. The stone on his chest indicates a death by stoning. Together the images may document a death related to natural disaster. As the glosses and images in the migration section make clear, significant natural phenomena are often recorded. The motif of a tree and a flow of water may mark the calendar month of this event, Atlcahualo.

Folio 25v

1527: ARRIVAL OF FRAY JULIÁN GARCÉS, THE FIRST BISHOP IN MEXICO

The upper register of folio 25v depicts a bishop on horseback, wearing his miter and ecclesiastical clothing. Behind the bishop is a seated indigenous ruler depicted in the same manner as Cuauhtemoc on the previous page. Two Spanish men on horseback follow the bishop in procession. All of the men on horseback carry red and yellow umbrellas. A female figure, depicted slightly smaller and on the lower part of the page, joins the procession. This scene may depict the December 1528 arrival in New Spain of bishop-elect Juan de Zumárraga, who would be consecrated at a later point in 1533.[71] However, because he was not yet an acting bishop and because the previous page records information from 1526, it seems more likely that this represents the arrival in Mexico City of Fray Julián Garcés, bishop of Tlaxcala, in October 1527.[72] As López de Gómara states: "All the priests and friars of the city, bearing crosses, came out to welcome him, for he was the first bishop of the country."[73] A Dominican, Garcés had founded the first bishopric in 1519 at Santa María de los Remedios de Yucatan before becoming the first acting bishop of New Spain in 1525 in the Diocese of Tlaxcala.[74] Díaz del Castillo also describes his arrival and the processions that welcomed him: "Don Julián Garcés arrived from Spain, in order to enter upon the new bishopric of Tlascalla. . . . As intelligence of his approach had reached this town, the whole of the clergy in grand pomp, the chief authorities, the Conquistadores, and all the officers and soldiers then in Mexico went out to meet him."[75]

Reading this figure as Garcés suggests connections to the plot against Cortés recorded on the preceding page, folio 25r. According to López de Gómara, the day that Garcés arrived in the city was the same day that Alonso de Estrada exiled Cortés. Shortly after Cortés returned from the Honduran expedition in June 1526, his powers were curtailed when Luis Ponce de León arrived from Spain as the newly appointed governor of New Spain. Because it was politically expedient, Cortés accepted the authority of the royal appointee, but Ponce de León died that same month. Before dying, he appointed an elderly and ailing successor, Marco de Aguilar. According to López de Gómara, Aguilar had long suffered from syphilis and died from this and other complications shortly thereafter. Before he died, he appointed the treasurer Alonso de Estrada as his successor. López de Gómara summarized the event that led to Cortés's exile as follows:

> Now it happened that several retainers of Cortés stabbed a captain during a quarrel. One of them was arrested, and that very day Estrada had the man's right hand cut off and sent him to jail into the bargain—this to show his scorn of Cortés. He also exiled Cortés to prevent him from releasing the prisoner—such a scandalous act that Mexico was on the point of bloodshed that day, and even of ruin. Cortés, however, met the situation by leaving the city to begin his exile.[76]

This precipitous event occurred on the same day that Garcés had landed in Texcoco.[77] Garcés reconciled the two, but tensions persisted. Facing rumors that he had poisoned Ponce de León and Aguilar, and still trying to recover property taken when Paz was attacked, Cortés left New Spain for the Spanish court in March 1528.[78]

While the bishop is identifiable because of his clothing and miter, none of the figures are named.

If these images reflect the events of 1527, the seated indigenous governor would most likely represent either Motelchiuh, the governor of Tenochtitlan, or Temilotl, the governor of Tlatelolco. The figures on horseback are spread out over the page, in what appears to be a scenic expansion of the event. The horses and umbrellas indicate the high status of these individuals. While the two upper figures are clearly men, the gender of the lower figure is more ambiguous.

Both male and female identities have been proposed for this figure. Barlow has little to say but identifies it as female because of the sidesaddle riding position.[79] Castañeda de la Paz and Oudijk have noted the ambiguity of this figure as well, siding with an interpretation of the figure as a male cleric.[80] As these authors note, despite the sidesaddle position used by women and the appearance of long hair, it would be very unusual to depict a woman in a hat and pants. This figure probably represents a highly unusual woman, a Spaniard named María de Estrada who formed part of Cortés's expedition and is referenced in the writings of Diego Durán, Bernal Díaz del Castillo, Diego Muñoz Camargo, Francisco Cervantes de Salazar, Antonio de Herrera y Tordesillas, and Juan de Torquemada.[81] These accounts indicate that after the conquest she married Pedro Sánchez Farfán and later Alonso Martínez Partidor. They also cite her willingness to participate on the battlefield and her skill in battle, which rivaled that of men.

Diego Durán describes an episode featuring María de Estrada in the last chapter of his *History*, where he sums up some notable events that occurred in the years after the conquest: "After Cortés had conquered the Valley of Mexico, he went forth to subdue other provinces, especially those we now call the Marquesado, the hot country."

> Here is a story I was told about a woman who accompanied Cortés's army and who later was married to Martín Partidor. As Cortés was leaving Huaxtepec after having subdued the entire hot country, he passed through Ocuituco, where he was received in peace. After this he ascended to a town called Tetela, where the Indians were lined up in order to fight, having much confidence in the rugged nature of the place. Other Indians from Hueyapan, which faced Tetela across a deep ravine, also appeared in a warlike manner. When Cortés saw these forces, he ordered his men to prepare themselves. But this Spanish woman, advised by certain soldiers, mounted a horse, took a lance and leather shield, and asked the Spanish captain for permission to attack the Indians and demonstrate her personal valor. Cortés granted her this, whereupon she came forth and, spurring on the horse, she attacked the enemy, shouting, "Saint James, and at them!" The foot soldiers then followed her; when the Indians saw them all coming, some fled and others fell into the ravine. The town was taken and all the leading men came with their hands crossed to surrender to Cortés. When he realized the bravery of the woman, Cortés granted her the control of the two towns of Tetela and Hueyapan in the name of His Majesty.[82]

While Durán does not give the woman's name, he identifies her as later marrying "[Alonso] Martín Partidor," one of the conquistadors who would found the city of Puebla. This allows us to identify the Spanish woman he describes as María de Estrada. In Durán's account she demonstrates the bravery and valor of a male conquistador and is richly compensated.[83]

Like Durán, Bernal Diaz del Castillo notes that this woman accompanied Cortés's army, calling her the "courageous and excellent María de Estrada." He names her as one of the survivors of the Noche Triste and the only Spanish woman in their party at that time: "I have forgotten to write about the joy we felt in seeing alive doña Marina and doña Luisa, the daughter of Xicotenga, who some Tlaxcalans had saved at the bridges, and also a woman named María de Estrada, for she was the only Spanish woman we had with us in Mexico." Earlier in his text, when detailing the lineup of forces during the evacuation of Tenochtitlan on the Noche Triste, he does not include María de Estrada among the protected women: "three hundred Tlaxcalans and thirty soldiers were designated to take charge of the prisoners and doña Marina and doña Luisa."[84] Perhaps she was not as important as Cortés's primary translator or the daughter of his closest ally. But the conquistadors thought of her as quite capable of protecting herself. As Diego Muñoz Camargo writes: "María de Estrada displayed valor, doing marvelous, heroic deeds with a sword and buckler in her hands, fighting bravely with so much fury and spirit, that she outdid the effort of any man, no matter how brave and valiant he might be."[85] The figure at the lower left on folio 25r of Codex Azcatitlan blends both masculine and feminine traits, just as the brief references to María de Estrada in scripted sources suggest a woman who has taken on a male role.

As a prominent Spaniard, María de Estrada could have been among the party meeting Garcés on his arrival in 1527. Shortly after the conquest she had married Pedro Sánchez Farfán, who held an appointment as *regidor* (commissioner) of Mexico City between 1525 and 1527. She may later have had direct involvement with Garcés as well. After Sánchez Farfan's death in 1536, she married Alonso Martínez Partidor and helped found the city of Puebla de los Ángeles.[86] The young city, close to Bishop Garcés's rural establishment in Tlaxcala, built a large church. Garcés would later move the episcopal see to Puebla de los Ángeles in 1539.[87] If this figure represents María de Estrada, the male figure above may be her husband.

Folio 25v

THE LOST TREASURE OF MOTEUCZOMA

The remaining figures on the lower register of folio 25v constitute another scene. A Spaniard holds something in his hand as he approaches two figures that stand on raised platforms and are bound to tall poles. The bound figures have closed eyes, signaling that they are deceased. The prisoner closest to the Spaniard has a shaved head and wears a long robe with no shoes. He is bound at the hands and neck. The other figure has his hands bound to the pole. He has long loose hair and wears a *maxtlatl*. A treasure box appears to the right of these figures. Above it a dotted line connects two bundles and a *xiuhhuitzolli*. A glyph formed of a reed and water frames the treasure box on the left and lower sides.

These images correspond to another event described in the final chapter of Durán's *History*:

> While the new city was being planned and Cortés rested, the Spaniards began to seek the treasure that had been found in the secret chambers. The Tlatelolcas, by command of their leader, had concealed it in a deep pool in the city that the Aztecs feared, due to a certain religious superstition. It was believed that this spring was the place discovered by their ancestors, where the red and blue waters flowed, where lived the white fish, the white frogs, the white snakes. This pool was never seen by the Spaniards, nor has anyone ever discovered its exact location. In order to find it Cortés ordered that many Indians be hunted down by dogs, others hanged, and yet others be burned alive so that the secret might be revealed. However, it never came to light, nor has it been discovered in our times. In fact, it never will be found, as those who might have known about it are no longer alive. If this secret is in the possession of anyone, it would belong to the lords of Tlatelolco, to whom it was entrusted. For this treasure, the conquerors wept more tears than for the wicked deeds they had committed.[88]

The images to the right of María de Estrada in the lower register of Codex Azcatitlan folio 25v depict a scene of torture and a treasure box. The two figures who are dead at the hands of a Spaniard appear to have suffered punishments that were regularly employed in New Spain by conquistadors both during and after the conquest. In his scathing indictment of the conquistadors' behavior, for example,

Bartolomé de las Casas describes conquistadors burning indigenous people at the stake and engaging in acts of torture as methods of intimidation and seeking financial gain.[89] The two deceased figures are bound upright to a pole, so it is possible that this scene is meant to depict burning at the stake. On the previous folio the flames have not been painted onto the candles that surround the figure of Paz. If the *tlacuilo* intended to add flames here, that would account for the figures being deceased. The Spaniard may be depicted holding an incendiary device. The prisoner at left has a rope around his neck, so he may have been garroted before burning.

This kind of punishment is also consistent with Spanish Inquisition practices. Inquisition records of the 1530s indicate that punishments against the indigenous people included, among other things, binding hands and feet, forcing the punished to stand with bare feet, stripping clothing, shearing hair, and, in extreme cases, burning at the stake.[90] The upper register shows the arrival of a bishop, so it is possible that this is a generic representation of Inquisition punishments. The presence of the treasure chest to the right, however, suggests that this scene relates to the ongoing torments described by Durán.

Durán makes reference to a treasure that the Spaniards had won and lost earlier in the conquest: "While the new city was being planned and Cortés rested, the Spaniards began to seek the treasure that had been found in the secret chambers." He is referring to the royal treasure that was sealed into a secret chamber in the palace that was built by Moteuczoma Ilhuicamina (Moteuczoma I). When the Spaniards arrived in Tenochtitlan for the first time, Moteuczoma Xocoyotl (Moteuczoma II) housed them in his grandfather's palace and was soon held prisoner within these same walls. In chapter 74 of his *History* Durán relies on the account of a conquistador who had later become a friar to describe how the Spaniards found this treasure:

> He told me of the intense search that was made for the secret treasure chambers of Motecuhzoma. One day the Spaniards' eagerness and hunger for gold led them to a small low door that had been filled in and recently plastered, a mystery that intrigued them. They were ordered to open it and when they passed through a narrow door they found a spacious chamber in the middle of which stood a pile of gold, jewelry, and rich stones, the whole pile as high as the tallest man. If we wish to know what this pile of riches was, we see that according to the *Historia* the treasure did not consist of things acquired by Motecuhzoma, nor were they objects for his own use. This was the treasure that had belonged to all the kings who were his ancestors, which they had deposited there but which could not be used by the present ruler. When a king died, on that very day all his wealth in gold, gems, feathers, and weapons and his entire wardrobe were placed in that room and guarded as if they were sacred or divine things. The king who was about to reign would then begin to acquire wealth so that it could not be said he used the treasures of his ancestors. So it was that the treasure was guarded as a testimony to the greatness of the city of Mexico-Tenochtitlan.[91]

Codex Azcatitlan folio 25v shows two bundles above the treasure box that connect to a ruler headdress. As Durán stated in the passage above: "This was the treasure that had belonged to *all* the kings" (emphasis added). Although there are no name glyphs on folio 25v, the *xiuhhuitzolli* probably did not have one. Like the diadem in the *tecpan* on folio 25r, this is a reference to rulership, not an individual ruler. In conjunction with the bags and locked chest, the image suggests that this is a royal treasure, but not identified with any one king. Durán goes on to describe the different kinds of objects and goods that formed the treasure and how Cortés ordered the chamber resealed and guarded.[92]

Later Durán describes how the treasure was lost when the Spanish fled Tenochtitlan on the Noche Triste: "Cortés ordered them not to carry any of the treasure or to be greedy in taking gold and jewels that might hinder their flight. He realized that anyone carrying these things would be unable to flee, and he told them to leave all the treasures since they would find them when they returned."[93] Bernal Diaz del Castillo offers a similar account, describing how Cortés, on the Noche Triste, ordered all of the jewels, gold, and silver brought out and then ordered his secretary and the king's notaries to "[g]ive me written testimony that I can't do anything more to guard this gold; here in this building and hall we have more than seven hundred thousand gold pesos, and as you have seen, it can neither be weighted nor put in a safer place, I hereby give it to those soldiers who would like to take some of it, otherwise it's going to be left here lost among these dogs."[94] In his letter to the Spanish king Cortés downplays what was left behind and focuses on his attempts to leave with as much as possible: "I begged and commanded the alcaldes and regidores and all those who were present to help me to carry it [the gold and jewels] out and save it; and for this purpose I gave them one of my mares onto which they loaded as much as possible. . . . Having abandoned the fortress with great riches belonging to Your Highness, the Spaniards, and myself, I went out as secretly as possible."[95] He goes on to describe great losses of treasure and life during the escape from Tenochtitlan. As the passage in Durán's conclusion indicates, the treasure was never regained.

Durán's concluding chapter describes the treasure as concealed in a deep pool associated with whiteness and the sacred springs of the Tlatelolca ancestors. In the context of Durán's *History* the deep pool simultaneously represents Aztlan and Tenochtitlan. His language explicitly echoes his own earlier descriptions of the time when the migrating Mexica encountered the eagle on the nopal cactus, the sign given by Huitzilopochtli that foretold the end of their journey:

> And wandering in this way, among the reeds and rushes, they came upon a beautiful spring and saw wondrous things in the waters. These things had been predicted to the people by their priests, through the command of Huitzilopochtli, their god.
>
> The first thing they beheld was a white bald cypress, all white and very beautiful, and the spring came forth from the foot of the tree.
>
> The second thing they saw was a group of white willows around the spring, all white, without a single green leaf.
>
> There were white reeds, and white rushes surrounding the water.
>
> White frogs came out of the water, white fish came out, white water snakes, all shiny and white.
>
> The spring flowed out from between two large rocks, the water so clear and limpid that it was pleasing to behold. . . .
>
> Cuauhtlequetzqui informed the people that the mysterious and wonderful things seen the day before in the spring had been placed there by the hand of the god: white water snakes, white frogs, white fish, white willows and white bald cypress, everything white. . . .
>
> Thus again they found the spring they had seen the day before. But the water on that day had been clear and transparent, and it now flowed out in two streams, one red like blood, the other so blue and thick it filled the people with awe. Having seen these mysterious things [where the red and blue waters flowed as one], the Aztecs continued to seek [the omen of] the eagle whose presence had been foretold. Wandering from one place to another, they soon discovered the prickly pear cactus. On it stood the eagle with his wings stretched out toward the rays of the sun, basking in their warmth and the freshness of the morning.[96]

Durán also describes Aztlan as a place of whiteness, albeit with less detail.[97] Since the Templo Mayor was purported to be the location of the eagle on the nopal cactus, the location of the "deep pool," according to Durán's description, would have been nearby.

In Codex Azcatitlan the reed-water glyph that signifies Aztlan (the place of whiteness) is found on the island of Aztlan on folio 2r and again framing the lower and left sides of the treasure box on folio 25v (figure 5.6). As discussed earlier, the reed-water

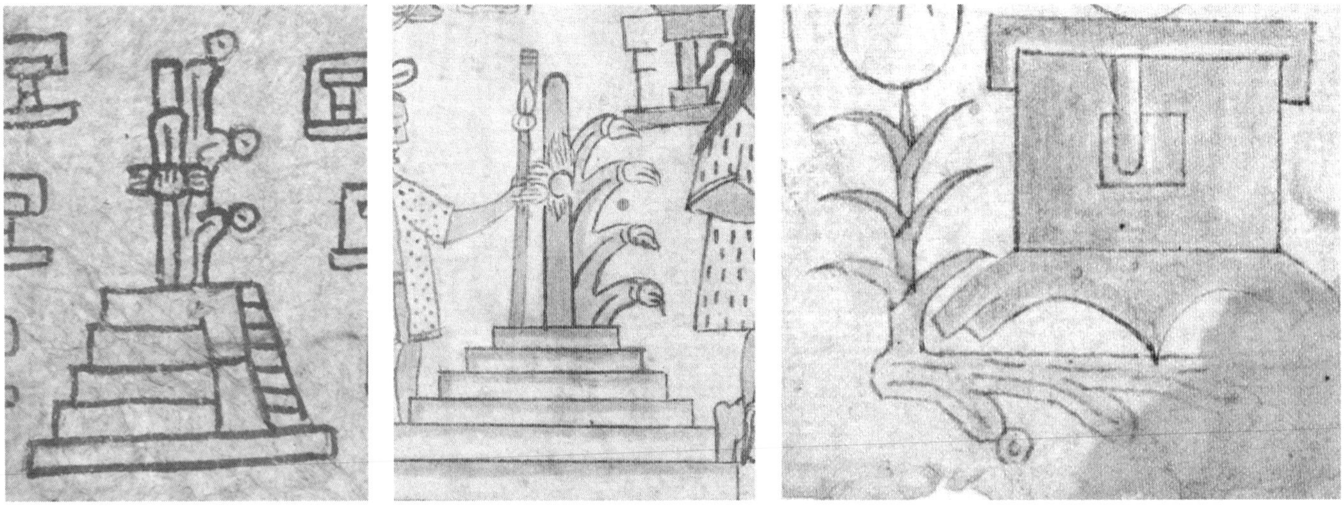

Figure 5.6. Left: The glyph representing Aztlan from Codex Boturini, folio 1 (detail). CONACULTA-INAH-MEX; reproduced with permission of the Instituto Nacional de Antropología e Historia. Center and right: Codex Azcatitlan (details), folios 2r and 25v. Courtesy of the Bibliothèque Nationale de France.

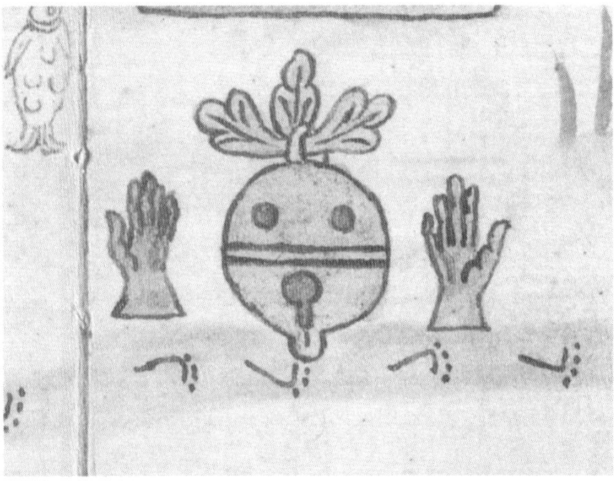

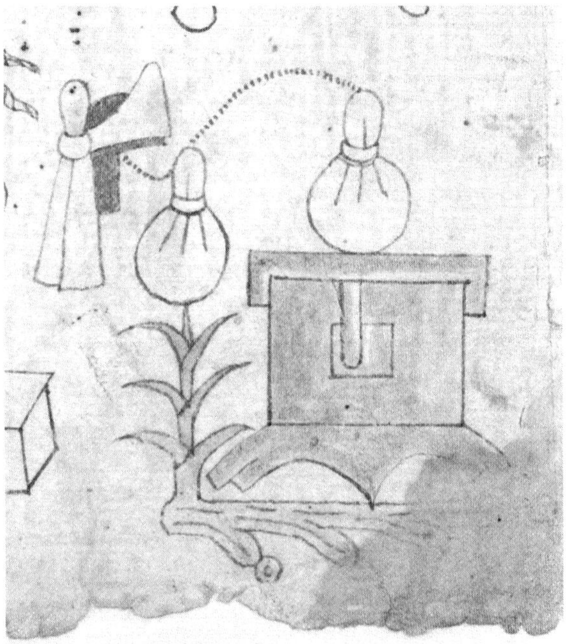

Figure 5.7. References to the treasure of the Mexica tlatoque on Codex Azcatitlan, folios 13r (detail) and 25v (detail). Courtesy of the Bibliothèque Nationale de France.

glyph on folio 2r appears on the "Tenochtitlan" part of the island of Aztlan, just as the site of the eagle on the nopal cactus and surrounding springs would have been in Tenochtitlan. When Durán references the place of the red and blue waters, it is associated with the founding of Tenochtitlan and the site of the hidden treasure. In Codex Azcatitlan the founding of Tenochtitlan is depicted nominally by the nopal cactus growing from the sacrificed body of Copil on folio 12r. But in terms of the *tlacuilo*'s Tlatelolco-based pictorial narrative the real foundation occurs on folios 12v–13r when the Tlatelolca separate from the Tenochca. At the bottom of the scene depicting the separation of the Tlatelolca from the Tenochca is a reference to the disposal of the treasure. Beneath the reedy waters, teeming with fish and fowl, appear two hands and a Spanish colonial lockplate (figure 3.11, figure 5.7). This visual prolepsis is not unique to Codex Azcatitlan and occurs in the Historia Tolteca-Chichimeca, a manuscript produced on European paper in Cuauhtinchan between 1545 and 1563.[98] These anachronistic elements signal a future moment and show how the *tlacuilo* layers meaning and how he uses retrospective knowledge to help his audience understand and access the past.

Conclusion

The postconquest pages of Codex Azcatitlan record a narrative that ends in 1527. As in the conquest section, the protagonists of this narrative continue to be high-ranking indigenous and Spanish officials. Although many of the events take place away from Tenochtitlan-Tlatelolco, in Colhuacan, Hueymollan Acallan, Tlatlauhquitepec, Coyoacan, and other areas surrounding Lake Texcoco, the postconquest section still begins and ends with the island city. The very first images record the departure after the devastating effects of the conquest. The last images reference the location that marked the very heart of the city. In contrast to the often personal and local entries in Codex Aubin, the Codex Azcatitlan *tlacuilo* depicted major events of widespread importance, indicating that he envisioned an audience beyond the immediate confines of his *parcialidad*. As also evident in the earlier parts of the manuscript, that audience was indigenous. The tales of traitors and intrigue that enliven the postconquest account are not particularly flattering to the Spanish. The story ends with events that occur on the day of Cortés's exile from Tenochtitlan.

The *tlacuilo*'s decision to end with the treasure of the *tlatoque* and its location at the site of the reed-water glyph suggests a cosmic overlay that stretches through the extent of the manuscript. With this image he connects Aztlan, the foundation of the Mexica at Tenochtitlan and Tlatelolco, and the final narrative moment. In essence the *tlacuilo* projects the migration narrative forward as a way to understand and interpret the history of the Mexica from the period after they settle at Tenochtitlan-Tlatelolco to 1527. The migration from Aztlan to the foundation of Tenochtitlan and Tlatelolco is one great narrative cycle that dominates the first half of the manuscript, defining who the Mexica people were and how they separated to pursue their independent destinies as the Tenochca and Tlatelolca. This separation is marked by the installment of the first rulers of Tenochtitlan and Tlatelolco on folios 12v–13r. The second half of the manuscript traces their parallel histories through the actions of the ruling elites until their fortunes begin to merge again in the form of Cuauhtemoc, a leader of both Tenochca and Tlatelolca lineage. The manuscript details his unjust death, ending shortly thereafter.

Just as Colhuacan, the Place of the Bent Hill, anchors the beginning and end of the migration narrative, it appears at both ends of the second half of the manuscript. The first *huey tlatoani* listed in the ruler history is Acamapichtli, and the first place documented in his reign on folio 13v is Colhuacan. The head of a Huitzilopochtli impersonator is just above the place glyph. On folio 24v Colhuacan appears just before the death of the last pre-Hispanic *huey tlatoani* of Tenochtitlan, Cuauhtemoc. Although the meaning of the accompanying glyphs is uncertain, the *tlacuilo* may allude to the postconquest hiding of Huitzilopochtli idols at Colhuacan around 1523.[99]

Codex Azcatitlan begins and ends with sacred waters. The swirling, turbulent waters of Aztlan and Chicomoztoc are tamed, controlled, and bountiful when Huitzilopochtli's promise is fulfilled and Tenochtitlan and Tlatelolco are established. The sacred springs, as discussed in Durán's passage above, are as much a sign from their god as the sighting of the eagle on the nopal cactus. Barbara Mundy speaks to similar themes in her recent reinterpretation of the foundation scene depicted on the back of the Teocalli stone. She argues that the eagle on the nopal cactus emerges from the tamed and sacrificed body of the female water goddess Chalchiuhtlicue rather than from an earth deity: "As expressed in the Teocalli, it was the sacrifice of Chalchiuhtlicue that made the foundation of the city possible, much as on the experiential plane, it was the taming of the lakes in the fifteenth century that allowed the city to survive."[100] Later, when the Spanish lay siege, the swirling waters reappear on Ecatl's tunic. Despite his valiant acts, the Annals of Tlatelolco and Florentine Codex tell us that Huitzilopochtli will imminently withdraw his favor. Folios 12v–13r depict the beginning of Tlatelolca identity and the abundance promised to the Aztecs when they departed Aztlan. When the Codex Azcatitlan *tlacuilo* painted the hands and the lockplate beneath this scene, he referenced the later return of that abundance, centuries of accumulated wealth, to the sacred waters at the end of an era. The image of the treasure of the *tlatoque* on the final page of the manuscript reminds the audience that, despite Spanish torture and acts of cruelty, the true treasure is in the font of sacred waters. As Durán's informant tells us, it cannot be defiled by Spanish greed: if anyone knows the secret of the treasure, it is the Tlatelolca.

CHAPTER 6

CODEX AUBIN AND THE INFLUENCE OF PRINTED BOOKS

BOTH CODEX AZCATITLAN and Codex Aubin append the migration history presented in Codex Boturini to a ruler history and later conquest and postconquest history. In contrast to the Codex Azcatitlan *tlacuilo*, who relied on pictorial modes of expression, promoted a Tlatelolca perspective, and painted for an indigenous audience without regard for Spanish concerns, the Codex Aubin *tlacuilo* took a very different and much more cautious tack. Though he too put paint to paper in the context of the newly rebuilt colonial capital, he appears to have written for a more intimate audience. His entries in the conquest history reflect a Tenochca viewpoint and those of the colonial period record events that relate to San Juan Moyotlan, one of the four *parcialidades* of the city, located to the southwest. As explicated in this chapter, he likely grew up in this neighborhood, training at the nearby school of San José de los Naturales and later honing his skills at the Colegio de Santa Cruz in Tlatelolco. Although the *tlacuilo* records events of importance to the Basin of Mexico region that are commonly found in other annals, his entries are peppered with local and very personal information. This, along with the diminutive size of the manuscript, suggests a more personal consumption, designed for an individual or a neighborhood rather than for a government or religious functionary.

Nevertheless, although the *tlacuilo* wrote in Nahuatl script, ostensibly directing his history to an indigenous audience, the materiality of the manuscript and its facture reveal a cautious consideration of how best to construct preconquest and postconquest history in a fraught colonial present. The Codex Aubin *tlacuilo* worked hard to preserve the narrative content of Codex Boturini's record as faithfully as possible (see chapter 2). Yet he opted for a very different vehicle, combining written text, pictorial images, and a new bound book format. As Dana Leibsohn puts it in her exploration of the intersection of indigenous and European modes of recordkeeping in the Historia Tolteca-Chichimeca: "The questions that now beckon concern a different tension, that between preservation and innovation."[1] Although he does not direct his narrative to a Spanish audience, the armature of the Codex Aubin *tlacuilo*'s narrative is built to withstand Spanish scrutiny. His fidelity and his caution stand in contrast to the Codex Azcatitlan *tlacuilo*, who freely adapted the Mexica migration history of Codex Boturini to emphasize the Tlatelolca presence that runs throughout his manuscript and to give shape and meaning to a postmigration history that makes no move to placate Spanish religious and political officials.

Although Codex Aubin incorporates pre-Hispanic history and pictorial writing, the *tlacuilo* chose to emulate the format of printed and bound books from Europe (codices in the truest definition of the word) that circulated widely in New Spain. Through close examination of the manuscript's binding and composition and comparison with contemporary printed texts, the first part of this study demonstrates how the *tlacuilo* emulated his models. The second part places the manuscript in historical context, examining how the *tlacuilo*'s choices reflect sixteenth-century educational practices in New Spain, the epidemic disease outbreaks that made recording history a matter of urgency, and the climate of censorship created by Spanish Catholicism and Inquisition practices. This study offers a more nuanced understanding of how and why Codex Aubin was produced. Codex Aubin reveals a strong impetus toward the faithful recording of canonical pre-Christian indigenous history and a consideration of how to make that history palatable in a sixteenth-century colonial context. By using printed books as a model, the *tlacuilo* lent authority to the pre-Hispanic history that he presented.

Background

While the details of Codex Aubin's provenance are unknown, the consistency of page layouts, images, and handwriting through the entry of 1591 indicates the work of a single *tlacuilo*. After 1591 additional hands add to the manuscript, recording dates as late as 1608 (figure 6.1).[2] While it is possible that one artist wrote the alphabetic script and another produced the pictographic imagery, this scenario seems unlikely: both the images and the handwriting change abruptly in 1591. Since the postconquest entries become more detailed in the 1550s and include personal references by 1564, it appears that the *tlacuilo* began his project around that time and continued to work on it for the next thirty years. Charles Dibble suggests a start date of 1562 because the Nahuatl text entries shift from beginning with *nican* (here) to incoporating *axcan* (today).[3]

As was customary at the time, the primary *tlacuilo* never names himself, but he does include some references in the postconquest section of the annals that signal information about his identity. Numerous references to the governors of San Juan Moyotlan, for example, indicate that Codex Aubin is a product of this *parcialidad* of Tenochtitlan. Amid entries that discuss the comings and goings of viceroys, archbishops, and the San Juan Moyotlan community leaders, the *tlacuilo* indicates that he participated in the labor tax, which signals his indigenous descent. Several additional references document personal events. For example, he documents the construction of his home in 1564. On Monday, May 5, 1567, he reports the birth of a daughter named Juana López. After work ceased on the manuscript in 1608, it may have stayed in the San Juan Moyotlan community, perhaps remaining with his family or passing into the hands of local officials until Lorenzo Boturini Benaduci collected it more than one hundred years later.

Walter Lehmann and Gerdt Kutscher's *Geschichte der Azteken: Codex Aubin und verwandte Dokumente* (1981) helped to make Codex Aubin widely available to scholars in the twentieth century. In addition to a discussion of the relationship between Codex Aubin and other manuscripts, *Geschichte der Azteken* offered scholars a transcription of the Nahuatl text in Codex Aubin with a German translation and high-quality black-and-white images. No other significant monographic works have been published on Codex Aubin since then, but many scholars have addressed this important manuscript as part of their studies. For example, Elizabeth Hill Boone has contextualized it in relation to other historical manuscripts in *Stories in Red and Black* and has also discussed its narrative qualities.[4] María Castañeda de la Paz has published an article that examines the relationship between Codex Aubin and its source material.[5] Camilla Townsend has recently provided a discussion of indigenous historiography that comments on the way in which multiple sources are employed in the Codex Aubin.[6] These studies and others have broadened our knowledge of the manuscript.

Codex Aubin and the Printed Book as Model

Many scholars mention in passing the small booklike format of Codex Aubin when discussing its colonial properties. Codex Aubin resembles a printed and bound book in size and in style. It is small and easy to hold (15.5 cm high and 13.4 cm wide: octavo size).[7] The *tlacuilo* used European paper, included a sizable amount of alphabetic text, and bound the manuscript. To consider more fully how the European printed book influenced the Codex Aubin *tlacuilo*, this study begins with an examination of the binding, which incorporates endpapers that are recycled from a sixteenth-century Latin edition of Julius Caesar's *Commentarii de Bello Gallico* (Commentaries on the Gallic War).[8] While it is impossible to determine the date of the binding definitively, evidence suggests probable coeval production, raising the possibility

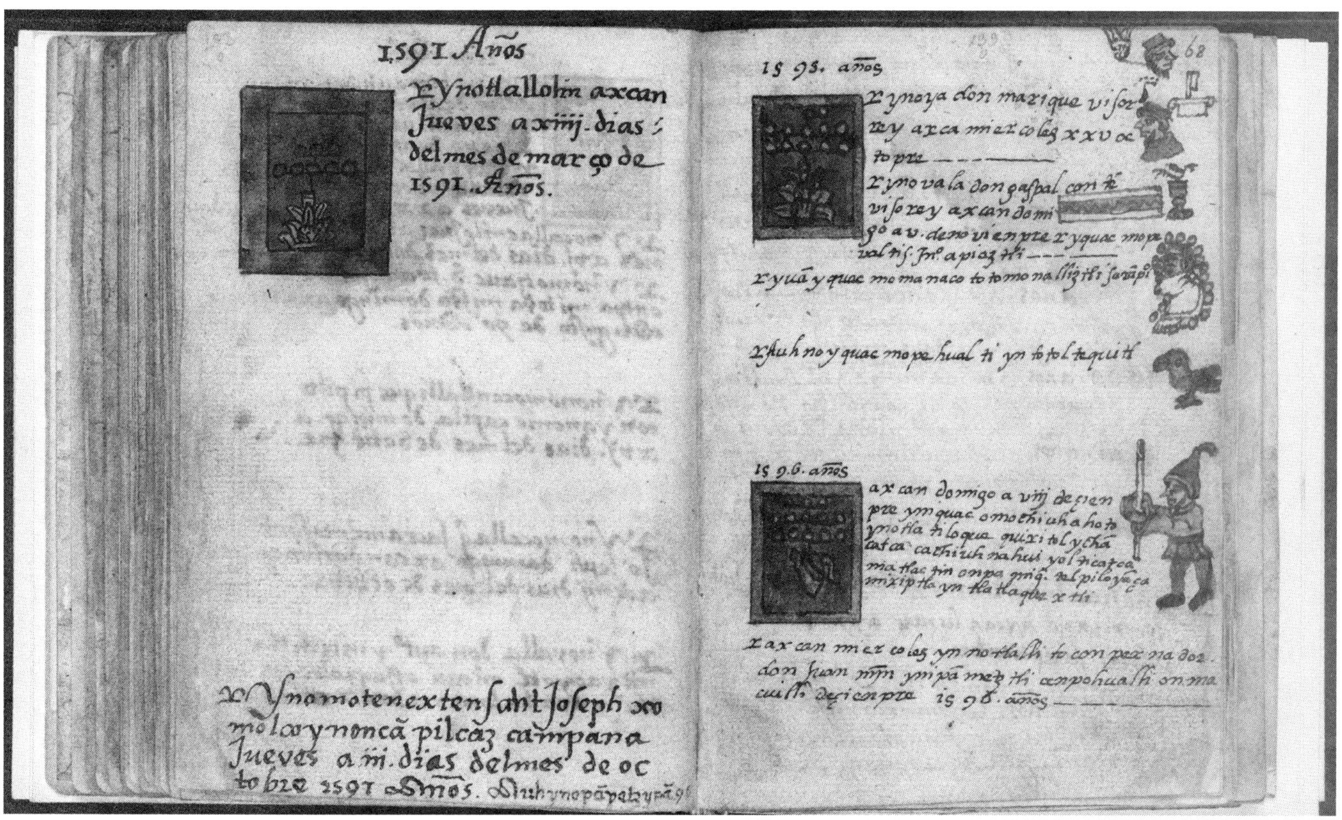

Figure 6.1. The primary *tlacuilo* ceases work on the manuscript after 1591. A new *tlacuilo* with different handwriting and different formatting takes over in 1595, altering the one year per page layout. Codex Aubin, folios 67v and 68r. © The Trustees of the British Museum. All rights reserved.

that the endpapers and the book from which they came directly influenced the *tlacuilo*. An examination of individual page layouts reveals that the *tlacuilo* mimicked printed books by reproducing the printer's marks, justifying the text blocks, and employing a variety of fonts. These compositional choices reflect a break with earlier pre-Hispanic models. Although the *tlacuilo* reproduced almost all of the images related to Mexica migration history found in a purely pictographic manuscript like Codex Boturini, he organized the alphabetic writing and pictographic writing on the page so that the pictographs resemble illustrations in a printed book. Finally, this section considers conceptual links to the printed book and ideas of authorship by examining the title page of the manuscript.

Perhaps because of the lack of documentation and available reproductions, the binding of Codex Aubin has not been addressed in previous studies.[9] Within the red leather binding that the British Library applied in 1969, Codex Aubin is bound up with a vellum cover and a few endpapers that come from a sixteenth-century Latin edition of Julius Caesar's *Commentarii de Bello Gallico*. The *Commentarii* consists of eight books written by this Roman military and political leader about his experiences in the first century B.C.E. fighting local armies in Gaul that opposed Roman domination. Like Codex Aubin, it is an annals history. The *Commentarii de Bello Gallico* has been in print almost since the birth of the printing press in the West and circulated in manuscript form before that. The Aubin endpapers are nearly identical to an edition produced in 1534 by Sebastian Gryphius of Lyon, France.[10] The British Museum has no documentation related to the binding, but the juxtaposition of the painted manuscript and the early printed text invites comparison and consideration of why and how the *tlacuilo* chose to mimic the printed book format (figure 6.2). While the vellum cover and endpapers may have been added after the manuscript's production, I argue here that it is highly likely that they formed part of the original manuscript binding applied in 1576 and that books like this served as a model for the Codex Aubin *tlacuilo* as he worked.

First, this particular binding technique (a limp vellum cover with recycled endpapers) was most common in the sixteenth and seventeenth centuries. In *The British Library Guide to Bookbinding History and Techniques* P. J. M. Marks writes: "Although it was in use much earlier, vellum is often found on sixteenth- and seventeenth-century texts which were sold ready bound." He describes the virtues of the material: "Vellum or parchment (any skin treated with lime and dried under tension) is strong, light and cheap. The surface is hard, smooth and generally white, although it can be stained any colour."[11] In their book on *Bookbinding and the Conservation of Books* Matt Roberts, Don Etherington, and Margaret Brown state: "Limp vellum or limp-parchment bindings were used frequently in the 16th and 17th centuries, and were sometimes gilt but were also often not embellished. In later centuries vellum has been more commonly used like leather, that is, as the covering for stiff board bindings." In their discussion of endpapers the authors state that

> during the first several centuries of the codex, endpapers consisted of little more than two or four leaves of vellum folded and sewn along with sections of the book. When paper became the common material for book production, it then became necessary to reinforce the folds of the endpapers. A common type of endpaper, used in the first part of the 16th century, consisted of a fold of white paper employing a strip of vellum for reinforcement. The use of printer's waste for the fly leaves of endpapers was not uncommon during the 16th century.[12]

Codex Aubin's binding, made from recycled endpapers with a strip of vellum for reinforcement, is entirely consistent with sixteenth-century binding practices.

Just as limp vellum bindings were common in the sixteenth century and fell out of use in the seventeenth century, the use of recycled endpapers was most common in the sixteenth century. In places where paper was still somewhat expensive, it was not uncommon for bookbinders to "recycle" paper and use it for endpapers and paste-downs. Recycled papers would become less common later. In the sixteenth century European paper was imported to New Spain and was still expensive. By the late sixteenth century paper had become more widely available and less costly as Mexican paper factories began production.[13] Furthermore, marbled paper was introduced to Europe in the sixteenth century and quickly became the standard for endpapers of the seventeenth and eighteenth centuries.[14] If recycled endpapers are a function of paper availability and cost, the Codex Aubin binding probably dates to the mid- to late sixteenth century.

The recycled endpapers used in these early books came in different forms. In his study *Early Printed Books* E. Gordon Duff quotes from the papers of Henry Bradshaw, a nineteenth-century librarian and historian who makes a distinction between

> what may be called respectively binder's waste and printer's waste. When speaking of fragments of books as *binder's waste,* I mean books which have been in circulation, and have been thrown away as useless.... But by *printer's waste* I mean ... waste, proof, or cancelled sheets in the printer's office, which in the early days when printers were their own bookbinders, would be used by the bookbinder for lining the boards, or the centres of quires, of books bound in the same office of the printer who printed them.[15]

An example of a book binding in the Princeton University Library Rare Books collection provides an interesting comparison. Roughly contemporary with

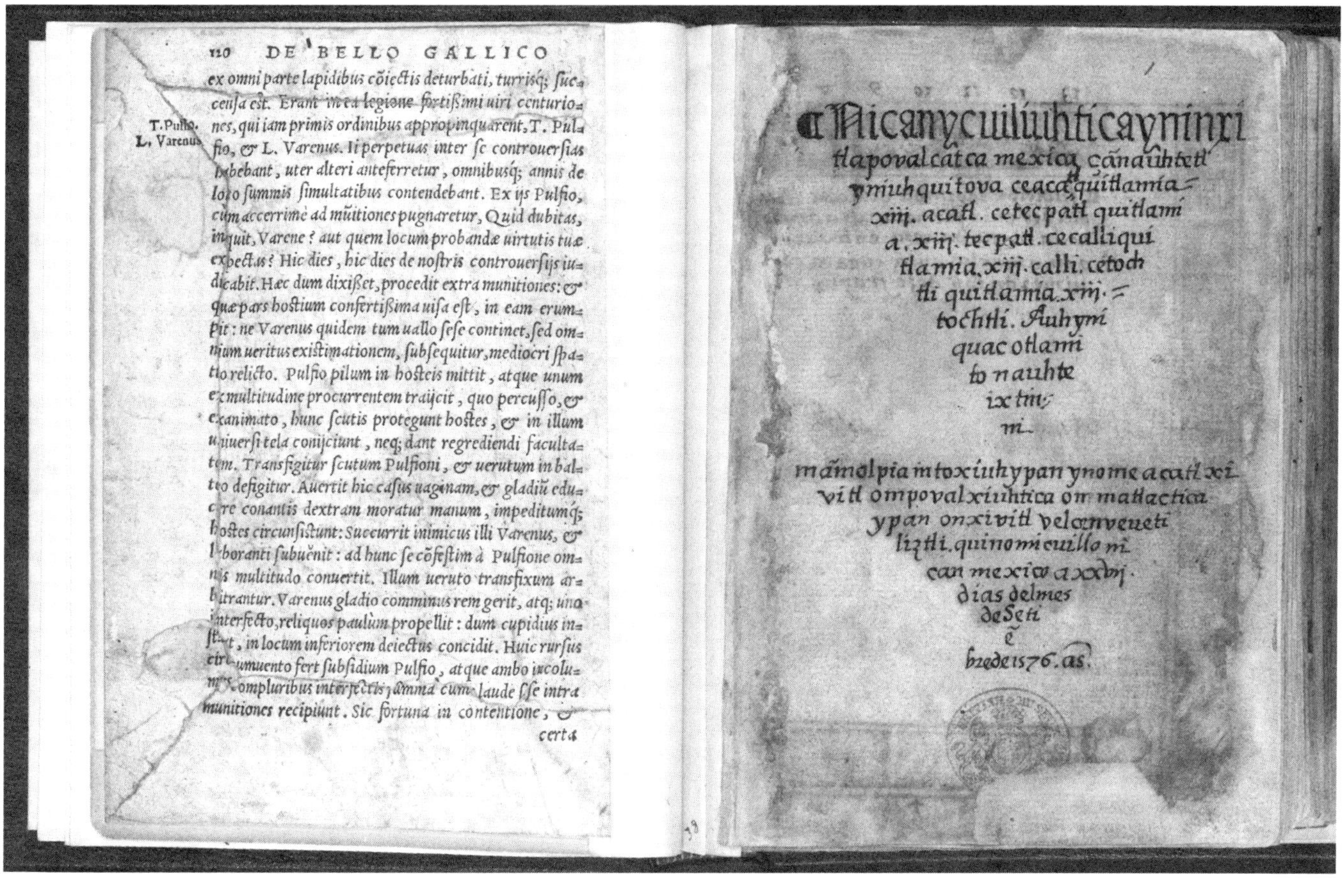
110 DE BELLO GALLICO

T. Pulfio. L. Varenus

ex omni parte lapidibus cõiectis deturbati, turrisq; succensa est. Erant in ea legione fortißimi uiri centuriones, qui iam primis ordinibus appropinquarent, T. Pulfio, & L. Varenus. Ii perpetuas inter se controuersias habebant, uter alteri anteferretur, omnibusq; annis de loco summis simultatibus contendebant. Ex ijs Pulfio, cùm accerrimè ad mũitiones pugnaretur, Quid dubitas, inquit, Varene? aut quem locum probandæ uirtutis tuæ expectas? Hic dies, hic dies de nostris controuersijs iudicabit. Hæc dum dixißet, procedit extra munitiones: & quæ pars hostium confertißima uisa est, in eam erumpit: ne Varenus quidem tum uallo sese continet, sed omnium ueritus existimationem, subsequitur, mediocri spatio relicto. Pulfio pilum in hosteis mittit, atque unum ex multitudine procurrentem traijcit, quo percusso, & exanimato, hunc scutis protegunt hostes, & in illum uniuersi tela conijciunt, neq; dant regrediendi facultatem. Transfigitur scutum Pulfioni, & uerutum in balteo defigitur. Auertit hic casus uaginam, & gladiũ educere conantis dextram moratur manum, impeditumq; hostes circunsistunt: Succurrit inimicus illi Varenus, & laboranti subuẽnit: ad hunc se cõfestim à Pulfione omnis multitudo conuertit. Illum ueruto transfixum arbitrantur. Varenus gladio comminus rem gerit, atq; uno interfecto, reliquos paulùm propellit: dum cupidius instat, in locum inferiorem deiectus concidit. Huic rursus circumuento fert subsidium Pulfio, atque ambo incolumes, compluribus interfectis, summa cum laude sese intra munitiones recipiunt. Sic fortuna in contentione, &

certa

Figure 6.2. Paste-down from *De Bello Gallico* and Codex Aubin, folio 1r.

the Codex Aubin, the 1583 book by William Fulke is titled *A Defense of the Sincere and True Translations of the Holie Scriptures into the English*, but the waste endpapers are leaves from an edition of the *Digesta*. The Fulke book, with its imperfectly printed endpapers, provides an example of "printer's waste." The relatively pristine printed pages of the *Commentarii de Bello Gallico* that protect the Codex Aubin manuscript are "binder's waste." In other words, they come from a well-printed edition that was probably worn out and discarded. The earliest printers working in Mexico produced primarily religious texts, so Codex Aubin may have been bound at a location like the Colegio de Santa Cruz in Tlatelolco, where bookbinding was taught.

The limp vellum cover with recycled endpapers was already falling out of use in the seventeenth century and it is unlikely that such a binding would be applied in the eighteenth and nineteenth centuries. In the eighteenth century Codex Aubin circulated through many institutional collections in New Spain after the government seized Lorenzo Boturini Benaduci's collection in January 1743.[16] Thereafter it passed through the hands of J. M. A. Aubin and Jules Desportes before being sold to the British Museum. In the eighteenth and nineteenth centuries institutions paid little historical attention to bookbindings and often removed old bindings that were damaged, replacing them with blank endpapers and standardized bindings.[17] In the 1960s E. Gordon Duff lamented this practice:

> In the last century no regard whatever seems to have been paid to old bindings, the very fact of their being old prejudiced librarians against them; if they became damaged or worn they were not repaired, but destroyed, and the book rebound. Nor did they fare better in earlier times. Somewhere in the first half of the seventeenth century all the manuscripts in the Cambridge University Library were uniformly rebound in rough calf, to the utter destruction of every trace of their former history.[18]

In the eighteenth and nineteenth centuries there was no shortage of paper, so it seems unlikely that the British Library or any of the earlier owners would rebind Codex Aubin with recycled endpapers or with vellum, which was already more of a specialty paper.[19] The British Museum stamp appears on the vellum cover as well as on various pages throughout the manuscript, perhaps indicating that it was part of the object as it came into that collection.

The edition of the *Commentarii de Bello Gallico* that is bound with Codex Aubin represents one of the most popular and influential print formats introduced in the sixteenth century. The printer, Sebastian Gryphius, was a German who had worked in Venice and had become the most prominent printer in Lyon. A scholar and Latinist, he was well known for his fine editions. The editions of the *Commentarii de Bello Gallico* that he produced in the early part of the sixteenth century were reprints of the work of Aldus Manutius, the foremost humanist scholar-printer in Renaissance Italy. Although Gryphius issued his reprint legally, printers had been pirating Aldine's work since the beginning of the sixteenth century. H. George Fletcher, former Astor Curator of Printed Books and Bindings at the Pierpont Morgan Library in New York, described this as a form of flattery:

> Aldus's competitors "honored" him in their own way by pirating his books. Some printers, however, would embrace the enchiridion format as a legitimate tribute to Aldus's creative genius.
>
> The earliest counterfeiting of typography, format, and texts can be found, within Italy, by Soncino in Fano and the Giunti in both Florence and Venice (this, at least, Aldus quashed by lawsuit). Outside Italy, the great commercial center of Lyon was a burgeoning printing locale, and the counterfeiting enterprise was only the beginning of an era that would see Lyon become a dominant location during the first half of the sixteenth century. We should also note that because so many copies of these piracies are still found in contemporary Italian bindings, the Lyonese must have

> sold into the Italian market deliberately, and this tactic must have been part of their agenda from the beginning.[20]

Aldus Manutius is perhaps best known for making classical Greek and Latin texts widely available and for introducing in 1501 the *enchiridion* (handbook) printed on octavo paper. Handbooks were designed to be held comfortably in the hand and were later incorrectly referred to as "pocketbooks."[21] This portable format overturned the tradition of heavy tomes and became popular in the sixteenth century because of its convenience and lower cost. Aldus Manutius had made a name for himself as an editor, translator, scholar, typographer, and printer. In the sixteenth century his books were exceedingly popular in both original and pirated print editions. When the Codex Aubin *tlacuilo* set to work in the second half of the sixteenth century, he chose to work on octavo-sized paper and created his own handbook, adopting one of the most widely used print formats of his era. This format was not at all common for pictographic manuscripts. In John Glass's census of indigenous pictorial manuscripts, no other work approximates the octavo size; most are considerably larger.[22]

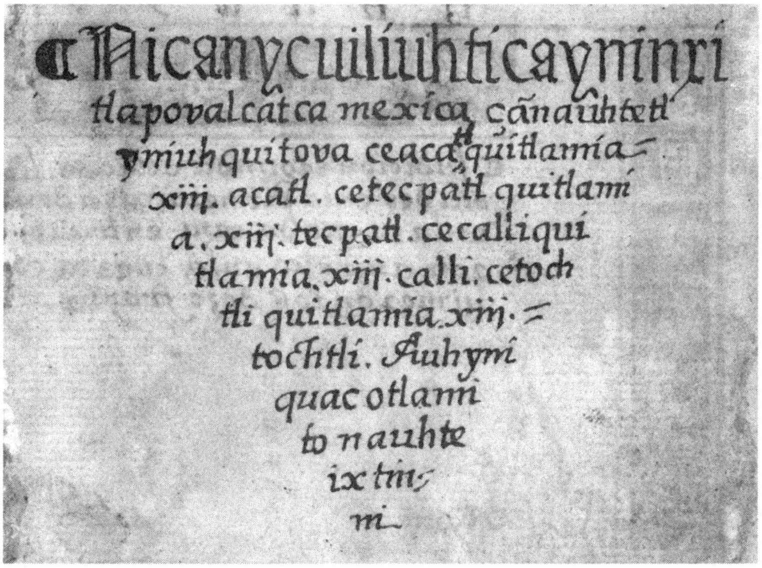

Top: Figure 6.3. Detail of text on Codex Aubin, folio 1r. © The Trustees of the British Museum. All rights reserved.

Left: Figure 6.4. Two details of the word *nican* from Codex Aubin, folios 1r and 3v. © The Trustees of the British Museum. All rights reserved.

The parallels between Codex Aubin and the *Commentarii de Bello Gallico* endpapers clearly demonstrate the impact of early printed texts on this late sixteenth century *tlacuilo*. Aside from the octavo size, European paper, binding, and emphasis on alphabetic text, the *tlacuilo* mimics many of the printer's techniques and marks. He uses justification, capitulum marks, and a variety of fonts. Figure 6.2 shows the small justification marks used to form the printed text into a neat margin. Justification marks are used frequently throughout this edition of Caesar's *Commentarii de Bello Gallico* and other early printed texts, and the Aubin artist employs them often in his manuscript (see figure 6.3), particularly in the lengthy text passages. In both the *Commentarii de Bello Gallico* and the painted manuscript "C"-shaped capitulum marks appear often; they serve as precursors to the paragraph indentations that are used today to designate a shift in the text's subject matter (figures 6.3 and 6.4).

Codex Aubin also mimics works like the 1534 *Commentarii de Bello Gallico* by employing a variety of fonts. Figure 6.4 shows two details of the Nahuatl word *nican* (here) that appear in the Codex Aubin manuscript. A comparison of the style of the letters of Codex Aubin folio 1r with the text that follows shows that the artist uses a gothic style for the opening words and switches to a roman style for the rest of the manuscript. In Konrad Haebler's study of incunabula, the earliest printed texts, he describes European printers' growing interest in typeface variety:

> The custom was developing of cutting types in a great variety of forms. While the earliest printers at first usually printed only with a single size of type, as time went on it became more and more customary to use a great many types of various sizes in the

> same book. It was not long before certain printers were seized with the ambition to provide themselves with an extensive stock of the most varied kinds and sizes.[23]

The Codex Aubin artist would have seen multiple typefaces in the sixteenth-century books circulating in New Spain and used this variety for aesthetic purposes in his own work.

While the Codex Aubin *tlacuilo* mimics the format and composition of a printed text, he does not use printer's marks unless they serve some useful or aesthetic purpose. For example, he does not mimic the "headers," "signatures," or "catchwords" that appear on the *Commentarii* endpapers. These marks at the top and bottom of the page helped the printer assemble the book after it was printed on large sheets of paper and cut down but served no purpose for the Codex Aubin *tlacuilo*, who already had the year dates to signal the proper order of the pages.

In adopting the format of a printed book, the Codex Aubin *tlacuilo* chose to include a title page, a further signal that he conceptualized his work as a European book. Although the title page of the 1534 edition of Caesar's *Commentarii* does not appear in the Codex Aubin endpapers, it is typical of Renaissance books and provides an instructive comparison with folio 1r of Codex Aubin (figure 6.5). Both are designed to inform the reader of the contents of the work as well as the date and location of production. Aesthetically, they employ similar composition, constructing the text into a decorative inverted pyramid with a large font at the top and a smaller font at the bottom. The title announces the contents of the book, Julius Caesar's *Commentarii*, with the printer's device and year below. On the Codex Aubin folio the Nahuatl text reads:

> Here is written the Mexica year count. It has four parts, as follows:
>
> 1 Reed ends with 13 Reed,
> 1 Flint ends with 13 Flint,
> 1 House ends with 13 House,
> 1 Rabbit ends with 13 Rabbit.
>
> And when all four are going to end, then our years are bound in the year 2 Reed. Fifty-two years is a complete cycle.
>
> Written here today in Mexico, the 27th of the month of September of 1576.[24]

The content is in annals form, recording the significant events of Mexica history, so the *tlacuilo* begins by informing the reader of the key components of the Mexica calendar system that are depicted on the following folios. Reproducing the date and the printer's information proved more difficult for the *tlacuilo* because there was no precedent for this in indigenous tradition. Both title pages record the date of the book at the very bottom, 1534 for the *Commentarii* and September 27, 1576, for Codex Aubin. While that date might refer to the day the *tlacuilo* created the title page, the manuscript could not have been produced in a single day: he and others continued to add entries until 1608. Codex Aubin was not printed and the idea of claiming authorship was foreign, so the *tlacuilo* compromised by obliquely acknowledging the act of creation with the words "written here today."

In many ways Codex Aubin evidences the *tlacuilo*'s efforts to convert indigenous content and indigenous systems of recording knowledge into the conceptual paradigm of a European printed book. Unlike many contemporary annals that were produced on indigenous fig bark paper or assembled like a pre-Hispanic screenfold, the Codex Aubin *tlacuilo* used introduced materials and an introduced format. Individual pages are designed to be read like a book, from top to bottom and from left to right. The small octavo format evoked Renaissance humanist scholarship and signaled a new context for consumption. In the pre-Hispanic period *tlacuiloque* produced pictographic writing that served as a mnemonic device. Trained orators would have elaborated the contents to an audience. Codex Aubin pairs the pictographic writing with extensive alphabetic Nahuatl text, effectively supplanting the orator's role. Rather than functioning as a tool for an orator elaborating a narrative before an audience that looked on at the painted images, the diminutive Codex Aubin caters to an individual reader. Finally, Codex Aubin's binding, though impossible to date definitively, is entirely consistent with sixteenth-century binding practices. The Gryphius edition of Julius Caesar's *Commentarii*, or works like it, provided direct inspiration to the *tlacuilo*. His choice of model reflects the growing impact of the codex or bound book in sixteenth-century New Spain.

Codex Aubin in Historical Context

The murals that adorn the walls of the Augustinian *convento* at Actopan in Hidalgo highlight the role of the codex in intellectual and spiritual life (figure 6.6). The stairwell murals, painted by indigenous artists in the sixteenth century, depict Augustinian church fathers and important saints, most with an open codex in front of them. The inkwells, quills, and quill holders on their desks imply that the venerated friars were producers as well as consumers of the knowledge contained in these books. If the stairwell murals celebrate the power and possibility of scholarship in written form, the large lunette-shaped mural on the north wall of Actopan's *sala de profundis* suggests that this power can be dangerous in the wrong hands (figure 6.7). In the midst of a rocky landscape filled with scenes of the founding of the monastic order, a half-human, half-animal devil creeps up the mountain path with a bound book on his back and a quill and inkwell dangling from his arm. As art historian Jeanette Peterson notes, the *tlacuilo* depicts the devil as a *tlameme* (indigenous porter), who carries his book with a tumpline.[25] Though the possibilities for understanding this provocative figure are multivalent, the image on at least one level can be interpreted as a reference to the Catholic Church's ongoing battle against heretical writings, particularly those authored by the indigenous inhabitants of New Spain. The Actopan murals reflect something of the prevailing attitude toward the bound book: originally written by hand and now produced with printing presses, the codex had become the preeminent knowledge bearer in sixteenth-century New Spain. The ideas contained in these books were powerful, and the Catholic Church maintained that content had to be tightly regulated. The Inquisition carried this out by censoring books that were considered dangerous or heretical.

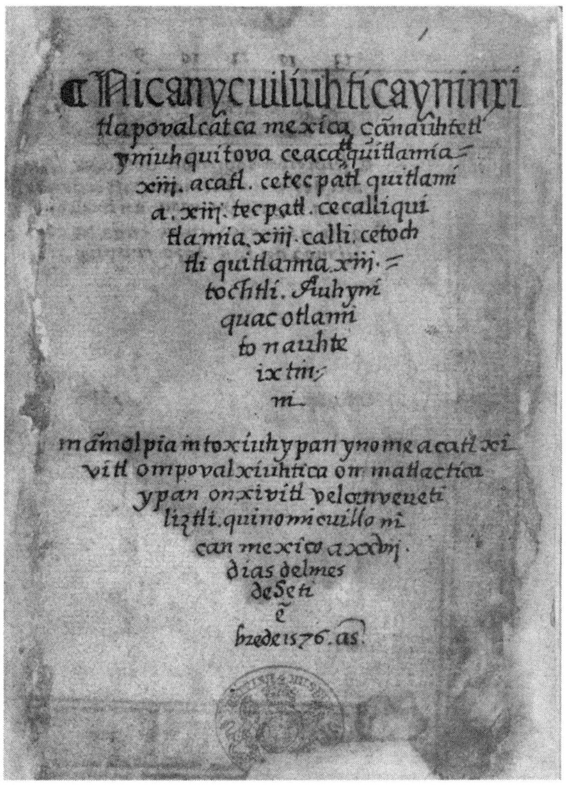
Nicanycuiliuhticaynixquich
tlapovalcâtca mexica cânauhtetl
yniuhquitova ceacatl quitlamia
xiij. acatl. cetecpatl quitlami
a. xiij. tecpatl. cecalliqui
tlamia xiij. calli. cetoch
tli quitlamia xiij.
tochtli. Auhyni
quac otlami
to nauhte
ixtin
mâmolpia intoxiuhypan ynome acatl xi
vitl ompovalxiuhtica on matlactica
ypan onxivitl yeloenveueti
liztli. quinomicuillo ni
can mexico a xxbij.
dias delmes
de Seti
e
bre de 1576. as.

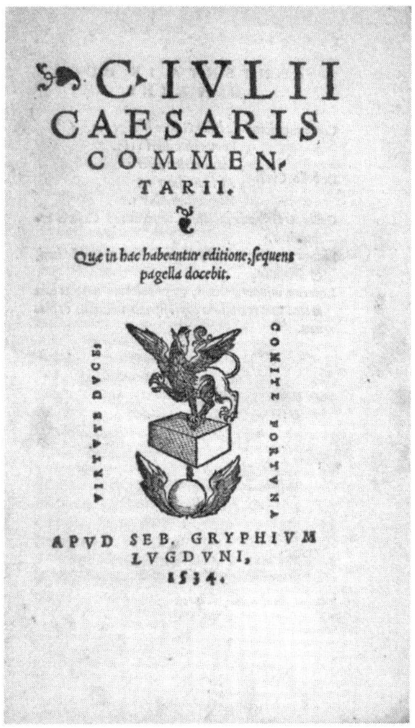
C. IVLII
CAESARIS
COMMEN-
TARII.

Quae in hac habeantur editione, sequens
pagella docebit.

VIRTVTE DVCE
COMITE FORTVNA

APVD SEB. GRYPHIVM
LVGDVNI,
1534.

Figure 6.5. Left: Codex Aubin, folio 1r. © The Trustees of the British Museum. All rights reserved. Right: Title page of Julius Caesar's *Commentarii* (Lyon: Seb. Gryphius, 1534). Courtesy of the Charles E. Young Research Library, Department of Special Collections at the University of California, Los Angeles.

The Inquisition monitored the printing presses, required ships to list the titles of the books that they imported on their manifests, and destroyed or suppressed suspect texts by indigenous authors. Against this ideological backdrop the *tlacuilo* began his training and conceived and produced Codex Aubin.

THE EDUCATIONAL ENVIRONMENT

The Codex Aubin *tlacuilo*'s ability to write alphabetic Nahuatl and Spanish indicates that he was trained in the Franciscan schools established in the decades after the conquest for the children of indigenous elites. In this educational system the *tlacuilo* would have learned to read and write alphabetic Nahuatl, Spanish, and Latin, while studying arts, Christian doctrine, and music.[26] Though the alphabetic text in the manuscript is primarily written in Nahuatl, a short Spanish inscription at the beginning of the manuscript written in the primary *tlacuilo*'s hand demonstrates that he was versed in more than one language. The *tlacuilo* acquired basic reading and writing skills sometime before he began work on the manuscript. His higher education probably occurred before or concurrently with initial production of the manuscript.

The *tlacuilo* notes the death of Fray Pedro de Gante (who established and taught at the monastery school of San José de los Naturales) in 1572 and makes frequent mention of the chapel of San José, where the school was located, so it is likely that he began his studies there.[27] After 1530 San José de los Naturales began to focus on teaching practical job skills, including many artistic professions such as painter, sculptor, embroiderer, silver worker, and gold worker.[28] The *tlacuilo* may have developed his painting skills at the school. Perhaps he even made the "stone image" or sculpture that decorated his home.[29] He also would have developed a basic knowledge of Spanish and Latin at San José de los Naturales. The Catholic masses were given in Latin in sixteenth-century New Spain, and it was considered imperative that students understand the basic prayers and rites. It is unlikely, however, that the *tlacuilo* encountered the printed books that he would use as a model at this school. As historian Michael Mathes notes, at San José de los Naturales "the only books available were the personal and highly valued property of the friars," which meant that "a substantial part of educational process was involved in the verbatim copying of dictation into bound paper copybooks."[30]

The *tlacuilo*'s interest in emulating printed and bound books probably developed at the Colegio de Santa Cruz in Tlatelolco, the first European school of higher education in New Spain. The Franciscan friars that created it amassed the first academic library there. A highly selective school geared toward children of the indigenous elite, the Colegio de Santa Cruz only admitted students who had excelled in monastery schools like San José de los Naturales. Students entered at eight to ten years of age with a command of alphabetic reading and writing and a basic knowledge of Latin. At the Colegio de Santa Cruz, they spent about three years advancing their grammatical skills and command of Latin, while studying subjects such as the arts, theology, rhetoric, logic, philosophy, music, and indigenous medicine.[31] In this setting students had access to printed books that covered a diversity of subject matter. If the Codex Aubin *tlacuilo* found his model in this library, it was probably a Latin text. Latin was considered a universal language and studies there went far beyond the rites of the Catholic mass, so the overwhelming majority of books in the library were in Latin.[32] Students left the school and returned to their home communities before the age of fifteen, unless they returned to assist with teaching, administration, or other projects.[33]

Codex Aubin is also the kind of endeavor that students of the Colegio de Santa Cruz at Tlatelolco developed and pursued, particularly after 1540, when the school became secular and began to focus on linguistic projects. José María Kobayashi has described this period in New Spain as a time of "historiographic revitalization," born of the encounter between Mexica historiographic traditions and the Latin alphabet. Hundreds of texts were written in Nahuatl in the postconquest period, mostly in the sixteenth

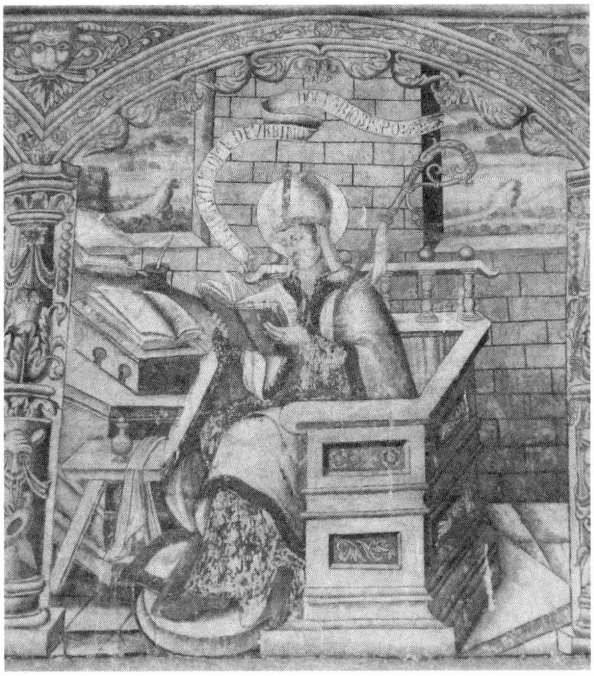

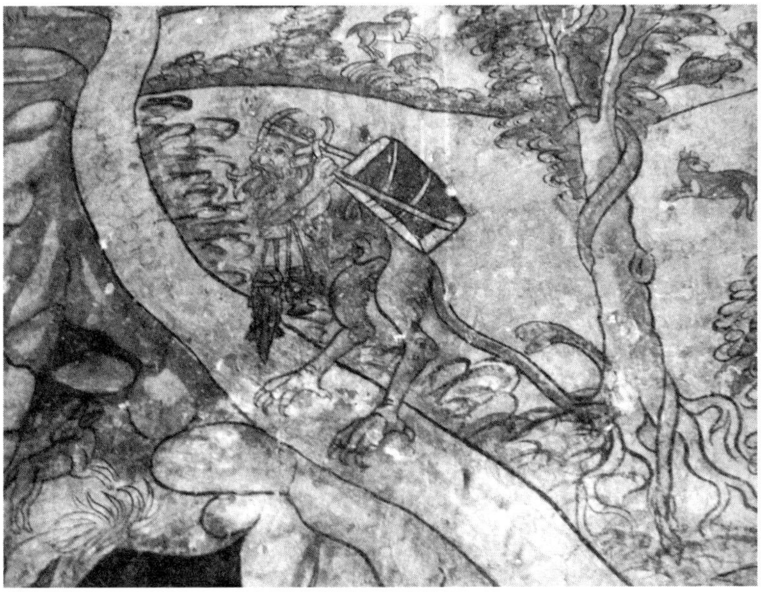

Top: Figure 6.6. Stairway mural from the Augustinian *convento* at Actopan in Hidalgo, Mexico. Courtesy of author.

Bottom: Figure 6.7. Detail of the devil figure at the center of the lunette-shaped mural in the sala de profundis of the Augustinian *convento* at Actopan in Hidalgo, Mexico. Courtesy of author.

century; more than sixty were dedicated to recording memories and knowledge about the pre-Hispanic past. Well-known authors that studied at the Colegio de Santa Cruz at Tlatelolco and addressed the pre-Hispanic past in their writings include Fernando Alvarado Tezozomoc, Fernando de Alva Ixtlilxochitl, Juan Bautista Pomar, and Domingo Francisco de San Antón Muñón Chimalpahin Quauhtlehuanitzin.[34]

In 1560, around the time the *tlacuilo* began work on the Codex Aubin, Bernardino de Sahagún was working with students of the Colegio de Santa Cruz on his *Historia general de las cosas de Nueva España*, now known as the Florentine Codex (written in Nahuatl with later Spanish translations). Sahagún coordinated production of this multivolume history of pre-Hispanic central Mexican culture over several decades with the assistance of indigenous informants.

A relationship with the Colegio de Santa Cruz de Tlatelolco, as student or alumnus, also would have made the binding of Codex Aubin in the 1570s possible. A 1572 inventory shows that the school had purchased the tools and presses needed for bookbinding and had begun to teach book-related arts.[35] This was an academic setting rather than a professional printer's office, so it makes sense that recycled endpapers would consist of binder's waste rather than printer's waste. The Gryphius edition of Julius Caesar's *Commentarii de Bello Gallico* is exactly the kind of text that might have been available for reuse. Most of the books in the school's library were written in Latin and a substantial number of these were classical texts, considered an important part of a humanistic education. Documentation shows that another 1543 edition of Julius Caesar's *Commentarii de Bello Gallico* once formed part of the collection. Furthermore, Mathes's analysis of the library inventory shows that at least 102 of the 277 books known to have formed a part of the collection were published in France; 51 of these were published in Lyon.[36] These facts are important because the library inventories also reflect significant losses at this time.

In his discussion of the Colegio de Tlatelolco's struggles of the 1570s, Mathes notes that "the library suffered losses from theft, and was also depleted by the sale of books." As he accounts for some of the depletions in the inventory, Mathes quotes Sahagún as stating that the "Indians in the colegio . . . said that some [books] had worn out due to age and others had been lost."[37] If the Codex Aubin *tlacuilo* was an alumnus or had a relationship with the school, he might have had access to some of these worn-out volumes. Alternatively, he could have purchased books from the school; under serious financial hardship in 1574, the Colegio de Tlatelolco sold part of its library.[38] If the Codex Aubin *tlacuilo* bound his book, he most likely did so in the midst of these developments, in the year 1576, when he produced the title page of the manuscript.

THE IMPACT OF EPIDEMIC DISEASE

I argue that the *tlacuilo* produced his title page and bound his manuscript in the year 1576 because he had good reason to believe that he might not survive one of the most deadly epidemic disease outbreaks in the history of New Spain. Under the entry for 1576, the *tlacuilo* records one of his most personal entries:

> The guardians who had been prisoners for a *tomín* [coin, monetary unit] were released; they had to pay 5 *tomines* of tribute in the palace today, Saturday, August 18. And also in August disease spread. Blood flowed from the nose. Only in our houses the priests gave us confession and gave us food. And the doctors healed us. And it was when the bells remained silent, they did not toll for the burials, as if we were abandoned in the church.
>
> Sunday, September 16, there was a procession in Santa Lucía, due to the disease. And on Monday they cured my groin.[39]

The *tlacuilo* references the devastating epidemic that had begun to sweep through Mexico in 1576 and its most conspicuous symptom: excessive bleeding from the nose. According to one medical study, this was one of the largest epidemics in New Spain, "causing at least two million deaths in Mexico, out of a total population of 4.4 million, representing a 45% mortality in the entire population." Some thirty years earlier the 1545 epidemic had already wiped out 80 percent of the indigenous population.[40]

The results were catastrophic. Franciscan friar Juan de Torquemada documented the destruction:

> In the year 1576, a great mortality and pestilence that lasted for more than a year overcame the Indians. It was so big that it ruined and destroyed almost the entire land. The place we know as New Spain was left almost empty. It was a thing of great bewilderment to see the people die. Many were dead and others almost dead, and nobody had the health or strength to help the diseased or bury the dead. In the cities and large towns, big ditches were dug, and from morning to sunset the priests did nothing else but carry the dead bodies and throw them into the ditches without any of the solemnity usually reserved for the dead, because the time did not allow otherwise. At night they covered the ditches with dirt.[41]

Both the Codex Aubin scribe and Fray Juan de Torquemada note the departure from the typical rites for the dead. The indigenous *tlacuilo* presents himself as a Christian, but in the face of such devastating illness he finds his faith tested and writes that it was "as if we were abandoned in the church." In the same passage he mentions that they cured his groin. This statement directly follows a reference to the procession in Santa Lucía "due to the disease," so it is possible that the scribe himself contracted the disease. In any case he would have had just cause to question his chances for survival, which may have prompted him to complete the title page eleven days later with the words "written here today in Mexico, the 27th of the month of September of 1576." I suspect that he bound the manuscript at this time as well. The scribe may have included blank pages at the end because his work, like many annals histories, was meant to be maintained and continued as a record of the community.

While the epidemic caused great devastation, the

artist-scribe survived. The last entry under 1576 continues in the same hand, although the ink is clearly different, indicating that it was written later:

> But on Holy Thursday there was no procession; so there was a rest. Whoever held a procession would have to pay five pesos; there would only be prayer. This is how it was done.[42]

The scribe is still referring to the disruptions in typical activities due to the epidemic, but he backtracks to Easter week of 1576. He may have retrospectively decided to include this detail after watching the epidemic gain momentum during the year.[43] He goes on to fill in the events of 1577. The handwriting and pictographic imagery remain consistent until 1591. Thereafter at least two additional hands appear. The catastrophic devastation wrought by epidemic diseases undoubtedly contributed a sense of urgency to the "historiographic revitalization" of sixteenth-century New Spain, spurring authors to record their histories before no one was left to tell them.

THE IMPACT OF SPANISH CATHOLICISM AND INQUISITION PRACTICES

In addition to contending with the immediate concern of disease, the Codex Aubin *tlacuilo*, throughout his project, had to take into consideration the significant influence that the Catholic Church wielded over society and cultural production. As discussed above, education was provided and overseen by the Catholic mendicant orders, primarily the Franciscans in the first half of the sixteenth century. As in Europe, written works produced by these schools' teachers, students, and graduates were subject to the scrutiny of the church. Orthodoxy in the practice of Catholicism remained a major concern of the church throughout the sixteenth century in both Europe and New Spain and was enforced through the Holy Office of the Inquisition. Prior to 1571, before the establishment of a formal tribunal in New Spain, canon law allowed bishops to act as ordinary inquisitors in the absence of a delegated inquisitor. In November 1571 inquisitor general Pedro Moya de Contreras established the first formal tribunal of the Holy Office of the Inquisition in Mexico.[44] Both before and after 1571, indigenous manuscripts and native-language texts were subject to review and possible destruction.

In the first half of the sixteenth century the elimination of these manuscripts was considered part of the process of eradicating indigenous spiritual practices and not necessarily a matter to be brought before the Inquisition. Juan de Zumárraga, who served as apostolic inquisitor from 1536 to 1543, notoriously destroyed hundreds of Nahua images and manuscripts. The friars, and even their indigenous students, often aided him in this task. In his *Historia general de las cosas de Nueva España*, Bernardino de Sahagún describes how the friars' students had helped destroy pyramid-temples and their contents.[45] In the mid-sixteenth century Diego de Landa ran the local inquisition in Yucatan. He infamously destroyed Maya idols, Maya books, and several Maya heretics in his auto-da-fé of 1562 in Maní.

Certainly the *tlacuilo* was aware of the Catholic leadership and some of their major activities. He records the death of Bishop Juan de Zumárraga in 1548 but does not record Zumárraga's arrival or the exact day of his death, which presumably occurred well before his time. Alonso de Montúfar, archbishop, is mentioned by name twice. The *tlacuilo* records his arrival on June 23, 1554, and his death on March 7, 1572. The arrival of Moya de Contreras is noted in 1571: "Here came our spiritual lord the Inquisitor. We went to Acaxic, Monday, September 3." In 1571 viceroy Martín Enríquez sent people to the towns along the road from Veracruz to Mexico City to greet the new inquisitor and his party. The *tlacuilo*'s entry suggests that he was among a group sent to Acaxic (Acajete), a site near the modern city of Puebla that was along the route. In 1574 he notes: "Here the spiritual lord, the inquisitor, disclosed the different sins that we commit, during Sunday he disclosed them." He then refers to the Holy Office's first great public auto-da-fé, where several English corsairs who had been convicted of heresy were turned over to the secular arm for burning at the stake: "On February 28 they burned the lords who had killed our beloved father on the coast, Vera Cruz." At the end of the entry for 1574 the *tlacuilo* notes: "The archbishop [Moya de Contreras] was consecrated today, Sunday, the 5th of the month of December." In 1586 the *tlacuilo* recapitulates his career:

> And the archbishop don Pedro Moya departed today, Wednesday, the 11th of the month of June of the year 1586. First he was the inquisitor, then the archbishop, then the viceroy, this is how he came to undertake three posts. And he came to improve the main church, and he expelled the *regidores*, who were Spaniards.[46]

According to Chimalpahin, Pedro Moya de Contreras departed for Spain in 1586, where he was made president of the Royal Council of the Indies.[47] He remained there until his death in 1592. The arrival of his successor, Alonso Fernández de Bonilla, in 1592 was not recorded because the primary *tlacuilo* had stopped writing in 1591. After several years of neglect, another *tlacuilo* took over in 1595 (figure 6.1). He recorded the major autos-da-fé of 1596 and 1605, the death of Fernández de Bonilla in 1600, and the return of the next archbishop, García de Santa María Mendoza y Zúñiga, to San Francisco in 1603. The entries in Codex Aubin indicate that the primary *tlacuilo* began his project in an environment shaped by Alonso de Montúfar's policies and created his title page and probably the binding about five years after Pedro Moya de Contreras established the Holy Office of the Inquisition in New Spain.

The Codex Aubin *tlacuilo* began his project at a time when owning, copying, and writing books and manuscripts could bring unwanted attention from the religious authorities. He notes a local example of this in 1560 by recording an act of censorship. His first entry under that year states: "On March 17 the books [*amatl*] were burned." His accompanying image shows flames beneath pages with text and images.[48] In an environment hostile to books, the *tlacuilo*'s decision to exercise care would have been wise. Even if he intended his manuscript for a limited local audience, it would have been important to safeguard the work from church authorities.

Further complicating matters, early Inquisition practices in New Spain lacked uniformity: documentation reflects jurisdictional struggles for control within the church as well as conflicts between the church and the political establishment.[49] At the time of its initial production, Codex Aubin (and its early migration sequence in particular) was the kind of project that would have been embraced by the Franciscans, who valued native-language texts and translations as tools for understanding and converting indigenous neophytes. Despite this potential support among the clergy, ideological conflict in New Spain was growing as the Catholic Church in Europe debated the issues raised by the Protestant Reformation at the Council of Trent (1545–1563).

The Dominican Alonso de Montúfar, second archbishop of Mexico (1554–1571), fomented dissent in the religious community in New Spain by promoting conservative antihumanist counterreform.[50] Inquisition scholar Martin Austin Nesvig has described Montúfar in conjunction with Vasco de Quiroga, the bishop of Michoacan, as leading

> the attack on Franciscan and Augustinian projects of native-language publication, expansion of the non-Dominican mendicant missions, and mendicant privileges generally speaking, though Montúfar cast a blind eye to his own order in many illegal actions designed to benefit the Dominican presence.[51]

Informants were placed in the schools as Montúfar investigated monastery and school life. Book censorship rose, particularly after 1560, when the aging archbishop brought Bartolomé de Ledesma to Mexico to serve as administrator of the diocese, provisor, and censor of printed matter.[52] Montúfar's attack was uneven, and the Franciscan clergy bore the brunt of increased scrutiny. Some of the well-known

Franciscan works censured include Zumárraga's *Doctrina*, Maturino Gilberti's *Diálogo* (written in Purepecha, the dominant indigenous language of Michoacan in western Mexico), and Bernardino de Sahagún's *Historia general de las cosas de Nueva España*. By the late 1560s the relative merits and dangers of the latter were even debated among the Franciscans themselves.[53] Sahagún noted that between 1570 and 1575 "it has been impossible to deal with this work because of the great disfavor that existed on the part of those who should have favored it."[54] The Spanish king Phillip II banned circulation of the *Historia general* in 1577.[55] As the Codex Aubin *tlacuilo* began his project, conservative secular forces in the church were growing increasingly critical of the powerful mendicant orders and increasingly suspicious of the Christian humanist ideas and projects freely promoted just a decade earlier.

The conservative trend escalated when Pedro Moya de Contreras stepped in as inquisitor general in 1571 and established the Holy Office of the Inquisition. As he continued Montúfar's centralizing reforms, he introduced more systematic attempts to enforce the Index of Prohibited Books. The Inquisition examined Franciscan monasteries and libraries thoroughly and established port controls, however poorly enforced, at Veracruz. As Nesvig has noted, even the printers became suspect: "Two high-profile cases against the typographer Pedro Ocharte and his blockcutter Juan Ortiz in 1572 underscored the new emphasis Moya de Contreras would place on the regulation not only of books but also of the people who physically created them."[56] Simply knowing of someone who possessed or had read a prohibited book and not reporting it could result in excommunication.[57] Moya de Contreras's focus on heresy related to printed matter and books had profound consequences. As Nesvig explains:

> The enforcement of the Index, the ban on Indian language scripture, and the *motu propio* ban on various other works were part of a strategy to clamp down on humanism, Erasmianism, and cultural production that went afoul of the conservative forces that came to dominate the Mexican Church after the brief period of humanist projects of prior decades. It is difficult to gauge, in quantitative terms, the effects on cultural production this trend had, but one can safely assume it had an impressive chilling effect. Certainly the Franciscans bore the brunt of this assault as their libraries and schools came under increasing scrutiny. But the laity surely also understood the terrible consequences of flouting the inquisitorial apparatus. At the same time prohibited books continued to circulate in wide numbers in Mexico despite the best efforts of inquisitors and censors.[58]

Though the Holy Office of the Inquisition focused its formal censorship activities on books and ideas associated with Protestantism (bringing their authors, owners, and readers to trial), works in indigenous languages, like Sahagún's *Historia general*, were still regarded with great suspicion and faced potential destruction or removal from circulation. As the Codex Aubin *tlacuilo* began his project and observed changing attitudes in the church as he continued to work, he surely considered the potential vulnerability of his enterprise.

While the latter part of the Codex Aubin history includes no controversial content, the initial migration sequence and ruler history might have attracted unwelcome attention from conservative religious authorities because these narratives reference pre-Hispanic ritual practice and feature pre-Hispanic deities. As in the primarily pictographic renditions of the migration story in Codex Boturini and Codex Azcatitlan, Huitzilopochtli (the hummingbird god) plays a prominent role in the narrative. The *tlacuilo* emphasized that the deity provided the inspiration and the guiding force behind the journey. According to the narrative shared in all three manuscripts, Huitzilopochtli identified the Mexica as his chosen people and led them on a 200-year journey filled with hardships until they founded the city of Tenochtitlan and their great empire. For the pre-Hispanic Mexica, the glory that Huitzilopochtli provided did not come without costs; sacrificial offerings and strict adherence to a ritual calendar ensured the continuation of privilege. In the migration sequence and in the ruler history Codex Aubin makes reference to the building of altars and temples and the sacrifices dedicated to the pre-Hispanic deities. Although the *tlacuilo* clearly presents himself as a practicing Catholic, inclusion of pre-Hispanic religious content in a manuscript written in an indigenous language posed certain risks.

As the *tlacuilo* worked, he balanced a desire for fidelity to his source material with the need to mitigate that risk. As demonstrated in chapter 2 and tables 1.1 and 2.1, the key elements of the migration narrative in Codex Aubin, including dates, stops along the migration route, and significant events, are identical to those in Codex Boturini and nearly identical to those in Codex Azcatitlan. Many colonial manuscripts include a chronology of Mexica rulers, and the Codex Aubin *tlacuilo* records the dates and reigns of the rulers faithfully. Unlike the migration sequence and ruler history, no well-established narrative existed for the postconquest annals portion of the manuscript. For the most part the postconquest events that he deemed worthy of recording are similar to those in other annals: events related to the activities of indigenous and Spanish political leaders, religious activities, and notable illnesses and natural phenomena. With so much of his content already scripted, the *tlacuilo* opted to innovate, and to mitigate risk, through form and layout.

The *tlacuilo*'s choices seem designed to lend authority to his content while mollifying potential Spanish critics. By presenting his manuscript as a codex, he delivered his content in a familiar, legible format associated with scholarship and knowledge. The decision to use pages from Julius Caesar's *Commentarii* may have been another move to counter vulnerability. Although Franciscan libraries suffered major losses in 1572, under Ledesma's enforcement of the primarily Dominican-authored Index of Prohibited Books, Latin classics largely escaped censure.

As Mathes explains, these texts were allowed to circulate for the purposes of Latin instruction:

> This exception was commonly employed as a means of retaining otherwise prohibited humanistic works, particularly in conventual libraries, for such grammatical or rhetorical works as those of Cicero and Quintillian were generally introduced by humanist authors and were considered an integral part of the humanist revival of classical intellectual values.

Inquisition records indicate that the Holy Office permitted buying and selling of Julius Caesar editions in New Spain and that these editions figured in the collections of both conventual and private libraries.[59] Although we cannot know for sure if the primary *tlacuilo* applied Codex Aubin's binding, it is appealing to imagine him consciously couching his history in endpapers from an uncensored and highly esteemed Latin edition of Julius Caesar's *Commentarii de Bello Gallico*, one of Renaissance Europe's most compelling pre-Christian annals histories.

Conclusion

In making a connection between pre-Hispanic culture and Europe's pagan past, the *tlacuilo* would not have been alone. Serge Gruzinski discusses the influences of pre-Columbian imagery, Ovid, and European pagan grotesques on the images that line the walls of the Augustinian monastery of Ixmiquilpan in Hidalgo, Mexico (figure 6.8).[60] He suggests that, as part of a complicated and multilayered process of mestizo mélange, indigenous and mestizo artists placed their cultural past in the same context as Europe's pagan past. Like Ovid, who could be read through a Christian filter, and the grotesques that had become decorative elements rather than potent references to actual pagan practice, indigenous Mexican culture and aesthetics could become an admired and accepted part of late sixteenth-century New Spain by placing it in a kind of classicized past.

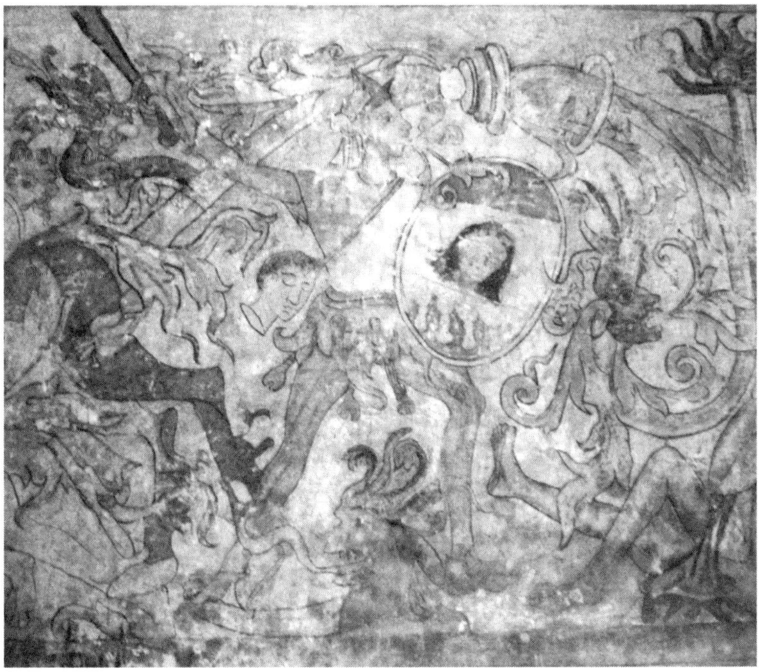

Figure 6.8. Detail of the murals at the Augustinian *convento* at Ixmiquilpan in Hidalgo, Mexico. Courtesy of author.

The *tlacuilo* encouraged his reader to view the viceregal present as an extension of the pre-Hispanic past. The narrative content of Codex Aubin spans five centuries and draws the pre-Hispanic past, conquest, and postconquest events into one historical continuum, albeit a continuum that at times backtracks and is therefore not always linear. The narrative begins with the migration of the Mexica people as they follow their supreme deity, Huitzilopochtli. At the end the annals reflect a world dominated by Christianity.

Throughout, the *tlacuilo* presents himself as an unwavering Catholic. In a successful manipulation of the codex format, he manages to convey all of the essential information about Huitzilopochtli's role in the Mexica migration while highlighting his own steadfast Christianity. While images of Huitzilopochtli, or the priests that channel him, appear regularly in Codex Boturini and Codex Azcatitlan, the Codex Aubin *tlacuilo* eliminates them almost entirely. This once-powerful Mexica deity is relegated to the alphabetic text, where the *tlacuilo* could control perception by referring to him as "the devil Huitzilopochtli." By mitigating the role of Huitzilopochtli and using the physical format of a printed book and some of its aesthetic forms, the artist-scribe at once posits his subject matter as "history" worthy of being recorded in a "book" and neutralizes that part of the history that at one time had significant ritual overtones.[61]

Drawing inspiration from pictographic manuscripts and printed books, the *tlacuilo* struck a balance designed to persuade his audience to accept the legitimacy of his work. As a historian trying to preserve something of the past, he chose to retain pictographic writing in his manuscript rather than produce a purely alphabetic text. Likewise, he recorded the pre-Hispanic narrative content of his sources with great fidelity. He responded to some of the primary threats to his project, like epidemic disease and church censorship, with innovation. By drawing on his education and the availability of new materials, he created a hybrid work meant to channel the legitimacy and prestige of a European codex. In 1576, when his own death might have seemed a foregone conclusion, he wrapped things up by producing a title page. If he went to the trouble to create a title page, he probably also sought to have the work bound, using the resources and technology available to him in sixteenth-century New Spain. If he selected pages from Julius Caesar's *Commentarii de Bello Gallico* as his endpapers, perhaps he hoped to stimulate a new ideological framework by inviting comparison between Europe's classical pagan past and the pre-Christian past of his own ancestors. In any case, the *tlacuilo*'s work represents a negotiation between the perceived legitimacy of pre-Hispanic and European modes of expression and communication. In our own era it has become increasingly clear that the pre-eminent knowledge bearer of today is shifting from printed books to digitalized media. The Codex Aubin *tlacuilo* and his work remind us that navigating major shifts in how we communicate and receive knowledge is nothing new in the scheme of history.

CHAPTER 7

CONCLUSION

Central Mexican Manuscript Painting in Transition

CODEX BOTURINI, Codex Azcatitlan, and Codex Aubin are linked by the migration history they share. The studies included here explore the methods and motivations of their makers, elucidating some of the creative strategies that the *tlacuiloque* deployed to make the Mexica migration history relevant and accessible to their audiences. By way of conclusion I offer some final thoughts on how these three manuscripts might have intersected as they circulated among Nahua intellectuals in the Basin of Mexico in the sixteenth and seventeenth centuries.

The first of the three manuscripts to come into existence was Codex Boturini. This document was begun by a *tlacuilo* working in the early part of the sixteenth century before, during, or shortly after the conquest. His goal was to record the migration history of the Mexica people. Archival evidence and the reinforced seams on the verso of the screenfold indicate that he did not intend to add additional content. He recorded a story that was already known and shared through oral tradition. It was a narrative that cemented existing power dynamics by reinforcing the early presence of the Mexica in many locations that had become tribute-paying subjects of the Mexica Empire. The narrative privileged and set the Mexica apart from other groups inhabiting the Basin of Mexico and therefore must have been created there. The *tlacuilo* may have had access to pictorial manuscripts that depicted this migration with a different composition or had access to this narrative through oral traditions. The evidence of compositional editing and revision suggests that he was not making an exact copy of another manuscript.

He was either giving an existing visual template his own twist or constructing an aesthetic and mnemonic record based on his own interpretation of oral accounts.

It seems likely that the *tlacuilo* was born and educated before the conquest. He worked with traditional materials and in a traditional style. His symmetrical narrative highlighted the cyclical nature of time and the mythic connections between Aztlan and Tenochtitlan, suggesting that he commanded knowledge of Mesoamerican cosmology. The *tlacuilo* or another manuscript specialist assembled this *amatl* in a screenfold format, anticipating its use in oral presentations of the whole or parts on required occasions. The religious component of the manuscript is not obscured in any way. Huitzilopochtli is given pride of place as a central protagonist. There are no aesthetic or conceptual concessions meant to assuage a European audience uneasy or openly hostile to pre-Hispanic religion. The codex has few or no introduced European stylistic traits. If it was produced before the conquest, the *tlacuilo* probably put black and red pigment to paper in the close vicinity of a temple where he anticipated this cultural history might be used. His skilled even hand reveals him to be an experienced artist. If the codex was produced before the conquest, recording this history may have been part of his duty as a *calmecac* priest that taught children of the elite in the Mexica capital. Or perhaps it was a history requested by Moteuczoma himself.

While the *tlacuilo* laid out his entire composition in draft and went over the contour lines with a deep black, he did not have the opportunity to apply the pigments whose color and material composition would have added additional meaning to the images. Perhaps he died in the conquest or perished from the introduced diseases sweeping through the indigenous populations. Maybe he worked after the conquest and abandoned his project as he saw painted manuscripts targeted for destruction. We may never know. We do know that someone else who valued this history preserved it. The Annals of Tlatelolco describes indigenous elites carrying their codices with them in the aftermath of the conquest.[1] Codex Boturini was guarded and preserved through a period when painted manuscripts were actively sought and destroyed.

In the 1550s or early 1560s the Codex Aubin *tlacuilo* began work on his manuscript. As presented in chapter 2, I believe that he worked directly from the Codex Boturini manuscript. In chapter 6 I link him to the Colegio de Santa Cruz in Tlatelolco. At midcentury this school was a locus for the production of historical manuscripts. The *tlacuilo* may have encountered Codex Boturini there. Perhaps it had entered its collection or become the personal property of a friar. Or it may have belonged to one of the students whose father had also been a *tlacuilo*. Although pre-Hispanic histories were being recorded, it was also a time of censorship. The Codex Aubin *tlacuilo* approached his subject cautiously. Direct references to Huitzilopochtli and sacrifice are usually addressed in the text rather than pictorially. The *tlacuilo*, a product of the Franciscan schools, was keen to preserve the history of his people and to continue the annals tradition by recording the events of his day. With studied effort he reproduced a remarkably faithful account of the migration history in a completely new format designed for the edification of his Nahuatl-speaking peers as well as to survive in an era of censorship. The new format lent his history the authority of a printed book, the premier vehicle for recording knowledge in the European world. His deliberate choices reflected a successful merging of the Tenochca past and present as well as a sea change in the way communication and dissemination of knowledge were understood.

The small, carefully rendered, and brilliantly pigmented pages recorded a history that could only be viewed by one person at a time. The context for producing and consuming knowledge had changed. The content of Codex Aubin is general enough that its history was probably intended as a communal document for the cabildo of San Juan Moyotlan. Nevertheless, a few personal references remind us that behind this communal history is an individual who, like many of us, provided labor, had children, and feared death.

After recording the migration and imperial history, the *tlacuilo* may have kept the document with him, adding important events throughout the year. When he fell ill during the intense plague of 1576, he went to the Colegio de Santa Cruz and bound his manuscript. Perhaps as part of his overall defensive strategy, he couched it within the pages of Julius Caesar's *De Bello Gallico*, offering the reader a classical framework with which to understand the material contained therein.

Codex Azcatitlan seems to draw on Codex Boturini rather than on Codex Aubin for content. The Codex Azcatitlan *tlacuiloque* use the same glyph for Aztlan as found in Codex Boturini and do not draw on Codex Aubin's imperial, conquest, or postconquest history. Both Codex Aubin and Codex Azcatitlan manipulate the contents of the Codex Boturini narrative. While the Codex Aubin *tlacuilo* couched his content in an innovative new format meant to protect, communicate, and preserve this history, the Codex Azcatitlan master *tlacuilo* expanded and edited the contents for his own ends. The focus on Tlatelolco indicates that the *tlacuiloque* probably produced Codex Azcatitlan there. They too might have accessed Codex Boturini at the Colegio de Santa Cruz in Tlatelolco, perhaps working on Codex Azcatitlan together as teacher and student.

Codex Azcatitlan represents an elite Mexica history designed for a Tlatelolca audience. I suspect that the conquest and postconquest history was originally narrated by the Tlatelolca warrior Ecatl or his descendants. As outlined in chapter 4, the conquest history highlights the role of Ecatl and positions him as a cosmic hero. The postconquest history devotes a significant amount of attention to the Honduran expedition. Ecatl survived the Honduran expedition and would have had the firsthand experience necessary to pass down a detailed description of Cuauhtemoc's death. As chapter 5 details, the Codex Azcatitlan narrative ends with events of the year 1527. The Annals of Tlatelolco tells us that by 1528 Ecatl was a stowaway on Cortés's ship to Spain.[2] He may have shared his experiences and his memories of Tlatelolca history with a *tlacuilo* in 1527 or 1528 before departing on this dangerous expedition. Records in Nahuatl script were not yet common at this early date, and the resulting manuscript would have been pictographic. In addition to drawing on Codex Boturini, I believe that the Codex Azcatitlan *tlacuiloque* drew on this early manuscript, no longer extant.

Furthermore, I believe that this early manuscript and Codex Azcatitlan are linked to the Annals of Tlatelolco. As described earlier in the book, MS 22 may have been produced around 1545 and MS 22bis (a copy) was produced later, perhaps as late as the late seventeenth or eighteenth century. As Lockhart writes:

> [T]he more I have studied the texts, the more I have returned to my first thought, that the later manuscript is a direct copy of the earlier, with some digressions based on other late texts, oral tradition, or the writer's imagination. The vast majority of the relatively minor variations between the texts prove to stem from the later writer's inability to read the older text (in which it is easy to have sympathy with him). Some of the added material is clearly discordant with the early manuscript; passages not in the earlier version often have to do with Quauhtemoc [Cuauhtemoc], whose popularity grew with every passing generation.[3]

The newer text, MS 22bis, claims to be a copy of an older text of 1528. The inscription states that "it was done a long time ago here in Tlatelolco, in the year of 1528."[4] Lockhart rejected this claim out of hand, definitively arguing that MS 22 does not date to such an earlier period. However, the scribe may be referring to MS 22 as a later transcription of a pictographic narrative recorded in 1528. Or perhaps he refers to the "digressions," the additional content that he added when he copied MS 22. Codex Azcatitlan was clearly not made in 1528, but its content ends there. It may be based on an older pictographic manuscript produced around 1528. The additions to MS 22bis that relate to conquest and postconquest history, such as the account of Cuauhtemoc's death, align closely to pictorial content in Codex Azcatitlan and merit further study.

Kevin Terraciano has linked Ecatl to MS 22bis:

> The story in the List of Rulers [Document 1] resembles the annals tradition in that the narrative abruptly shifts in the end to focus on a single individual, Ecatzin, who not only survived the voyage to Spain but returned to Tlatelolco and received some compensation from the king, apparently. It is very likely that Ecatzin or his descendants were involved in the writing or relating of the account. Why else would he appear so prominently? The narrative ends with his return to Tlatelolco, where the List of Rulers was written.[5]

Around 1533 Ecatl returned from Spain; he not only survived the journey but claimed to have had an audience with the Holy Roman Emperor Charles V. After establishing himself in Tlatelolco, he sought to share his story as he aged, like several of the Spanish conquistadors. He may have been one of the informants who provided information for Sahagún's project. As Terraciano notes:

> We know that Sahagún was in Tlatelolco in 1555. He took his writing to another altepetl named Tepepulco and returned to Tlatelolco in 1561. In the prologue to book II, Sahagún stated that the indigenous governor of Tlatelolco and his councilmen "assigned me as many as eight or ten leaders" who were "very capable in their language and in their ancient customs." These men worked closely with a few students of the College of Santa Cruz de Tlatelolco, established by the Franciscans to house and instruct the most gifted sons of the native nobility in reading, writing and the Christian doctrine. Thus many of the Nahua writers of book XII came from Tlatelolco. Few, if any, came from Tenochtitlan.[6]

While Cuauhtemoc's extreme youth is recorded in conquest accounts, Ecatzin's is not. If he had been around twenty years old at the time of the conquest, he would have been in his fifties in 1555. At this age he would have been considered one of the elders who had survived the conquest and was therefore a font of firsthand knowledge.

It seems likely that Codex Azcatitlan was produced in the vicinity of the Colegio de Santa Cruz in the late 1560s or 1570s and possibly later. The *tlacuiloque* painted it sometime after the colonial city was rebuilt and probably after the Manila galleons had started circulating in 1565. Graulich has claimed that the colored parasols that appear on the last folio were Chinese import items.[7] As the *tlacuiloque* began work on Codex Azcatitlan, the master artist determined the framework of the narrative. Perhaps working for Ecatl directly, he determined to highlight the Tlatelolca presence in a shared Mexica history. He trained the apprentice, perhaps assigning him the Codex Boturini as a template. The *tlacuiloque* worked on expensive European paper and were influenced by introduced woodcuts, paintings, and illustrations.

As in the case of Codex Boturini, the work on Codex Azcatitlan was interrupted. The composition and color were never finished. The latter part of the history required a more thorough reconciling of dates and material that did not come to fruition. If one *tlacuilo* died, we might expect the other to have completed the manuscript. Perhaps the manuscript attracted the negative attention of the Catholic Church. Unlike Codex Aubin, the migration history depicts Huitzilopochtli frequently and includes several images of sacrifice. It highlights indigenous victory over the Spanish. The missing pages may have contained more explicit sacrifice scenes. Perhaps the master *tlacuilo* tried to mediate the content by belatedly adding the image of the Holy Spirit to the Spanish banner and by painting the image of a devil on Acamapichtli's cape. Or perhaps the project ended when Ecatl died. After work stopped, the manuscript appears to have stayed in Tlatelolco and may have been used at a later point by the author of MS 22bis. By the early eighteenth century all three of these manuscripts entered the collection of Lorenzo Boturini Benaduci. Their history thereafter is traced in the epilogue.

EPILOGUE

LIFE AFTER PRODUCTION

THE NARRATIVES RECORDED IN Codex Boturini, Codex Azcatitlan, and Codex Aubin would eventually leave the communities of their production and circulate far and wide. They apparently stayed in the capital of New Spain until the eighteenth century, at which time they were collected and eventually inventoried by a Milanese aristocrat named Lorenzo Boturini Benaduci (1702–1755). Boturini would amass a large collection of manuscripts between March 1736, when he arrived at the capital of New Spain and January 31, 1743, when the viceroy, Pedro Cebrián y Agustín, Conde de Fuenclara (1742–1746), ordered his arrest, imprisonment, and eventual exile. The viceroy charged him with failing to observe legal protocol in organizing a coronation ceremony for a statue of the Virgin of Guadalupe, a major impetus for Boturini's trip to New Spain.[1] It was his search for historical documents relevant to the cult of the Virgin of Guadalupe that initially led Boturini to study, copy, and collect pre-Hispanic and colonial manuscripts. According to John Glass, parts of the Boturini collection may trace back to the collections of Fernando de Alva Ixtlilxochitl and Carlos de Sigüenza y Góngora.[2] This epilogue charts the early movements of Codex Boturini, Codex Azcatitlan, and Codex Aubin, from their first appearance in Boturini's inventories to the museum and library collections where they are currently located.

The Boturini Collection Inventories

Lorenzo Boturini Benaduci first began cataloguing his collection while in prison. An unpublished manuscript dated July 15, 1743, currently in the Archivo General de las Indias (AGI) in Seville, Spain, is the first record of his collection.[3] The viceroy ordered Boturini to make an official catalogue of the collection later that year. Beginning on September 16, 1743, Boturini was released from prison each day under guarded surveillance to assist in the cataloguing of his confiscated documents. Descriptions of the codices (without identifying titles) appear in this 1743 judicial catalogue of his collection. A second government inventory, produced without Boturini's assistance, used the same catalogue numbers and was published by order of the viceroy in 1745.

Although Boturini never returned to New Spain and never reclaimed his collection after his deportation to Spain in October 1743, he produced a third catalogue of his collection, the 1746 *Catálogo del Museo Histórico Indiano del Caballero Lorenzo Boturini Benaduci, Señor de la Torre, y de Hono*. This inventory indicates that he consulted and copied books and manuscripts from many important archives in New Spain and made several trips to areas outside the city center, such as Metztitlan (in the present-day Mexican state of Hidalgo), Huexotzinco (in the present-day Mexican state of Puebla), Cholula (in the present-day Mexican state of Puebla), and Tlaxcala (in the present-day Mexican state of Tlaxcala). In Mexico City the archives he worked in included the Cabildo de la Catedral, Archivo de la Real Audiencia, and Biblioteca de la Universidad. Boturini copied several manuscripts—including works by Alva Ixtlilxochitl, Chimalpahin, and Tezozomoc—from the collection of don Carlos de Sigüenza y Góngora housed in the Jesuit Colegio Máximo de San Pedro y San Pablo.[4]

After 1746 Codex Azcatitlan and Codex Aubin do not appear in subsequent inventories of the Boturini collection. Codex Boturini, however, continues to appear in subsequent lists of the Boturini collection through the 1804 inventory produced by Ignacio de Cubas.[5] By the time Cubas prepared an 1823 inventory of the collection, all three manuscripts were listed as missing.[6] The manuscript entries for the 1743 judicial inventory and the 1746 catalogue inventory are cited below.

1743 JUDICIAL INVENTORY, MEXICO CITY

[Codex Boturini 2-33]

33———Item. A map, on agave paper, relating to Mexican history, in eleven folds.[7]

[Codex Azcatitlan 2-32]

32———Item. Another map, covered with figures and characters; treats of the history of the Mexican nation and the conquest made by the Spaniards; all being very much damaged, and in twenty-five sheets, enveloped in parchment.[8]

[Codex Aubin 2-17]

17———Item. Another history in octavo, manuscript, in the Mexican language, interspersed with many paintings; it treats of Mexican History, and is written by various Indian authors and is original, in seventy-nine sheets.[9]

1746 CATÁLOGO DEL MUSEO INDIANO ENTRIES, SPAIN

[Codex Boturini 7-1]
Paragraph 7 Heading: "Historia Mexicana" (Mexican History)

1. An Indian paper map with folds like a piece of cloth, and it extends like a bundle, we can say that it represents about 23 pages. It paints the departure of the Mexicans from the island of Aztlan and their arrival at the continent of New Spain, with the stays that they made in each place and the years of these, signified in their characters, and finally the wars that followed in service to Coxcox, king of Culhuacan. [Original.][10]

[Codex Azcatitlan 7–3]
Paragraph 7 Heading: "Historia Mexicana" (Mexican History)

> 3. Another map on European paper, of 25 leaves, perhaps translated from another ancient one. Explains the Mexican history; the arrival of their people to New Spain; stays that they made in places, with characters of the years and symbols of the days; the arrival of the Spanish, preaching of the holy scriptures and rites of our sacred religion. [Copy.][11]

[Codex Aubin 8–14]
Paragraph 8 Heading: "Manuscritos de Autores Indios" (Manuscripts by Indian authors)

> 14. Another history of the Mexican nation, part in figures and characters and part in prose, in *nahuatl*, written by an anonymous author in the year 1576, and continues in the same way with other Indian authors until the year 1608. The first paintings show the four *triadecatéridas* of the Indian calendar, and the last some figures of the Mexican kings and other Christian rulers, with the symbols of the years they ruled. [Volume 9 in octavo, original.][12]

Boturini's 1746 catalogue was a labor of love. He cared deeply for his collection, calling it "the only estate that I have in the Indies, and so precious, that I wouldn't exchange it for gold and silver, for diamonds and pearls."[13] As he began work on his catalogue in Spain, he had to rely on limited documentation and his own powers of recollection. As manuscript scholar Francisco González-Hermosillo Adams writes in his summary of "Lorenzo Boturini y su colección de códices indios novohispanos" (Lorenzo Boturini and His Collection of Indian Codices from New Spain):

> Unfortunately, Boturini had to mentally reconstruct the document list in Spain, without the judicial inventory constructed at the time he was apprehended.
>
> The collection that they seized from him was distant and mutilated, the techniques of memory his only recourse. From memory, after falling into disgrace, he had already determined to reconstruct the collection in his mind. Once on the peninsula, when at last he could have his catalogue printed, Boturini could not include a multitude of undoubtedly important loose pieces. He declared of them: "I cannot humanly remember."[14]

Although Boturini did have to rely on his memory, he must have had a core (if limited) set of notes to work with in Spain. Boturini's unpublished July 15, 1743, version of his catalogue is held in Seville, so it is likely that he brought that manuscript to Spain and used it as a source to produce a more finished version in 1746. That version has too many details (such as the frequent references to the number of pages in a manuscript, as we see in the descriptions of the Codex Boturini and Codex Azcatitlan) for the document to have been produced at a great distance from the originals. Boturini's statement on the difficulty of remembering (cited by González-Hermosillo above) may relate to the difficulty of remembering at the time he was producing his initial manuscript (the July 15, 1743, version) while incarcerated. A comparison of the 1743 judicial and 1746 entries indicates that the 1746 version is somewhat more detailed, although the 1746 catalogue is less comprehensive, as Glass points out.[15] Once in Spain, Boturini reorganized the entries into categories like "Mexican history" and "Manuscripts by Indian authors."

Another difference between the two entries cited above is that Boturini's 1746 catalogue terminates each description with a note on the status of the document as an original or copy and sometimes includes a volume number or description of the size (folio, quarto, octavo). Interestingly, he describes the Codex Azcatitlan as a copy. This does not indicate that Boturini made or commissioned a copy: he explains when such a situation occurs. For example, his note on the pictorial manuscript known as the Tira de Tepechpan (2–4) states that he had a copy made (now lost). Likewise, his prose sources often mention the circumstances of production, such as the *Relación sucinta* by Alva Ixtlilxochitl (4–2): "The copy was made from the original, and it can be found in said Volume 2."[16] Since Boturini did not commission the Codex Azcatitlan, he was probably told that the manuscript was a copy of older sources when he obtained it, or his assessment may have relied on stylistic considerations. The categorization as "copy" does not seem to be based on the European paper that is used, because the pictorial Nezahualcoyotl manuscript (3–6) is described as both original and on European paper. Finally, in addition to describing the Codex Aubin as "original," Boturini describes it as "volume 9 in octavo," referring to the small size of the manuscript and identifying it as one of the twenty "tomos" in Boturini's collection. Glass identifies the twenty "tomos" in a chart in *The Handbook of Middle American Indians*, but the exact relationship among these manuscripts is unknown.[17]

The 1746 catalogue also provides information about the preservation of the manuscripts. The extant Codex Azcatitlan and Codex Aubin still have the same number of pages described in the eighteenth-century listing. This indicates that the missing folios in Codex Azcatitlan were removed earlier, probably in the mid- to late sixteenth century, as theorized in the conclusion. Codex Boturini, by contrast, still had twenty-three folios in the eighteenth century. The remaining folio and a half was lost in the nineteenth century, as described below.

Copying the Manuscripts in the Eighteenth Century: Antonio León y Gama (1735–1802) and Father José Pichardo (1748–1812)

Once Boturini's collection was seized in 1743 and deposited in the Real Caja (treasury), it moved to several different locations where scholars were able to consult, study, and copy the manuscripts. The collection then moved to the following locations: to the Escribanía de Gobierno in the mid-eighteenth century; to the library of the archbishop of Mexico in the second half of the eighteenth century; to the university library in 1771; to the Secretaría de Cámara del Virreinato in 1787–1788; to the hands of Fray Manuel de Vega in 1790; to the Secretaría de Cámara del Virreinato again in 1795; and to the Secretaría de Estado y Relaciones in 1821. Parts of the collection were deposited in the university's newly formed Museo Nacional in 1826 and probably in the newly formed Archivo General, founded in 1823. According to Glass, the 1791, 1804, 1823, and 1917–1918 inventories reflect the slow dispersal of the collection. "Although the collection suffered some depletion by 1771, the most important losses seem to have occurred between 1771 and 1788, the period also when [Antonio de] León y Gama was engaged in copying many of its documents."[18]

Born and raised in New Spain, Antonio de León y Gama studied at the Colegio de San Ildefonso and developed interests in astronomy and pre-Columbian archaeology and history, though he occupied an unrelated bureaucratic post in the administration of New Spain for nearly forty years.[19] In the second part of his *Descripción histórica y cronológica* León y Gama describes how he began to copy indigenous manuscripts as a means of learning about the Nahuatl language and the history and origins of the indigenous Mexicans:

> Among so much that I attained to instruct me sufficiently to be able to penetrate the spirit of these narratives, I was allowed to make copies, not only of the many that the gentleman Boturini collected, both in our characters as in paintings that existed in the Royal University, as well as others that were found in the possession of some curious persons, who gave me the honor of copying, as well as other originals that I was able to attain, in which collection I spent much time and work, and not a little money.[20]

In this manner León y Gama amassed a collection of documents, many copied from the Boturini collection. The majority of his collection is accessible today in the Bibliothèque Nationale de France.

Among the reproductions that León y Gama made are the earliest copies of Codex Azcatitlan and Codex Aubin (partial).[21] These copies provide an important chronological marker, indicating that the manuscripts were still in Mexico and available for study there around 1780. The order of León y Gama's pages show that the reversed initial pages of the Codex Azcatitlan (folios 1r and 1v) remained so from the late eighteenth century until 1959, when the manuscript underwent restoration. At that time the pages were reordered, mounted on muslin, and bound with a red leather cover.[22]

Upon León y Gama's death in 1802, his collection passed into the hands of another scholar, his testamentary executor, Father José Antonio Pichardo. Born in New Spain, Pichardo was a member of the Catholic Oratory of San Felipe Neri in Mexico City and wrote several religious treatises as well as a publication on the boundaries of Louisiana and Texas. Like León y Gama, Pichardo had an interest in Nahua culture. He also copied the Codex Azcatitlan and perhaps part of the Codex Aubin, among other manuscripts.[23] Though Pichardo had León y Gama's manuscript collection in his possession for some time, the documents were eventually sold by Gama's descendants. Parts of the collection were acquired by the Prussian naturalist Alexander von Humboldt and the French scientist Joseph Marius Alexis Aubin.[24]

Nineteenth-Century Collection History

Many of the manuscripts that formed the original Boturini collection made their way into private collections and public institutions during the late eighteenth and nineteenth centuries. Codex Boturini was taken to Europe in the early nineteenth century but was returned to Mexico and is held today in the Biblioteca Nacional de Antropología e Historia. Codex Azcatitlan entered the private collections of two Frenchmen, Joseph Marius Alexis Aubin and then E. Eugène Goupil, before being left to the Bibliothèque Nationale de France in Paris in 1898, where it resides today. Codex Aubin, as its name indicates, also belonged to J. M. A. Aubin and apparently was sold to Jules Desportes. The British Museum in London acquired it from Desportes, and it remains there today. A more detailed description of these transfers follows.

CODEX BOTURINI

As a material object Codex Boturini bears traces of its life after initial production. In conjunction with archival evidence, a gold border and a museum label on the last page bear witness to the exhibition of the manuscript in the nineteenth century and the damage that occurred around that time. The museum label corresponds to the first exhibition of Codex Boturini in Europe in 1824 (figure E.1). William Bullock, an Englishman known as a jeweler, taxidermist, naturalist, entrepreneur, and showman, traveled to Mexico in 1823, just two years after independence. In 1824 and 1825 he exhibited objects, flora, fauna, and plaster casts of stone sculpture and architecture that he brought back from his journey. This exhibit, shown in multiple incarnations, represented the first British exhibition of Mexican natural and cultural history. In June 1824 he published the first edition of the very popular account of his travels called *Six Months' Residence and Travels in Mexico: Containing Remarks on the Present State of New Spain, Its Natural Productions, State of Society, Manufactures, Trade, Agriculture, and Antiquities, &c.*

Codex Boturini was among the objects that Bullock brought back to London for exhibition in his gallery spaces at the Egyptian Hall in Piccadilly. On April 8, 1824, he opened two complementary

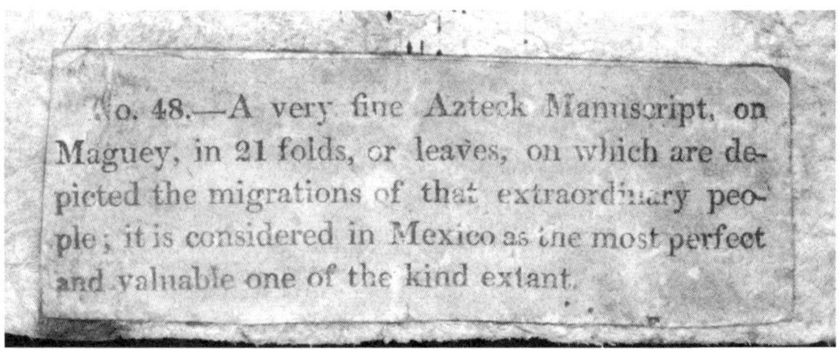

Figure E.1. The label that appears on the last half-folio of Codex Boturini. Secretaría de Cultura-INAH-MEX; reproduced with permission of the Instituto Nacional de Antropología e Historia.

exhibits: "Ancient Mexico" and "Modern Mexico."[25] Each exhibit had its own accompanying catalogue: *A Description of the Unique Exhibition Called Ancient Mexico* and *Catalogue of the Exhibition, Called Modern Mexico*. As attendance at the immensely popular exhibition slowed, perhaps in November 1824, selected works from the two galleries were combined in an exhibition called "Ancient and Modern Mexico," with a third catalogue version: *A Descriptive Catalogue of the Exhibition, Entitled Ancient and Modern Mexico*.

Codex Boturini still bears a label, pasted onto the last half-folio, from Bullock's "Ancient Mexico" exhibition. The wording on the label matches exactly the number, description, punctuation, and spelling from the accompanying 1824 catalogue. In fact it appears to be cut directly from that catalogue:

> No. 43.—A very fine Azteck Manuscript, on Maguey, in 21 folds, or leaves, on which are depicted the migrations of that extraordinary people; it is considered in Mexico as the most perfect and valuable one of the kind extant.[26]

Codex Boturini disappears from the inventory lists in Mexico during the exhibition years, further corroborating the loan of this manuscript to Bullock. It is included in Ignacio de Cubas's 1804 census of the Boturini collection then held in the Secretaría de Cámara del Virreinato under the title "Colección de memorias de Nueva España," where it appears as entry 7–1.[27] Cubas produced another inventory in 1823. Codex Boturini is not listed there and is instead recorded on a list of missing manuscripts.[28] While Bullock's catalogue entry and the label on the manuscript indicate that the original Codex Boturini was exhibited, the lithographic image of the "Ancient Mexico" exhibit included in the catalogue appears to show a copy on display (figure E.2). The artist who produced the lithograph, Agostino Aglio, depicts an oversized version of the Codex Boturini with the individual folios spaced at regular intervals as they encircle the room.

Bullock appears to have exhibited both the original and the copy in his "Ancient Mexico" exhibit, but only the copy, enlarged and in clear view, could

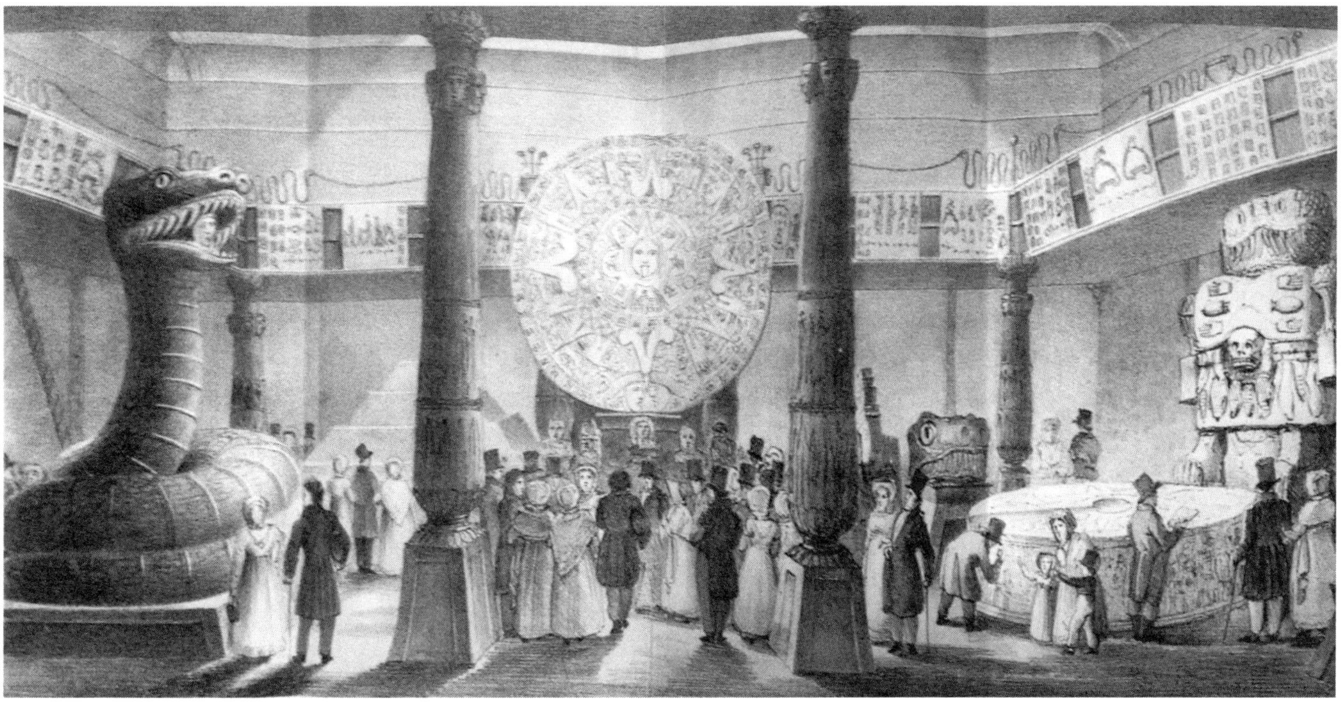

Figure E.2. Agostino Aglio engraving published in *A Description of the Unique Exhibition Called Ancient Mexico: Collected on the Spot in 1823 by the Assistance of the Mexican Government and Now Open to Public Inspection at the Egyptian Hall, Picadilly by W. Bullock* (London, 1824).

be reproduced in the lithograph. As Diana Fane has pointed out, the illustrations in Bullock's catalogues are not a true documentation but reflect the lithographers' creative license.[29] As it would be impossible to represent the many smaller objects exhibited on pedestals and in vitrines, Aglio had to make choices. His image highlighted the model of a pyramid temple and the casts taken of some of the largest works, monumental sculptures that Bullock wrote about extensively. In lieu of smaller pieces that would be impossible to reproduce, Aglio populated the scene with a crowd of intrigued nineteenth-century viewers. The right half of the room includes a man peering at the Tizoc Stone with a magnifying glass, a mother with her two children, and a man gazing into a book, presumably the very guidebook that Aglio was illustrating.

Aglio included the copy of Codex Boturini in his lithograph for several reasons. First, if the Boturini copy was on display as it appears in this image, it would have been highly visible and a natural addition to the composition. While no copy is listed in the catalogue of the "Ancient Mexico" exhibit, the later version from the "Ancient and Modern Mexico" exhibition eliminates the original manuscript from the inventory and lists a copy as item number 69:

> No. 69.—Copy of a very fine Azteck Manuscript, on Maguey, in 21 folds, or leaves, on which are depicted the migrations of that extraordinary people; it is considered in Mexico as the most perfect and valuable one of the kind extant.—It encircles the room.[30]

Bullock modified the original data on Codex Boturini first by adding the word "copy" and "encircles the room," a description that matches Aglio's image in the "Ancient Mexico" catalogue. Second, Bullock considered Codex Boturini of great importance. In the "Ancient Mexico" catalogue he discusses the rarity of the painted manuscripts in his exhibit:

> After the conquest, every document of this description that could be procured was destroyed, and very few have reached our time. The Baron Humbolt [*sic*] brought some fragments, which he has published; but so rare are these Azteck MMS. that neither of the Museums or Libraries of Paris or London possess one. Mr. B. were [*sic*], however, so fortunate as to discover several, and by the permission of the Mexican government, allowed to bring them to this country, on the express condition of their being returned at the close of the Exhibition.[31]

As "the most perfect and valuable one [painted manuscript] of the kind extant," the Codex Boturini merited inclusion as an exemplar of the genre. Finally, and not least, Aglio himself had been commissioned by Bullock to produce the copy of Codex Boturini. By including it prominently in the lithograph, he celebrated his own creative work.

In *Six Months' Residence and Travels* Bullock indicates that making copies of the painted manuscripts was one of his goals in securing the loans from the Mexican government:

> They are articles of such interest, and so much prized by the government, that, though I experienced from the public authorities the greatest liberality, and every assistance in my pursuit for information concerning the ancient state of the country, yet no offers of mine could induce them to part with these MSS. until I had given them an assurance that, after they had been copied in England, I would transmit them again to Mexico.[32]

Ian Graham notes that Aglio's enlarged copy of the Codex Boturini greatly pleased Bullock and also attracted the attention of Edward King, Lord Kingsborough, a frequent visitor to the exhibition. Before Bullock could commission additional copies of other manuscripts, Lord Kingsborough had engaged Aglio to make one hundred facsimiles of the

Codex Boturini and later a copy of Codex Bodley (in September 1824).[33] Perhaps the original Codex Boturini was removed from the exhibition as part of the process of making these additional facsimiles. In any case, when Bullock condensed and combined the "Ancient Mexico" and "Modern Mexico" exhibitions sometime around November 1824, the entry for the original Codex Boturini was replaced with the listing of the copy.[34]

Though Bullock credited the cooperation of the Mexican government frequently in his publications, the loan of painted manuscripts may not have been as straightforward as he suggested. Michael Costeloe's biographical account of William Bullock explains:

> In fact, it seems that he did not have permission to take them out of the country. On 27 March 1825, Lucas Alamán, Mexico's Minister of Internal and External Affairs, wrote to the Mexican minister in London, Mariano Michelena, telling him that Bullock had removed them without permission. He had been stopped at Veracruz but promised that once copies had been made, he would return them. He had not done so, and Alamán instructed that they should be retrieved as soon as possible.
>
> The two most important manuscripts—the Codex Boturini and the Plano—are now to be found in the Mexican Museo Nacional de Antropología.

As Costeloe has noted, the circumstances of the manuscripts' return to Mexico are unknown, but "it would seem probable that Bullock himself, not wanting to antagonize the Mexicans on his return in the autumn of 1825, may have personally taken them back."[35]

The circumstances of the manuscripts' return are also commented upon in two nineteenth-century sources. Ian Graham writes that "according to one source the request was made to the British Museum by General Mariano Michelena, then Mexico's representative in London, at the urging of Isidro Icaza and Manuel Orozco y Berra."[36] Father Isidro Ignacio Icaza was the director of the first incarnation of the museum in the 1820s. The Frenchman Eugène Boban provided his own account in an 1891 publication, *Documents pour servir à l'histoire du Mexique*, a catalogue raisonné of Eugène Goupil's collection of painted manuscripts. Catalogue Entry No. 93 for the "Copie de la Tira del Museo" (Copy of the Codex Boturini) reads as follows:

> The original figurative painting on agave paper is folded like a folding screen. The lithographic copy that we examine appears to be made in London at Mr. Delafield's. An English traveler, Mr. Bullock, author of a work entitled *Mexico in 1823, or relations of a voyage in New-Spain*, collected some antiquities during his stay in Mexico City. He obtained authorization from the Mexican government to take to London several manuscripts belonging to the museum to make some copies in England.
>
> Among these manuscripts was the *Tira del Museo*, whose copy concerns us at this moment. After some time, the Mexican government, not seeing the return of the documents on loan, instructed its minister to go to London to reclaim them, and thus the *Tira* is currently deposited with the National Museum of Mexico.[37]

It is not surprising that there may have been some tension surrounding the return of the loaned objects. After Bullock's exhibitions closed, just as he was preparing to sell the bulk of objects he had collected, Mexico was beginning to restrict the exportation of antiquities in anticipation of the forming of a new national museum. Although he probably intended to return the borrowed manuscripts to protect his interest in a mine that he had bought in Mexico, Bullock was eager to keep in Britain the objects he had purchased and the copies he had made.[38] Codex Boturini did return to Mexico. Although it was missing from Cubas's 1823 inventory, it does appear in subsequent lists. The collection that Cubas inventoried in 1823 was transferred to Mexico's newly formed Museo Nacional (in the university) that was established in

1825 and later to the Museo Nacional de Antropología in 1919.[39] Today Codex Boturini is held in the Biblioteca Nacional de Antropología e Historia in the Bodega de Códices as Manuscript 35–38.

Codex Boturini suffered damage sometime between 1804 and the exhibition of the manuscript in 1824. Both Lorenzo Boturini Benaduci's 1746 catalogue and Ignacio de Cubas's 1804 inventory list Codex Boturini as having twenty-three folios. Like the 1746 catalogue entry, Cubas's 1804 entry records the manuscript under the number 7–1:

> A map of one *quarto* width and about five *varas* length of thick maguey paper divided into 23 panels that are decorated with symbols and many other places that the first founders of this America made in their peregrination, towns that they founded on their journey from Culiacan to Chapultepec, and wars that they stirred up there.[40]

In contrast, Bullock's catalogue entry describes Codex Boturini as having twenty-one folios. To be more precise, the manuscript then, as now, consisted of twenty-one and one half folios. Bullock's label appears on the lower part of the last half-folio, indicating that it was displayed in London in that state. It is atypical for preconquest or postconquest Mesoamerican manuscripts to begin or end with partial folios, so Codex Boturini's current state reflects the loss of a folio and a half. Though very general, both the 1746 and 1804 descriptions indicate that the manuscript's narrative terminated with the wars near Chapultepec that the Mexica undertook in service to Coxcox. This corresponds generally to the final folios of Codex Boturini as it exists today, so it is unlikely that the narrative continued much further on the missing folios.

In addition to the label, the borders of Codex Boturini bear traces of gold paint that were added at a later date. Traces of the gold border appear on the outer edges of the manuscript, including the final partial folio. While it is possible that these were added for the Bullock exhibition, they may instead reflect the later exhibition of the manuscript in the Museo Nacional. We know that Codex Boturini, a copy of the Lienzo de Tlaxcala, and other manuscripts were on display after 1880, when the Museo Nacional was in the Casa de Moneda location. In the early twentieth century, when the collections were reorganized, Codex Boturini was included in a display hall dedicated to indigenous paintings with thirty original manuscripts and twelve copies.[41]

CODEX AZCATITLAN AND CODEX AUBIN

Although the original Codex Azcatitlan and Codex Aubin were copied in the late eighteenth century by Antonio León y Gama and may have been known to Father José Pichardo, their whereabouts thereafter are unknown until they resurfaced in the collection of Joseph Marius Alexis Aubin (1802–1891), a Parisian scholar who came to Mexico to conduct scientific research in 1830.[42] Aubin describes the acquisition of his collection in his 1849 *Mémoires sur la peinture didactique*:

> Some unhappy circumstances having deprived me of my instruments of observation, and not being able anymore to completely achieve the principal goal of my voyage, I sought to compensate with a thorough study of the monuments placed before my eyes. I was able to acquire some of the manuscripts and paintings coming from the succession of the sons of the famous American astronomer Gama, appreciated so well by Baron Humboldt. Later, a great number of chronicles in Nahuatl, or Mexican, written by the first natives instructed in the use of our letters, having become my property, I decided to learn this language, without which it is impossible to take a step in this kind of research. The abundance of historical documents soon no longer allowed me to simultaneously study the monuments of art. Thus, I limited myself to the ancient history of the country, leaving to the archaeologists the exploration of the antiquities themselves, etc., etc.[43]

Although Aubin does not provide the exact details of acquisition, his collection included several manuscripts from the Boturini collection and the collections of León y Gama and Pichardo. The original Codex Azcatitlan, original Codex Aubin (known as the Codex of 1576 before it was named after Aubin), and copies of both manuscripts were among the items acquired. He returned to France in 1840.[44] In 1889, financially ruined by his investment in France's disastrously unsuccessful attempts to build the Panama Canal, Aubin sold his collection to Eugène Goupil, a Parisian art dealer of French and Mexican heritage and a longtime friend of Aubin. A French antiquarian, Eugène Boban, orchestrated the sale.

By 1880, however, Codex Aubin was no longer in Aubin's possession. Eugène Boban discussed five of the most important original manuscripts that disappeared from Aubin's collection, including the Codex Aubin, in his catalogue raisonné of Goupil's collection, *Documents pour servir à l'histoire du Mexique*:

> Among the original documents which had formed part of the Aubin collection and are currently missing, a certain number were lent by their former owner to people who neglected to return them to him, others were withdrawn by him [Aubin] and doubtless sold in secret.
>
> We will note only the principal ones in giving the same description Mr. Aubin gave in his *Note on a Collection of Mexican Antiquities*; perhaps this information will serve to put our friends on the trail of the documents which we seek.[45]

Aubin's description is quoted as follows:

> 4) *Codex of 1576*, described by Mr. Aubin on page 17 of his *Note*:
>
> § VIII, N 14.—"History of the Mexican nation, part in figures and characters, part in Nahuatl prose, written anonymously in 1576, and continued in the same way by other Indian authors until 1608." The Mexican text is the explanation of the figures. I have the original and the copy by Gama, which sometimes cites this work, sufficient in itself to give the key to Mexican writing and iconography.[46]

Boban concludes:

> The original of this document was withdrawn while with Mr. Aubin; a well-informed person assured us that this original figurative painting had been offered for sale to several Parisian collectors, not long ago.
>
> We truly hope to trace it. The Goupil collection has a copy of it made by Leon y Gama (No. 35 of our catalogue).[47]

Boban's passage suggests that Aubin himself had offered the manuscript for sale in a discreet attempt to raise money. The files of the British Museum, where Codex Aubin resides today, state that it was acquired from "M. J. Des Portes" in 1880, most likely a misspelled reference to French lithographer Jules Desportes, who produced several lithographic reproductions of Aubin's Mexican manuscripts in the mid-nineteenth century.[48] Perhaps Desportes sold the manuscript on Aubin's behalf or had purchased it from Aubin himself. The transfer of ownership is unclear.

Boban wrote a lively version of events surrounding the 1889 sale of the Aubin collection (in which he plays a starring role) in *Documents pour servir à l'histoire du Mexique*. In March of that year the Mexican scholar Dr. Antonio Peñafiel, whom Boban had introduced to Aubin, broached the subject of a sale. Boban recounts Peñafiel's "astonishing" attempts to convince Boban and Goupil that the manuscripts were of only "relative value" and writes of Peñafiel's near success in purchasing the collection secretly. Mexico narrowly missed regaining its lost patrimony when Aubin, who had been asked to keep the sale quiet, shared information regarding the impending transaction with Boban. Boban asked Aubin to stall the sale two days and forthwith convinced a somewhat reluctant Eugène Goupil to purchase the collection. Boban praised Peñafiel's *stratagème de bonne guerre* but clearly benefited from the outcome he had orchestrated.[49]

The collection remained in France until Goupil's death in 1898, when his widow left it to the Bibliothèque Nationale in Paris. A brief inscription in French at the top of folio 1v of Codex Azcatitlan identifies the manuscript as belonging to the E. Eugène Goupil collection and lists the place and date: Paris 1889. Throughout the manuscript large purple stamps mark the entry of the work into the library and identify it as No. 59–64, "Collection E. Eug. GOUPIL à Paris, Ancienne Collection J. M. A. AUBIN." Later red circular stamps identify the work as part of the Bibliothèque Nationale's manuscripts division.

In the hands of J. M. A. Aubin the collection had been studied and occasionally published. Aubin examined the manuscripts he collected and added handwritten notes in French on many of the original manuscripts and copies. He had a remarkable body of materials to work with. In addition to the original Codex Azcatitlan (BNP 59–64) and original Codex Aubin (BM Anales Mexicanos 1, Add. MS 31219), he had a lithographic copy of the Codex Boturini in his possession (BNP 93), Léon y Gama's copy of the Codex Azcatitlan (BNP 90–1) and partial copy of the Codex Aubin (BNP 35–36), and Pichardo's copy of the Codex Azcatitlan (BNP 89–3). He made his own notes and copy of the Codex Aubin (BNP 346, 333) and Codex Boturini (BNP 96) and catalogued his entire collection (BNP 351). Aubin's substantial publication *Mémoires sur la peinture didactique* drew on these observations. Several lithographic reproductions of codices were produced to accompany the text.[50] The inventory portion of *Mémoires* was published separately in 1851.[51] Forced to sell his collection for financial reasons in 1889, rather than leaving it to the Bibliothèque Nationale as he had intended, Aubin respected the integrity of his collection and sought to keep it together as a whole.[52]

Once Goupil purchased Aubin's collection, he charged Eugène Boban with organizing and cataloguing it. According to Boban, the collection was in substantial disarray, as Aubin had indiscriminately mixed original leaves with copies when he left Mexico to evade that country's cultural patrimony law and successfully pass through customs.[53] After organizing Goupil's holdings, Boban published a three-volume catalogue raisonné of the collection called *Documents pour servir à l'histoire du Mexique* that offered brief descriptions and analyses of items in the collection and an atlas of photographic reproductions.

Codex Boturini, Codex Azcatitlan, and Codex Aubin remain, respectively, in the Biblioteca Nacional de Antropología e Historia in Mexico City, in the Bibliothèque Nationale de France in Paris, and in the British Museum in London. While the manuscripts have ceased their physical migrations for the time being, they are gaining new life through the dissemination of high-quality digital reproductions.

APPENDIX 1: TRANSLATION OF THE NAHUATL GLOSSES IN CODEX AZCATITLAN

Table A.1.
Translation of the Glosses of Codex Azcatitlan

PLATE #	NAHUATL GLOSSES	TRANSLATION
1r	no glosses	
1v	Ascatitla	Azcatitlan
2r	no glosses	
2v	matlatzinca	Matlatzinca
	tepaneca	Tepaneca
3r	[c]hichimeca	Chichimeca
	mal linalca	Malinalca
	cui tlahuaca	Cuitlahuaca
	xoch millca	Xochimilca
	Chalca	Chalca
	huex xotzinca	Huexotzinca
	tecpaneca	Tecpaneca
	tlacochcal [degraded area]	Tlacochcalca
3v	tepemaxalco	Tepemaxalco
	ymauh	their water
4r	no glosses	
4v	Chicomostoc	Chicomoztoc
	ymauh	their water
	omca motetzahuique nauhxihuitl. onca quissaia ssin/tocoian yntlaca cuitlaxcolli petlatl onca quincauh ynteuh	there they have been bewitched for four years. There they will leave for Cintocoyan. Their god left them the human entrails on the mat.
5r	homca mixpolloque tepetla cuauhtla texcallco can cani neneca mexica	here they were lost among the mountains, in the forests, in rocky spots, the Mexica followed their path wherever it led
	quimama inteo	god-bearers
	tepetla	among the mountains
	cuauhtla	in the forests
	texcallco	in rocky spots
5v	Cohuatlycamac motlallico mex[i]ca	the Mexica came to establish themselves at Coatlicamac
	huacaltepec motlallico mexica	the Mexica came to establish themselves at Huacaltepec
5v–6r	motlallico huixachtitlan in mexica	the Mexica came to establish themselves at Huixachtitlan
6r	otlica inpan tlaiohhuac yeilhuitl amo tlanes yhuan [n]auh yohual yc tlanes citlalli	on the way night fell above them and for three days the sun did not rise; for four nights the stars shone
	tlatlamacazque in mexica	priests of the Mexica

PLATE #	NAHUATL GLOSSES	TRANSLATION
	coh huatepec	Coatepec
	xiuhcohuatl onca temoc	at this spot the Fire Serpent descended
6v	tescatepec motlallico mex[i]ca	the Mexica came to establish themselves at Tezcatepec
	xiuhcococan inpan tlequiauh	at Xiuhcococan they followed a shower of fire
7r	tollan motlallico in mexica	the Mexica arrive at Tula [Tollan]
	huehuetoca motlallico mexica	the Mexica came to establish themselves at Huehuetoca
7v	honca tlachixtiuh yn ma nquistepetl onpaqui[n]huica mex[i]ca	he goes to see the mountain Maquistepetl, he follows the Mexica there
	tlemaco motlallico in mexica	the Mexica came to establish themselves at Tlemaco
	Apasco motlallico in mexica	the Mexica came to establish themselves at Apazco
8r	Tzonpanco onca quicocoque yntzonteco	Tzompanco, they spread out their heads [skulls] on the altar
	Mexican	Mexica
	Huitzillopochtli	Huitzilopochtli
	xaltocamotlallico yn mexica	the Mexica came to establish themselves at Xaltocan
8v	Acolhuacan motlallico in mexica	the Mexica came to establish themselves at Acolhuacan
	Ecatepec motlallico in mexica	the Mexica came to establish themselves at Ehecatepec
	to[l]petlac motlallico mexica	the Mexica came to establish themselves at Tolpetlac

PLATE #	NAHUATL GLOSSES	TRANSLATION
	Tecpaioca motlallico mex[i]ca	the Mexica came to establish themselves at Tecpayocan
9r	Yohualltecatl	it got dark [perhaps a reference to New Fire ceremony]
	in mexica	the Mexica
	Omca tza tzaia innacaio ym mex[i]ca	at this spot the bodies of the Mexica were cracked [an act of self-sacrifice?]
	Pantitlan motlallico mexica	the Mexica came to establish themselves at Pantitlan
	Tepetzinco	Tepetzinco
	inpa tlalloll[i]n mex[i]ca	the Mexica experience a trembling of the earth [an earthquake]
	tenaiocan tepetl	Tenayuca
9v	mexica	Mexica
	huitzilih huitzin motlallico chapoltepec	Huitzilihuitl installed himself, set up an establishment at Chapultepec
	Chapoltepec	Chapultepec
	Acocolco motlallico honca temactlan que mexica atlaquinemilltique naucanpa huiloqe	they came to establish themselves at Acocolco; there the Mexica ended up in the hands of those who were there; they were forced to live in the water; the native people broke out from all around
	Mexica	Mexica
	Mexica	Mexica
	Mexica	Mexica
	mexica	Mexica

PLATE #	NAHUATL GLOSSES	TRANSLATION
	xalto	Xalto[cameca]
	colhuaque	Colhuaque
	tepaneca	Tepaneca
	mexica	Mexica
	huitzillihuitzin	Huitzilihuitzin
10r	xiuhchimalli macoc in huitzillihuitzin ihuan xiuhtilmatli	the turquoise shield [the royal shield] and the turquoise cape, cloak were given to Huitzilhuitzin
	mexica	Mexica
	mexica	Mexica
	mexica	Mexica
	xaltocameca	Xaltocameca
	ascapotzalca	Azcapotzalca
	Chalca	Chalca
	colhuaque	Colhuaque
	chimalxoch	Chimalxoch
	tospanxoch	Tospanxoch
	huitziliqui	Huitzilihuitl
	xaltocameca	Xaltocameca
	[i]ichpochhuan huitzillihuitzi huicoque xaltocan quinmamatiaque in chimallaxoch yhua tospanxoch y momextin huicoq[u]e yn ipilhua	the daughters of Huitzilihuitl had been taken away at Xaltocan; they had taken Chimaloaxoch and Tospanxoch away; their two daughters had been taken away
	coiohuaca [degraded area]	Coyoacan
	onca mique in mexica	the Mexica died here

PLATE #	NAHUATL GLOSSES	TRANSLATION
10v	Comtitla honoca in mexica honca nauhxiuhtique moxinachoque mopilhuatiaia yhua onca motetlaquehui cocolhuaque ytlatocauh cocoxtli	the Mexica remain in Contitlan for an extended period of time; they spent four years there; they breed and have children; they were at the service of the lord of the Colhua and of the Cocoxtli; this was why they went to war with the Xochimilca; the Mexica persevered until they arrived at Cuauhtizaapan, the Mexica triumphed there, bearing swords covered with strips of obsidian
	Chalchiuhtlato nall	Chalchiuhtlatonall
	tellitl	Tellitl
	cocoxtli	Coxcoxtli
	acamapich	Acamapichtli
	mexica	Mexica
	huitzillihui	Huitzilihuitl
	omca mique yxpan cihuacohuatl colhuacan in mexica	they died there [the Mexica], in the presence of the captain general [*cihuacoatl*] of Colhuacan
	tospaxocq	Tospanxoch
	Chimalaxocq	Chimalaxoch
	Colhuaque tetoca	the Colhuaque pursued them
11r	mexica	Mexica
	mexica tlatlamacasque	the Mexica priests
	acatzintitla	Acatzintitlan
	huehuetl	drum

PLATE #	NAHUATL GLOSSES	TRANSLATION
	maltique xochmillca inic polhuhque nauhtecpa[n]tin	they captured [took prisoners] some of the Xochimilca, 80 were defeated
	xochmillca	Xochimilca
	ticaapan	Tizapan
	colhuaque monamique xochmillca	the Colhua met the Xochimilca
	onca mique maltique xochmillca	there they died [were killed], there they bathed [in a ritual fashion] the Xochimilca
	mexica	Mexica
	hualchimalpanoque in mexica amoxtli quimoquentique ycuac quihualtototaque	the Mexica crossed [the river] on their shields; they dressed themselves with the amoxtli plant so that they could not be followed
11v	miquisteuctli	the rulers died
	coquatlcycham	Coatlinchan
	mexica	Mexica
	Mexicatzinco	Mexicatzinco
	Nexticpac	Nexticpac
	ystacallco	Iztacalco
	hualachieia tzatzitepetl in onpa itztihui	around here they saw the Tzatzitepetl, over there was where they set their sights
	yctlatlamaia	it is with them that they fished
	ictlatlamaia	it is with them that they fished
	mixiuhcan	Mixiuhcan
	Temascaltitlan	Temazcaltitlan

PLATE #	NAHUATL GLOSSES	TRANSLATION
12r	no glosses	
12v	no glosses	
13r	no glosses	
13v	12 tecpatl mic tecocomoc	in 12 Flint [1400] Tezozomoc died
14r	ommotlati maxton	Maxton was installed as governor
14v	no glosses	
15r	5 tochi in mic matlato	in the year 5 Rabbit [1406] Maxtlaton died
15v	no glosses	
16r	no glosses	
16v	no glosses	
17r	no glosses	
17v	no glosses	
18r	Chalcoatenco	Chalcoatenco
	Chalca	Chalco
	acolman	Acolman
18v	no glosses	
19r	no glosses	
19v	no glosses	
20r	no glosses	
20v	no glosses	
21r	no glosses	
21v	no glosses	
22r	no glosses	
22v	no glosses	
23r	no glosses	
23v	no glosses	
24r	no glosses	
24v	no glosses	
25r	no glosses	
25v	no glosses	

APPENDIX 2: TRANSLATION OF THE NAHUATL TEXT IN CODEX AUBIN

English translation by Debra Nagao of the Spanish translation of Codex Aubin provided in *Historia de la nación mexicana*, translated and with commentary by Charles E. Dibble. Nagao was assisted by Alfredo López Austin and Leonardo López Luján, who clarified certain passages. Nagao's additions appear in angle brackets; brackets and parentheses in the text have been preserved. Dibble's brief commentary and notes are not reproduced here. The equivalent folio numbers for Codex Aubin appear next to Dibble's page designations.

PAGE 1 <FOLIO 1R>

Here is written the Mexica year count. It has four parts, as follows:

> 1 Reed ends with 13 Reed,
> 1 Flint ends with 13 Flint,
> 1 House ends with 13 House,
> 1 Rabbit ends with 13 Rabbit.

And when all four are going to end, then our years are bound in the year 2 Reed. Fifty-two years is a complete cycle.

Written here today in Mexico, the 27th of the month of September of 1576.

PAGE 2 <FOLIOS 1V–2R>

Second iudicion [*sic*] <judición> of the house called *ce acatl* has thirteen years and three olympiads <presumably this has an astrological meaning> in the first house where the hand is, this land was discovered, in the second house the Spaniards entered it, in the third they defeated Mexico, in the fourth they began to build Mexico, in the sixth the twelve friars came.

PAGE 3 <FOLIO 3R>

The Huexotzinca, the Chalca, the Xochimilca, the Cuitlahuaca, the Malinalca, the Chichimeca, the Tepaneca, the Matlatzinca came to Quinehuayan.

PAGE 4 <FOLIO 3V>

Here is written the history of the Mexica who came from a place called Aztlan. So from there in the middle of the water the four *calpulli* departed. And to do penance, they came in boats to put their fir branches there in the place called Quinehuayan. In that place there is a cave from where the eight *calpulli* left: the first *calpulli* of the Huexotzinca, the second *calpulli* of the Chalca, the third *calpulli* of the Xochimilca, the fourth *calpulli* of the Cuitlahuaca, the fifth *calpulli* of the Malinalca, the sixth *calpulli* of the Chichimeca, the seventh *calpulli* of the Tepaneca, the eighth *calpulli* of the Matlatzinca.

When those who were inhabitants of Colhuacan remained there, they [the Aztecs] crossed over to here from Aztlan; there those of Colhuacan came out to receive them. When the inhabitants had seen them, then they said to the Aztecs: "Our lords, where are you going? We are willing to accompany you."

Then the Aztecs said: "Where are we going to take you?"

Then the eight *calpulli* said: "It does not matter, our lords, so we shall accompany you."

And then the Aztecs said: "So be it, accompany us!"

PAGE 5 <FOLIO 4R>

From Colhuacan they left carrying the devil who they worshipped as a god, the Huitzilopochtli. When they came they brought a woman by the name of Chimalma from there, from Aztlan. They divided into four as they walked.

In the year 1 Flint they departed from Colhuacan. Four of them bore the devil on their back: a person by the name of Quauhcohuatl, a second <by the name of> Apanecatl, a third by the name of Tezcacohuacatl, a fourth by the name of Chimalma.

PAGE 6 <FOLIO 4V>

And when they arrived at the foot of the tree, then they settled there. The tree was very wide. Then they formed an altar there on which they put the devil. When they had made the altar, then they had their provisions. But just as they were ready to eat, then the tree broke on top of them.

PAGE 7 <FOLIO 5R>

Then, as a result, they left what they were eating, they were with their heads bowed for a long time. And then, the devil called them and said to them: "Send the eight *calpulli* who accompany you, and say to them: 'We will not continue ahead, we will go in another direction.'"

When they had told them this, the eight *calpulli* became very sad. When they had been sent, then the eight *calpulli* said: "Our lords, where shall we go? Since we accompany you."

Then again, they said to them: "Do not go."

Then first the eight *calpulli* departed. They abandoned them [the Aztecs] there at the foot of the tree; they remained there for a long time. Afterward when they left on the path, the "owl men" came to descend on them. Among the bisnagas (barrel cacti) they were falling, and some of them were falling at the foot of the mesquites.

These were called *mimixcoa*: the first by the name of Xiuhneltzin, the second by the name of Mimichtzin, the third, a woman, their older sister.

Again, there the devil Huitzilopochtli called them; he said to them:

PAGE 8 <FOLIO 5V>

"Take what is among the bisnagas. They will be the first tribute."

And at once, there, he changed the name of the Aztecs. He said to them: "From now on, your name is no longer *Aztec*, you are now *Mexica*."

There he painted their ears black; in this way the Mexica took their name. And there they were given the arrow and the bow and the little net. Whatever flew overhead, the Mexica shot them well with bows and arrows.

They came to leave from there to Cuextecatlichocayan and Coatlicamac in the year 2 House.

PAGE 11 <FOLIO 7R>
[2 Reed]

There, in this <year>, they bound the years for the first time in Coatlicamac. On the hill of Coatepetl, they made new fire in the year 2 Reed.

PAGE 12 <FOLIO 7V>
[3 Flint]

And then the Mexica moved to Tula.

PAGE 13 <FOLIO 8R>
[9 Reed]

In (the year) Reed the Mexica had been there in Tula for twenty years.

PAGE 14 <FOLIO 8V>
[10 Flint]

And then the Mexica moved to Atlitlalacyan.

[7 Rabbit]

There the Mexica had been in Atlitlalacyan for eleven years.

PAGE 15 <FOLIO 9R>
[8 Reed]

And then the Mexica moved to Tlemaco.

[12 Reed]

In (the year) Reed, in this <year>, the Mexica had been in Tlemaco for five years.

PAGE 16 <FOLIO 9V>
[13 Flint]

At once the Mexica moved to Atotonilco.

[3 Reed]

In this <year> the Mexica had been in Atotonilco for four years.

PAGE 17 <FOLIO 10R>
Year 4 Flint

At once the Mexica moved to Apazco.

Year 2 Reed

At once, in this <year>, the Mexica bound the years there in Apazco. They made new fire on (the hill) called Huitzcol.

PAGE 18 <FOLIO 10V>
Year 3 Flint

At once the Mexica moved to Tzompanco.

Year 6 Reed

In this <year> the Mexica had been in Tzompanco for four years.

PAGE 19 <FOLIO 11R>
Year 7 Flint

At once the Mexica moved to Xaltocan.

Year 10 Reed

In this <year> the Mexica had been there in Xaltocan for four years.

PAGE 20 <FOLIO 11V>
Year 11 Flint

And then the Mexica moved to Acalhuacan.

Year 1 Reed

In this <year> the Mexica had been there in Acalhuacan for four years.

PAGE 21 <FOLIO 12R>
Year 2 Flint

It was when the Mexica moved to Ehecatepec.

Year 5 Reed

In this <year> the Mexica had been in Ehecatepec for four years.

PAGE 22 <FOLIO 12V>
Year 6 Flint

It was when the Mexica moved to Tolpetlac.

Year 13 Reed

In this <year> the Mexica had been there in Tolpetlac for eight years.

PAGE 23 <FOLIO 13R>
Year 1 Flint

And then the Mexica moved to Cohuatitlan.

PAGE 24 <FOLIO 13V>
Year 7 Reed

In this <year> the Mexica had been there in Cohuatitlan for twenty years. And then they went to get maguey at Chalco. And they also collected honey [from the maguey]. Later the Mexica gave *octli* to drink <the subject is ambiguous here, whether the Mexica gave someone else *octli* or if they were given *octli*; perhaps Dibble compared this incident with another account> in Cohuatitlan.

PAGE 25 <FOLIO 14R>
Year 8 Flint

At once the Mexica moved to Huixachtitlan.

Year 11 Reed

In this <year> the Mexica had been in Huixachtitlan for four years.

PAGE 26 <FOLIO 14V>
[12 Flint]

And then the Mexica moved to Tecpayocan.

[2 Reed]

In this <year> they were there in Tecpayocan for four years. There in this <place> it happened that they were surrounded by the enemies. There those by the name of Tecpatzin and Huitzilihuitzin died; also Tetepantzin. There in this <place> the years were bound. They made new fire on [the hill of] Tecpayo.

PAGE 27 <FOLIO 15R>
Year 3 Flint

At once the Mexica moved to Pantitlan.

Year 6 Reed

In this <year> the Mexica had been in Pantitlan for four years. In this <place> disease spread there; the entire body split open.

PAGE 28 <FOLIO 15V>
Year 7 Flint

At once the Mexica moved to Amallinalpan, there in Azcapotzalco.

Year 1 Reed

In this <year> they had been in Amallinalpan for eight years. In this <year>, Tezozomoctli was lord of Azcapotzalco.

PAGE 29 <FOLIO 16R>
Year 2 Flint

At once the Mexica moved to Pantitlan.

Year 5 Reed

In this <year> the Mexica had been in Pantitlan for four years.

PAGE 30 <FOLIO 16V>
Year 6 Flint

At once the Mexica moved to Acolnahuac.

Year 9 Reed

In this <year> the Mexica had been in Acolnahuac for four years.

PAGE 31 <FOLIO 17R>
Year 10 Flint

At once the Mexica moved to Popotlan.

Year 13 Reed

In this <year> the Mexica had been in Popotlan for four years.

PAGE 32 <FOLIO 17V>
Year 1 Flint

At once the Mexica moved to Techcatitlan.

Year 2 House

It was when Tenochtli began to reign.

160 years

Year 4 Reed

In this <year> the Mexica had been in Techcatitlan for four years.

PAGE 33 <FOLIO 18R>
Year 5 Flint

It was when the Mexica moved to Atlacuihuayan.

Year 8 Reed

In this <year> the Mexica had been in Atlacuihuayan for four years. There they discovered the *atlatl* (spear-thrower) and the dart; therefore the Mexica called it Atlacuihuayan.

PAGE 34 <FOLIO 18V>
[9 Flint]

It was when the Mexica moved to Chapultepec.

PAGE 35 <FOLIO 19R>
[2 Reed]

In Chapultepec it was when the Mexica were conquered, since they were taken to the four directions. The Tepanec and the Colhua fought against them.

PAGE 36 <FOLIO 19V>

There in Chapultepec they had been there for twenty years. In mid-year they moved to Acocolco. There the Mexica were surrounded by their enemies. There the Mexica became captives. In this place, it was (the year) to bind the years. And there they covered themselves with an aquatic plant.

There they took Huitzilihuitl together with his daughter, Azcalxoch by name; and her older sister, by the name of Tozpanxoch, was taken to the desert. Only they (two) <Huitzilihuitl and Azcalxoch> were taken to Colhuacan. They were naked, they no longer wore anything. And the lord of that place, of Colhuacan, his name was Coxcoxtli. And Huitzilihuitl felt great pity for his daughter, who did not have anything on. The lord said: "Have <the> compassion to give my daughter a little thing <to wear>, oh lord!"

And then the (lord) said to him: "I do not want to, she must walk like this."

PAGE 37 <FOLIO 20R>

It will start here <in this year>.

Year 3 Flint

At once the Mexica moved to Colhuacan. They settled in Contitlan, there in Tizaapan-Colhuacan.

Year 6 Reed

In this <year> the Mexica who had remained in Contitlan had been in Colhuacan for four years. Given that they remained in Contitlan,

PAGE 38 <FOLIO 20V>

secretly they procreated children in Contitlan.

In [the year] Reed the Colhua waged war against the Xochimilca. When the Colhua were in danger, then Lord Coxcoxtli said: "The Mexica! Aren't they here? Have them come!"

Then at once they call them. Then they appeared before the lord. Then he said to them: "Come quickly! The Xochimilca are about to conquer us! I grant you that the eight thousand that you apprehend shall be your captives."

Right away the Mexica said to him: "As you wish, sir! Help us with the shields and *macanas*."

Then the lord said: "You cannot do this. You shall walk just as you are."

But the Mexica then united and said: "What thing shall we carry?"

Then they said: "At least our blades

PAGE 39 <FOLIO 21R>

(made) of obsidian, we shall cut off our captives' noses. If we cut off their ears, wouldn't they say that perhaps we had cut them off on two sides? This will not happen with their noses. Therefore, we shall put on large bags because we shall count how many there may be."

Then when they were given their large bags, at once they went to fight; some of them fought on boats. They waged battle there in Cohuaapan.

At this moment, it so happened that a captain from Colhuacan, by the name of Tetzitzilin, who wore a mantle covered with bark as insignia, said to them: "Mexica! Come here. While the captives are prisoners they look frightened; they continue weeping, when one says to them, come here, Mexica!"

Then they arrived at the doors of the Xochimilca. The Mexica came at once. Then they counted their captives before Lord Coxcoxtli. Then the Mexica said: "Our captives are enough, because there are 3,200 that we have taken."

And then [Coxcoxtli] warned their fathers, then he said to them: "The Mexica are inhuman. How did they do what I asked them to do? Since I was only mocking them."

PAGE 40 <FOLIO 21V>

The Mexica frightened many of (the Colhua). And they even kept four of their captives alive; they did not show them to Lord Coxcoxtli. Then they built their altar there in Tizaapan. And when they had built it, then they went to say to the lord: "Now, sir, give us some little thing as the heart of our altar."

Then the lord said: "So be it. You have earned it. Let the priests make a heart."

Then they ordered the priests, they said to them: "Now make them a heart of excrement and hair, plus a stupid bird."

Then they went to put a heart [in the altar] at night.

And then the Mexica said: "What thing have you placed as the heart of our altar?"

And then they saw the heart [of the altar]. And when they had seen it, many of them were saddened. When they saw the excrement that

PAGE 41 <FOLIO 22R>

had been placed as the heart of their altar, then they destroyed it. Those Mexica placed a heart of huisache and fir branches <there>.

And when they had finished, then they went to invite the Lord. And when he came<,> then he sees that they sacrificed their captives, he sees everything with which they made sacrifices: they made sacrifice with the crosspieces of quetzal feathers and turquoise shields with quetzal feather banners. However, it was not true, it only looked that way.

And above, they made new fire. With this they solemnly celebrated when they bound their years at Chapultepec. They still had not made new fire, when they were captured by their enemies.

When this happened, Coxcoxtli was angry. He said: "Who are these barbarians? Cast them out!"

Then they were cast out. They moved to Acatzintitlan, to Mexicatzinco. With thick reed mats they crossed, on rush mats they sailed. [The Colhua] came, shooting them with darts.

PAGE 42 <FOLIO 22V>
Year 7 Flint

In this year the Mexica had been in Mexicatzinco for a year.

PAGE 43 <FOLIO 23R>
Year 8 House

At once the Mexica moved to Nexticpac.

Year 11 Flint

In this <year>, the Mexica had been there in Nexticpac for four years.

PAGE 44 <FOLIO 23V>
12 House

It was when the Mexica moved to Iztacalco.

13 Rabbit

In this <year>, the Mexica had been there in Iztacalco for two years. There they made a hill of bark. At night they made music; there they intoned songs to the captain of Colhuacan called Tetzitzillin. They sang: "Tetzitzillintzin, Tetzitzillintzin. Owner of insignia of twisted paper! Weeping on the path," etc.

PAGE 45 <FOLIO 24R>
Year 1 Reed

It was when they moved to Zoquipan. In the year 1 Reed, one of the women of the Mexica gave birth there, in Zoquipan. And then they made their sweatbath there in Temazcaltitlan. Being there, then they had a sweatbath. From there they arose, they went in search.

They walked for 196 years.

Axolohua and also the one called Quauhcohuatl, both went, they went in search, they went to enter among the reeds. There is a prickly pear <nopal>

PAGE 46 <FOLIO 24V>

on which is perched an eagle. At the foot is its nest, its bed, all the different fine feathers; of the red bird, of the blue bird; all the precious feathers.

And then comes along a man called Quauhcohuatl. Then he tells them, he says to them: "The water that we have come to see is like blue ink."

But there they submerged Axolohua. And when they had submerged

Axolohua, right away Quauhcohuatl returned. So he went to say to his companions: "There died Axolohua. Since they submerged him there where we saw among the reeds a prickly pear on which is perched an eagle, and his nest is there at the foot [of the prickly pear], his bed <is> entirely of different precious feathers, and the water like blue ink. There they submerged Axolohua."

Quauhcohuatl informed them of this. Only on the next day, Axolohua came out. Then he says to his companions: "Since I went to see Tlaloc, because he called me, he said: 'My son Huitzilopochtli has arrived,

PAGE 47 <FOLIO 25R>

since his house shall be here. Since he shall dedicate it here because we shall live united on the earth.'"

And when they were informed, then they went to look, to see the prickly pear. When they had seen it, then they sweep. At the foot of the prickly pear they shaped an altar.

[To make the] base [of the altar], they were rejoicing; there they found a captain of Colhuacan, then they brought him. When he had been brought, still alive, they put him in their altar; they made the captain called Chichilquahuitl, the captain of Colhuacan, as the heart [of the altar].

The year in which they made their altar is the year 2 Flint.

PAGE 49 <FOLIO 26R>

When the Chichimecs arrived, the Chichimecs of Colhuacan, it was when [the Mexica] had made at the foot of the prickly pears nothing more than their small reed huts that they dwelled in. But now they had begun to catch fish with nets.

And when those who were on solid ground surrounded them, they saw that they were making smoke, and how the filth rose spreading. When many smelled it, they died and they swelled up. And many times they wanted to conquer them but they couldn't.

PAGE 52 <FOLIO 27V>
[1 Flint]

The reign of Acamapichtli began. In the year 1 Flint he began to reign.

PAGE 53 <FOLIO 28R>
[8 Reed]

20 years

PAGE 55 <FOLIO 29R>
[7 Reed]

Acamapichtli died here.

PAGE 56 <FOLIO 29V>
[8 Flint]

How the second lord Huitzilihuitl was established.

PAGE 57 <FOLIO 30R>
[2 Reed]

Here they bound our years; for the fifth time they are bound. And here the locusts descended.

40 years

PAGE 60 <FOLIO 31V>
[2 Flint]

Huitzilihuitl came to die here.

[3 House]

How Chimalpopoca, the third lord, then was established. This was under Tepanec domination.

PAGE 61 <FOLIO 32R>
[9 Reed]

60 years
[10 Flint]

Chimalpopoca died here. The Tepanecs took him.

[11 House]

Then Itzcoatzin was established as the fourth lord.

PAGE 62 <FOLIO 32V>
[1 Flint]

Here they intercepted those from Quauhnahuac in the year 1 Flint.

PAGE 64 <FOLIO 33V>
[9 Flint]

Here those from Quauhnahuac perished. Once vanquished, they lasted a year in servitude, then they paid tribute to the house of Itzcoatzin only for two years.

[10 House]

Itzcoatzin died here.

11 Tochtli

In this <year> Ilhuicaminatzin Huehue Moteuczoma was established as fifth lord.

PAGE 65 <FOLIO 34R>
[3 Reed]

80 years

PAGE 66 <FOLIO 34V>
[6 Rabbit]

Here locusts devoured something. The locusts descended. It was when there was hunger.

PAGE 67 <FOLIO 35R>
[13 House]

Here the cornstalks froze. Here hunger began.

[1 Rabbit]

Here hunger was suffered <literally: "Here they passed the quality of 1 Rabbit" = hunger>, they were taken with a stick <attached to collars; cf. Durán>, it was when they were made slaves.

[2 Reed]

Here they bound our years; for the sixth time they are bound. And it was when no one gave their tortilla to anyone else. The buzzards remained only among the dead; [the buzzards] ate them. No other person. No one else buried them.

PAGE 68 <FOLIO 35V>
[4 House]

In the year 4 House came rain; there was abundance. In all parts, maize grew on the roofs. Wherever raindrops fell, chía <sage>, amaranth, beans grew there.

PAGE 69 <FOLIO 36R>
[10 Reed]

100 years

[12 House]

Here the Chalca perished.

PAGE 70 <FOLIO 36V>
[4 Rabbit]

Here the Cuetlaxteca perished.

PAGE 71 <FOLIO 37R>
[5 Reed] 1471

Here Ilhuicaminatzin died. Then Axayacatzin, the sixth lord, was established. It was then the inhabitants of Xochitlan perished.

[7 House] 1473

Here the Tlatelolcas perished. Soon afterward, Axayacatzin vanquished Moquihuix together with Teconal, who pretended to be valiant. If it were not for Quaquauhtzin who spoke for them [the Tlatelolca], they would have been destroyed.

[9 Reed] 1475

Here there were many earthquakes. Many hills collapsed, all the houses sank.

PAGE 72 <FOLIO 37V>
[10 Flint] 1476

Here those of Ocuilan perished.

[11 House] 1477

Here those of Icpatepec perished.

[12 Rabbit] 1478

Here those of Calimayan, the Matlatzinca, perished. There they wounded Axayacatzin. The name of he who wounded him in the thigh was Tlilcuetzpal, originally from Xoquipilco.

[13 Reed] 1479

Here the sun was eaten. All the stars appeared. It was when Axayacatzin died.

[1 Flint] 1480

And then Tizocicatzin, the seventh lord, was established.

PAGE 73 <FOLIO 38R>
[4 Reed] 1483

Here the foundations of what would be the temple of Huitzilopochtli were placed.

160 years

[5 Flint] 1484

Here Ahuitzotzin, the eighth lord, began to reign.

PAGE 74 <FOLIO 38V>
[8 Reed] 1487

Here the temple was dedicated. It was dedicated with the Tziuhcohuaca, the Mazateca. It was when lords were again named in the four towns: Quauhnahuac, Tepoztlan, Huaxtepec, Xilloxochitepec.

[10 House] 1489

Here there was an earthquake. It was when Moyohuallitohua [the ghost] became visible.

[11 Rabbit] 1490

Here hail fell. All the fish died in the water.

PAGE 75 <FOLIO 39R>
[12 Reed] 1491

Here locusts devoured something; locusts descended.

PAGE 76 <FOLIO 39V>
[4 Flint] 1496

Here there were many earthquakes. All the earth cracked open.

[5 House] 1497

Here those of Xochitlan perished.

[6 Rabbit] 1498

Here those of Amaxtlan perished. It was when Tlacahuepatzin went to die in Huexotzinco.

[7 Reed] 1499

Here (the streambed) Acuecuexatl rose, which flooded the cornstalks that were beginning to sprout cobs. Ahuitzotzin sent messengers (and) the lord of Coyohuacan<,> Tzotzo-matzin<,> did not give (water to him). So the house <Tzotzomatin's> was burned. Tzotzomatzin did not work with the Tepanecs, so he <Ahuitzotzin> wanted to kill him.

PAGE 77 <FOLIO 40R>
[9 House] 1501

Here they went to excavate stone in Malinalco. Of those who did not go, many of them were locked up.

Here Ahuitzotzin died.

[10 Rabbit] 1502

And then Moteuczomatzin was established as the ninth lord.

[11 Reed] 1503

Here again they went to excavate stone in Malinalco.

140 years

[12 Flint] 1504

Here cacao arrived.

[13 House] 1505

Here the Tzitzimitl descended.

PAGE 78 <FOLIO 40V>
[1 Rabbit] 1506

Here those of Zozolla perished.

[2 Reed] 1507

Here our years were bound; they bind them for the seventh time since the Mexica departed from Aztlan.

[3 Flint] 1508

Here the Tlacahuilome descended.

[4 House] 1509

Here a hole appeared. It was when the round column of stone descended. It was when the Christians set out, since our Lord revealed to them that they would arrive here.

PAGE 79 <FOLIO 41R>
[6 Reed]

Here those of Icpatepec and some from Xochitepec perished.

[7 Flint]

Here those of Tlachquiyauhco perished.

[9 Rabbit]

Here dust rose so that there was hunger.

[10 Reed]

Here, for the third time, they went to excavate stone in Malinalco. It was when those from Huexotzinco entered as servants. They came to spy.

PAGE 80 <FOLIO 41V>
[1 Reed]

Here Moteuczomatzin came to die. And it was when the marquis arrived.

It was when the Christians conquered the Mexica. They did not come in vain, since by orders of Our Lord, the Holy Father <the pope> sent the message to them: "Order the knights to send the 12 friars."

PAGE 82 <FOLIO 42V>

In this <year>, the prostitutes who were going to be concubines of Moteuczomatzin died. The Christians said: "Women will come, they shall be your maidens."

Moteuczomatzin said: "Let the Mexica hear it."

In this <year> the men from Castile arrived, the 25th of November in [the month] of Quecholli. Still [in] ten days we will reach [the end] of Quecholli; then the 25th of December came to be established. Atemoztli, Tititl, Izcalli, 5 [of the *nemontemi*], Cuahuitlehua, Xilopehualiztli, Tozoztontli, Huey Tozoztli, Toxcatl.

In Toxcatl they raised a devil; they made sacrifices while they began the chants. As they began the preparatory chants, Moteuczoma asked, he said to Malintzin: “Let god listen: as we have arrived at the festival of our gods; it is ten days from now. And we always celebrate this as <an> important <event>. Well, we have to burn incense; we will only do a dance when they take up the bread made of amaranth. We will make a lot of noise; well, that is all.

And then the captain said: “So be it. Do as I have heard.”

Then they began, they went to make other men from Castile return, those who came. Only that Tonatiuh remained. And when the moment of the count came, then Moteuczoma said: ¨Listen to this you who are here:

PAGE 83 <FOLIO 43R>

I say to god: As we have reached the day on which we shall celebrate our god.”

Then [Tonatiuh] said to him: “Do it. Now somehow we shall be.”

Then the nobles said: “Call the captains.”

And when they came, then they order them, they say to them: “We made great efforts to do this.”

And the captains said: “Let the effort be made!”

At once, general Ecatzin said: “Let the man who is in charge of us understand how it happened in Cholula when they were only locked up at home. That now something similar is happening to us! Let every wall make room to hide shields!”

Then Moteuczoma said: “Are we at war? Let it be! <It’s too small to worry us!>”

Then the general said: “So be it.”

Then the chant begins. A brave, young soldier goes before the people. He has put on his lip plug; his name Tolnauacatl Quatlazol. When the chant began, at once one after another, the Christians come out on their own; they push through among the people. Then they went to occupy the entrances in groups of four.

Then they were to injure with a stick the one who guided them. They injured the nose of a man who was the image of the devil. Then they came to strike those who were playing the drums. There were two of them who were playing their drums,

PAGE 84 <FOLIO 43V>

one of them was playing it on the shore of the water. Then some trample one another; everyone is lost.

A man, an incenser, who came from Acatliyacapan, suddenly shouted, he said quickly: “Mexicans, what are you doing? No one else has confidence! Who have the captives’ shields in their hands?”

Their sticks were only fir sticks. When they saw it they began to flee, it was as if they pushed one another.

Then [the Spaniards] returned to the houses; they were locked up in houses during the twenty days of Etzalqualiztli.

In Etzalqualiztli, it is when the word of Moteuczoma was secretly revealed. He said to the captains: “Listen, Mexica, the deer of the gods <horses> have not eaten anything for two days now. The piles of reeds that feed them have come to an end. And now only two days have passed since they became stirred up. And so the captains must be warned so that we not perish. As it is for the prudence of the captains.”

Then they said: “So be it.”

Then they ordered that only at night food be given to the deer.

Then the captain came after five days had passed since they entered the house of those who went to Tlaxcala, at Tecuilhuitontli. It was when Moteuczoma died.

Having died, then one by the name of Apanecatl came to carry him.

PAGE 85 <FOLIO 44R>

Then he took him there to Huitzillian, but they chased him away from there. Then he took him there to Necatitlan; right there they shot at him with arrows. Then he took him to Tecpantzinco, they just chased him away. Again he took him to Acatliyacapan. At once there they received him. Apanecatl said: “Our lords, Moteuczoma is annoyed. Perhaps I should continue carrying him?”

Then the nobles said: “Receive him.”

Then the mayordomos took their burden, then they burned him.

Then Huey Tecuilhuitl, Tlaxochimaco, Xocotlhuetzi, Ochpaniztli. It was when Cuitlahuatzin began to reign. Then Ecoztli, then Tepeilhuitl. Then at Quecholli, Cuitlahuatzin died. Panquetzaliztli, then Atemoztli, Tititl, Izcalli, Atlacahualo. At this <time> Cuauhtemoctzin began to reign.

Tlacaxipehualiztli was when those of Chalco and those of Xocotitlan were conquered. Then they saw that with others they were painted with stripes of two colors.

Tozoztontli at this <time> there died the nobles: Tzihuacpopoca, Xoxopehualoc, Tzihuactzin, Tencuecuenotl, Axayacatl, Totlehuicol.

PAGE 86 <FOLIO 44V>

When Tzihuacpopoca died, Cuauhtemoc called for the incensers of Amatlan; he said to them: "Captains, Tzihuacpopoca has been with me for two days now. May nothing bad happen to me!"

Then the captains said: "Do not be offended. He will be punished. Let's let him go."

Then the priests were named, and also those captains who were to be sacrificed.

Then they search for him everywhere. When they found him, they were laughing.

Cuauhtemoctzin at once went to grab his neck, he said to him: "Come here my younger brother!"

Then he beat him.

Huey Tozoztli, then Toxcatl, Etzalqualiztli. At this <time> the Christians completely conquered us. Tecuilhuitontli, Huey Tecuilhuitl, then Miccailhuitontli.

In eighty days what was Mexican, what was Tenochca, came to an end.

[2 Flint 1520]

As the tenth lord, Cuitlahuactzin began to reign in the month of Ochpaniztli. He only governed eighty days. It ended in the month of Quecholli, in which he died. He died of boils, when the men from Castile went to Tlaxcalla.

PAGE 87 <FOLIO 45R>
[3 House] 1521

As the eleventh lord, in the *nemontemi* of the month of Quauitleua, Cuauhtemoctzin began to reign. And there what was Mexican, what was Tenochca, was defeated when the Spaniards as a group came to enter.

4 Rabbit 1522

The marquis was in Coyohuacan. It was there when he met the lords Cuauhtemoctzin, Tlacotzin, Oquiztzin, and Uanitzin. It was when the marquis went to Pantlan, Cuextlan. It was when the wax candles appeared. With this Alonso Tlacamatlaca, Martín Tochpain rose.

[5 Reed] 1523

Here Cihuacohuatzintli Tlacotzin began to reign. He did his job as lord when there was a solar eclipse. It was when the candles of fat appeared. Morales and Rodrigo Hernández, who again greeted the marquis in Mexico, showed their superiority.

160 [Years]
[6 Flint] 1524

Here began the faith. It was when the priests began to preach to us.

[7 House] 1525

Here Cuauhtemoctzin came to die at Hueymollan.

PAGE 88 <FOLIO 45V>
[9 Reed] 1527

Here Guzmán left for Guatemala. It was when Motelchiuhtzin was consul.

[10 Flint] 1528

Here the Tenochca, who went to Colhuacan for the first time, set out. It was when the canal of Chapultepec was installed.

[11 House] 1529

Here marriage began.

PAGE 89 <FOLIO 46R>
[13 Reed] 1531

Here don Pablo Xochiquen was established. It was when for the second time they set out for Colhuacan. It was when the fourteenth lord suffered from boils.

[1 Flint] 1532

Here the president arrived. It was when the play was presented at Santiago. And it was when the cape was placed and women were covered. And <it is> when don Pablo dispersed the Tenochca. And when the road to Chapultepec was installed.

[2 House] 1533

Here the market of Santo Domingo was set up. And it was when there was an earthquake; <the earth> moved a lot, very often. And it was when for the first time the staff <"staff" throughout clearly is simply a reference to authority> was given to Francisco Tziuacxilotl.

PAGE 90 <FOLIO 46V>
[5 Flint] 1536

Don Diego Panitzin began to reign here as the twelfth lord. It was when don Antonio de Mendoza, viceroy, came and when the *tomines* <Spanish weight unit and small coin> appeared. Then the president began here.

[7 Rabbit] 1538

Here the church of wood was built. It was when the Tenochca were hidden at Acalco.

[8 Reed] 1539

Here they left for the New Land; the Tenochca went. In the middle of the year don Diego Panitzin died.

[9 Flint] 1540

Don Diego Teuetzquititzin began to reign here as the thirteenth lord.

PAGE 91 <FOLIO 47R>
[10 House] 1541 Years

Here those of Xochipillan were conquered.

[11 Rabbit] 1542 Years

Here the copper four-*tomines* appeared. It was when the Tenochca who had gone to the New Land arrived. Those who went to Xochipillan entered as a group.

[12 Reed] 1543 Years

Here dust rose, so there was hunger. It was when the Atempanecatl Bartolomé made public proclamations in the church. And it was when the cave of Tetzicapan was found.

180 Years
[13 Flint] 1544 Years

[1 House] 1545 Years

Here disease spread. It was when blood came from our noses. It lasted one year. It was when they put the market at San Hipólito.

PAGE 92 <FOLIO 47V>
[2 Rabbit] 1546 Years

[3 Reed] 1547 Years

Here San José was dedicated. It was when there was an earthquake and when a canal was installed at Apepetzpan.

[4 Flint] 1548 Years

Here bishop don Fray Juan de Zumárraga died. It was when the fountain of San Miguel was enlarged. There they summoned Francisco Ocelotecatl. It was then the judges of Huexotzinco Mateo Xuárez, Francisco Vásquez entered.

[5 House] 1549 Years

Here for the first time *alcaldes* were established. Francisco Aneztoc began the *alcalde* system. It was when tribute began; each one paid two *reales* in tribute.

[6 Rabbit] 1550 Years

Here they would hang the Tenochca: Pablo Ezuauacatl, Miguel Atlaua, Baltasar Xochimitl. They only went to Atenco <it is unclear whether Atenco [literally, "by the water": on the coast, on the lakeshore, etc.] means a specific town or simply a place near water: according to Alfredo López Austin in some cases it is used to designate a low region, such as Atenco Chalco versus Amaquemecan Chalco [considered "high"]>. It was when don Luis de Velasco, viceroy, came. It was when there was disease; fever struck in the throat. It was when the canal of Citlaltepec was installed.

PAGE 93 <FOLIO 48R>
[7 Reed] 1551 Years

Here the Tenochca captured on the 6th of the month of February were forced to leave for Atenco.

[8 Flint] 1552 Years

Here don Luis de León Romano arrived. He sought out everything necessary for life. It was when he left for Zacatlán. It was when the Ixmatlatepetl at Chalco collapsed. It was when [the representation of] the Resurrection of Our Lord ended. It was when the little canal of San Francisco was enlarged.

PAGE 94 <FOLIO 48V>
[9 House] 1553 Years

Here the wall of San Francisco was renovated.

It was when <don Luis de León Romano> left for Zacatlán again.

And it was when the fine metalsmiths were crushed in the church, March 12.

And it was when the news arrived that the viceroy died in Peru.

PAGE 95 <FOLIO 49R>
[10 Rabbit] 1554 Years

Here don Diego Teuetzquititzin died on May 11.

It was when the staff was given to don Esteban de Guzmán, judge, on June 26. They needed to investigate don Diego Teuetzquititzin. They no longer found him; they only investigated his parents.

Fray Alonso de Montúfar, archbishop, came on June 23.

It was also when Montealegre came on July 16. The *oidores* <judges of an *audiencia*> were investigated: Messías (*sic*), Quezada, Herrera.

PAGE 96 <FOLIO 49V>
[11 Reed] 1555 Years

Here the Tenochca who had gone to Atenco arrived. They are Francisco Ocelotecatl, Gabriel Tlamiyauh, Baltasar Xochimitl. They arrived Saturday, February 16.

They laid the turf at San Lázaro, where there are huts; again it was begun on February 28.

At this <day> the viceroy spoke of the public work, during Sunday, September 22. He said: "On Monday eight hundred ninety of the commoners will be put <to work>.

And he said: "It will be necessary for a hospital to be built, that from there food will be given; the workers will eat four hundred pesos."

And the singers will eat three hundred pesos.

Only once was there a market at San Hipólito on Wednesday, October 12.

In this <place> the stone wall was begun on Friday, December 6.

It was also when portable platforms were made.

PAGE 97 <FOLIO 50R>
[12 Flint] 1556 Years

Here the stone wall was finished.

Fish fell on May 14.

Here the Hospital and Sacristy of San José was begun.

On November 11 the road behind the grove of chestnut trees was installed; it goes straight to Xochitlan.

PAGE 98 <FOLIO 50V>
[13 House] 1557 Years

Here the sacristy of San José was finished.

Here the church of San Miguel was begun.

Here don Cristóbal de Guzmán Cecetzin began to reign on January 6.

Here the canal of Teuiloyocan was installed on March 26.

On June 6 here the lords met to explain that the emperor had given up his power; it was given to prince don Felipe. So there was a procession, three days of rejoicing.

Here the little house of the Sacrament was completed and it was presented with full festivities and a play to San Francisco.

It was when the market was reinstated on Wednesday, October 13.

PAGE 99 <FOLIO 51R>
[1 Rabbit] 1558 Years

Here the locusts came out of the forest on May 28.

The Chichimecs, lords of Tlaixco, arrived on Saturday, May 28.

At the festival of San Juan it was when [the church] of San Miguel was dedicated.

PAGE 100 <FOLIO 51V>
1559 Years

Here the locusts passed today on Saturday, April 15.

The viceroy left, he went to embark people on Monday, the 24th of the month of April. He went to embark those who went to Florida.

The drainage pipe began on Monday, the 29th of the month of May.

[2 Reed] 1559 Years

Here our years were bound; they are bound for the eighth time.

The viceroy arrived, who had gone to embark the people, on Saturday, the 8th of the month of July.

On August 12 don Esteban de Guzmán began his post as judge. He came to fix the <matter> of the lands of the *calpulli*.

At the festival of San Andrés it was when prayers were said for don Carlos the emperor.

PAGE 101 <FOLIO 52R>
[3 Flint] 1560 Years

On March 17 the books were burned.

On May 9 the prisoners left; they were by way of war.

Here Dr. Ceynos came again.

Here Juan Gallego and don Esteban de Guzmán, judge, took a census of us.

August 10, some more arrived who were going to Florida.

October 8, again water came to fall outside the palace.

Monday, October 28, don Esteban de Guzmán, judge, went to place himself as lord of Tlatelolco.

On December 11 the viceroy went to spend some time in San Miguel. They put Spanish boats in a pool; the fireworks exploded.

PAGE 102 <FOLIO 52V>
[4 House] 1561 Years

Here doña Ana, the wife of Diego de Vara, daughter of don Luis de Velasco, viceroy, came. She was from Zacatlán.

PAGE 103 <FOLIO 53R>
[5 Rabbit] 1562 Years

Here the *alcaldes* don Pedro de la Cruz Tlapaltecatl and Martín Cano were favorably established. They took the staff.

Friday, the 7th of the month of August, a canal was dug behind the church, where water is extracted with a pump.

At this <time> the little girls gathered. They learn the doctrine today Monday, August 31.

In September the corn was lost. A single *almud* <old grain measure> was equivalent to a *tomín*. The *alcaldes*, the *regidores*, personally took charge.

Don Cristóbal de Guzmán Cecetzin died today Saturday, October 17.

Here the archbishop consecrated people; he consecrated three priests.

PAGE 104 <FOLIO 53V>
[6 Reed] 1563 Years

The son of the marquis arrived today, Sunday, the 17th of the month of January.

Today confirmation was held on Tuesday, the 9th of the month of March.

Don Luis de Santa María Cipac began to reign today, Tuesday, the 30th of the month of August.

The bishop of San José was installed today, Sunday, the 12th of the month of September.

200 Years

The *visitador* came on Monday, the 20th of the month of September.

Here began the *zahuatl* measles. This lasted a year. The priests helped us. Only in our very highly polished <public> houses they gave us confession and they instructed us in the doctrine.

PAGE 105 <FOLIO 54R>
[7 Flint] 1564 Years

Finally they began to whitewash the church today, Tuesday, the 10th of the month of February.

Monday, the 29th of May<,> I began my little house. There is a stone image.

Thursday, July 13, it was said that it would be necessary to give a peso and three *tomines* in (each) house in tribute. And when he finished the speech, then they cast stones at the governor and an *alcalde*. When the court was held, they went to sentence the Mexica. They sold them; some were forced to serve for five years, others for two years.

On July 31, Monday, don Luis de Velasco, viceroy, was buried in Santo Domingo.

On August 16, Wednesday, those who were in court were moved, they went there to the new court that was renovated this year. Then it was over when the different officials took their posts there.

On September 13, Wednesday, Captain Miguel López left. He was closing the march of those who went to China. They only assembled.

On December 25, Monday, the altarpiece of San José was placed.

PAGE 106 <FOLIO 54V>
[8 House] 1565 Years

Instruction was given in the main church for the priests to work all over. And today, Sunday, January 8, they will leave home.

And instruction was given in San José today, Sunday, the 21st of the month of January.

On the second day of June the text of Juan Gallego was printed.

On December 28, Friday, don Luis de Santa María, governor, was buried.

PAGE 107 <FOLIO 55R>
[9 Rabbit] 1566 Years

On the second day of January, Wednesday, the *oidores*, Dr. Puga, etc., took the staff.

The *visitador* departed today, Monday, the 25th of the month of March.

On the 9th of April, Holy Tuesday, the Audiencia was toppled; Martín Cano died there.

On July 16th, Tuesday, the marquis, Alonso Dávila, and his younger brother were taken prisoner; they were locked up. And Alonso Dávila and his younger brother, don Pedro González, died on Saturday, the 3rd day of the month of August. There will be exactly nineteen prisoners locked up.

Viceroy don Gastón de Peralta arrived today, Monday, the 21st of the month of October.

The text of Juan Grande was printed today, Wednesday, the 5th of the month of June of the year 1566.

PAGE 108 <FOLIO 55V>
[10 Reed] 1567 Years

The marquis left today, Monday, the 10th of the month of March.

Here the judges Alonso Carrillo and Muñoz investigated.

On May 5, Monday, they began to excavate canals everywhere. So the City of Mexico was converted into two.

Today Juana López was born.

PAGE 109 <FOLIO 56R>
[11 Flint] 1568 Years

On the 8th of the month of January, Thursday, they hung three mayordomos who belonged to Alonso Dávila; also the one who was going to go to Castile. And at midday they hung the third. At night they chopped them into pieces. The next day, Friday, they slit the throat of two: Baltasar Pérez and his younger brother don Pedro.

Don Francisco Jiménez arrived Sunday, the 18th of January. The next day there was public proclamation for him in the church. It was when the house of Alonso Dávila began to be destroyed, on February 9.

Don Gastón de Peralta, viceroy, left on Wednesday, March 3; he received the ashes in Tepeyacac.

Then don Martín Enríquez, viceroy, arrived.

The judge Alonso Carrillo went to Castile, on Saturday, March 20. He took the prisoners who were to die upon disembarking.

They began to excavate a canal at Totoltepec today, Wednesday, July 2.

The *alcaldes* changed today, Thursday, in the afternoon, on the 13th of the month of May. Don Diego de Tovar and Juan García, *alcaldes*, took the staff.

The *visitador* departed today, Monday, in the early morning, the 20th of the month of September; he went to meet the *regidores* who were already on the way. At vespers Pedro Calixto left.

Dr. Ceynos died today, Friday, December 10. He was buried in San Francisco.

PAGE 110 <FOLIO 56V>
[12 House] 1569 Years

On July 14, Thursday, judge don Francisco Jiménez left early.

It was when they buried Ana Núñez.

And don Francisco Jiménez arrived today, Saturday, the 27th of the month of August.

PAGE 111 <FOLIO 57R>
[13 Rabbit] 1570 Years

Baltasar Quauhtli left for China today, Saturday, February 4.

Work began on excavating a canal at Acaxochic. Again we went behind the Santa Cruz today, Monday, the 6th of the month of February.

We went to fill six spots with turf as our work today, Friday, the 15th of the month of September.

PAGE 112 <FOLIO 57V>
[1 Reed] 1571 Years

Here came our spiritual lord the inquisitor.

We went to Acaxic, Monday, September 3.

PAGE 113 <FOLIO 58R>
[2 Flint] 1572 Years

The archbishop don Fray Alonso de Montúfar died today, Friday, the 7th of the month of March.

The blacks were taken prisoners in Santo Domingo today, Thursday, March 17.

The canal of San Juan was excavated.

There was prayer for those who had died in the water and for those taken captive today, Wednesday, the 9th of the month of April.

Our beloved father Fray Pedro de Gante was buried today, Sunday, April 20.

A church was built with a theatrical purpose. The lords were dressed up as the conquered Moors. In this way they began as if it were at home, and so they did it: first they made them arrive, they fought on boats; then they fought on horseback; afterward they made them arrive on foot. They set siege on the roof. It was presented today, Friday, the 25th of the month of July.

Here the Theatine clerics arrived.

The second day of Advent, water fell at Santa Fe. There they became ill.

PAGE 114 <FOLIO 58V>
[3 House] 1573 Years

Don Francisco Jiménez died today, Friday, at midnight. The messengers arrived on January 4.

The judge Antonio Valeriano came today, Sunday. He began his post, on the 18th of the month of January.

He gave possession to the Chalca today, Thursday, the 29th of the month of January.

It began, the foundations of the shops in the market of San Hipólito were dug today.

PAGE 115 <FOLIO 59R>
[4 Rabbit, 1574 Years]

Here the spiritual lord, the inquisitor, disclosed the different sins that we commit, during Sunday he disclosed them. On February 28 they burned the lords who had killed our beloved father on the coast <here Atenco probably means near the water or coast>, Vera Cruz.

Here as a group the image of Our Lord was carried in procession today, Holy Thursday, the 8th of the month of April.

Don Martín Hernández, *Alcalde.*
Gaspar García, *Alcalde.*
Toribio Lucas, *Alcalde.*

The archbishop was consecrated today, Sunday, the 5th of the month of December.

Friday, July 30, we went to destroy the church of San José, which was made of wood.

PAGE 116 <FOLIO 59V>
[5 Reed] 1575 Years

The priests of San Pablo and San Augustín entered today, Saturday, the 30th of the month of July. Then they said mass there.

They began to whitewash the little canal of San Miguel today, Friday, the 4th of the month of November.

PAGE 117 <FOLIO 60R>
[6 Flint] 1576 Years

The guardians who had been prisoners for a *tomín* <coin, monetary unit> were released; they had to pay 5 *tomines* of tribute in the palace today, Saturday, August 18. And also in August disease spread. Blood flowed from the nose. Only in our houses the priests gave us confession and gave us food. And the doctors healed us. And it was when the bells remained silent, they did not toll for the burials, as if we were abandoned in the church.

Sunday, September 16, there was a procession in Santa Lucía, due to the disease. And on Monday they cured my groin. But on Holy Thursday there was no procession; so there was a rest. Whoever held a procession would have to pay five pesos; there would only be prayer. This is how it was done.

PAGE 118 <FOLIO 60V>
[7 House] 1577 Years

An eagle descended to the chapel of San José today, Tuesday, the 8th of the month of October of the year 1577.

And Juan Grande took a census of the houses today, Friday, the 11th of the month of October of the year 1577.

The star began to make smoke today, Wednesday, the 6th of the month of November of the year 1577.

PAGE 119 <FOLIO 61R>
[8 Rabbit] 1578 Years

PAGE 120 <FOLIO 61V>
[9 Reed] 1579 Years

On the day of the Saints, the Holy Cross was taken in procession. It came from Rome shortly before. Our Savior died on it.

And it was when there was also much hunger. The viceroy and the *alcaldes* took over the sale of maize.

In October water fell in Tlatzcan.

On December 27, it was when the sons of Santa Clara moved.

PAGE 121 <FOLIO 62R>
[10 Flint] 1580 Years

Here many fish appeared.

On the 23rd of the month of September of the year 1580, Friday, don Martín Enríquez, viceroy, left.

On the 4th of the month of October, Tuesday, viceroy don Lorenzo entered. It was when the banner was completed with which they went to receive him.

PAGE 122 <FOLIO 62V>
[11 House] 1581 Years

On March 20, Holy Monday, the iron clock with bell, hung there in San Augustín, fell.

On Tuesday, April 11, there was an earthquake two times; once in the morning, once at midday.

On May 8, the judge Alonso de Nava took a census of the houses.

On June 15, the news arrived that the wives of the lords died; the wife of the king of Castile and the wife of the viceroy here. Therefore there was fasting.

On June 24, on the day of St. John the Baptist, they drowned a Spaniard, who went to swim there, where there is white water.

On September 11, Monday, there were many earthquakes at night.

PAGE 123 <FOLIO 63R>
[12 Rabbit] 1582 Years

It was when Sebastiana was born, today Tuesday, the 23rd of January of the year 1582; a day 6 Aquarius, golden number 10 <1 + 2 + 3 + 4 = 10 as a "golden" number as per the golden mean or else perhaps astrological>; 6 o'clock 8 Mars.

Again we were delivered at San Sebastián; today, Saturday, the 8th of the month of September mass was held.

Water fell today, Friday, the 14th of December of the year 1582. Lord don Lorenzo Suárez de Mendoza has still not been seen; he parried <or fought for his life>.

PAGE 124 <FOLIO 63V>
[13 Reed] 1583 Years

Here the canal was begun; it was dug on all sides. In the second week it was when it was very cold, so that there was much misery, Monday, February 4 of the year 1583.

It was when the drainpipe of San Pablo was begun.

220 Years

Friday, March 22, Our Lord entered San Pablo, who left Totolapan.

Sunday, April 14, there was a procession and joy because there were war captives in Castile. And at sunset fires were lit on all the rooftops. And whoever did not light a fire would pay ten pesos, this was the order.

March, June 4, Our Lord entered San Augustín when night fell, it was Wednesday when he came, he stayed there all day.

Saturday, June 29, Lord don Lorenzo Suárez de Mendoza died.

Tuesday, festival day, the festival of San Lucas was celebrated. There marked the beginning that only the 21st of each month would be counted.

PAGE 125 <FOLIO 64R>
[1 Flint] 1584 Years

The trumpeters went today, Friday, January 27. Santiago de Vara took them; they only accompanied the Spaniards.

Friday, June 30, the gold was buried there where the college was to be completed, where the sons of the lords were to be taught. The bishop consecrated the gold and silver chains.

Work to demolish the main church began today, Tuesday, the 12th of the month of September of the year of 1584. It was when mass was said for Juana López.

The bishop entered there in the main palace today, Saturday, October 7.He will do justice.

The mayordomo Melchor Dávila fell from the main church today, Tuesday, at seven o'clock, on the 12th of December of the year 1584.

San Augustín was completed. Mass was said there on Advent.

PAGE 126 <FOLIO 64V>
[2 House] 1585 Years

The main church was demolished, today, Monday, January 15 of the year 1585.

On January 21, Sunday, the bishops held a procession. There are always eight, plus the lords. In October they went to their different tasks.

Sunday, November 18, the viceroy don Francisco de Alvaro came.

Mariatón was born today, Sunday, the 25th of the month of February of the year 1585 on the day 9 Sagittarius, 8 Jupiter, Aureus 8 <8 is not a "golden" number, so perhaps "Aureo" [Latin for "golden"] is a term from astrology>.

PAGE 127 <FOLIO 65R>
[3 Rabbit] 1586 Years

The priests of San Sebastián entered, Sunday, January 19.

Here the *tomín* ended and corvée labor.

And the archbishop don Pedro Moya departed today, Wednesday, the 11th of the month of June of the year 1586. First he was the inquisitor, then the archbishop, then the viceroy, this is how he came to undertake three posts. And he came to improve the main church, and he expelled the *regidores*, who were Spaniards.

PAGE 128 <FOLIO 65V>
[4 Reed] 1587 Years

Here the collection of tribute of 13 *tomines* began.

And here again the sacristy of San José was renovated. In that <sacristy> our beloved father friar Alonso Martínez and Francisco çapovan [*sic*] spoke.

And again it was when acts of compassion were conducted for the sick. On August 23, for seven days, it was when the arrival of the twelve *fanegas* <1.6 bushels in Spain> of corn and seven peso *tomines* began to arrive. There they were given to the people in the house of the marquis. Our beloved father gave people <something> with which to buy meat.

PAGE 129 <FOLIO 66R>
[5 Flint] 1588 Years

PAGE 130 <FOLIO 66V>
[6 House] 1589 Years

It was when don Alonso began his post as judge, today, Monday, the 10th of the month of April of the year 1589.

Today, Tuesday, the 11th of April, Wednesday, and Thursday, for two days, there were many earthquakes. And the last fifteen days, also on Wednesday, when there were two earthquakes.

Monday, the 3rd of the month of July of 1589, the foundations of the entrance to the chapel of San José were dug; it was whitewashed.

Sunday, the 9th of the month of July of 1589, the daughter of the viceroy died. She died in Coyohuacan and was buried here in San Francisco.

Tuesday, first day of the month of August of 1589, here Our Lady Santa María passed a day here in the barrio of Tequixquipan. It <the image> has just arrived from Castile.

Thursday, the 30th of November of the year 1589, on the day of San Andrés, mass was said. We were delivered at San Juan and Santa María.

PAGE 131 <FOLIO 67R>
[7 Rabbit] 1590 Years

Don Francisco Alvaro, viceroy, departed today, Thursday, the 18th of January of the year 1590.

Don Luis de Velasco, viceroy, arrived today, Thursday, the 25th of January.

It was when judge don Alonso took a census of the houses today, Friday, the 6th of the month of July of 1590.

San Francisco was closed, since mass is not given there anymore; Sunday, the 26th of August of the year 1590.

In this [year] the boys congregated in the new chapel; Sunday, the 16th of the month of September.

The Sacrament entered San José; today, Sunday, the 14th of the month of October.

Don Antonio came. The war ends with him. Here the court closed when he came; Monday, the 29th of October.

PAGE 132 <FOLIO 67V>
[8 Reed] 1591 Years

There was an earthquake today, Thursday, the 14th of the month of March of the year 1591.

San José Xomolco was whitewashed; there a bell will be hung; Thursday, the third of the month of October of the year 1591. And it went up in the year 1596.

PAGE 133 <FOLIO 68R>
[12 Reed] 1595 Years

Don Manrique, the viceroy, left today, Wednesday, the 25th of October.

Don Gaspar, count viceroy, came today, Sunday, the 5th of November.

It was when the drainpipe of San Juan was begun.

And it was when they came to spread the boils of measles.

And it was also when the tribute of turkeys began.

[13 Flint] 1596 Years

Today, Sunday, the 8th of December, was when an auto-da-fé was issued. Nine people were burned in the house of the inquisitor; ten died there in the prison. They burned ten only in effigy.

Today, Wednesday, our governor don Juan Martín was established; on the 25th of the month of December of the year 1596.

PAGE 134 <FOLIO 68V>
[1] House 1597 Years

Here the priests entered in San Francisco. They went to establish themselves in Santa María, on the 10th of October.

Sunday, the 19th of October, was when the Señora de la Asunción <Our Lady of the Assumption> was taken in procession there in Santa María.

[2] Rabbit 1598 Years

On the 6th of February, there in Santa María, the procession began on Friday of Lent by orders of father Fray Lope Izquierdo.

[3] Reed 1599 Years

On the 10th of February was when news arrived that Our Lord king don Felipe died there in Castile.

[4] Flint 1600 Years

On the 3rd of May was when the news arrived that the archbishop don Alonso Fernández de Bonilla died there in Peru.

[5] House 1601 Years

Here the celebration of the festival of San Blas began. It was a festival to keep.

[6] Rabbit 1602 Years

Here appeared the monument; it was put in the building on Holy Thursday. It was very big and completely white.

Our beloved father the *comisario* of San Francisco came today, Monday, the 23rd of the month of September.

[7] Reed 1603 Years

It was when the archbishop don Fray García de Santa María returned to San Francisco. The priests received him with much esteem. And he also marveled over the interior of the house of the Holy.

PAGE 135 <FOLIO 69R>
8 Flint 1604

Here our reverend father Fray Francisco de Gamboa, who was the guardian of Tlatilolco, died; on Thursday on the day of Santa María Magdalena <St. Mary Magdalene>.

And it was also when there was a flood here in Mexico; when the wall of stone that was here in Ahuatzalpan rose.

9 House 1605

Friday, 25th of March of the year 1695, was when an auto-da-fé was issued in Santa Domingo, when thirty-two people were exposed.

10 Rabbit 1606

Today, Friday, the 3rd of the month of March, was when the judge don Gaspar de Monterrey took a census of us.

11 Reed 1607

Today, Sunday, on the 8th of the month of July, the viceroy don Luis de Velasco entered.

PAGE 139 <FOLIO 70R>

Tenotzin *tlatoani* [52 Years].

PAGE 140 <FOLIO 70V>

Acamapichtli. 40 Years.

PAGE 141 <FOLIO 71R>

Huitzilihuitzin. 22 Years.

PAGE 142 <FOLIO 71V>

Chimalpopocatzin. 12 Years.

PAGE 143 <FOLIO 72R>

Itzcoatzin. 13 Years.

PAGE 144 <FOLIO 72V>

Huehue Moteuczoma Ilhuicaminatzin. 29 Years.

PAGE 145 <FOLIO 73R>

Axayacatzin. 14 Years.

PAGE 146 <FOLIO 73V>

Tizocicatzin. 4 Years.

PAGE 147 <FOLIO 74R>

Ahuitzotzin. 17 Years.

PAGE 148 <FOLIO 74V>

Motecuzomatzin. 19 Years.

PAGE 149 <FOLIO 75R>

Cuitlahuactzin. 80 [Days].

PAGE 150 <FOLIO 75V>

Cuauhtemoctzin. 2 Years.

PAGE 151 <FOLIO 76R>

Cihuacohuatl Tlacotzin [5 Years].
Motelchiuhtzin [5 Years].
Don Pablo Xochiquen [3 Years].

All the three Mexica-Tenochca captains were *cónsules* <antiquated form for *caudillos*: chiefs, leaders, commanders>.

PAGE 152 <FOLIO 76V>
Don Diego Huanitzin [4 Years].
Don Antonio de Mendoza.

PAGE 153 <FOLIO 77R>

Don Luis de Velasco.
Don Diego Teuetzquititzin [18 Years].
Judge don Esteban de Guzmán.

PAGE 154 <FOLIO 77V>

Don Cristóbal de Guzmán [Cecetzin] [6 Years].

PAGE 155 <FOLIO 78R>

Don Luis Cipac [3 Years].
Don Gastón de Peralta, viceroy [2 Years].

PAGE 156 <FOLIO 78V>

Don Martín Enríquez, viceroy [5 Years].
Don Francisco Jiménez, judge, inhabitant of Tecamachalco.
Don Antonio Valeriano, judge, inhabitant of Azcapotzalco [23 Years].

PAGE 157 <FOLIO 79R>

Don Juan Martín, inhabitant of this place, governor of Mexico.
Don Gerónimo López, judge, governor, inhabitant of Xaltocan.

Here the viceroy don Juan de Mendoza arrived.

Here the archbishop don Fray García de Santa María arrived.

NOTES

CHAPTER 1. INTRODUCTION

1. Domingo Francisco de San Antón Muñón Chimalpahin Quauhtlehuanitzin (hereinafter Chimalpahin), *Codex Chimalpahin*, 1:61.

2. Alvarado Tezozomoc's writings are incorporated into the "Mexican History" produced by the Nahua intellectual Chimalpahin, who wrote at the beginning of the seventeenth century. See Susan Schroeder, "The Truth about the Crónica Mexicayotl."

3. While the term "Aztec" is often used in North American scholarship to refer to the indigenous group that dominated central Mexico between the fourteenth and sixteenth centuries, it is something of a misnomer. The term "Aztec" best applies to the original inhabitants of Aztlan. The descendants of the Aztecs who came to dominate the political structure in central Mexico, as Spanish conquistador Hernando Cortés encountered it, identified themselves as "Mexica."

4. The Acolhua inhabited the eastern part of the Basin of Mexico with their capital at Tetxcoco. Like the Mexica, they claimed Chichimec ancestry but maintained separate traditions of their early history. Named for the first three rulers of Tetxcoco, Codex Xolotl, the Tlohtzin Map, and the Quinatzin Map use a cartographic format to record the history of Acolhua polities from their foundation to the fifteenth and mid-sixteenth centuries. They differ from the Mexica histories: while they show the arrival of ancestors in the Basin of Mexico, they do not depict Chicomoztoc or Aztlan as a place of origin and do not place great emphasis on the migratory journey and the foundation.

5. Diego Durán, *The History of the Indies of New Spain*, 549–557 (quotation on 557).

6. Ibid., 558.

7. Ibid., 20, 562 (quotation), 563.

8. The school was located within the monastery of San Francisco in the southwest part of the city, in the indigenous *parcialidad* (neighborhood) of San Juan Moyotlan.

9. Arts and crafts would also become a part of the curriculum. For more on the early educational systems in New Spain, see José María Kobayashi, *Le educación como conquista*; and Robert Ricard, *The Spiritual Conquest of Mexico*.

10. For observations on the structuring of time in these manuscripts, see Donald Robertson, *Mexican Manuscript Painting of the Early Colonial Period*; Elizabeth Hill Boone, *Stories in Red and Black*; and Federico Navarrete, "The Hidden Codes of the Codex Azcatitlan."

11. Eloise Quiñones Keber, *Codex Telleriano-Remensis*, 204–205.

12. John B. Glass (in collaboration with Donald Robertson), "A Census of Native Middle American Pictorial Manuscripts," 100.

13. María Castañeda de la Paz and Michel R. Oudijk, "La conquista y la colonia en el *Códice Azcatitlan*."

14. María Castañeda de la Paz, "Los codices históricos mexicas," "Los tlatelolcas y su ascendencia tepaneca en las fuentes mexicas," "El Códice X o los anales del 'Grupo de la Tira de la Peregrinación,'" "Codex Azcatitlan and the Work of Torquemada," and "Filología del corpus pintado (siglos xvi–xviii)"; Navarrete, "The Hidden Codes of the Codex Azcatitlan," 158.

15. Dana Leibsohn, *Script and Glyph*, 5.

16. Frances F. Berdan and Patricia Rieff Anawalt, eds., *The Codex Mendoza*; Walter Lehmann and Gerdt Kutscher, trans. and eds., *Geschichte der Azteken*; Eloise Quiñones Keber, *Codex Telleriano-Remensis*; Robert Barlow and Michel Graulich, eds., *Codex Azcatitlan*.

17. Lori Boornazian Diel, *The Tira de Tepechpan*; Eduardo de J. Douglas, *In the Palace of Nezahualcoyotl*.

18. Angélica Jimena Afanador-Pujol, *The Relación de Michoacán (1539–1541) and the Politics of Representation in Colonial Mexico*; Leibsohn, *Script and Glyph*; Alessandra Russo, *The Untranslatable Image*.

19. See, for example, Federico Navarrete, "The Path from Aztlan to Mexico," "The Hidden Codes of the Codex Azcatitlan," and "Writing, Images, and Time-Space in Aztec Monuments and Books"; Maria Castañeda de la Paz, "Los códices históricos mexicas," "Los tlatelolcas y su ascendencia tepaneca en las fuentes mexicas," "De Aztlan a Tenochtitlan," "El Códice X o los anales del 'Grupo de la Tira de la Peregrinación,'" "Codex Azcatitlan and the Work of Torquemada," "Filología del corpus pintado (siglos xvi–xviii)," and *Conflictos y alianzas en tiempos de cambio*; Castañeda de la Paz and Michel Oudijk, "La conquista y la colonia en el Códice Azcatitlan."

20. Diana Magaloni Kerpel, *The Colors of the New World*; Barbara E. Mundy, *The Death of Aztec Tenochtitlan, the Life of Mexico City*.

21. See, for example, the work of Arthur J. O. Anderson, James Lockhart, Susan Schroeder, and Doris Namala in Chimalpahin, *Annals of His Time* and *Codex Chimalpahin*; Susanne Klaus, trans. and ed., *Anales de Tlatelolco*; James Lockhart, *The Nahuas after the Conquest*, *Nahuas and Spaniards*, and *We People Here*; Kevin Terraciano, "Three Views of the Conquest of Mexico from the *Other* Mexica"; Camilla Townsend, *Annals of Native America*.

CHAPTER 2. CODEX BOTURINI: A PICTOGRAPHIC PARADIGM

1. Dinorah Lejarazu Rubin and Manuel Hermann Lejarazu, *Códice Boturini o Tira de la Peregrinación*.

2. Elizabeth Hill Boone, "Migration Histories as Ritual Performance."

3. Castañeda de la Paz, "De Aztlan a Tenochtitlan."

4. Navarrete, "The Path from Aztlan to Mexico."

5. Rafael Tena, "La cronología de la *Tira de la Peregrinación*."

6. Patrick Johansson Keraudren, *Códice Boturini*.

7. Thanks to the generous assistance of Carolusa González, former guardian of the Bodega de Códices, this study draws on observations of the original Codex Boturini and further study of the high-quality digital reproductions that were provided to me by the Biblioteca Nacional de Antropología e Historia.

8. The Museo Nacional de Antropología keeps a copy of Codex Boturini on display in the Sala Mexica.

9. http://www.codiceboturini.inah.gob.mx/codex.php.

10. Paul Radin, "The Sources and Authenticity of the History of the Ancient Mexicans," 6, 11.

11. Robertson, *Mexican Manuscript Painting*, 86.

12. Ibid., 84, 86 (quotation).

13. Pablo Escalante, "El trazo, el cuerpo, y el gesto," 166–169.

14. The Spanish Council of the Indies (both East and West Indies) was created in 1510 by a special Privy Council. Peter Martyr became the chronicler and was appointed a full member in 1518. Erich Woldan, "Petrus Martyr de Angleria."

15. Martyr quoted in Philipp J. J. Valentini, "Mexican Paper," 65–66.

16. Hans Lenz, *Cosas del papel en Mesoamérica*, 211–212, 417–420.

17. For a brief overview of the physical aspects of painted books produced in the pre-Columbian and early colonial periods, see Boone, *Stories in Red and Black*, 23–24.

18. For detailed information on Aztec papermaking traditions and use, see Valentini, "Mexican Paper"; Victor Wolfgang von Hagen, *Aztec and Maya Papermakers*; Bodil Christensen and Samuel Martí, *Brujerías y papel precolombino*; Hans Lenz, *El papel indígena mexicano*; Lenz, *Cosas del papel*; and Alan R. Sandstrom and Pamela E. Sandstrom, *Traditional Papermaking and Paper Cult Figures of Mexico*. For the use of the terms *amatl* and *amate*, see von Hagen, *Aztec and Maya Papermakers*, 37, 99. *Amatl* derives from trees in the botanical family Moraceae, genus *Ficus*. Several different varieties of *Ficus* were and still are used for papermaking in Mexico (e.g., *Ficus padifolia*, *Ficus petiolaris*, and *Ficus involuta*).

19. Motolinía [Toribio de Benavente], *Motolinía's History of the Indians of New Spain*, 333. Fray Bernardino de Sahagún's informants describe the tree from which paper is made (*amaquauitl*) as follows: "It is smooth, smooth overall; its leaves, foliage verdure gleam; its bark is herb-green. It is made into paper; it becomes paper. It is beaten." Bernardino de Sahagún, *Florentine Codex*, 11:111.

20. Philip Dark and Joyce Plesters, "The Palimpsests of Codex Selden," 532; Alfonso Caso, *Interpretación del Códice Colombino*, 91–92.

21. Sahagún, *Florentine Codex*, 11:243–244. See the entries on chalk (*tiçatl*), limestone (*tetiçatl*), and especially chimaltiçatl (*in chimaltiçatl*).

22. In some cases, such as the early colonial Codex Borbonicus, the preparatory base was applied to both sides of the native paper manuscript. Robertson, *Mexican Manuscript Painting*, 88.

23. For example, Donald Robertson refers to Codex Boturini as "totally without color" (ibid., 85). He makes reference to the black and white plates in Radin's work.

24. For a list of reproductions available prior to 1975, see John Glass's entry on Codex Boturini in Glass (and Robertson), "A Census," 100–101.

25. See descriptions of the pigments and their preparation in books 10 and 11 of Sahagún, *Florentine Codex*.

26. For the definition of *tlilli* and *tlapalli*, see Frances Karttunen, *An Analytical Dictionary of Nahuatl*, 289, 308.

27. Chimalpahin, *Codex Chimalpahin*, 1:181.

28. Sahagún, *Florentine Codex*, 10:190–191.

29. As quoted in Miguel León-Portilla, *The Aztec Image of Self and Society*, 69.

30. Some studies have incorporated a limited discussion of the use of line. For example, Robertson (*Mexican Manuscript Painting*) discusses the use of frame lines and Lejarazu Rubin and Hermann Lejarazu (*Códice Boturini*) briefly discuss the type of tool that the *tlacuilo* used. Patrick Johansson Keraudren includes some discussion of these topics in *Códice Boturini*.

31. The extreme fading of the red line may be due in part to unfavorable display conditions in the early part of the twentieth century. See Felipe Solís, "Adventures and Misadventures of the National Museum of Anthropology's Collections," 79, n. 49.

32. See, for example, Motolinía, *Motolinía's History*, 259.

33. Arthur G. Miller, "Introduction to the Dover Edition," xiii.

34. See, for example, Elizabeth Hill Boone, ed., *Painted Architecture and Polychrome Monumental Sculpture in Mesoamerica*.

35. Sahagún, *Florentine Codex*, 10:28.

36. See the locations designated on table 2.1, from Cuextecatlichocayan to Atotonilco.

37. For all references to the text in Codex Aubin, please refer to appendix 2, a translation of the Nahuatl text in Codex Aubin, unless otherwise noted.

38. Navarrete, "The Path from Aztlan to Mexico," 32.

39. Place identifications are based on Ernst Mengin, "Commentaire du Codex Mexicanus Nos. 23–24 de la Bibliothèque Nationale de Paris."

40. Navarrete, "The Path from Aztlan to Mexico," 45.

41. John Glass, "William Bullock and the Old Collection of Pictorial Manuscripts in the Mexican National Museum of Anthropology." I am grateful to Barbara Tenenbaum, Georgette Dorn, and Lewis Wyman of the Library of Congress for locating this document and providing me with a copy.

42. John Delafield Jr., *An Inquiry into the Origin of the Antiquities of America*.

43. Johansson Keraudren, *Códice Boturini*.

44. Boone, "Migration Histories as Ritual Performance," 144–145.

45. The term "Chichimec" (from the Nahuatl *chichimecatl*, plural *chichimeca*) encompasses groups that arrived into the Basin of Mexico from the north. Nahuatl accounts characterize the Chichimecs as nomadic or seminomadic people who wore animal-skin clothing, did not cut their hair, and typically carried bows and arrows used for hunting. The Mexica claimed that they migrated directly from the desert lands of the Chichimecs to the north. See Pedro Carrasco, *The Tenochca Empire of Ancient Mexico*, 41; and Sahagún, *Florentine Codex*, 10:165–175, 189.

46. Scripted accounts of the sixteenth and early seventeenth century, such as Diego Durán's *The History of the Indies of New Spain*, Fernando Alvarado Tezozomoc's *Crónica Mexicayotl*, Juan de Tovar's *Historia de la venida de los indios* (found in Tovar, *Origen de los mexicanos*), José de Acosta's *Historia natural y moral de las Indias*, the texts of Domingo de San Antón Muñón Chimalpahin Quauhtlehuanitzin, and Juan de Torquemada's *Monarquía indiana*, cite Aztlan as the Mexica point of departure.

47. *a[tl]* + *az[tapilli]* + *-tlan* (locative suffix): Eduard Seler, *Gesammelte Abhandlungen zur Amerikanischen Sprach- und Alterthumskunde*, 2:31.

48. Barlow and Graulich, *Codex Azcatitlan*, 40–43.

49. Durán, *History*, 21.

50. Mengin, "Commentaire du Codex Mexicanus."

51. The teeth emphasize the locative suffix: *a[tl]* + *az[tapilli]* + *-tlan[tli]*.

52. See Michel Oudijk, "Elaboration and Abbreviation in Mexican Pictorial Manuscripts," 157–158.

53. Appendix 2.

54. For some pictorial representations of Chicomoztoc with seven caves, see the Historia Tolteca-Chichimeca, Cuauhtinchan Map 2, and Codex Mexicanus.

55. They are named on Codex Aubin folio 4r. The same god-bearers are also found in Codex Azcatitlan on folios 2v–3r; for the identification of these figures, see Barlow and Graulich, *Codex Azcatitlan*, 46–49, n. 12.

56. Appendix 2.

57. Sahagún, *Florentine Codex*, 1:1.

58. Chimalpahin, *Codex Chimalpahin*, 1:185.

59. Joaquín Galarza and Krystyna M. Libura, *Para leer la Tira de la Peregrinación*, 29.

60. Chimalpahin, *Codex Chimalpahin*, 1:71.

61. Chimalpahin's "History or Chronicle with Its Calendar of the Mexica Years" (found in Chimalpahin, *Codex Chimalpahin*, vol. 1) states that they stayed in this location three and a half years: "It was in this same year, One Flint, 1064, that they had settled at the foot of the cypress tree. They spent three and a half years [where] it was." Chimalpahin, *Codex Chimalpahin*, 1:183.

62. Torquemada, *Monarquía indiana*, 114.

63. Chimalpahin, *Codex Chimalpahin*, 1:73.

64. Durán describes the sixteenth-century Mimixcoa as servants of the god Mixcoatontli: Diego Durán, *Book of the Gods and Rites and the Ancient Calendar*, 148.

65. Chimalpahin, *Codex Chimalpahin*, 1:67.

66. The *xiuhmamalhuaztli* resembles the one shown in the representation of the New Fire ceremony attached to the date cartouche 2 Reed on folio 6 (plate 2.6).

67. Chimalpahin, *Codex Chimalpahin*, 1:73.

68. For some visual examples of the presence of the eagle at foundation, see the Tira de Tepechpan, Codex Mendoza, and Codex Aubin.

69. Chimalpahin, *Codex Chimalpahin*, 1:103.

70. Lori Diel notes that human sacrifice is specifically associated with the Mexica in the Tira de Tepechpan and other colonial-period documents: *The Tira de Tepechpan*, 38–40.

71. Appendix 2.

72. Appendix 2.

73. Many Mexica migration histories claim that the eagle on the nopal cactus appeared at the site where Copil's sacrificed heart was thrown into Lake Texcoco. A divine figure, Copil is identified as the son of Malinalxochitl, who was the sister of Huitzilopochtli.

74. Barlow and Graulich, *Codex Azcatitlan*, 52–53.

75. Durán, *History*, 22–23.

76. The same events in the same order are also described in Chimalpahin, *Codex Chimalpahin*, 1:76–81. Barlow suggests a shared source material for these accounts that he calls "Crónica X": "La Crónica 'X.'"

77. Durán, *History*, 23–25.

78. Acosta, *Historia natural y moral de las Indias*, 382.

79. Durán states that some indigenous accounts "say that the Indians were born of pools and springs": *History*, 3–4.

80. For all references to the glosses in Codex Azcatitlan, refer to appendix 1.

81. Chimalpahin, *Codex Chimalpahin*, 1:71.

82. Tom Cummins, "Here, There, and Now," 87–89.

83. The text in Codex Aubin notes each of these developments; see appendix 2.

84. For example, the Mexica are called "Culhua-Mexica" in Hernando Cortés's letters to the Spanish king Charles V: *Letters from Mexico*, 47, 74, 142–152, 166–168, 173, 178, 180, 217, 231, 397, 459, n. 1.

85. The Toltecs were the people of Tula or "Tollan," meaning "Place of the Reeds." Tula was at its most populous circa 950–1200 C.E. The archaeological remains of the city, known to the pre-Hispanic Mexica, are located north of the Basin of Mexico in what is now the Mexican state of Hidalgo. The Toltecs were understood to be from the Chichimec region to the north. The Codex Azcatitlan, Codex Boturini, and Codex Aubin include Tula as a stop along the migration journey.

86. See Nigel Davies, *The Toltec Heritage*; Richard Diehl, *Tula*; and Alba Guadalupe Mastache de Escobar, Robert H. Cobean, and Dan M. Healan, *Ancient Tollan*.

87. See Sahagún, *Florentine Codex*, 10:165–170.

88. Appendix 2.

89. Appendix 2.

90. Appendix 2.

91. Durán, *History*, 41.

92. Carrasco, *The Tenochca Empire of Ancient Mexico*, 428.

93. Boone, "Migration Histories as Ritual Performance," 142–143.

94. Ibid. (throughout).

CHAPTER 3. MASTER AND APPRENTICE: THE MULTIPLE ARTISTIC HANDS IN CODEX AZCATITLAN

Some of the ideas in this chapter were initially proposed in Angela Marie Herren, "Writing Collaborative Histories."

1. Barlow and Graulich, *Codex Azcatitlan*, 22. This 1995 publication reproduces in full Barlow's original 1949 study: "El Códice Azcatitlan."
2. Barlow and Graulich, *Codex Azcatitlan*, 22.
3. Robertson, *Mexican Manuscript Painting*, 69.
4. Barlow and Graulich, *Codex Azcatitlan*.
5. Navarrete, "The Hidden Codes of the Codex Azcatitlan," 158.
6. Ibid., 155.
7. Elizabeth Hill Boone, "Manuscript Painting in Service of Imperial Ideology," 192.
8. Boone, *Stories in Red and Black*, 209.
9. Barlow and Graulich, *Codex Azcatitlan*, 16–17.
10. John Bierhorst, trans. and ed., *Ballads of the Lords of New Spain*, 1–23.
11. Oudijk, "Elaboration and Abbreviation in Mexican Pictorial Manuscripts," 158.
12. Though it is difficult to see this in the Codex Azcatitlan facsimile, the original manuscript depicts the priest figure in a darker tone.
13. Though Barlow interpreted this glyph as Amimitl, Michel Graulich expanded upon Eduard Seler's initial interpretation to offer a convincing argument for reading this glyph as Aztlan; the name derives from *aztapilli* (a kind of sedge associated with whiteness) and *atl* (water): Barlow and Graulich, *Codex Azcatitlan*, 40–45 and n. 7.
14. See, for example, Navarrete, "The Hidden Codes of the Codex Azcatitlan"; and Castañeda de la Paz, "Los códices históricos mexicas," "Los tlatelolcas y su ascendencia tepaneca en las fuentes mexicas," "El Códice X o los anales del 'Grupo de la Tira de la Peregrinación,'" "Codex Azcatitlan and the Work of Torquemada," and "Filología del corpus pintado (siglos xv–xviii)."
15. Boone, "Migration Histories as Ritual Performance."
16. Barlow and Graulich, *Codex Azcatitlan*, 42–43, n. 8; see also R. A. M. van Zantwijk, *The Aztec Arrangement*, 64.
17. Carrasco, *The Tenochca Empire of Ancient Mexico*, 93–94.
18. Barlow and Graulich, *Codex Azcatitlan*, 40–41, n. 7.
19. The glyph for Xaltocan in the Codex Aubin also shows a darkened insect.
20. Michael E. Smith, *Aztec City-State Capitals*, 69. For a thorough recent treatment of Azcapotzalco's legacy and its relationship to other *altepetl*, see María Castañeda de la Paz, *Conflictos y alianzas en tiempos de cambio*.
21. Quoted in Peter B. Villella, *Indigenous Elites and Creole Identity in Colonial Mexico, 1500–1800*, 85–86. The Valeriano quotations come from a letter of the governors and officers of Azcapotzalco to Felipe II, Azcapotzalco, February 10, 1561, 218–221.
22. Villella, *Indigenous Elites and Creole Identity*, 85. Codex Aubin also notes Valeriano's assumption of the office in 1573: "The judge Antonio Valeriano came today, Sunday. He began his post, on the 11th of the month of January" (appendix 2).
23. Appendix 2.
24. This warrior-like incarnation of the god appears intermittently in the manuscript. On folio 6r he appears atop a temple at Coatepec carrying a spear and shield. On folio 8r Artist B draws a version of this figure carrying a shield and darts and a serpent staff, subjugating an enemy whose head is behind the shield. Since the bird looks different here, the figure has been glossed "Huitzilopochtli."
25. The meaning of the toponym is taken from María Elena Bernal-García, "The Dance of Time," 71, n. 13.
26. The glyph for Tepemaxalco that appears on the *Relación geográfica* of Cempoala also shows agave at the base of the toponym (Nettie Lee Benson Latin American Collection, University of Texas Libraries).
27. Alfonso Caso's map of Tenochtitlan and Tlatelolco, showing the twenty indigenous neighborhoods, appears in "Los barrios antiguos de Tenochtitlan y Tlatelolco." A reproduction of this map is published as figure 7.3 in Mundy, *The Death of Aztec Tenochtitlan*, 136, 137 (quotation). Mundy defines *tlaxilacalli* as "the basic unit for collective identification within the city, one step up from the household and one step down from the parcialidad" (137).
28. Klaus, *Anales de Tlatelolco*, 29. Barlow states that both rulers were installed in the same year, 1376, when their territories were elevated from the category of *cuauhtlahtollo*: Barlow and Graulich, *Codex Azcatitlan*, 98–99.
29. Barlow identified a similar glyph in the Codex García Granados: Barlow and Graulich, *Codex Azcatitlan*, 98–99. The same glyph appears again on folio 14r.

30. Chimalpahin, *Codex Chimalpahin*, 2:59, 111–113. The author of the Annals of Cuauhtitlan writes: "For while he [Tezozomoc] was still alive, still ruling, while it was still in his time, he kept setting up his children as rulers of cities, sending them off to rule in distant parts": John Bierhorst, trans. and ed., *History and Mythology of the Aztecs*, 81–82.

31. The figure on the upper right part of folio 13r is shown seated, but the image is unfinished and his circular chair has not yet been painted.

32. Chimalpahin, *Codex Chimalpahin*, 1:61; appendix 2; and Durán, *History*, 558–559.

33. Navarrete, "The Path from Aztlan to Mexico," 40.

34. Boone, *Stories in Red and Black*, 208.

35. Indigenous sources often list conflicting dates for the various rulers' reigns. I am following Robert Barlow's dates here: Barlow and Graulich, *Codex Azcatitlan*.

36. The mummy bundles do not appear in the reigns of Moteuczoma I, Axayacatl, and Moteuczoma II. The first two rulers have extensive conquests documented. The *tlacuilo* may have felt that there was not enough pictorial space to show the mummy bundle. Moteuczoma II's reign extended into the period of Spanish contact, which is treated in the following folios.

37. Barlow suggested that it might represent a ceremony that took place, while Graulich notes that many indigenous sources mark Colhuacan as the first Mexica conquest: Barlow and Graulich, *Codex Azcatitlan*, 104 and n. 60.

38. Chimalpahin, *Codex Chimalpahin*, 1:113.

39. Ibid., 1:115.

40. In the Florentine Codex book devoted to "Rhetoric and Moral Philosophy," the ruler is often described as a substitute and speaker for Tezcatlipoca: Sahagún, *Florentine Codex*, 6:17–20.

41. Chimalpahin, *Codex Chimalpahin*, 1:117.

42. Durán also offers a version of these events: *History*, 48–50.

43. Barlow and Graulich, *Codex Azcatitlan*, 104.

44. An account of Maxtla usurping the throne of his brother Tayatzin can be found in Fernando de Alva Ixtlilxochitl, *Obras históricas*, 1:353–354. As Eduardo de J. Douglas notes, Chimalpopoca supported Maxtla's brother Tayatzin as the successor to Tezozomoc, and the two were killed for plotting against Maxtla. Page 8 of Codex Xolotl depicts the garroting of Tayatzin and the imprisonment but not the death of Chimalpopoca: Douglas, *In the Palace of Nezahualcoyotl*, 226, n. 74. Codex Azcatitlan folio 16r shows the mummy bundle of Chimalpopoca facing another unidentified mummy bundle, perhaps Tayatzin.

45. Frances F. Berdan and Patricia Rieff Anawalt, *The Codex Mendoza*, 2:9.

CHAPTER 4. DON MARTÍN ECATZIN: CODEX AZCATITLAN'S COSMIC HERO

1. For the sake of convenience, in discussing questions of organization and content in Codex Azcatitlan I refer to the *tlacuilo* in the singular, with the understanding that this means the master *tlacuilo* who presumably made or led composition and content decisions.

2. For a discussion of the complicated relationship between MS 22, MS 22bis, and the different parts of the Annals of Tlatelolco, see Klaus, *Anales de Tlatelolco*; Lockhart, *We People Here*, 37–43; and Terraciano, "Three Views of the Conquest," 15–40.

3. These are the designations used in Klaus, *Anales de Tlatelolco*.

4. H. B. Nicholson, "Fray Bernardino de Sahagún," 24, 29.

5. Francisco López de Gómara, *Cortés*, 140.

6. Sahagún, *Florentine Codex*, 12:43, n. 1, 45.

7. Durán, *History*, 530.

8. Lockhart, *We People Here*, 257.

9. Mundy, *The Death of Aztec Tenochtitlan*, 97.

10. Sahagún, *Florentine Codex*, 12:53.

11. According to Anderson and Dibble, "These were, respectively, the south gate of the main temple square to the Iztapalapan road; the west gate to the Tlacopan road; and, probably, the north and east gates": Sahagún, *Florentine Codex*, 12:55, n. 2.

12. Ibid., 12:55.

13. Lockhart, *We People Here*, 257, 259 (quotation).

14. Ibid., 259.

15. Sahagún, *Florentine Codex*, 12:57.

16. Ibid., 2:167, 168, 170, 171.

17. Lockhart, *We People Here*, 257, 259 (quotation).

18. Ibid., 138.

19. The account is found under the year 1 Reed (before 1520) in appendix 2.

20. Lockhart, *We People Here*, 267.

21. Bernal Díaz del Castillo describes the rapid construction of two small ships shortly after Moteuczoma was taken prisoner. The master shipwrights, Martín López

and Andrés Núñez, had constructed them from materials brought from Villa Rica. Díaz del Castillo describes accompanying Moteuczoma to a nearby island for a hunting expedition, but I have found no reference to these ships being used during the Noche Triste: Bernal Díaz del Castillo, *The True History of the Conquest of New Spain*, 234–238.

22. Barlow, "El Códice Azcatitlan," 130. For examples of indigenous people referring to Alvarado as Tonatiuh, see Díaz del Castillo, *The True History*, 266 and 409. The nickname derived from Alvarado's red hair.

23. Barlow, "El Códice Azcatitlan," 130.

24. Díaz del Castillo, *The True History*, 390.

25. López de Gómara, *Cortés*, 264.

26. Díaz del Castillo, *The True History*, 398; see also López de Gómara, *Cortés*, 269.

27. Cortés, *Letters from Mexico*, 238. Díaz del Castillo states that sixty-six soldiers were taken alive and eight horses were killed: *The True History*, 406.

28. Cortés, *Letters from Mexico*, 238–239.

29. Díaz del Castillo, *The True History*, 406.

30. Durán, *History*, 554. Biscay is a province in northern Spain in the Basque country.

31. Cortés, *Letters from Mexico*, 238–239.

32. López de Gómara, *Cortés*, 278–279.

33. Durán, *History*, 553.

34. Díaz del Castillo, *The True History*, 411.

35. Castañeda de la Paz and Oudijk, "La conquista y la colonia," 10–12.

36. Fernando de Alva Ixtlilxochitl, *The Native Conquistador*, 49–50.

37. Lockhart, *We People Here*, 212. The information in brackets is clarified in the Spanish text. The indigenous scribe refers to a location in what would become the San Martín Atezcapan area of Tlatelolco.

38. Alva Ixtlilxochitl, *The Native Conquistador*, 49.

39. Lockhart, *We People Here*, 202–203.

40. Díaz del Castillo, *The True History*, 399.

41. Durán, *History*, 555–556.

42. Lockhart, *We People Here*, 216.

43. Ecatl's costume in these images, though uncolored, aligns with the Codex Mendoza's written and pictorial descriptions of the *tlacatecatl* (commanding general), a title that he carried. See the references to folio 67r in Berdan and Anawalt, *The Codex Mendoza*.

44. Klaus, *Anales de Tlatelolco*, 45.

45. Lockhart, *We People Here*, 265, 267, n. 30.

46. Klaus, *Anales de Tlatelolco*, 145 (quotation); Lockhart, *We People Here*, 267, 313, n. 30.

47. Cited in Emily Umberger, "Appendix 3," 257.

48. Lockhart, *We People Here*, 265, 267, n. 30.

49. Sahagún, *Florentine Codex*, 12:100, n. 14; Caso, "Los barrios antiguos," 35.

50. Lockhart, *We People Here*, 216.

51. Durán, *History*, 40–44 (quotation on 43).

52. Appendix 2.

53. See, for example, the account described earlier in the Florentine Codex, Lockhart, *We People Here*, 216.

54. Justyna Olko, *Insignia of Rank in the Nahua World*, 134–135.

55. See Carmen Aguilera, "Of Royal Mantles and Blue Turquoise"; and Patricia Rieff Anawalt, "Riddle of the Emperor's Cloak."

56. For a brief overview of Tecuichpotzin's marriages, see Donald Chipman, *Moctezuma's Children*, 40–42.

57. Cortés, *Letters from Mexico*, 264–265.

58. Ibid., 262.

CHAPTER 5. TRAITORS, INTRIGUE, AND THE COSMIC CYCLE IN CODEX AZCATITLAN

1. Ecatl's role is discussed in chapter 4. Moteuczoma would have been imprisoned but alive during the feast of Toxcatl depicted on plate 23r, the second page of the conquest material. The reverse, folio 23v, depicts Ecatl battling after Moteuczoma's death, during the time when Cuauhtemoc led the forces. Thus, Moteuczoma's death and Cuitlahua's brief reign were never recorded. While Cuauhtemoc does not appear in the extant folios, it seems logical that he would have appeared surrendering on the folio opposite folio 24r. In folios 23v and 24r of the conquest material, Cuauhtemoc's role is at least implicit.

2. Terraciano, "Three Views of the Conquest," 25. He cites Chimalpahin, *Codex Chimalpahin*, 2:79.

3. Barlow and Graulich, *Codex Azcatitlan*; and Castañeda de la Paz and Oudijk, "La conquista y la colonia."

4. As Lockhart notes, this passage was popularized through Ángel María Garibay's translation. Lockhart corrected his translation of this passage, noting that "Garibay recast the section as a verse lament, and he translated 'omitl' as 'darts' (mitl is arrow, dart, or spear), which then gave rise to the English 'Broken Spears.' Garibay did so even though both previous translators had correctly ren-

dered the word as 'bones,' and there is no room for doubt that 22bis says 'omitl'; it is one of the clearest things in the manuscript and is entirely consonant with the rest of the passage, which has none of the earmarks of Nahuatl song and verse": Lockhart, *We People Here*, 313, n. 31.

5. Lockhart, *We People Here*, 313, n. 31.

6. Ibid., 269.

7. Sahagún, *Florentine Codex*, chapters 39–40; Lockhart, *We People Here*, 242–251.

8. Lockhart, *We People Here*, 246.

9. Berdan and Anawalt, *The Codex Mendoza*, 4:83, 69.

10. See the entry for "Aztahuatzin" in Pilar Máynez, *El calepino de Sahagún*.

11. Lockhart, *We People Here*, 269.

12. Ibid. The Florentine Codex does not list the month. There is some discrepancy in the dating in the Florentine Codex conquest account, but it also places the end of the conquest in the year 3 House.

13. Sahagún, *Florentine Codex*, 2:16.

14. Lockhart, *We People Here*, 271, 273.

15. Ibid., 273, n. 43.

16. For an illuminating look at the developments in Tenochtitlan immediately after the conquest, see chapter 3, "The City in the Conquest's Wake," in Mundy, *The Death of Aztec Tenochtitlan*.

17. See, for example, Mundy's discussion of how the postconquest rivalry between Tenochtitlan and Tlatelolco played out in the naming of the city: *The Death of Aztec Tenochtitlan*, 130–135.

18. Durán, *History*, 559–560.

19. Cortés, *Letters from Mexico*, 334.

20. Durán, *History*, 560.

21. Annabeth Headrick, *The Teotihuacan Trinity*, 148–154 (quotation on 150).

22. Castañeda de la Paz and Oudijk have noted that the *palo volador* was a part of the 1566 celebrations honoring the arrival of Gastón de la Peralta and may be functioning similarly here: "La conquista y la colonia," 15.

23. Mundy, *The Death of Aztec Tenochtitlan*, 108.

24. For a description of this event, see Durán, *History*, 112.

25. Cortés, *Letters from Mexico*, 321.

26. Castañeda de la Paz, Oudijk, and Graulich have noted a series of similar glyphs on folio 90v of Codex Vaticanus A under the year 9 Reed (1527), where the use of baptized slaves to build the Chapultepec aqueduct is recorded: Castañeda de la Paz and Oudijk, "La conquista y la colonia," 16–18; and Barlow and Graulich, *Codex Azcatitlan*, 144.

27. According to Durán, the symbol for the third month of the year, Tozoztontli (Small Perforation), was a bird pierced through with a bone: *Book of the Gods and Rites*, 418. Michel Graulich suggested that this glyph represents the following month, Tozoztli (Great Perforation), which is marked by a similar glyph: Barlow and Graulich, *Codex Azcatitlan*, 146. However, the accompanying glyphs and the correspondence to Cuauhtemoc's death indicate that the earlier month is recorded.

28. Susan Milbrath, *Heaven and Earth in Ancient Mexico*, 18–36; López de Gómara, *Cortés*, 356; Alva Ixtlilxochitl, *The Native Conquistador*, 92.

29. Sahagún, *Florentine Codex*, 2:5–6, 57–60.

30. The glyph shows the hat of the deity Yopi, another name for Xipe Totec. See Caso, "Los barrios antiguos," 13. Yopico is also the name of a *tlaxilacalli* in Tenochtitlan in the *parcialidad* of San Juan. Mundy, *The Death of Aztec Tenochtitlan*, table 7.3.

31. Sahagún, *Florentine Codex*, 2:60.

32. Klaus interprets a reference in Document 5 to Cuauhtemoc being bound or hung from a beam as a brief reference to his death: *Anales de Tlatelolco*, 37, n. 85. This passage occurs during the description of Cuauhtemoc's torture by Cortés during the search for gold after the conquest. Like Lockhart, I believe that the context indicates that Cuauhtemoc was hung or tied to a beam while his feet were being burned with hot oil. Lockhart, *We People Here*, 271.

33. While MS 22bis may include passages of now-eroded text from MS 22, I suspect that MS 22bis incorporates information from another source, as do Klaus, *Anales de Tlatelolco*; Lockhart, *We People Here*, 37–43; and Terraciano, "Three Views of the Conquest." Similarities between Codex Azcatitlan and much of the additional content in MS 22bis indicate that Codex Azcatitlan may have been one of the additional sources used by the MS 22bis scribe.

34. Klaus, *Anales de Tlatelolco*, 35, 37.

35. Chimalpahin, *Codex Chimalpahin*, 2:169.

36. Terraciano, "Three Views of the Conquest," 15.

37. Alva Ixtlilxochitl, *The Native Conquistador*, 91.

38. Durán, *History*, 39.

39. The *tlacuilo* depicts this figure wearing a *temillotl* hairstyle, which denoted high-ranking military status. The

style was frequently worn by rulers and is most common in the Basin of Mexico region but was also found outside the core of the Aztec Empire. Justyna Olko, *Turquoise Diadems and Staffs of Office*, 109–112.

40. This account claims that Cuauhtemoc's head was cut off and impaled on a ceiba tree. Matthew Restall, Lisa Sousa, and Kevin Terraciano, *Mesoamerican Voices*, 56–62.

41. Ibid., 57.

42. Alva Ixtlilxochitl, *The Native Conquistador*, 89.

43. Klaus, *Anales de Tlatelolco*, 43.

44. Alva Ixtlilxochitl, *The Native Conquistador*, 93.

45. Cortés, *Letters from Mexico*, 367.

46. The quetzal takes an odd form here because the pigment has not yet been applied. The two points on the left of this form, however, recall the overlapping tips of the feathers that make up the quetzal halos that appear behind the rulers' heads in the ruler list.

47. MS 22bis lists the three victims in order of importance: Cuauhtemoc, Coanacoch, and Tetlepanquetzal. Klaus, *Anales de Tlatelolco*, 41.

48. Klaus, *Anales de Tlatelolco*, 43.

49. Under an entry for "Acala," William Bright writes: "The Mexican place name represents Nahuatl (Aztecan) *acallan* 'place of boats,' from *acalli* 'boat,' lit. 'water-house,' composed of *a(tl)* 'water' and *calli* 'house'": *Native American Placenames of the United States*, 20–21.

50. Chimalpahin, *Codex Chimalpahin*, 1:169.

51. Bernal Díaz del Castillo, *The Memoirs of the Conquistador*, 313, 315 (quotation).

52. The modern town, called Nochixtlan, is north of Oaxaca city in the Mexican state of Oaxaca.

53. "Tlatlauhquitepec" in Codex Mendoza references a location in the eastern Sierra Madre in the modern Mexican state of Puebla: Berdan and Anawalt, *The Codex Mendoza*, 2:128. Alva Ixtlilxochitl describes Iztapan and Tlatlahuitlapan (written as Ytztepec and Tlatlauhquitepec in Codex Mendoza) as stops made early in the Honduran expedition as they headed south: *The Native Conquistador*, 86. I am proposing that "Tlatlauhquitepec" may have been used to reference the same site in the Mixteca Alta that Chimalpahin's informants call Nochiztlan. Nochiztlan (Place of Scarlet or Where There Is Much Cochineal) helped the province to contribute forty bags of the red dye called cochineal annually: Berdan and Anawalt, *The Codex Mendoza*, 2:102.

54. Olko, *Insignia of Rank*, 338.

55. Tlacotl and his successor Motelchiuh did not descend from royal lineage. As others have noted, indigenous accounts often distinguish between the "legitimate" rulers of proper descent and "interim" ones. See, for example, Mundy, *The Death of Aztec Tenochtitlan*, 80–84. It is unclear, however, if that is the case here; the figure on folio 25v wearing a *xiuhhuitzolli*, seated on a *petlatl icpalli*, and carrying a staff may represent Motelchiuh.

56. Folio 23r depicts the events that lead up to Moteuczoma's death and folio 23v depicts a battle that took place when Cuauhtemoc was in power.

57. Lockhart, *We People Here*, 204.

58. Ibid.

59. For an account of the plot, see López de Gómara, *Cortés*, 339–345. A very detailed account of this plot appears in Hubert Howe Bancroft's *History of the Pacific States of North America*, 193–237.

60. Alva Ixtlilxochitl, *The Native Conquistador*, 79.

61. As Alva Ixtlilxochitl writes: "If it seemed they had mistreated the natives before, it was much worse during these revolts, in which they did them a thousand wrongs and stole their properties": ibid., 83.

62. The candles were only recently available in New Spain and probably signal Paz's status. Codex Aubin states that the wax candles appeared in 1522 and the candles of fat in 1523. See appendix 2.

63. Alva Ixtlilxochitl, *The Native Conquistador*, 82, n. 87.

64. Ibid., 84. Alva Ixtlilxochitl's account is in part a response and correction to López de Gómara.

65. This may or may not have been the case. Mundy points to the power vacuum, compromised infrastructure, uncertain provisioning, and frayed relations among different indigenous groups as obstacles to an uprising: *The Death of Aztec Tenochtitlan*, 116.

66. Bancroft, *History of the Pacific States*, 218–219.

67. Díaz del Castillo, *The Memoirs*, 285.

68. Lockhart, *We People Here*, 271. See also Klaus, *Anales de Tlatelolco*, 153.

69. López de Gómara, *Cortés*, 295, 296.

70. Ibid., 296.

71. Richard E. Greenleaf, *Zumárraga and the Mexican Inquisition, 1536–1543*, 12, n. 46.

72. Because of their important role in the conquest, the Tlaxcalans were granted the first bishopric.

73. López de Gómara, *Cortés*, 385.

74. Greenleaf, *Zumárraga*, 12, n. 46.

75. Díaz del Castillo, *The Memoirs*, 324.

76. López de Gómara, *Cortés*, 383–384.

77. Ibid., 384.

78. J. H. Elliott, "Cortés, Velázquez, and Charles V," xxxvi.

79. Barlow and Graulich, *Codex Azcatitlan*, 152.

80. Castañeda de la Paz and Oudijk, "La conquista y la colonia," 25. They suggest that what appears to be long hair may be a veil.

81. Juan Francisco Maura, *Women in the Conquest of the Americas*, 105–115.

82. Durán, *History*, 560, 561.

83. Although María de Estrada did participate in a skirmish shortly after the conquest, Durán conflates this with an earlier battle that took place in the spring of 1521, after the Noche Triste and before the siege.

84. Díaz del Castillo, *The True History*, 317, 323.

85. Cited in Maura, *Women in the Conquest*, 106.

86. Robert Himmerich y Valencia, *The Encomenderos of New Spain, 1521–1555*, 239.

87. Catholic historian Charles Herbermann wrote: "Bishop Garcés reached New Spain in 1527 and took possession of his see. Subsequently finding that it was impossible to hold the choir office at Tlaxcala because there was no cathedral, but only an altar covered with thatch work, and as a sumptuous church with three naves had been erected in the new city of Puebla de los Ángeles, the bishop declared that the chapter should pass to the latter city, and transferred thither the episcopal see on 3 October, 1539": *The Catholic Encyclopedia*, 748.

88. Durán, *History*, 558–559.

89. Bartolomé de las Casas, *An Account, Much Abbreviated, of the Destruction of the Indies with Related Texts*, 28–47. See, for example, the account on pages 44–45 describing an incident associated with Pedro Beltrán Nuño de Guzmán: "He later laid hold of this king because he was famed for being rich in gold and silver, and so that the king might give him great treasures the tyrant began to lay upon him the following torments: He put him in the stocks by the feet and with the body extended and bound by the hands to a piece of timber, and he held burning coals to his feet, and a boy with a horsetail reed wetted with oil would from time to time sprinkle them with oil to roast the flesh the better; on one side was a cruel man with an iron crossbow pointed at his heart, and on the other, another such a one, setting on him a terrible raging dog, which in the space of a Hail Mary would have torn him to pieces; and thus they tormented and tortured him so that he would reveal to him the treasures that the captain pretended that he had, until, a certain Franciscan priest having been advised of all this, he took the poor creature from the captain's hands, although from these torments the Indian later died. And in this wise they tormented and tortured and killed many lords and caciques in those provinces so that they might give them gold and silver."

90. See chapter 3 in Greenleaf, *Zumárraga*.

91. Durán, *History*, 532.

92. Descriptions of this treasure can be found in other accounts as well. See Díaz Del Castillo, *The True History*, 218–220, 238.

93. Durán, *History*, 543.

94. Díaz del Castillo, *The True History*, 317–318.

95. Cortés, *Letters from Mexico*, 137–138.

96. Durán, *History*, 40–44.

97. Ibid., 21. See also the description of Aztlan as a place of whiteness on 213.

98. Dana Leibsohn notes an example of this on folio 33r of the manuscript: "A kind of visual prolepsis is put into play, the arrows foreshadowing events that will occur two centuries hence, when Tlatelolcans conquer the latter-day Teuhctlecozauhqui and Tepexoch ilama": *Script and Glyph*, 57.

99. Luis González Obregón, ed., *Procesos de indios idolatras y hechiceros*. See also Greenleaf, *Zumárraga*, chapter 3.

100. Mundy, *The Death of Aztec Tenochtitlan*, 49.

CHAPTER 6. CODEX AUBIN AND THE INFLUENCE OF PRINTED BOOKS

An earlier version of this chapter appears in Merideth Paxton and Leticia Staines Cicero, eds., *Constructing Power and Place in Mesoamerica*.

1. Leibsohn, *Script and Glyph*, 66. See also her explication of these issues in chapter 3.

2. For the purposes of this study, I focus on the primary *tlacuilo* who produced the bulk of the manuscript and made decisions about format and content and hence refer to him in the singular.

3. Charles E. Dibble, *Historia de la nación mexicana*, 12.

4. Boone's *Stories in Red and Black* and "Migration Histories as Ritual Performance."

5. Castañeda de la Paz, "El Códice X."

6. Camilla Townsend, "Glimpsing Native American Historiography."

7. In early printing practices designations like octavo, cuarto, and folio referred to the number of pages printed on a standard sheet. Octavo printing produced eight pages front and back on a standard sheet that was then folded three times to create a gathering of eight leaves or sixteen pages.

8. "Endpapers" are the few leaves placed in the front and back of the book between its covers and the text block. The leaf closest to the cover is called the "paste-down" or "board paper."

9. The British Museum has recently made high-resolution digital color images of the manuscript available to the public on its website. For the first time it is easy to access full-color reproductions of each page of the painted manuscript and a few images of the endpapers that protect it. http://www.britishmuseum.org/research/collection_online/collection_object_details.aspx?objectId=3008812&partId=1.

10. The endpapers that surround the Codex Aubin do not have a title page. The edition can be identified, however, by comparing the size of the page, the language of the text, the type, the number of lines per page, the headers, signatures, catchwords, and so forth. A selective examination of the British Library's 400 volumes of the *Commentarii de Bello Gallico* indicated that this was clearly an early Latin edition and that it was most similar to those books published by Aldus Manutius in Venice in the sixteenth century. I did not find a close match until I visited the collection of books published by Aldus Manutius and his followers (the Aldine collection) at the University of California at Los Angeles. The book that most closely resembles the Codex Aubin endpapers is an Aldine reprint produced in 1534 by Sebastian Gryphius of Lyon, France. Page 117 of the *Commentarii de Bello Gallico*, for example, is identical in the 1534 book and the Aubin endpapers. Page 120 is identical except that the catchword has been shortened on the page in the Aubin endpapers. An examination of the Gryphius collection at the John Rylands Library in Manchester indicated that the Gryphius editions of the *Commentarii de Bello Gallico* changed format in 1545. Thus the pages that surround Codex Aubin appear to date between 1534 and 1545.

11. P. J. M. Marks, *The British Library Guide to Bookbinding History and Techniques*, 44.

12. Matt Roberts, Don Etherington, and Margaret R. Brown, *Bookbinding and the Conservation of Books*, 91, 277.

13. Sigfred Taubert, *The Book Trade of the World*, 221.

14. Marks, *The British Library Guide*, 34–35. See also Roberts, Etherington, and Brown, *Bookbinding*, 166.

15. E. Gordon Duff quotes from Henry Bradshaw's Memoranda No. 5, *Notice of the Bristol Fragment of the Fifteen Oes: Early Printed Books*, 195. In the second half of the nineteenth century Henry Bradshaw (1831–1886) worked with the book collections at Cambridge University Library.

16. For a complete list of locations where the Boturini collection was held, see chapter 2, "Tracing the Manuscripts through Time: A Collection History," in Angela Marie Herren, "Portraying the Mexica Past," and the epilogue to this book.

17. The British Library website, for example, discusses this problem in relation to its eighteenth-century collection of Sloane's printed books: "In many cases, evidence of identity was lost by the early practice of binding or re-binding in a Museum style which involved removing the preliminary leaves where Sloane's identification marks are often found": http://www.bl.uk/catalogues/sloane/History.aspx.

18. Duff, *Early Printed Books*, 186.

19. Although the British Museum owned the manuscript, the British Library handled its binding requests. It is also worth noting that, unless it had been completely destroyed, a 1534 edition of *De Bello Gallico* would have been something worth keeping or selling in one of the many duplicate sales that the British Library had in the nineteenth century. By contrast, in the late sixteenth century a 1534 octavo edition of the *Commentarii de Bello Gallico* would have been fairly common and not old enough to be considered rare.

20. H. George Fletcher, *In Praise of Aldus Manutius*, 55.

21. Ibid., 49.

22. Glass (and Robertson), "A Census."

23. Konrad Haebler and Lucy Eugenia Osborne, *The Study of Incunabula*, 88.

24. Appendix 2.

25. Jeanette F. Peterson, "Image/Texts in Sixteenth-Century Mexican Murals (A Devil in the Details)," 17.

26. Kobayashi, *La educación como conquista*, 174, 180, 185–186, 194–198.

27. "Our beloved father Fray Pedro de Gante was buried today, Sunday, April 20" (folio 58r, appendix 2).

28. Kobayashi, *La educación como conquista*, 195.

29. Under the entry for 1564 he describes a "stone image" at the site of his home (appendix 2).

30. W. Michael Mathes, *The America's First Academic Library*, 6.

31. Kobayashi, *La educación como conquista*, 214, 216, 222.

32. According to Michael Mathes, of 277 books known to have formed part of the library at the Colegio de Santa Cruz in Tlatelolco, 255 were Latin, 20 Spanish, 1 Italian, and 1 Nahuatl/Purepecha: *The America's First Academic Library*, 87.

33. Kobayashi, *La educación como conquista*, 217, 253.

34. Ibid., 261.

35. Mathes, *The America's First Academic Library*, 33.

36. Ibid., 60, 87.

37. Ibid., 31, 32–33.

38. Kobayashi, *La educación como conquista*, 247.

39. Appendix 2.

40. Rodolfo Acuña-Soto, Leticia Calderón Romero, and James H. Maguire, "Large Epidemics of Hemorrhagic Fevers in Mexico 1545–1815," 733.

41. Torquemada cited in Rodolfo Acuña-Soto, Leticia Calderón Romero, and James H. Maguire, "Large Epidemics of Hemorrhagic Fevers in Mexico 1545–1815," 733.

42. Appendix 2.

43. The artist-scribe generally lists events in chronological order, but this is not always the case. Discrepancies in chronology, for example, occur in the entries under 1566 and 1568.

44. Martin Austin Nesvig, *Ideology and Inquisition*, 134.

45. Sahagún, *Florentine Codex*, introductory vol.: 79–80.

46. Appendix 2 (all quotations in this paragraph are from this source); Greenleaf, *The Mexican Inquisition of the Sixteenth Century*, 159.

47. Chimalpahin, *Annals of His Time*, 153.

48. Appendix 2. Byron Hamann (personal communication, May 19, 2012) has suggested that the entry under 1560 may relate to a decree of December 6, 1559, in which Montúfar instituted a blanket book inspection. He notes that March 17, 1560, was the second Sunday in Lent, so an "appropriate" date for an auto-da-fé type of spectacle. Francisco Fernández del Castillo, comp., *Libros y libreros en el siglo XVI*.

49. See Nesvig, *Ideology and Inquisition*; Martin Austin Nesvig, "'Heretical Plagues' and Censorship Cordons"; Greenleaf, *The Mexican Inquisition*; Greenleaf, *Zumárraga*.

50. Nesvig, "'Heretical Plagues,'" 17.

51. Nesvig, *Ideology and Inquisition*, 120.

52. Greenleaf, *The Mexican Inquisition*, 126, 119.

53. Miguel León-Portilla, *Bernardino de Sahagún*.

54. Sahagún, *Florentine Codex*, intro. vol., 46–47.

55. León-Portilla, *Bernardino de Sahagún*, 161–180.

56. Nesvig, *Ideology and Inquisition*, 161.

57. Nesvig, "'Heretical Plagues,'" 15.

58. Nesvig, *Ideology and Inquisition*, 162–163.

59. W. Michael Mathes, "Humanism in Sixteenth- and Seventeenth-Century Libraries of New Spain," 412–435 (quotation on 422).

60. Serge Gruzinski, *The Mestizo Mind*.

61. Dana Leibsohn describes a similar tactic at work in the Historia Tolteca-Chichimeca, where pre-Hispanic deities are only referenced in the text and only in relation to the distant past: *Script and Glyph*, 40.

CHAPTER 7. CONCLUSION

1. Lockhart, *We People Here*, 273.
2. Klaus, *Anales de Tlatelolco*, 45.
3. Lockhart, *We People Here*, 38, 39 (quotation).
4. Ibid., 39, n. 94.
5. Terraciano, "Three Views of the Conquest," 23.
6. Ibid., 21.
7. Barlow and Graulich, *Codex Azcatitlan*, 152, n. 100.

EPILOGUE

1. See Antonio Peñafiel, *Monumentos del arte mexicano antiguo*. Though later exonerated, Boturini was never able to return to Mexico and reclaim his collection of manuscripts. See also Miguel León-Portilla, "Estudio preliminar," xiii.

2. John B. Glass, "The Boturini Collection," 473.

3. Ibid., 474.

4. León-Portilla, "Estudio preliminar," ix–lxxii.

5. Glass, "The Boturini Collection," table 2, 479–482; Ignacio de Cubas and Barbara Hermanns. *Catálogo Boturini del Hamburgo, 1804: CBH*.

6. John B. Glass, *The Boturini Collection and a Concordance*, 18–19.

7. Peñafiel, *Monumentos del arte mexicano antiguo*, 56–68.

8. Ibid.

9. Ibid.

10. Lorenzo Boturini Benaduci, *Idea de una nueva historia general de la América septentrional*, 116–117.

11. Ibid., 117.

12. Ibid., 119.

13. Ibid., 114.

14. Francisco González-Hermosillo Adams and Luis Reyes García, *El códice de Cholula*, 38.

15. Glass, "The Boturini Collection," 473.

16. Boturini Benaduci, *Idea de una nueva historia general*, 115.

17. Glass, "The Boturini Collection," table 1, 476–477.

18. Ibid., 475. For an interesting discussion and more specific information on the late eighteenth-century dispersion, see John B. Glass, *The Boturini Collection and the Council of the Indies, 1780–1800*.

19. Roberto Moreno, "La Colección Boturini y las fuentes de la obra de Antonio de León y Gama."

20. Ibid., 258 (quotation); Antonio de León y Gama, *Descripción histórica y cronológica de las dos piedras*.

21. Both copies are in the Bibliothèque Nationale de France. The Codex Azcatitlan copy is catalogued as *Manuscrit mexicain no. 90–1* and the Codex Aubin copy is catalogued as *Manuscrit mexicain no. 35–36*.

22. Barlow and Graulich, *Codex Azcatitlan*, 16–17.

23. The Codex Azcatitlan copy by Pichardo is catalogued as *Manuscrit mexicain no. 89–3* in the Bibliothèque Nationale de France. John Glass suggests that a partial copy of the Codex Aubin in the Staatsbibliothek Stiftung Preussischer Kulturbesitz (SSPK Ms. Amer. No. 5) in Berlin may be by Pichardo: Glass (and Robertson), "A Census," 89. My observations of León y Gama's and Pichardo's copies indicate that Pichardo's version of the manuscript is closer to León y Gama's than to the "original" Azcatitlan. Pichardo probably copied directly from León y Gama.

24. Moreno, "La Colección Boturini," 259.

25. Michael Costeloe, "William Bullock and the Mexico Connection," 277.

26. Bullock, *A Description of the Unique Exhibition Called Ancient Mexico*, 50.

27. Cubas and Hermanns, *Catálogo Boturini del Hamburgo*, 14.

28. In addition to the 1823 inventory, the documents from Lorenzo Boturini Benaduci's 1745 inventory that were no longer in the collection were reported as missing on a *Lista*. Glass declares the *Lista* "demonstrably inaccurate," but Codex Boturini's absence does correlate with Bullock's presence in Mexico. Glass, *The Boturini Collection and a Concordance*, 10.

29. Diana Fane, "Reproducing the Pre-Columbian Past."

30. Bullock, *A Descriptive Catalogue of the Exhibition, Entitled Ancient and Modern Mexico*, 28.

31. Bullock, *A Description of the Unique Exhibition Called Ancient Mexico*, 47.

32. Bullock, *Six Months' Residence and Travels in Mexico*, 329.

33. Ian Graham, "Three Early Collectors in Mesoamerica," 60–61.

34. Costeloe, "William Bullock," 286.

35. Ibid., 269–290.

36. Graham, "Three Early Collectors in Mesoamerica," 63.

37. Boban, *Documents pour servir à l'histoire du Mexique*, 2:257.

38. Graham, "Three Early Collectors in Mesoamerica," n. 13.

39. Felipe Solís, "Adventures and Misadventures of the National Museum of Anthropology's Collections," 61.

40. Cubas and Hermanns, *Catálogo Boturini*, 14. Cubas's census was produced for the Secretaría de Cámara del Virreinato under the title "Colección de memorias de Nueva España."

41. Solís, "Adventures and Misadventures," 67, 79. While I have not had the opportunity for a systematical examination of the other original manuscripts listed in late nineteenth and early twentieth century Museo Nacional exhibition catalogues for gold borders, I did note the presence of a gold border on the Museo Nacional de Antropología's Mapa de Coatepetl (MS 35–19). John Glass has identified eight of the manuscripts now present in the Museo Nacional de Antropología collections that match descriptions in Bullock's exhibition catalogues: Codex Boturini, Codex Huamantla (three or four fragments), Codex de la Cueva, Lienzo de Tlaxcala, and Plano en papel de maguey: John Glass, *Catálogo de la colección de códices*, 22. The presence or absence of the gold border on one or the other set of manuscripts should indicate when it was applied.

42. Boban, *Documents pour servir à l'histoire du Mexique*, 1:23–30.

43. Aubin cited in ibid., 1:24.

44. Ibid., 1:25.

45. Ibid., 1:17–19.

46. Ibid.

47. Ibid.

48. Jules Desportes was clearly familiar with the Codex Aubin (Codex of 1576), having produced a lithograph of it in 1851. He produced other lithographs from Aubin's collection as well, such as the Mapa Quinatzin, Mapa Tlotzin, Aubin Tonalamatl, and Tira de Tepechpan.

49. Boban, *Documents pour servir à l'histoire du Mexique,* 1:10–13.

50. J. M. A. Aubin, *Mémoires sur la peinture didactique et l'écriture figurative des anciens mexicains.* See also J. M. A. Aubin, *Memorias sobre la pintura didáctica y la escritura figurativa de los antiguos mexicanos.*

51. J. M. A. Aubin, *Notice sur une collection d'antiquités mexicaines (peintures et manuscripts).*

52. Boban, *Documents pour servir à l'histoire du Mexique,* 1:10.

53. Ibid., 1:14.

BIBLIOGRAPHY

Acosta, José de. *Historia natural y moral de las Indias*. Edited by Edmundo O'Gorman. Mexico City: Fondo de Cultura Económica, 1962. Reprint of 2nd edition, 1979.

Acuña-Soto, Rodolfo, Leticia Calderón Romero, and James H. Maguire. "Large Epidemics of Hemorrhagic Fevers in Mexico 1545–1815." *American Journal of Tropical Medicine and Hygiene* 62:6 (2000): 733–739.

Afanador-Pujol, Angélica Jimena. *The Relación de Michoacán (1539–1541) and the Politics of Representation in Colonial Mexico*. Austin: University of Texas Press, 2015.

Aguilera, Carmen. "Of Royal Mantles and Blue Turquoise: The Meaning of the Mexican Emperor's Mantle." *Latin American Antiquity* 8:1 (1997): 3–19.

Alva Ixtlilxochitl, Fernando de. *The Native Conquistador: Alva Ixtlilxochitl's Account of the Conquest of New Spain*. Edited and translated by Amber Brian, Bradley Benton, and Pablo García Loaeza. University Park: Pennsylvania State University Press, 2015.

———. *Obras históricas*. Edited by Edmundo O'Gorman. 2 vols. Mexico City: Universidad Nacional Autónoma México, Instituto de Investigaciones Históricas, 1975–1977.

Alvarado Tezozomoc, Fernando. *Crónica Mexicayotl*. Translated and edited by Adrián León. Primera serie prehispánica 3. Mexico City: Universidad Nacional Autónoma México, Instituto de Investigaciones Históricas, 1949. Reprint 1992.

Anawalt, Patricia Rieff. "Riddle of the Emperor's Cloak." *Archaeology* 46:3 (May/June 1993): 30–36.

Aubin, J. M. A. *Mémoires sur la peinture didactique et l'écriture figurative des anciens mexicains*. Paris: P. Dupont, 1885.

———. *Memorias sobre la pintura didáctica y la escritura figurativa de los antiguos mexicanos*. Edited and introduction by Patrice Giasson. Mexico City: Universidad Nacional Autónoma México, 2002.

———. *Notice sur une collection d'antiquités mexicaines (peintures et manuscripts)*. Paris: P. Dupont, 1851.

Bancroft, Hubert Howe. *History of the Pacific States of North America*, vol. 5, *Mexico*, vol. 2, *1521–1600*. San Francisco: A. L. Bancroft & Company Publishers, 1883.

Barlow, Robert. "El Códice Azcatitlan." *Journal de la Société des Américanistes* 38 (1949): 101–135. Accompanied by a facsimile of the codex in a separate album.

———. "La crónica 'X': Versiones coloniales de la historia de los Mexica-Tenochca." *Revista Mexicana de Estudios Antropológicos* (Mexico City: Sociedad Mexicana de Antropología) 7 (1945): 65–87.

Barlow, Robert, and Michel Graulich, eds. *Codex Azcatitlan*. Facsimile, with commentary by Robert Barlow revised by Michel Graulich. Spanish translation by Leonardo López Luján. French translation by Dominique Michelet. Paris: Bibliothèque Nationale de France and Société des Américanistes, 1995.

Berdan, Frances F., and Patricia Rieff Anawalt, eds. *The Codex Mendoza*. 4 vols. Berkeley: University of California Press, 1992.

Bernal-García, María Elena. "The Dance of Time: The Procession of Space at Mexico-Tenochtitlan's Desert Garden." In *Sacred Gardens and Landscapes: Ritual and Agency*, edited by Michael Conan, 69–114. Dumbarton Oaks Colloquium on the History of Landscape Architecture 26. Washington, DC: Dumbarton Oaks, 2007.

Bierhorst, John, trans. and ed. *Ballads of the Lords of New Spain: The Codex Romances de los Señores de la Nueva España*. Austin: University of Texas Press, 2009.

———, trans. and ed. *History and Mythology of the Aztecs: The Codex Chimalpopoca*. Tucson: University of Arizona Press, 1998.

Boban, Eugène. *Documents pour servir à l'histoire du Mexique: Catalogue raisonné de la collection de M. E.-Eugène Goupil (ancienne collection J. M. A. Aubin): Manuscrits figuratifs, et autres sur papier indigène d'agave mexicana et sur papier européen antérieures et postérieures à la conquête du Mexique (XVIe siècle)*. 2 vols. Paris: E. Leroux, 1891.

Boone, Elizabeth Hill. "Manuscript Painting in Service of Imperial Ideology." In *Aztec Imperial Strategies*, by Frances F. Berdan, Richard E. Blanton, Elizabeth Hill Boone, Mary G. Hodge, Michael E. Smith, and Emily Umberger, 181–208. Washington, DC: Dumbarton Oaks, 1996.

———. "Migration Histories as Ritual Performance." In *To Change Place: Aztec Ceremonial Landscapes*, edited by Davíd Carrasco, 121–151. Boulder: University of Colorado, 1991. Reprint, Boulder: University Press of Colorado, 1999.

———. *Painted Architecture and Polychrome Monumental Sculpture in Mesoamerica*. Washington, DC: Dumbarton Oaks, 1985.

———. *Stories in Red and Black: Pictorial Histories of the Aztecs and Mixtecs*. Austin: University of Texas Press, 2000.

Boturini Benaduci, Lorenzo. *Idea de una nueva historia general de la América septentrional* [1796]. Mexico City: Editorial Porrúa, 1974.

Bright, William. *Native American Placenames of the United States*. Norman: University of Oklahoma Press, 2004.

Bullock, William. *Catalogue of the Exhibition, Called Modern Mexico; Containing a Panoramic View of the City, with Specimens of the Natural History of New Spain, and Models of the Vegetable Produce, Costume, etc.* London: Printed for the Proprietor, 1824.

———. *A Description of the Unique Exhibition Called Ancient Mexico; Collected on the Spot in 1823, by the Assistance of the Mexican Government, and Now Open for Public Inspection at the Egyptian Hall, Piccadilly*. London: Printed for the Proprietor, 1824.

———. *A Descriptive Catalogue of the Exhibition, Entitled Ancient and Modern Mexico; Containing A Panoramic View of the Present City, Specimens of the Natural History of New Spain. Models of Its Vegetable Produce, Habitations, Costume, etc. etc., and of the Colossal and Enormous Idols, the Great Calendar and Sacrificial Stones, Temples, Pyramids, and Other Existing Antique Remains. The Whole Forming the Rationally Instructive and Interesting Exhibition, Which Is Now Open, for Public Inspection, at the Egyptian Hall, Piccadilly*. London: Printed for the Proprietors, 1824.

———. *Six Months' Residence and Travels in Mexico: Containing Remarks on the Present State of New Spain, Its Natural Productions, State of Society, Manufactures, Trade, Agriculture, and Antiquities, &c.* London: John Murray, 1824.

Bullock, William, John Scott Ripon, Maurin de Pompigny, Henry Petty-Fitzmaurice Lansdowne, and Robert Banks Jenkinson Liverpool. *Le Mexique en 1823, ou, Relation d'un voyage dans la Nouvelle-Espagne: Contenant des notions exactes et peu connues sur la situation physique, morale et politique de ce pays; accompagné d'un atlas de vingt planches*. Paris: Alexis-Eymery, 1824.

Carrasco, Pedro. *The Tenochca Empire of Ancient Mexico: The Triple Alliance of Tenochtitlan, Tetzcoco, and Tlacopan*. Norman: University of Oklahoma Press, 1999.

Casas, Bartolomé de las. *An Account, Much Abbreviated, of the Destruction of the Indies with Related Texts*. Translated by Andrew Hurley. Edited by Franklin W. Knight. Indianapolis: Hackett, 2003.

Caso, Alfonso. *Interpretación del Códice Colombino*. Accompanied by a facsimile of the codex. Mexico City: Sociedad Mexicana de Antropología, 1966.

———. "Los barrios antiguos de Tenochtitlan y Tlatelolco." *Memorias de la Academia Mexicana de la Historia* 15 (1956): 7–62.

Castañeda de la Paz, María. "Codex Azcatitlan and the Work of Torquemada: A Historiographic Puzzle in the Aztec-Mexica Sources." *Latin American Indian Literatures Journal* 24:2 (2009): 151–194.

———. *Conflictos y alianzas en tiempos de cambio: Azcapotzalco, Tlacopan, Tenochtitlan y Tlatelolco (siglos XII–XVI)*. Mexico City: Universidad Nacional Autónoma México, Instituto de Investigaciones Antropológicas, 2013.

———. "De Aztlan a Tenochtitlan: Historia de una peregrinación." *Latin American Indian Literatures Journal* 8:2 (2002): 163–212.

———. "El Códice X o los anales del 'Grupo de la Tira de la Peregrinación': Copias, duplicaciones y su uso por parte de los cronistas." *Tlalocan* 15 (2005): 183–214.

———. "Filología del corpus pintado (siglos xvi–xviii): Códices, techialoyan, pinturas y escudos de armas." *Anales del Museo de América* 17 (2009): 78–90.

———. "Los códices históricos mexicas: El Códice Azcatitlan." *Estudios de Historia Social y Económica de América* 14 (1997): 273–299.

———. "Los tlatelolcas y su ascendencia tepaneca en las fuentes mexicas." *Expresión Antropológica* 8–9 (1999): 38–53.

Castañeda de la Paz, María, and Michel Oudijk. "La conquista y la colonia in *Códice Azcatitlan*." *Journal de la Société des Américanistes* 98–2 (2012). Published online: http://jsa.revues.org/12322.

Chimalpahin Quauhtlehuanitzin, Domingo Francisco de San Antón Muñón. *Annals of His Time*. Edited and translated by James Lockhart, Susan Schroeder, and Doris Namala. Stanford: Stanford University Press, 2006.

———. *Codex Chimalpahin: Society and Politics in Mexico Tenochtitlan, Tlatelolco, Texcoco, Culhuacan, and Other Nahua Altepetl in Central Mexico*. 2 vols. Edited and translated by Arthur J. O. Anderson and Susan Schroeder. Norman: University of Oklahoma Press, 1997.

Chipman, Donald. *Moctezuma's Children: Aztec Royalty under Spanish Rule, 1520–1700*. Austin: University of Texas Press, 2005.

Christensen, Bodil, and Samuel Martí, *Brujerías y papel precolombino*. Mexico City: Ediciones Euroamericanas, 1971.

Cortés, Hernando. *Letters from Mexico*. Edited and translated by Anthony Pagden. New Haven: Yale University Press, 1986.

Costeloe, Michael. "William Bullock and the Mexico Connection." *Estudios Mexicanos* 22:2 (Summer 2006): 275–309.

Cubas, Ignacio de, and Barbara Hermanns. *Catálogo Boturini del Hamburgo, 1804: CBH*. Hamburg: Wayasbah, 1988.

Cummins, Tom. "Here, There, and Now: Deictics and the Transposition of Orality to Image in Colonial Imagery." *Art in Translation* 7:1 (2015): 65–93.

Dark, Philip, and Joyce Plesters. "The Palimpsests of Codex Selden: Recent Attempts to Reveal the Covered Pictographs." In *Proceedings of the 33rd International Congress of Americanists*, 530–539. San José, Costa Rica: Lehmann, 1959.

Davies, Nigel. *The Toltec Heritage: From the Fall of Tula to the Rise of Tenochtitlan*. Norman: University of Oklahoma Press, 1980.

Delafield, John, Jr. *An Inquiry into the Origin of the Antiquities of America*. Cincinnati: N. G. Burgess, 1839.

Díaz del Castillo, Bernal. *The Memoirs of the Conquistador*. London: Hatchard, 1844.

———. *The True History of the Conquest of New Spain*. Translated by Janet Burke and Ted Humphrey. Indianapolis: Hackett, 2012.

Dibble, Charles E. *Historia de la nación mexicana: Reproducción a todo color del Códice de 1576 (Códice Aubin)*. Madrid: J. Porrúa Turanzas, 1963.

Diehl, Richard. *Tula: The Toltec Capital of Ancient Mexico*. New York: Thames & Hudson, 1983.

Diel, Lori Boornazian. *Tira de Tepechpan: Negotiating Place under Aztec and Spanish Rule*. Austin: University of Texas Press, 2008.

Douglas, Eduardo de J. *In the Palace of Nezahualcoyotl: Painting Manuscripts, Writing the Pre-Hispanic Past in Early Colonial Period Tetxcoco, Mexico*. Austin: University of Texas Press, 2010.

Duff, E. Gordon. *Early Printed Books*. New York: Haskell House, 1968.

Durán, Diego. *Book of the Gods and Rites and the Ancient Calendar*. Edited and translated by Fernando Horcasitas and Doris Heyden. Foreword by Miguel León-Portilla. Norman: University of Oklahoma Press, 1971. Reprint 1975.

———. *The History of the Indies of New Spain*. Edited and translated by Doris Heyden. Norman: University of Oklahoma Press, 1994.

Elliott, J. H. "Cortés, Velázquez, and Charles V." In Hernando Cortés, *Letters from Mexico*, edited and translated by Anthony Pagden, xi–xxxvii. New Haven: Yale University Press, 1986.

Escalante, Pablo. "El trazo, el cuerpo, y el gesto: Los codices mesoamericanos y su transformación en el Valle de México en el siglo XVI." Ph.D. dissertation, Universidad Nacional Autónoma de México, 1996.

Fane, Diana. "Reproducing the Pre-Columbian Past: Casts and Models in Exhibitions of Ancient America, 1824–1935." In *Collecting the Pre-Columbian Past*, edited by Elizabeth Hill Boone, 141–176. Washington, DC: Dumbarton Oaks, 1993.

Fernández del Castillo, Francisco, comp. *Libros y libreros en el siglo XVI*. Mexico City: Archivo General de la Nación, Fondo de Cultura Económica, 1982.

Fletcher, H. George. *In Praise of Aldus Manutius: A Quincentenary Exhibition*. New York: Pierpont Morgan Library, 1995.

Fulke, William. *A Defense of the Sincere and True Translations of the Holie Scriptures into the English Tong*. London: printed by Henrie Bynneman, 1583. Published online: http://libweb5.princeton.edu/visual_materials/hb/cases/endleaves/index.html.

Galarza, Joaquín, and Krystyna M. Libura, *Para leer la Tira de la Peregrinación*. Mexico City, Ediciones Tecolote, 1999.

Glass, John B. "The Boturini Collection." In *Handbook of Middle American Indians*, vol. 15, edited by Robert Wauchope and Howard F. Cline, 473–486. Austin: University of Texas Press, 1975.

———. *The Boturini Collection and a Concordance of the Inventories, 1742–1918*. Lincoln Center, MA: Conemex Associates, 1978.

———. *The Boturini Collection and the Council of the Indies, 1780–1800*. Lincoln Center, MA: Conemex Associates, 1976.

———. *Catálogo de la colección de códices*. Mexico City: Museo Nacional de Antropología, Instituto Nacional de Antropología e Historia, 1964.

———. "William Bullock and the Old Collection of Pictorial Manuscripts in the Mexican National Museum of Anthropology." Handbook of Middle American Indians Working Papers 22, Box 40, Howard F. Cline papers, Manuscript Division, Library of Congress, Washington, DC.

Glass, John B. (in collaboration with Donald Robertson). "A Census of Native Middle American Pictorial Manuscripts." In *Handbook of Middle American Indians*, vol. 14, edited by Robert Wauchope and Howard F. Cline, 81–252. Austin: University of Texas Press, 1975.

González-Hermosillo Adams, Francisco, and Luis Reyes García. *El códice de Cholula: La exaltación testimonial de un linaje indio—estudio, paleografía, traducción y notas*. Mexico City: Instituto Nacional de Antropología e Historia, 2002.

González Obregón, Luis, ed. *Procesos de indios idolatras y hechiceros*. Publicaciones del Archivo General de la Nación. Mexico City: Guerrero Hermanos, 1912.

Graham, Ian. "Three Early Collectors in Mesoamerica." In *Collecting the Pre-Columbian Past*, edited by Elizabeth Hill Boone, 49–80. Washington, DC: Dumbarton Oaks, 1993.

Greenleaf, Richard E. *The Mexican Inquisition of the Sixteenth Century*. Albuquerque: University of New Mexico Press, 1969.

———. *Zumárraga and the Mexican Inquisition, 1536–1543*. Washington, DC: Academy of American Franciscan History, 1962.

Gruzinski, Serge. *The Mestizo Mind: The Intellectual Dynamics of Colonization and Globalization*. New York: Routledge, 2002.

Haebler, Konrad, and Lucy Eugenia Osborne. *The Study of Incunabula*. New York: Grolier Club, 1933.

Hagen, Victor Wolfgang von. *Aztec and Maya Papermakers*. New York: J. J. Augustin, 1944.

Headrick, Annabeth. *The Teotihuacan Trinity: The Sociopolitical Structure of an Ancient Mesoamerican City*. Austin: University of Texas Press, 2007.

Herbermann, Charles. *The Catholic Encyclopedia: An International Work of Reference on the Constitution, Doctrine, Discipline, and History of the Catholic Church*. Vol. 14. New York: Robert Appleton Co., 1912.

Herren, Angela Marie. "Portraying the Mexica Past: A Comparison of Sixteenth-Century Pictorial Accounts of Origin in Codex Azcatitlan, Codex Boturini, and Codex Aubin." Ph.D. dissertation, City University of New York, 2005.

———. "Writing Collaborative Histories: Codex Azcatitlan and the Painter's Workshop in Early Colonial New Spain." *Latin Americanist, Annals Issue* 56:4 (March 2012): 1–13.

Himmerich y Valencia, Robert. *The Encomenderos of New Spain, 1521–1555*. Austin: University of Texas Press, 1996.

Johansson Keraudren, Patrick. *Códice Boturini, Tira de la Peregrinación*. Mexico City: Instituto Nacional de Antropológia e Historia, 2015. Published online: http://www.codiceboturini.inah.gob.mx/codex.php.

Karttunen, Frances. *An Analytical Dictionary of Nahuatl*. Austin: University of Texas Press, 1983.

Kerpel, Diana Magaloni. *The Colors of the New World: Artists, Materials, and the Creation of the Florentine Codex*. Los Angeles: Getty Research Institute, 2014.

Klaus, Susanne, trans. and ed. *Anales de Tlatelolco: Los manuscritos 22 y 22bis de la Bibliothèque de France*. Markt Schwagen, Germany: Verlag Anton Saurwein, 1999.

Kobayashi, José María. *La educación como conquista*. Mexico City: El Colegio de México, 2002.

Lehmann, Walter, and Gerdt Kutscher, trans. and eds. *Geschichte der Azteken: Codex Aubin und verwandte Dokumente*. Berlin: Gebr. Mann, 1981.

Leibsohn, Dana. *Script and Glyph: Pre-Hispanic History, Colonial Bookmaking and the Historia Tolteca-Chichimeca*. Washington DC: Dumbarton Oaks, 2009.

Lejarazu Rubin, Dinorah, and Manuel Hermann Lejarazu. *Códice Boturini o Tira de la Peregrinación: Investigación, estudio, y paleografía*. Mexico City: Taller de Artes Gráficas, Grupo Gisma, 1991.

Lenz, Hans. *Cosas del papel en Mesoamérica*. Mexico City: Editorial Libros de México, 1984.

———. *El papel indígena mexicano*. Mexico City: Secretaría de Educación Pública, 1973.

León-Portilla, Miguel. *The Aztec Image of Self and Society: An Introduction to Nahua Culture*. Introduction by J. Jorge Klor de Alva. Salt Lake City: University of Utah Press, 1992.

———. *Bernardino de Sahagún: Pionero de la antropología*. Mexico City: Universidad Nacional Autónoma de México, Instituto de Investigaciones Históricas, 1999.

———. "Estudio preliminar." In *Idea de una nueva historia general de la América septentrional* [1796], by Lorenzo Boturini Benaduci, ix–xxxiii. Mexico City: Editorial Porrúa, 1974.

León y Gama, Antonio de. *Descripción histórica y cronológica de las dos piedras: Reproducción facsimilar de las primeras ediciones mexicanas, primera parte, 1792, segunda parte, 1832*. Mexico City: M. A. Porrúa, 1978.

Lienzo de Tlaxcala. Mexico City: Alfredo Chavero, 1892.

Lockhart, James. *The Nahuas after the Conquest: A Social and Cultural History of the Indians of Central Mexico, Sixteenth through Eighteenth Centuries*. Stanford: Stanford University Press, 1992.

———. *Nahuas and Spaniards: Postconquest Central Mexican History and Philology*. UCLA Latin American Studies, vol. 76, Nahuatl Series 3. Stanford: Stanford University Press; Los Angeles: UCLA Latin American Center Publications, University of California, Los Angeles, 1991.

———, ed. and trans. *We People Here: Nahuatl Accounts of the Conquest of Mexico*. Repertorium Columbianum, 1. Berkeley: University of California Press and UCLA Center for Medieval and Renaissance Studies. Reprint: Eugene, OR: Wipf & Stock Publishers, 2004.

López de Gómara, Francisco. *Cortés: The Life of the Conqueror by His Secretary*. Edited and translated by Lesley Byrd Simpson. Berkeley: University of California Press, 1965.

Marks, P. J. M. *The British Library Guide to Bookbinding: History and Techniques*. Toronto: University of Toronto Press, 1998.

Mastache de Escobar, Alba Guadalupe, Robert H. Cobean, and Dan M. Healan. *Ancient Tollan: Tula and the Toltec Heartland*. Boulder: University Press of Colorado, 2002.

Mathes, W. Michael. *The America's First Academic Library: Santa Cruz de Tlatelolco*. Sacramento: California State Library Foundation, 1985.

———. "Humanism in Sixteenth- and Seventeenth-Century Libraries of New Spain." *Catholic Historical Review* 82:3 (1996): 412–435.

Maura, Juan Francisco. *Women in the Conquest of the Americas*. Translated by John F. Deredita. New York: Peter Lang, 1997.

Máynez, Pilar. *El calepino de Sahagún: Un acercamiento*. Mexico City: Universidad Nacional Autónoma de México and Fondo Cultura Económica, 2002.

Mengin, Ernst. "Commentaire du Codex Mexicanus Nos. 23–24 de la Bibliothèque Nationale de Paris." *Journal de la Société des Américanistes* 41:2 (1952): 387–498.

Milbrath, Susan. *Heaven and Earth in Ancient Mexico: Astronomy and Seasonal Cycles in the Codex Borgia*. Austin: University of Texas Press, 2013.

Miller, Arthur G. "Introduction to the Dover Edition." In *The Codex Nuttall: A Picture Manuscript from Ancient Mexico*, edited by Zelia Nuttall, vii–xviii. New York: Dover Publications, 1975.

Moreno, Roberto. "La Colección Boturini y las fuentes de la obra de Antonio de León y Gama." *Estudios de Cultura Nahuatl* 9 (1971): 253–270.

Motolinía [Toribio de Benavente]. *Motolinía's History of the Indians of New Spain*. Edited and translated by Francis Borgia Steck. Washington, DC: Academy of American Franciscan History, 1951.

Mundy, Barbara. *The Death of Aztec Tenochtitlan, the Life of Mexico City*. Austin: University of Texas Press, 2015.

Navarrete Linares, Federico. "The Hidden Codes of the Codex Azcatitlan." *RES: Anthropology and Aesthetics* 45 (Spring 2004): 155–158.

———. "The Path from Aztlan to Mexico: On Visual Narration in Mesoamerican Codices." *RES: Anthropology and Aesthetics* 37 (2000): 31–48.

———. "Writing, Images, and Time-Space in Aztec Monuments and Books." In *Their Way of Writing: Scripts, Signs, and Pictographies in Pre-Columbian America*, edited by Elizabeth Hill Boone and Gary Urton, 175–195. Washington, DC: Dumbarton Oaks, 2011.

Nesvig, Martin Austin. "'Heretical Plagues' and Censorship Cordons: Colonial Mexico and the Transatlantic Book Trade." *Church History* 75:1 (2006): 1–37.

———. *Ideology and Inquisition: The World of the Censors in Early Mexico*. New Haven: Yale University Press, 2009.

Nicholson, H. B. "Fray Bernardino de Sahagún: A Spanish Missionary in New Spain, 1529–1590." In *Representing Aztec Ritual: Performance, Text, and Image in the Work of Sahagún*, edited by Eloise Quiñones Keber, 21–39. Boulder: University Press of Colorado.

Olko, Justyna. *Insignia of Rank in the Nahua World: From the Fifteenth to the Seventeenth Century*. Boulder: University Press of Colorado, 2014.

———. *Turquoise Diadems and Staffs of Office: Elite Costume and Insignia of Power in Aztec and Early Colonial Mexico*. Warsaw, Poland: Polish Society for Latin American Studies and Centre for Studies on the Classical Tradition, University of Warsaw, 2005.

Oudijk, Michel. "Elaboration and Abbreviation in Mexican Pictorial Manuscripts: Their Use in Literary Themes." In *Their Way of Writing: Scripts, Signs, and Pictographies in Pre-Columbian America*, edited by Elizabeth Hill Boone and Gary Urton, 149–174. Washington, DC: Dumbarton Oaks, 2011.

Paxton, Merideth, and Leticia Staines Cicero, eds. *Constructing Power and Place in Mesoamerica: Pre-Hispanic Paintings from Three Regions*. Albuquerque: University of New Mexico Press, 2017.

Peñafiel, Antonio. *Monumentos del arte mexicano antiguo: Ornamentación, mitología, tributos y monumentos*. Berlin: A. Asher, 1890.

Peterson, Jeanette F. "Image/Texts in Sixteenth-Century Mexican Murals (A Devil in the Details)." In *Sources and Methods for the Study of Postconquest Mesoamerican Ethnohistory*, by James Lockhart, Lisa Sousa, and Stephanie Wood, 1–21. Eugene, OR: Wired Humanities Project, University of Oregon, 2007. Published online: http://whp.uoregon.edu/Lockhart/Peterson.pdf.

Quiñones Keber, Eloise. *Codex Telleriano-Remensis. Ritual, Divination, and History in a Pictorial Aztec Manuscript*. Austin: University of Texas Press, 1995.

Radin, Paul. "The Sources and Authenticity of the History of the Ancient Mexicans." *University of California, Publications in American Archaeology and Ethnology* (Berkeley: University of California Press) 17:1 (1920): 1–150, 17 pls.

Restall, Matthew, Lisa Sousa, and Kevin Terraciano. *Mesoamerican Voices: Native Language Writings from Colonial Mexico, Oaxaca, Yucatan, and Guatemala*. Cambridge: Cambridge University Press, 2005.

Ricard, Robert. *The Spiritual Conquest of Mexico*. Berkeley: University of California Press, 1966.

Roberts, Matt, Don Etherington, and Margaret R. Brown. *Bookbinding and the Conservation of Books: A Dictionary of Descriptive Terminology*. Washington, DC: Library of Congress, 1982.

Robertson, Donald. *Mexican Manuscript Painting of the Early Colonial Period: The Metropolitan Schools*. New Haven: Yale University Press, 1959. Reprint, Norman: University of Oklahoma Press, 1994.

Russo, Alessandra. *The Untranslatable Image: A Mestizo History of the Arts in New Spain, 1500–1600*. Translation by Susan Emanuel. Joe R. and Teresa Lozano Long Series in Latin American and Latino Art and Culture. Austin: University of Texas Press, 2014.

Sahagún, Bernardino de. *Florentine Codex: General History of the Things of New Spain*. 13 vols. (Cited by original book number.) Translated by Arthur J. O. Anderson and Charles E. Dibble. Santa Fe, NM: School of American Research and University of Utah, 1950–1963.

Sandstrom, Alan R. and Pamela E. Sandstrom. *Traditional Papermaking and Paper Cult Figures of Mexico*. Norman: University of Oklahoma Press, 1986.

Schroeder, Susan. "The Truth about the Crónica Mexicayotl." *Colonial Latin America Review* 20:2 (2011): 233–247.

Seler, Eduard. *Gesammelte Abhandlungen zur Amerikanischen Sprach- und Alterthumskunde*. 6 vols. Berlin: Asher et Behrend, 1902–1923.

Smith, Michael E. *Aztec City-State Capitals*. Gainesville: University Press of Florida, 2008.

Solís, Felipe. "Adventures and Misadventures of the National Museum of Anthropology's Collections." In *National Museum of Anthropology*, 59–83. New York: Harry Abrams in association with CONACULTA-INAH, 2004.

Taubert, Sigfred. *The Book Trade of the World: Volume II: The Americas, Australia, New Zealand*. Wiesbaden, Germany: Verlag für Buchmarkt-Forschung, 1976.

Tena, Rafael. "La cronología de la *Tira de la Peregrinación*." *Estudios de Cultura Nahuatl* 40 (January 2010): 121–129. Published online: http://www.ejournal.unam.mx/ecn/ecnahuatl40/ECN04000006.pdf.

Terraciano, Kevin. "Three Views of the Conquest of Mexico from the *Other* Mexica." In *The Conquest All Over Again: Nahuas and Zapotecs Thinking, Writing, and Painting Spanish Colonialism*, edited by Susan Schroeder, 15–40. Portland: Sussex Academic Press, 2010.

Torquemada, Juan de. *Monarquía indiana*. Mexico City: Editorial Porrúa, 1969.

Tovar, Juan de. *Origen de los mexicanos (Códice Ramírez)*. Barcelona: Linkgua, 2009.

Townsend, Camilla. *Annals of Native America: How the Nahuas of Colonial Mexico Kept Their History Alive*. Oxford: University Press, 2017.

———. "Glimpsing Native American Historiography: The Cellular Principle in Sixteenth-Century Nahuatl Annals." *Ethnohistory* 56:4 (2009): 625–650.

Umberger, Emily. "Appendix 3: Material Remains in the Central Provinces." In *Aztec Imperial Strategies*, edited by Frances Berdan et al., 247–264. Washington DC: Dumbarton Oaks, 1996.

Valentini, Philipp J. J. "Mexican Paper: An Article of Tribute; Its Manufacture, Varieties, Employment and Uses." *Proceedings of the American Antiquarian Society* (Worchester: Press of Chas. Hamilton) (October 21, 1880): 58–81.

Villella, Peter B. *Indigenous Elites and Creole Identity in Colonial Mexico, 1500–1800*. Cambridge: Cambridge University Press, 2016.

Woldan, Erich. "Petrus Martyr de Angleria: His Life and Works." In *Opera: Legatio Babylonica: De orbe novo decades octo. Opus epistolarum* [by Peter Martyr d'Anghiera], vii–xi. Graz: Akademische Druck- und Verlagsanstalt, 1966.

Zantwijk, R. A. M. van. *The Aztec Arrangement: The Social History of Pre-Spanish Mexico*. Norman: University of Oklahoma Press, 1985.

INDEX

Note: Italic page numbers refer to figures and tables.